BLACK HEARTS

BLACK

ONE PLATOON'S DESCENT INT

Harmony Books / New York

HEARTS

MADNESS IN IRAQ'S TRIANGLE OF DEATH

JIM FREDERICK

Library of Congress Cataloging-in-Publication Data

Frederick, Jim.

Black Hearts: one platoon's descent into madness in Iraq's triangle of death /

Jim Frederick. Includes bibliographical references and index.

1. Iraq War, 2003—Atrocities—Iraq—Mahmudiyah.   2. War crimes—Iraq—Mahmudiyah.

3. Murder—Iraq—Mahmudiyah.   4. Rape—Iraq—Mahmudiyah.   5. Iraq War, 2003—

Psychological aspects.   6. Soldiers—Iraq—Psychology.

7. United States. Army. Airborne Division, 101st.   I. Title.

DS79.766.M34F74 2010

956.7044'3—dc22   2009035537

ISBN 978-0-307-45075-3

Printed in the United States of America

Design by Leonard Henderson
Maps by Mapping Specialists Ltd.
Title page photograph courtesy of Eric Lauzier

1 3 5 7 9 10 8 6 4 2

First Edition

For my mother and father

In Memory Of:

America's service members killed in action during the Iraq War, especially the men of 1st Battalion, 502nd Infantry Regiment/2nd Brigade Combat Team, 101st Airborne Division deployed to Mahmudiyah, Yusufiyah, and Lutufiyah, Iraq, 2005–2006.

First Lieutenant Garrison Avery, 23, Lincoln, Nebraska
Specialist David Babineau, 25, Springfield, Massachusetts
Specialist Ethan Biggers, 22, Beavercreek, Ohio
First Lieutenant Benjamin Britt, 24, Wheeler, Texas
Specialist Marlon Bustamante, 25, Corona, New York
Sergeant Kenith Casica, 32, Virginia Beach, Virginia
Staff Sergeant Jason Fegler, 24, Virginia Beach, Virginia
Sergeant Matthew Hunter, 31, Valley Grove, West Virginia
Private First Class Brian Kubik, 20, Harker Heights, Texas
Specialist William Lopez-Feliciano, 33, Quebradillas, Puerto Rico
Private First Class Tyler MacKenzie, 20, Evans, Colorado
Staff Sergeant Johnnie Mason, 32, Rio Vista, Texas
Private First Class Kristian Menchaca, 23, San Marcos, Texas
Specialist Joshua Munger, 22, Maysville, Missouri
Staff Sergeant Travis Nelson, 41, Anniston, Alabama
Specialist Anthony "Chad" Owens, 21, Conway, South Carolina
Captain Blake Russell, 35, Fort Worth, Texas
Specialist Benjamin Smith, 21, Hudson, Wisconsin
Private First Class Thomas Tucker, 25, Madras, Oregon
Private First Class Caesar Viglienzone, 21, Santa Rosa, California
Specialist Andrew Waits, 23, Waterford, Michigan

The innocent victims of the Iraq War, especially the Rashid al-Janabi family, Yusufiyah, Iraq. March 12, 2006.

Qassim Hamzah Rashid al-Janabi
Fakhriah Taha Mahsin Moussa al-Janabi
Abeer Qassim Hamzah Rashid al-Janabi
Hadeel Qassim Hamzah Rashid al-Janabi

Compassion is of value and enriches our life only when compassion is severe, which is to say when we can perceive everything that is good and bad about a character but are still able to feel that the sum of us as human beings is probably a little more good than awful. In any case, good or bad, it reminds us that life is like a gladiators' arena for the soul and so we can feel strengthened by those who endure, and feel awe and pity for those who do not.

—*Norman Mailer*

CONTENTS

CONTENTS

FOREWORD

IN LATE SEPTEMBER 2008, CBS's *60 Minutes* aired a profile of U.S. Army general Ray Odierno, who, along with General David Petraeus, is credited with spearheading a new strategy that helped bring a dramatic decrease in violence to Iraq in 2007 and 2008. During that segment, he and correspondent Lesley Stahl walked around the marketplace of a town south of Baghdad called Mahmudiyah, one of the three corners of an area known as the Triangle of Death. As they walked and talked—neither, conspicuously, was wearing a helmet—Odierno told Stahl that the area was once occupied by just 1,000 U.S. soldiers, who coped with more than a hundred attacks against them and Iraqi civilians each week. Today, including Iraqi security forces, Odierno said, the region is patrolled by 30,000 men and experiences only two attacks per week. (That comparatively low level of violence held well into late 2009.)

This book is about the soldiers deployed to that area back when the Triangle of Death lived up to its name, when it was arguably the country's most dangerous region, at arguably its most dangerous time.

I first became interested in 1st Battalion, 502nd Infantry Regiment, 101st Airborne Division just after June 16, 2006. Working as *Time* magazine's Tokyo bureau chief, I read a news report about three soldiers who had been overrun by insurgents at a remote checkpoint just southwest of Mahmudiyah. One trooper was dead on the scene and two were missing, presumed taken hostage. It was a gut-wrenching story, inviting horrible thoughts about what torture and desecration terrorists could inflict on captive soldiers. News of the search played out over the next few days, and on the 19th, the bodies were found, indeed mutilated, beheaded, burned, and booby-trapped with explosives.

About two weeks after that, another story from Iraq caught my eye.

Four U.S. soldiers had been implicated in the March 2006 rape of a fourteen-year-old Iraqi girl, killing her, her parents, and her six-year-old sister. The crime was horrific and cold-blooded. The fourteen-year-old had been triply defiled: raped, murdered, and burned to a blackened char. The soldiers' unit: 1st Battalion, 502nd Infantry Regiment, 101st Airborne Division. Because I followed both stories somewhat distractedly at first, it took a while for me to piece together that the accused were not just from the same company as the soldiers who'd been ambushed several weeks prior but from the very same platoon: 1st Platoon, Bravo Company.

Two of the most notorious events from the war had flooded the headlines within days of each other, and they had happened within the same circle of approximately thirty-five men. What could possibly have been going on in that platoon? Were the two events related? As I was ruminating about such things, I got a call from Captain James Culp, a former infantry sergeant turned lawyer who was the Army's senior defense counsel at Camp Victory in Baghdad. He was a source for a story I had worked on a couple years back and he had since become a friend.

He phoned to tell me that he had been assigned to defend one of the soldiers accused of the rape-murders, and he implored me to look into Bravo Company, "if not for the sake of my client," he said, "then for the sake of the other guys in Bravo." He told me that he had been down to Mahmudiyah several times examining the crime scene and interviewing dozens of members of the company. He finished that first call with a chilling assessment. "America has no idea what is going on with this war," he said. "I'm only twenty miles away, and most of the people on Victory have no idea how bloody the fight is down there. What that company is going through, it would turn your hair white."

Intrigued by what Culp told me, I tracked the trials of the accused soldiers as they wended their way to court over the next three years, either attending in person or reading the court transcripts. I contacted several men from 1st Platoon, to see if they were willing to talk. Surprisingly, they were. Despondent over being judged for the actions of a criminal few in their midst, they were eager to share their stories. The tales they told were raw and harrowing. They described for me the devastating losses they had suffered (seven dead in their platoon alone), the nearly daily roadside bombs called IEDs (improvised explosive devices) they had experienced, the frequent firefights they had fought, their belief that the chain of command had abandoned them, and the medical and psychological problems they were coping with to this day.

They were generous with their time, unvarnished in their honesty. They suggested I widen my scope, arguing that I could not properly understand the crime and the abduction if I did not understand their whole deployment, and I could not understand 1st Platoon if I did not understand 2nd and 3rd Platoons, who had labored under exactly the same conditions but who had come home with far fewer losses and their sense of brotherhood and accomplishment more intact. Check it out, they suggested, it might lead you someplace interesting about how the whole thing went down.

I followed their advice, interviewing more soldiers from all of Bravo and requesting reams of documents through the Freedom of Information Act. Embedded with the Army in mid-2008, I traveled throughout 1st Battalion's old area of operations in Iraq, speaking to as many locals as I could. I interviewed the immediate relatives of the murdered Iraqi family.

Every opened door led to a new one. Most soldiers and officers I talked to offered to put me in touch with more. Some shared journals, letters and e-mails, photos, or classified reports and investigations. I interviewed scores more servicemen, crisscrossing the United States several times, and ultimately broadened my scope even further to encompass not just Bravo but, for context, the rest of 1st Battalion.

The story of 1st Platoon's 2005–2006 deployment to the Triangle of Death is both epic and tragic. It was an ill-starred tour, where nearly everything that could go wrong did, and a chain of events unfolded that seems inevitable and inexorable yet, in retrospect, also heartbreakingly preventable at literally dozens of junctures.

To some degree, the travails of Bravo Company are a study of the tactical consequences that flow from a flawed strategy. Their tour was part of the final deployments before counterinsurgency theory and tactics took hold, before the surge of 2007, before the cease-fires initiated by Muqtada al-Sadr's Mahdi Army became more or less permanent, before the Sons of Iraq program that paid insurgents to stop fighting Americans and start taking responsibility for their own neighborhood safety.

Virtually ignored by military planners before the summer of 2005, the 330-square-mile region south of Baghdad that encompassed the Triangle of Death had become one of the most restive hotbeds of insurgency in the country, a battleground of the incipient civil war between Sunnis and Shi'ites, as well as a way station for terrorists of every allegiance ferrying men, weapons, and money into the capital.

With far fewer troops and resources than were necessary for the job, the 1-502nd Infantry Regiment was flung out there with orders, essentially, to save the day. A light infantry battalion of about 700 men, the 1-502nd was assigned to root out insurgent strongholds, promote social and municipal revival, and train the local Iraqi Army battalions into a competent fighting force.

It was a mission easy to encapsulate, but depressingly difficult to achieve. There was no coherent strategy for how they were supposed to accomplish these feats. There was confusion about whether they should emphasize hunting and killing insurgents or winning the support of the people who were providing both passive and active assistance to the terrorists. This confusion flowed from the Pentagon, through the battalion's chain of command, all the way down to the soldiers. The 1-502nd arrived when America's prospects in the country were dim, and, despite some successes in certain areas, the situation was dispiritingly bleaker when they left, with insurgent attacks on the rise and the country threatening to come apart entirely.

The Triangle of Death was a meat grinder, churning out daily doses of carnage. During their year-long deployment, soldiers from the battalion either found or got hit by nearly nine hundred roadside IEDs. They were shelled or mortared almost every day and took fire from rifles, machine guns, or rocket-propelled grenades (RPGs) nearly every other day. Twenty-one men from the battalion were killed and scores more were wounded badly enough to be evacuated home.

The gore was unrelenting, not just for soldiers but also for civilians. Including Iraqi locals, just one of the battalion's three bases treated an average of three or four trauma cases each day. Every soldier has stories of getting hit by IEDs. Many could tell of getting hit by several IED explosions in one day. The unrelenting combat wore on their psychological health. More than 40 percent of the battalion were treated for mental or emotional anxiety while in country, and many have since been diagnosed with post-traumatic stress disorder or traumatic brain injury, or both.

Bravo was particularly hard-hit. Within Bravo's first ninety days in theater, all three of its platoon leaders, its first sergeant, a squad leader, and a team leader (in addition to several riflemen) had been wiped from the battlefield by death or injury. For 1st Battalion executive officer Major Fred Wintrich, the challenge doesn't get any starker: "How do you reseed a company with almost all of its top leadership while in a combat zone? That was the task." By the end of the deployment, 51 of Bravo's approximately 135 soldiers had been killed, wounded, or moved to another unit.

Human organizations are flawed because humans are flawed. Even with the best intentions, men make errors in judgment and initiate courses of action that are counterproductive to their self-interest or the completion of the mission. In a combat zone, ranks as low as staff sergeants make dozens of decisions every day, each with a direct impact on the potential safety and well-being of their men. A company commander or a battalion commander may make hundreds of such decisions a day. Fortunately, in complex environments, individual errors or even long chains of mistakes can often be corrected or they simply dissipate before they cause any adverse effect. Decisions from different people about the same goal either negate or reinforce each other, and, it is hoped, the preponderance of these heaped-together decisions pushes the task toward completion rather than failure. But sometimes, in the permutations of millions of decisions from thousands of actors converging on a battlefield over a period of weeks or even months, a singular combination comes together to unlock something abhorrent. These are what are known, in retrospect, as disasters waiting to happen.

March 12, 2006, was one such disaster. Nothing can absolve James Barker, Paul Cortez, Steven Green, and Jesse Spielman from the personal responsibility that is theirs, and theirs alone, for the rape of Abeer Qassim Hamzah Rashid al-Janabi, her vicious murder, and the wanton destruction of her family. It is one of the most nefarious war crimes known to be perpetrated by U.S. soldiers in any era—singularly heinous not just for its savagery but also because it was so calculated, premeditated, and methodical. But leading up to that day, a litany of miscommunications, organizational snafus, lapses in leadership, and ignored warning signs up and down the chain of command all contributed to the creation of an environment where it was possible for such a crime to take place.

I have sympathy for the many men of Bravo who simply want this episode to go away, who saw my inquiries as a continuation of a nightmare from which they have not been allowed to wake. Several times one or the other of them remarked to me, "No matter how screwed up the chain of command was, how strung out the men were, and how many risks the unit was taking, it was not so different from what happens all the time in the Army, and if March 12 hadn't happened, you wouldn't be here now, years later, in my living room, dredging it all up again." This is undoubtedly true, but there is a circularity to this logic: "If something exceptional hadn't taken place, you wouldn't find it exceptional." When the final variables clicked into place—an unsupervised foursome of men drunk and in a murderous mood on the afternoon of March 12—the unexceptional became exceptional, and the exceptional became history.

On several levels, the story of Bravo is timeless and could emerge from any war. It is about the heroic and horrible things that men do under the extreme stresses of combat. It is about men who fight despite their fear, who violently extinguish other people's lives, who watch the best friends they will ever have die before their eyes, who make decisions under conditions that most people can barely conceive of, who butt heads with their superiors and their subordinates, and who love some of their closest comrades in arms as intensely as they do any blood relative.

But Bravo's story is also inseparable from the buildup to March 12, the crimes committed that afternoon, and their aftermath, which still reverberate today. It is a story about how fragile the values that the U.S. military, and all Americans, consider bedrock really are, how easily morals can be defiled, integrity abandoned, character undone.

Not surprisingly, this deployment has produced deep, irreconcilable rifts between many of the men who served together. Especially within Bravo Company, and especially within 1st Platoon, the anger and bitterness that many of the men feel is difficult to overstate. When the abduction and the rape-murders became public in such close succession, the unit descended into a frenzy of finger-pointing. Seemingly everyone tried to pin a single, unified blame on a select few (and who was blamed depended on who was doing the blaming) while scrambling to absolve himself completely.

I had thought that the Army way was for everyone to accept a small piece of the responsibility for any debacle truly too big to be of any one person's making and spread the blame to all parties, which would not only make it easier for everyone to survive professionally but, perhaps more important, also make the fiasco something that the Army could study and learn from. But the ordeal generated so much bile and rancor for so many people that the Army seems more interested in forgetting about the tragedy entirely than in ensuring it never happens again.

Careers were ruined. Reputations tarnished. Medals withheld. Friendships broken. Prodigious resentments have festered because many men feel that blame was unfairly pushed down to the lower ranks and not shared by a higher command they believe was also culpable.

This is true. The events surrounding Bravo Company were so complex and intertwined that to lay all responsibility not for the crime, but for creating an atmosphere where the crime could occur, at the feet of the few and relatively powerless, is the very definition of scapegoating. And to assert that the battalion command climate was anything other than utterly dysfunctional, or to declare that the soldiers of 1st Platoon were, at any point in the deployment, being effectively managed and led, is simply a whitewash. The Army failed 1st Platoon time and time again.

It bears emphasizing that given the strain inherent in the eight and a half straight years it has been at war, the United States Army today is among the most-tested and best-behaved fighting forces in history. Rape and murder have been by-products of warfare since the beginning of time. Soldiers today, however, suffer mightily under the burden of "the Greatest Generation" mythos and the sanitized Hollywood depictions of World War II. There is a persistent and unfortunate sentiment among modern warriors that they will never live up to the nobility and bravery of those who saw off fascism. But anyone with a better than glossed-over understanding of "the Good War" knows that even Allied troops committed war crimes such as killing prisoners and raping foreign women at a rate that could be charitably called not infrequent. (One expert estimates that U.S. forces alone may have committed more than 18,000 rapes in the European theater between 1942 and 1945.) It is thus a testament to the control and discipline now exercised by the Army how rarely crimes such as this are actually committed today, and how swiftly the Army moves to investigate them.

   The rules of conduct have changed remarkably rapidly, as has society's tolerance for military malfeasance. Although most Vietnam War movies are works of fiction, it is fascinating how often misconduct or outright felonies figure in them, sometimes just as subplots or secondary narrative devices. In contrast, today's soldiers are required to be nothing less than warrior monks. Frequenting whorehouses and drinking anytime not on duty (and sometimes when on duty) in a war zone used to be tolerated, if not condoned, by the Army until just a few decades ago. Today, young men are expected to fight for months on end with zero sexual release and almost no social recreation whatsoever. The two-cans-of-beer-a-day ration is long gone, and even the possession of pornography is expressly forbidden.

This is as it must be, of course. The story of Steven Green proves that in today's media and propaganda environment, even one private with a rifle can affect the course of a war and dramatically harm America's image abroad. Only one out-of-control platoon needs just one Steven Green and a handful of coconspirators to significantly damage the gains that a nearly thousand-strong battalion worked hard to achieve. That is why the manner that every last private is managed, every minute of every day, warrants scrutiny.

Despite battalion commander Lieutenant Colonel Tom Kunk's insistence that he and his chain of command practiced what he incessantly calls "engaged leadership," facts demonstrate that he and his senior leaders were woefully out of touch with the realities on the ground. Despite numerous warnings, Kunk and his subordinates were either unable or unwilling to acknowledge how dire Steven Green's mental state was specifically, or how impaired 1st Platoon was generally. Kunk instead belittled 1st Platoon's incapacity, told them they were wallowing in self-pity, and blamed them and their platoon-level leadership for all their problems, which, in turn, exacerbated their feelings of isolation and persecution and contributed to their downward spiral.

Bravo Company commander Captain John Goodwin made several explicit requests for more troops in late 2005 and early 2006. Kunk denied them all, arguing alternately that the company had enough men but was using them inefficiently or that there were simply no troops available. Whether Kunk, or his boss, or his boss's boss could find combat power to spare is debatable. Many senior leaders say it was impossible, there were no surplus troops anywhere in theater, and they insist that an extra platoon or company cannot be generated out of thin air. Perhaps so, but when the three Bravo soldiers were captured on June 16, 2006, 8,000 soldiers were somehow mustered and flooded the area in less than seventy-two hours.

As I have met and interviewed most of the soldiers and officers involved in the main arc of the events described in this book, they have become utterly, completely human in my eyes. As I have gotten to know them, it has been increasingly difficult to employ the comforting Hollywood dichotomies of good guys and bad guys, heroes and villains. I believe there were good leaders and bad leaders in this battalion, and I think the facts demonstrate who was who, but I also believe that bad leaders had good days and good leaders had bad days. While the story abounds in compelling personalities and colorful characters, they are, of course, not characters in any novelist's sense. They are all, every last one of them, real people. And besides a few significant and felonious exceptions, they were all trying to do their best, making decisions on the fly and under fire, in unspeakably difficult and dangerous circumstances, for their men, their unit, and the mission.

My greatest privilege of the past three years has been getting to know so many soldiers from Bravo and the rest of 1st Battalion. There are so many clichés about "supporting our troops" or calling every soldier who has ever donned a uniform a "hero" that it debases serious tribute to genuine warriors, and trivializes the terrible sacrifices that real frontline fighters make. It has been my solemn honor to have been allowed into these veterans' lives and to hear their stories.

They do not ask for anyone's pity, but the troopers of 1st Platoon are not the same men they used to be. The majority of them are no longer in the Army. Some of them drink too much, some are in trouble with the law, some cannot hold a job, some get into frequent fistfights, some fly into storms of rage, some suffer from debilitating medical problems, and some are racked with depression, doubt, and despair. Most of them will cope and adjust, and work hard to make peace with what they have lived through, and ultimately they will be okay. But some of them will not.

The trust these men have invested in me has been humbling, and in their trust I feel a massive responsibility. I believe they understood my goal when I described it to them, which is why they frequently sat with me for days on end going over every last detail, no matter how unsavory. The goal of this book is not to make soldiers look bad, but unlike many popular military histories, it does not attempt to gloss over the inherently brutal and dehumanizing institution of warfare, it does not edit out everything unflattering, let alone upsetting, and it does not seek to make soldiers or the Army look good as an unquestioned end unto itself. I have aimed, instead, to provide an unburnished look at how the soldiers of 1st Platoon and Bravo Company actually lived, fought, strived, and struggled during their 2005–2006 deployment to the Triangle of Death. This book is dedicated to them.

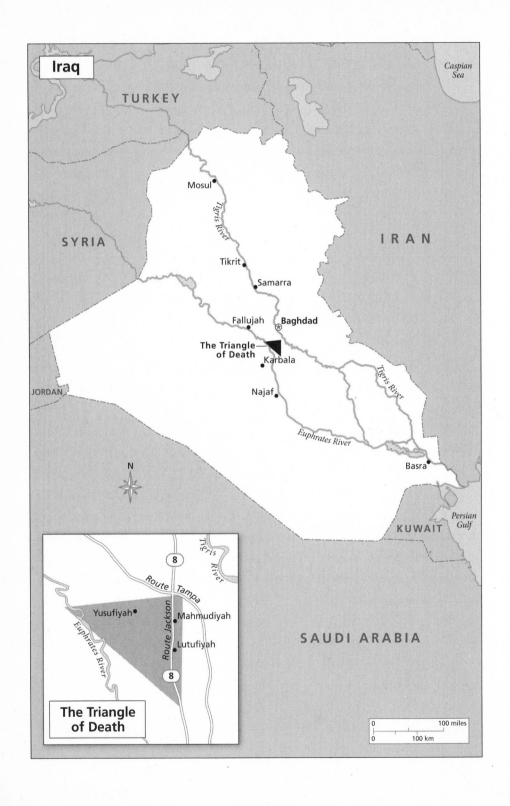

Iraq

TURKEY

Caspian Sea

SYRIA

IRAN

Mosul

Tigris River

Tikrit

Samarra

Fallujah

⊛ **Baghdad**

The Triangle of Death

Karbala

Najaf

JORDAN

Tigris River

Euphrates River

Basra

N

Persian Gulf

KUWAIT

SAUDI ARABIA

Tigris River

8

Route Tampa

Yusufiyah

Route Jackson

Mahmudiyah

Lutufiyah

Euphrates River

8

The Triangle of Death

0		100 miles
0		100 km

PRELUDE

___

March 12, 2006

IN THE LENGTHENING shadows of an afternoon sun, the masked men in black hurried from the farmhouse in a commotion. They had not left any witnesses.

About an hour later, Abu Muhammad heard a knock on his door. A balding, short, and hefty forty-nine-year-old with a salt-and-pepper mustache, Abu Muhammad had served fourteen years in the Iraqi Army and now worked for the Ministry of Health. Warily, he headed toward the window. You never knew who could be at the door. Everyone was tense since the invasion. Everyone was living in fear. To think people had originally welcomed the Americans, he often mused, welcomed the removal of Saddam! They never dreamed, never even considered, it would get worse after the dictator was gone, but it was so much worse now that people actually longed for Saddam—even the people who had hated him the most. Ever since the Americans came, there was no safety, there was no peace. Armed militias were roaming the countryside, both Sunni and Shi'ite, killing whomever they pleased. Bodies turned up every day.

Everyone feared the Americans, too. The soldiers were massive and intimidating, their hulking frames made all the more fearsome with their equipment and rifles and dark glasses, their massive trucks carrying even bigger guns, and their thuggish, arrogant ways. They shoved and slapped the men around, sticking guns in their faces, accusing them all of being terrorists while herding the women into a separate room where who knows what they could do to them? The Americans said they were here to bring democracy and freedom, but they could not even provide the small amounts of electricity and water that Saddam did. They brought death and chaos instead.

There was another knock. A good sign. A knock was better than the door getting kicked in. Looking out the window, Abu Muhammad thanked Allah—it was a man he knew, a neighbor of his cousin and her husband who lived not far away.

"You must come, Abu Muhammad," the man said, calling him by his nickname. "Abu" means "father of," and many Iraqi men carry such sobriquets. "You must come. Something has happened at your cousin's house, something terrible."

Abu Muhammad lived in a village just outside of Yusufiyah, about twenty miles south of Baghdad in the flatlands between the Tigris and the Euphrates. His cousin lived in an even smaller hamlet a mile away. Pulling his car onto the dirt driveway of his cousin's modest, one-story house, Abu Muhammad saw his cousin's boys, eleven-year-old Muhammad and nine-year-old Ahmed, outside. They had just returned home from school. There was smoke billowing out one window of the house. The boys were crying, inconsolable. They were screaming and wailing and blubbering; it was impossible to make sense of anything they said. Scared that danger lurked inside, Abu Muhammad circled the house, looking in the windows to ensure the scene was clear. In the house's sole bedroom he saw what looked like three bodies lying on the floor. There were big pools of blood. In the living room, he saw another body. This one was on fire.

"Stay here," he told the boys, as he entered the front door. The first thing that hit him was the smell: Propane. Musty smoke. Cooked flesh. Agitated and afraid, he scurried around the house. He went to the kitchen to turn off the propane tank, giving the valve a few solid turns. Then he moved to the bedroom.

Socked by dust storms and bleached by the sun, Iraq's usual color palette is filled with browns, beiges, and duns, as if the whole country were a sepia photograph. But here, inside the Janabi house, was a riot of colors, alarming in their vibrancy, a Technicolor brilliance of violence, concentrated and otherworldly. Abu Muhammad had seen what the insurgent death squads could do, but he had never witnessed anything like this. Each body was a different sort of travesty. Qassim, the father, was facedown in the far corner of the bedroom, in a lake of his own burgundy blood. His shirt was brightly patterned, striped with white, orange, and brown. The front of his skull had been blasted off. Gore and large chunks of gray matter stippled the walls in a wide, V-shaped pattern. A large mound of Qassim's brain, about the size of a fist, lay nearby on the intricately woven rug.

Not far from Qassim was Hadeel, just six years old. Wearing a bright pink dress, she was beautiful, her face almost pristine like a death mask, except that she was covered in blood, liters of it. It was everywhere, matting her hair, soaking her dress, covering her face in a thin dried sheen. A bullet fired from behind—perhaps she had been running away from her assailant—had blown the back right quadrant of her skull apart. A piece of it was lying several feet away, covered in skin and hair. Her hair band had been thrown across the room by the whiplash of the impact. In her right hand, she was still clutching some plants she had just picked, a kind of wild sweet grass that Iraqi children frequently gather and eat for fun.

Closest to the door was Fakhriah, the mother, wearing a black *abaya* and an emerald velveteen housedress embroidered with white flowers. She was lying on her back with her eyes wide open. Abu Muhammad thought his cousin might still be alive. He reached down to feel her pulse. Nothing. She was dead. He turned her over, and then he saw the hole. She had been shot in the back, but the rich, dark hues of her clothing obscured the full extent of her wound.

Shaken, Abu Muhammad moved into the living room. There was Abeer, only fourteen years old. What they had done to her, it was unspeakable. Her body was still smoking; her entire upper torso had been scorched, much of it burnt down to ash. Her chest and face were gone, with only the tips of her fingers, sticking out from the purple scraps of her dress sleeves, recognizably human. The lower half of her body, however, was mostly intact. Her thin, spindly legs were spread and, rigid in death, still bent at the knees. She was naked from the waist down, her tights and underwear nearby.

The stench was overpowering. Abu Muhammad ran to the kitchen and grabbed the only vessel he could see and came back to the living room. He dumped the teapot, including tea leaves, onto her, causing more smoke and a hiss. There was no running water in the house, so he hurried outside to the canal flowing nearby. He told the boys to stay where they were, plunged the teapot into the canal, and jogged back to the house to douse Abeer's body. This was slow, but he didn't know what else to do. He wasn't thinking clearly enough to try to find a bucket and wouldn't have known where to find one if he had been. It took five or six trips to the canal with the small vessel to put the fire out, until Abeer's remains were wet and cold.

"Come," he said to the boys, "come with me." Abu Muhammad got into his car with the boys and dropped them off at his home to stay with his wife. Then he drove to a nearby traffic control point known as TCP1 that was occupied by a dozen or so Iraqi Army (IA) soldiers and about the same number of U.S. soldiers. He found one of the Iraqis and told him that they needed to come because his cousin and her family, they had been murdered.

"Yribe! Hey, Yribe!" Staff Sergeant Chaz Allen called. Allen was 1st Squad's squad leader. Since 1st Platoon's platoon sergeant, Sergeant First Class Jeff Fenlason, was in another part of Bravo Company's area for much of the day, Allen was in charge of TCP1.

"What?" said Sergeant Tony Yribe, who was one of Allen's team leaders and one of 1st Platoon's most formidable warriors. Six feet tall and 210 pounds, Yribe was broad-shouldered, heavily muscled, and square-jawed. Just twenty-two years old, he was on his second tour in Iraq, a grizzled veteran more than familiar with the dark realities of being a trained killer that they don't show you in the movies and they don't tell you about in basic training. He looked like an action hero and radiated a confidence that cannot be learned. To most of the younger guys in the platoon, he was practically a god.

"The IAs got a guy saying some family was killed behind TCP2 or something," Allen said. "They took a look and say there are definitely bodies down there. I need you to go check it out."

Just another day in Yusufiyah, Yribe mused. The rate at which Iraqis were killing each other was astonishing sometimes. Every day, pretty much, soldiers were fishing dead bodies out of canals, coming across them in shallow graves, or finding them dumped by the side of the road after midnight executions. Of all the reasons to hate this country and its people, this was just another one: their utter disregard for each other.

As usual, Yribe noted, there were not enough men to mount a proper patrol. Ideally, they shouldn't be maneuvering around here with anything less than a squad, about nine or ten men. But that almost never happened. If the soldiers here in the Triangle of Death followed the directives specifying the minimum number of men for whatever task was at hand, they'd simply never get anything done. Three-, four-, five-man patrols were common to the point of being standard. Yribe pointed out that there were not enough soldiers even for that bare minimum. Allen told him to grab a guy from here and pick up two more men on his way to the house from TCP2, which was about three-quarters of a mile southwest. Allen would radio ahead so they would be waiting.

"And be sure to bring a camera," Allen said. "Battalion is going to want pictures."

Yribe grabbed another soldier and an interpreter and headed out. It was getting to be late afternoon. First Platoon, Bravo Company and all of 1st Battalion of the 502nd Infantry Regiment, 101st Airborne Division had been in theater for five and a half months. Five and a half more months to go. It felt like an eternity—with an eternity yet to come.

Yribe arrived at TCP2 and Cortez and Spielman were ready to go, suited up in full body armor, helmets, and weapons. Third Squad's leader, Staff Sergeant Eric Lauzier, was on leave for a month, so twenty-three-year-old Paul Cortez was acting squad leader, a job many in Bravo Company thought was beyond him. He wasn't even a sergeant, which is usually a requirement for leading a squad. He had passed the promotion board, but he wouldn't pin on his stripes for a few weeks, so he was technically a specialist promotable. A lot of Cortez's peers and superiors in Bravo thought he was a punk who shouldn't have been promoted at all. They found him immature, insecure, and a loudmouth, with a nasty streak to boot. He was probably the guy most desperate to prove he was as good a soldier and as tough a character as Yribe, but he wasn't and he never would be.

Cortez was in charge of a motley group of just six soldiers down at TCP2, some of whom had been on their own at this spartan, unfortified outpost for twelve days straight. They were pretty ragged and strung out. Twenty-three-year-old Specialist James Barker was next in seniority, a soldier renowned for being a smart aleck, mischief-maker, and master scrounge artist but also one of the platoon's coolest, deadliest heads in combat, with an uncanny memory and spatial awareness. Private First Class Jesse Spielman and Private First Class Steven Green had arrived from different TCPs just a couple of days ago to augment Cortez's understaffed position. Twenty-one-year-old Spielman was a quiet, unassuming trooper who generally just kept his head down and followed orders. But Green? Twenty-one-year-old Green was one of the weirdest men in the company. He was an okay soldier when he wanted to be, which wasn't often, but the oddest thing about him was that he never stopped talking. And the stuff that came out of his mouth was some of the most outrageous, racist invective many of the men had ever heard, which is saying something, considering the perpetual locker-room atmosphere of raunchy jokes and racial and ethnic taunts that are just part of the vernacular in any Army combat unit. Green could discourse on any number of topics, but they usually involved hate in some way, including how Hitler should be admired, how "white culture" was under threat in multiethnic America, and how much he wanted to kill every last Iraqi on the planet. He would go on and on and on like this until somebody literally would have to order him to shut up. Two more newbie privates who'd arrived late to the deployment fresh out of basic training rounded out the TCP2 group.

Yribe picked up Cortez and Spielman and the five-man patrol walked the quarter mile to the house. Some Iraqi Army soldiers were already there. They had surrounded the house but were waiting outside for the Americans to show up. Yribe and the three U.S. soldiers cleared the five-room house in textbook infantry fashion just in case some insurgents were lying in ambush. Once they determined the house was safe, they started surveying the scene.

It was grisly. Yribe started taking pictures and directed the other soldiers to look for evidence. Some Iraqi medics arrived to collect the bodies. As the men milled around trying to make sense of what they were seeing, Cortez started dry heaving. He looked green and pale and was drenched with sweat. He hacked and convulsed.

"Jesus, just go outside," Yribe told Cortez. What a pussy, Yribe thought as he looked around. This was some vile carnage, he reflected, but frankly, it was far from the worst he had ever seen in this God-forsaken country. Given the level of savagery he had watched Iraqis unleash on other Iraqis, the number of tortured, mutilated, executed bodies he had seen, the corpses bloated and stinking, human parts so traumatized by metal and heat that they had liquefied, or been ripped to shreds, nothing really shocked him anymore. And if Cortez can't handle this, he thought, that says a lot about him.

Yribe and Cortez had always been friends—their girlfriends were sisters, in fact—but Yribe wasn't sure how much he really respected him. Cortez had been a Bradley Fighting Vehicle driver with the 4th Infantry Division during the initial invasion in 2003, and he transferred to the 101st Airborne, a somewhat more prestigious division, because he wanted to be even closer to the action. Yribe had always teased him about that, being a driver. Everybody knows that they only put the shitbags, the fat kids, and the cowards behind the wheel, he would tell Cortez. He had always been kidding, but maybe, Yribe thought now, maybe it was true. Maybe Cortez just couldn't hack it.

Yribe took photos from every angle, so that higher headquarters could put together a "storyboard," a PowerPoint slide that described and illustrated major events in a one-page format for briefings and archiving. They made sketches of the house, noting where the bodies were lying. They emptied the pockets of the adults, looking for IDs, keys, or other identifiers. They picked up some AK-47 shell casings that were scattered about and dropped them into plastic bags. Every time Cortez had composed himself enough to come back in, he'd be able to last only a minute or two before he'd have to rush out gagging all over again. To get a full range of photos, Yribe told the other two soldiers to move the bodies around. They flipped some of the victims from front to back or vice versa to get shots of every corpse's face and wounds. Through the two or three hours it took to survey the house, Cortez was effectively useless, but Spielman, on the other hand, was cool and efficient, rolling over and moving whatever body Yribe told him to. The burned girl's remains were so disgusting, however, and there was so little of what could be called a body left, that they just left her where she was. The Iraqi medics had trouble getting her rigid, spread legs into a body bag.

As one of the men moved one of the many mattresses that were thrown about the bedroom floor, something small and green skittered across the ground. It was a spent shotgun shell.

That's odd, Yribe thought, Iraqis don't really use shotguns.

SUMMER 2005

1

"We've Got to Get South Baghdad

Under Control"

WHEN COLONEL TODD Ebel took command of the 2nd Brigade of the 101st Airborne Division in the summer of 2004, he knew he had little more than a year to get 3,400 men and women ready for a war that was becoming more complicated and dangerous every day. And by the fall of 2005, as the brigade approached deployment, the war was in its direst state yet.

The deterioration of Iraq since the April 9, 2003, toppling of Saddam Hussein's regime had been precipitous and unrelenting. The invasion itself was a stunning success, when 170,000 U.S. and British troops (less than one-third the number who fought in 1991's Operation Desert Storm) sprinted from Kuwait to Baghdad in twenty-one days, with just 169 killed in action.

After the initial euphoria wore off, however, nothing went according to plan because there was, quite simply, no plan. The first American transition team, formed just weeks before the invasion started and led by retired U.S. Army lieutenant general Jay Garner, was doomed before it could begin. With minimal staffing and funding, Garner proclaimed the Office of Reconstruction and Humanitarian Assistance

(ORHA) an agent of rapid power transfer back to the Iraqis, just as the White House said it intended. But when it became apparent that post-invasion Iraq was far more chaotic than the war's planners had envisioned and that there was no decapitated but functioning government to hand power to, ORHA's reason for existing vanished. On April 24, Secretary of Defense Donald Rumsfeld called Garner, who had made it to Baghdad only three days earlier, to tell him that he, and ORHA, were being replaced.

The White House appointed veteran diplomat L. Paul "Jerry" Bremer to head the Coalition Provisional Authority (CPA), ORHA's successor. After the stillbirth of ORHA, Bremer arrived with a desire to show early, decisive change. Unfortunately, his first two bold strokes—made over the objections of Garner, the CIA's Baghdad station chief, military commanders, and without the full blessing of the Bush administration—were disastrous. First, Bremer barred from government employment anyone who had held any position of consequence in Saddam's Baath Party. Under Saddam, party membership was common among public-service employees, whether they were true believers or not. By firing down to these levels, the United States jettisoned the midlevel doctors, bureaucrats, and engineers who actually provided essential public services to the people on a daily basis. Six days later, against even more opposition, Bremer dissolved the entire Iraqi military and national police force. In one week, he had thrown between 500,000 and 900,000 people, the majority of them armed and now humiliated men, out of work—on top of the already 40 percent of Iraqi adults estimated to be jobless.

The people who worked at the CPA, from Bremer on down, arrived with a kind of visionary—even missionary—idealism unsuited to the realities on the ground. For many, being Bush administration loyalists, rather than having experience in diplomacy or reconstruction, was their only qualification. Huge percentages of them never left the walled center of Baghdad known as the "Green Zone." Due to the CPA's weak administrative and financial controls, corruption and graft became rife among American and Iraqi contractors working with the organization.

Of the $12 billion disbursed by the CPA in just over a year, $9 billion remains unaccounted for. The CPA failed, repeatedly, to deliver on its promises, including Bremer's August 2003 pledge that "About one year from now, for the first time in history, every Iraqi in every city, town, and village will have as much electricity as he or she can use and will have it twenty-four hours a day, every single day."

Bremer and the CPA dramatically mishandled the complexities of the Iraqi ethnic, political, and social climate as well. Conducting himself with the imperiousness of a viceroy, Bremer confirmed most Iraqis' suspicions that the United States had arrived not as a liberator but as a conqueror bent on a lengthy occupation. He created an Interim Governing Council (IGC) and divided its twenty-five seats along demographic lines, with fourteen spots going to Shi'ites, five to Sunni Kurds, and four to Sunni Arabs. One seat went to a Christian and one to a Turkmen. While the Americans saw this as a simple matter of logic and fairness, and focused on the fact that they were bringing disenfranchised groups such as the Kurds and the Shi'ites into the fold, to the Sunni Arabs, this was the world upside down.

Sunnis had been the ruling class since the British cobbled the country together from three provinces of the Ottoman Empire, a continuation of the privileged status they had enjoyed under that regime, and for centuries before that. For the Americans, who talked a lot about democracy, to overturn the power structure so radically by diktat struck many Sunnis as hypocritical, vindictive, and proof of what they had always suspected: It wasn't just Saddam or even the Baathists the Americans had come to punish. They aimed to demolish Sunni hegemony outright. The Shi'ites, meanwhile, reveled in the realization that for only the second time in modern history (the 1979 Islamic revolution in Iran was the first), they were going to rule a country.

While the Bush administration and the CPA's ineptitude failed to provide virtually anything of value to Iraqis besides the removal of Saddam, an insurgency started flowering immediately. The large but sparsely populated Sunni-dominated western province of Anbar, where the city of Fallujah is located, was an early hot point. The insular tribes, whose sheikhs control ancient smuggling routes, had a reputation for fundamentalism and xenophobia even in Saddam's time. They extended the United States the least goodwill, and let it run dry the fastest. These burgeoning insurgents effectively employed hit-and-run shootings, but they were particularly fond of mortar attacks and especially IEDs (improvised explosive devices), homemade bombs planted under the road or disguised on the surface in bags, debris, or even animal carcasses. IEDs were the perfect terrorist weapon: they were cheap, lethal, and terrifying because they were so hard to spot or counteract.

Armed attacks on U.S. forces started as early as May 2003 and spread throughout that summer. The groups were small and disorganized at first but slowly added to their ranks and refined their tactics. Their motives were various. Some insurgents were religious, some were nationalists, some were simply opportunistic criminals. Disgruntled military personnel—some true Saddamists, others with no real allegiance to the defunct regime but humiliated over their loss of status and privilege—became increasingly active. Although the majority of the people did not actively support the insurgencies, armed groups drew recruits from every economic stratum. And those who did fight enjoyed the tacit approval of huge percentages of the population.

The insurgency was not limited to Sunnis, however. Among the United States' biggest and most lingering headaches was the surprising rise of Muqtada al-Sadr to become the most prominent voice of Shi'ite dissent to the American occupation. Until the invasion, al-Sadr was the undistinguished and politically insignificant thirty-year-old youngest son of a popular Shi'ite religious leader assassinated in 1999 by Saddam's security forces. Immediately after the invasion, however, he seized his moment. Because of his lineage, he could mobilize millions of faithful with a single speech. Unlike some other Shi'ite parties, which appealed to the middle and upper classes, al-Sadr's movement spoke to the poor, angry, alienated Shi'ite underclass whose pent-up rage was uncorked with the toppling of Saddam. And he had no time for America's expectations of gratitude. Al-Sadr's Friday sermons became increasingly virulent about the failings of the CPA.

Al-Sadr bolstered his power by running a kind of parallel govern-ment to provide the public services that the Iraqi state or the CPA sim-ply couldn't. He opened offices in cities and towns throughout the country, which served as community outreach centers, food banks, and water depots. They offered protection, infrastructure essentials, and dig-nity to a battered Shi'ite populace.

Despite his righteous mantle, however, al-Sadr was not above inciting or exploiting violence for more-nefarious purposes or material gains. Far from it. The line between a legitimate populist movement and a gi-gantic, theocratic organized-crime and terror ring was a thin one. What began as a ragtag crew of exceedingly violent al-Sadr followers grew into a committed, if unruly, militia called the Mahdi Army that numbered in the thousands. Al-Sadr's network of outposts served as Mahdi Army gar-risons, armories, and torture centers where militia members carried out reprisal killings, flying court trials, and pure criminal thuggery. The U.S. Army and Marines clashed directly with the Mahdi Army several times, and although they always delivered a severe tactical drubbing, al-Sadr emerged from every such conflict the strategic victor. He was more pow-erful than ever, a hero to millions and a major player on the national stage. For years to come, al-Sadr would remain a dangerous and un-predictable irritant to the United States.

The first response of the Bush administration and senior military leaders was to ascribe the violence to the death rattles of Saddam loyal-ists, denying, in Rumsfeld's words, that "anything like a guerrilla war or an organized resistance" was happening. In a persistent analytical mis-read, senior U.S. officials seemed unable to comprehend that there could be millions of Iraqis who considered themselves die-hard nation-alists and patriots while also despising Saddam. Well into 2007, the Army called the insurgents AIFs, for "anti-Iraqi forces," even though most non–Al Qaeda insurgent groups saw themselves as fiercely pro-Iraq but also anti–United States and, thus, against any government propped up by the United States.

As Washington lived in denial, the insurgency strengthened. In Au-gust 2003, for example, suicide bombers killed at least 180 people in a few weeks, and yet the United States declared victory whenever a major milestone was achieved, as when Saddam Hussein was captured in December 2003, or whenever the number of attacks dipped for more than a week or two.

Unfortunately, all lulls in violence proved transitory. And without enough troops, as increasing numbers of soldiers continued dying from these frustrating IEDs, many commanders on the ground panicked. Rough tactics became common. Leaders approved interrogation techniques that grew increasingly brutal. Without clearly formulated counterinsurgency theory or doctrine, the Army began using an array of techniques that were counterproductive. Units conducted huge sweeps of entire towns, hauling virtually every male over the age of ten into custody when only a tiny fraction of them were of any intelligence value.

As frontline commanders became increasingly desperate, the White House and senior military leaders remained bafflingly insouciant about the situation. When CENTCOM (Central Command) commander General Tommy Franks, who had planned and led the invasion, retired in July 2003, a new position was created to oversee all military units in Iraq. That job was not handed to another four-star general but to the most junior three-star general in the Army, Lieutenant General Ricardo Sanchez. Without enough experience or resources, Sanchez and his staff were all but guaranteed to fail.

In his memoir, Sanchez sounds overwhelmed by his role, with no real idea of what was happening around him, and no clear vision of what he was trying to accomplish. The specter of Abu Ghraib, the notorious Saddam-era prison that the U.S. military had turned into a hellhouse of torture themselves by late 2003, hangs over his tenure and his book. He seems dimly aware that something foul was going on in the prison—"I had received some worrisome reports from the field that prisoners were being treated too harshly," he writes—but he never seriously investigated. During this period, torture became more common across Iraq, not just at Abu Ghraib. One Human Rights Watch report detailed the systematic, daily abuse of detainees by members of the 82nd Airborne Division stationed near Fallujah in September 2003.

Many in the government and military downplayed the Abu Ghraib scandal as the actions of a few poorly trained reservists unprepared for the rigors of war, but even the most elite operatives in the U.S. military employed torture as standard practice. Another Human Rights Watch report described the 2003–2004 torture tactics of Task Force 121, a group of special operations forces units including Delta Force and SEAL Team Six.

For many Americans, the illusion that the Iraq War just might be going okay for the United States finally fell away on March 31, 2004, when four American private contractors ran into an insurgent ambush in Fallujah. A mob of locals dragged the bodies from their cars; burned, mutilated, and dismembered the corpses; and hung some of them from the support spans of a bridge. President Bush ordered the U.S. military to strike back with overwhelming force (against the objection of a Marine general who argued that this was exactly the overreaction the insurgents were hoping for). The military hit the city with 2,500 Marines and assorted armor groups on April 6. Arab television aired brutal and bloody images, broadcasting claims that hundreds of civilians were being killed. The backlash was enormous. Fighting erupted in several cities across Iraq. Sunni and Shi'ite militias actually united for a time against the common American enemy. The administration ordered Marine commanders, indignant at Washington's flip-flopping, to halt the attack three days after it began.

Even without the Fallujah debacle, Bremer's days as viceroy were numbered. In October 2003, Bremer had been summoned to Washington, where Rumsfeld and other members of the Bush administration told him to abandon his grand plans of an extended occupation and transfer sovereignty to the Iraqis as soon as possible. Ultimately, Bremer handed control of the country to Iraqi prime minister Ayad Allawi in a virtually secret ceremony on June 28, 2004, two days ahead of schedule. After Bremer's and General Sanchez's exit, John Negroponte, former ambassador to the United Nations, took over as ambassador to Iraq and four-star general George Casey became the head of U.S. military forces on the ground.

Casey arrived with a new initiative to attack the insurgency directly.

Casey's campaign plan dictated that the Army concentrate first on controlling the capital, then attempt to close off the Syrian border, then
battle for such insurgent safe-haven cities as Kirkuk and Mosul as well as
Hit, Ramadi, Fallujah, and Mahmudiyah, which are strung along the
Euphrates Valley between Syria and Baghdad. The idea was to clear and
hold territory rather than simply fight and withdraw, as happened with
the first battle of Fallujah.

Troop numbers, however, made this strategy untenable. U.S. troops
did the clearing, but there weren't enough soldiers to occupy recently
purged areas. Iraqi forces were supposed to do the holding, but there
were even fewer of them who were competent. A counterinsurgency
rule of thumb holds that 20 soldiers per 1,000 civilians are necessary to
run an orderly postwar reconstruction. At their peaks, NATO operations
in both Bosnia and Kosovo exceeded that ratio. Iraq's population of 25
million people suggested that an occupation force 500,000 strong would
be needed. During the planning for the war, however, Rumsfeld and
Deputy Secretary of Defense Paul Wolfowitz insisted that lighter, faster,
and technologically advanced troops could not only conquer a country
like Iraq with little more than 100,000 men but also hold it with even
fewer. When Army chief of staff General Eric Shinseki told the Senate
Armed Services Committee that "something on the order of several hundred thousand soldiers" would be needed to occupy Iraq, he was publicly ridiculed by both Rumsfeld and Wolfowitz. Shinseki retired four
months later, one year ahead of schedule.

The public pillorying of Shinseki stifled any dissent about troop levels from anyone in or out of uniform for years afterward. The subject
was so taboo that Bremer waited until he had just sixty days left in country to ask Rumsfeld, via a secret personal courier, for another division or
two. Whenever top Army commanders were asked if they had everything
they needed, they always said yes. Not until late 2006 did anyone with
real authority advocate increasing troop levels as a way of making American soldiers, and Iraqi civilians, substantially safer.

In late 2005, Casey received the result of a study he had commis-
sioned. Successful counterinsurgencies, the report said, emphasize intelligence rather than force, focus on the safety of the people, shut down

insurgent safe havens, and train competent security services. On nearly every count, the U.S. effort was failing. In 2005, the number of insurgent attacks climbed from 26,500 to 34,000. And yet, amid all of this, Casey unrelentingly, consistently, adamantly pushed for fewer troops in Iraq. His plans to reduce the number of combat brigades in country from fifteen in 2005 to five or six by the end of 2007 remained on the drawing board well into late 2006.

This was the environment in which Colonel Todd Ebel was leading his brigade to battle. The 101st Airborne's 2nd Brigade is the designated descendant of the 502nd Infantry Regiment, one of the most storied units in one of the Army's most legendary divisions. The 101st, along with the 82nd Airborne Division, pioneered large-scale, deep-strike paratroop warfare during World War II. Its exploits in the European theater, including the D-Day invasion of Normandy, Operation Market Garden, and the Battle of the Bulge, are almost mythical. Its screaming eagle shoulder patch is one of the most recognized military identifiers in the world. In Vietnam, the 101st continued its tradition as one of the Army's premier frontline forces. (Not knowing what a bald eagle is, the Vietcong were said to be terrified of the men who wore a chicken patch on their arms. They supposedly avoided the "Rooster Men" whenever possible.) During that conflict, the division overhauled its primary focus. Following the pioneering efforts of the 1st Cavalry Division, the 101st became one of the Army's first "Airmobile" units, dropping soldiers into battle not from planes thousands of feet in the sky but from helicopters briefly touching down on, or hovering just above, enemy territory. By 1974, the 101st had dispensed with the increasingly tenuous notion that it was a paratrooper unit and focused exclusively on this new martial art now called "Air Assault." After Vietnam, the 101st supported humanitarian relief efforts in Rwanda and Somalia, and supplied peacekeepers to Bosnia, Haiti, and Kosovo. Elements of the 101st were among the first to deploy for Operation Desert Storm and see combat in the post-9/11 invasion of Afghanistan. Today, the 20,000 men and women of the 101st, which is headquartered at Fort Campbell, Kentucky, constitute a special troops battalion and seven brigades: four infantry, two aviation, and a support brigade.

The 101st was called into action again for the 2003 invasion of Iraq under its then commanding general, Major General David Petraeus. The 101st was one of the war's primary attack forces, accompanying the 3rd Infantry Division from the south in the thrust to Baghdad. After the fall of the capital, the 101st moved north to stabilize Mosul, Iraq's third-largest city. With no guidance from the CPA, military commanders were left to pursue their own postwar reconstruction missions, to varying degrees of success. Petraeus would become the breakout leader of the war, mounting what is widely hailed as the best ad hoc rebuilding and counterinsurgency campaigns in the country.

Books such as *Band of Brothers* (and the ten-part HBO miniseries based on it), which followed a single company of soldiers from their pre-Normandy training all the way through World War II's end, cemented the 101st Airborne's reputation in the public's consciousness as some of history's greatest warriors. One of *Band of Brothers*'s indubitable strengths is its pinpoint focus on a small unit of men, Easy Company, 506th Parachute Infantry Regiment. But that strength created a significant side effect that rankles those with a broader view. "The funny thing about that book," opined 101st Airborne historian Captain James Page, "is that you could come away from it with the idea that Easy Company was almost like a commando unit accomplishing things no one else was, when, in truth, there was a company to their left, a company to their right, and thirty-five other rifle companies just from the 101st alone doing the exact same things they were doing all war long." Indeed, the glory was not restricted to Easy Company, or even the 506th. The 502nd Infantry Regiment (nicknamed "the Five-o-deuce," or just "the Deuce") played a crucial role in each of the division's major World War II campaigns, and was home to the division's only two Congressional Medal of Honor recipients for the whole war.

Although not technically the same, "2nd Brigade" and "502nd Infantry Regiment" are, today, effectively synonyms. Except in rare cases, regiments are an obsolete organizational unit in the U.S. Army, but to preserve a sense of history, tradition, and esprit de corps, certain groupings of battalions carry on the names of particularly illustrious regiments.

This continuum is entirely bogus, since so few Army units have been continuously active since their inceptions. The 101st itself, for example, has disbanded and reactivated no fewer than four times since World War II. When a new Army battle group is created, it often simply assumes the colors, crest, and regalia of some illustrious yet dormant unit from the past, even if it is based in a wildly different location or carries a vastly different purpose. Presto, instant history. And yet, this system of perpetuating noble lineages works: soldiers do not take much prodding to adopt a sense of pride and custodianship in the purported legacy and history of their unit. Modern warriors clearly long for a link between themselves and heroes of old.

Ebel had much to live up to, not just compared with the heroes of old but even his immediate predecessor. During the invasion, which the Army has come to call Operation Iraqi Freedom 1 (OIF1), Colonel Joseph Anderson commanded 2nd Brigade, which is also known as "Strike Brigade." He was a beloved and respected commander who had led his troops with impressive effectiveness and would shortly be promoted to brigadier general. As a quasi-official 101st history of OIF1 put it, "Second Brigade, simply put, was the MVP of the 101st during the push to Baghdad."

The son of a lieutenant colonel who served in Vietnam and a West Point grad, Ebel was promoted early to both major and colonel. Though not particularly tall, he has the lean build of the basketball player he once was, and the intellectual demeanor surprisingly common among senior Army officers, more in the mold of brainy Petraeus than brawny Franks. Subordinates occasionally derisively referred to Ebel as "The Professor." Along his rise, he had once declined the command of a brigade for family reasons, but after serving with General Petraeus in Iraq in 2004 training the new Iraqi Army, he returned to tell his wife that since their kids were older and moving on to college now, he thought the time was right. She obliged, and for Ebel the 101st's 2nd Brigade was his first choice.

Ebel took command just as Strike Brigade was, as part of the broader Army "transformation," expanding from three infantry battalions to six diverse battalions. Now called a brigade combat team (BCT), 2nd BCT comprised two infantry battalions, an artillery battalion, a support battalion, a reconnaissance battalion, and a special troops battalion (which includes headquarters, intelligence, engineers, and communications companies). The BCT concept was designed to make brigades more independent of their divisions and thus better suited to the rapid deployment necessary for the "small wars" commonly believed to be the threats of the future.

While 2nd Brigade was now a much larger entity, its headlining assets were still unquestionably its infantry battalions, known as the 1-502nd ("First Strike") and the 2-502nd ("Strike Force"). As part of the Army transformation, the 101st Airborne Division was also in the process of creating its fourth infantry brigade from scratch, which required seeding it with officers and noncommissioned officers (NCOs) from the other three brigades. Ebel would ultimately deploy with 90 percent of his allotted total staffing strength, but only 65 percent of a full complement of officers. In his infantry-focused brigade, for example, he had no infantry-qualified captains and only one infantry major on his headquarters staff.

Second Brigade as a whole is also less formally known as the "Black Heart Brigade" or simply the "Black Hearts" for the distinctive two-inch patch they wear on each side of their helmets. The Black Hearts name and the helmet marker tie indirectly back to World War II. During large-scale training exercises, as thousands of paratroopers scattered over drop areas, developing efficient ways for battalions to reconstitute themselves became a serious issue. One easy fix was visual: Each of the 101st's regiments adopted a suit from a deck of cards and stenciled it in white paint on the side of their helmets. As soldiers darted around open battlefields, they could identify close comrades quickly and without even speaking. The 327th wore clubs; the 501st, diamonds; the 506th, spades; and the 502nd, hearts. Although the practice fell out of favor after the Vietnam era, the convention was revived with gusto in 2001. But due to the muted-color imperatives and cloth helmet covers of modern uniforms, the insignia today are not white-paint stencils but black stitched patches. Over time, the 502nd thus added a new nickname to its collection.

Knowing that the 101st would deploy to Iraq sometime in the fall of 2005, Ebel trained his men the best he could considering, frustratingly, he did not know exactly where they were going. In the early summer he had the suspicion they would assume responsibility for convoy security along the main supply route from Kuwait all the way to Turkey, but he knew that was subject to change. And it did. In late August, the Multi-National Corps–Iraq commander called Ebel to tell him he had a new mission for him. There was a National Guard unit, the 48th Infantry Brigade out of Georgia, in South Baghdad, the vast, flat expanse south of the city spanning the stretch between the Tigris and the Euphrates, and, the general made clear, they were just not getting the job done.

"We've got to get South Baghdad under control," he told Ebel. Typically, a commander gets five to six months' notice to recon an area, talk to the leaders he will relieve, and modify training regimens. Ebel got less than six weeks.

After visiting the 48th in Iraq in late summer, he returned to tell his battalion commanders, "It is not going to be an easy road. They are not even sure of what they have in the area. It just feels bad. We can expect a real fight."

2

The Kunk Gun

A s PART OF GENERAL CASEY'S larger strategy to reclaim the Euphrates Valley, part of 2nd Brigade's mission would be to hold the region that had recently been dubbed the "Triangle of Death" for its relentless insurgent and sectarian violence, both against Americans and Iraqi-on-Iraqi. For the past three years, the area had been very lightly occupied by American forces, with no unit staying more than six months. Insurgents thrived wherever Americans were absent, and the area had become a deeply entrenched home base for a variety of insurgent groups, criminal gangs, and violent religious partisans. Insurgent organizations, including Al Qaeda in Iraq (AQI), enjoyed virtually unfettered transit from the Syrian border down the Euphrates River corridor, from Fallujah through to Yusufiyah or Mahmudiyah and up into Baghdad. Between the rivers and the roads, terrorists had multiple paths into the city and ample staging locations to stash weapons, build bombs, house fighters, and plan attacks. Ebel's mission would be to deny insurgents access to Baghdad throughout his area of operation (AO) and, as his units' intelligence increased, to uproot and destroy insurgent safe havens.

Simultaneously, however, he was tasked with helping to train the 4th

Brigade, 6th Division of the Iraqi Army (IA) so that they, ultimately, could ensure the stability of the region. These two broad goals would sometimes be at odds with one another. Rooting out insurgent hotbeds was the most immediate, life-or-death priority. But training the IA was what, in the long term, would allow the United States to leave Iraq.

The spearheads putting pressure on this terrorist stronghold would naturally be Ebel's two infantry battalions—First Strike, led by Lieutenant Colonel Tom Kunk, and Strike Force, led by Lieutenant Colonel Rob Haycock. But how to array them? Ebel decided it all came down to the personalities of his commanders. The eastern half of 2nd Brigade's territory was urban, featuring the towns of Mahmudiyah, Yusufiyah, and Lutufiyah. As such, it required a leader who could navigate the complex political and ethnic power struggles playing out not just at the end of gun barrels but in council meetings, tribal gatherings, and other ostensibly civil occasions. It required a lot of glad-handing and negotiations with sheikhs and other powerful men of the area whose loyalties were constantly shifting and always suspect. The western sector was far more rural, with smaller hamlets dotting wide swaths of agricultural land and isolated farmhouses, making it an ideal hiding locale for native insurgents, foreign Al Qaeda, and other sorts who didn't want to be found.

"Tom's more engaging," said Ebel. "He's more capable of communicating with others, in one sense. Rob was distinctly focused on fighting. Tom would be able, in my mind, to exercise restraint and go work with local officials. I sensed I needed Tom in the area where the population centers were."

When Tom Kunk first joined the Army, he never intended it to be his career. Growing up in Springfield, Ohio, he'd only enlisted in the Army in 1983 to earn some money for college. His branch was personnel administration. But he found he had a knack for Army life. He started taking college classes at night, completed his degree from the University of Maryland, and became an officer in 1988. He had also switched to infantry because if this was going to be his vocation, he figured, he wanted to be where the action was.

The competition for status between U.S. Army units is extreme, and the hierarchies of prestige between divisions are byzantine, with nuanced rivalries about which branches (or subsets of branches) are the most "hooah." ("Hooah" is the all-purpose word for anything that embodies the Army's most gung-ho ideals. Typically used as an adjective— "That is hooah" or "He is hooah"—it is also frequently, to the point of self-parody, used as a salutation, interjection, or alternative to the words "yes" and "okay.") Not surprisingly, the closer one gets to danger, and the more elite the unit, the greater the status. At the very pinnacle are the U.S. government's "black" or "gray" military and paramilitary units such as Delta Force, SEAL Team Six, the CIA, and the FBI's Hostage Rescue Team.

On the next rung of the status hierarchy are the elite units of the conventional Army, such as the 75th Ranger Regiment and Special Forces ("the Green Berets"). After that come the combat arms branches (infantry, armor, artillery, and attack aviation). Within this stratum, the ground units consider themselves tougher than the pilots, whom they resent for the undeniable glamour of flight, tease for being glorified taxi drivers, and constantly claim are too risk averse. Infantrymen, meanwhile, believe they are superior to artillery specialists and tankers because they fight at much closer quarters, usually within eyesight of the enemy.

Within infantry, there are still more substrata. Most infantry divisions today are mechanized, meaning they rely on Bradley Fighting Vehicles and other armored ground transportation to carry men into battle. But the light infantry divisions—the 101st Airborne, the 82nd Airborne, and the 10th Mountain—see themselves as the pure essence of ground combat: once they are dropped into enemy territory, they are on their own.

Beyond combat arms is the vast rest of the Army, which has virtually no status in the eyes of the war fighters. If combat arms soldiers pay the rear echelon branches any respect, it is only because support troops are necessary to make sure that they, the main event, get what they need. But the hooah status of quartermasters, chaplains, or the finance corps? Please, says the trigger-puller. If you want to serve your country, those branches might be for you. But so might the Post Office. If you want to fight for your country, the only job to have is in combat arms, and the only job in combat arms, says the light infantryman, is in light infantry.

Kunk served in 1991's Operation Desert Storm and deployed to Haiti and Kosovo before participating in OIF1 as the operations officer and then the executive officer of the 101st's 2-502nd Infantry Regiment. Coming back home, he completed a master's degree in human resources from Webster University and learned that when the 101st went back to Iraq, he would be commanding First Strike.

Kunk assumed command of the 1-502nd on March 16, 2005. Due to his enlisted service, he was, at forty-seven, several years older than the average battalion commander. At six foot five, 230 pounds, and possessing a thunderous basso profundo, he is almost always the dominant presence in the room. His large, shiny, hairless dome earned him the unit-appropriate nickname of "the Bald Eagle." Tough, uncompromising, even bullheaded, he distinguished himself in previous assignments by being a good organizer and planner, with a fine attention to detail. He had a small battery of Army clichés—"doing the harder right over the easier wrong," the importance of "engaged leadership," and how he always tried to "teach, coach, mentor"—that he repeated endlessly.

Rare for a light infantry battalion commander, Kunk did not have a Ranger Tab. The aura and the importance of the small black-and-yellow Ranger patch in the Army hierarchy of hooah is difficult to overstate. Worn on the top of the left sleeve, it may look inconspicuous, but it has talismanic properties. It signifies the wearer has graduated from Ranger School, one of world's most grueling leadership courses. Less than 40 percent of the men who start the course graduate. Sixty-one days long (if completed without having to repeat a section), it focuses on small-unit combat tactics (everyone is stripped of rank, and everyone takes turns leading), through harsh conditions in mountain, swamp, and forest settings. Instructors design scenarios to induce maximum stress and confusion, and students go weeks with severe sleep deprivation and caloric restriction. It is common for already fit men to lose thirty to forty pounds, and almost every graduate has at least one story about hunger- and exhaustion-induced hallucinations he experienced.

For virtually every other branch of the Army, the Ranger Tab is an elite trophy. For infantry units, however, and especially light infantry units, it is almost a requirement for officers and senior NCOs. Graduates of Ranger School, like graduates of West Point, have a strong subculture within the Army (though the Ranger club is open to enlisted men). When one soldier meets another, the top left shoulder is the second thing he looks at after rank. And for those in infantry leadership positions without one, not having a Ranger Tab is a constant source of insecurity, a noteworthy deficiency no matter how sterling the résumé otherwise. It is certainly possible to rise to general without the tab, but if a tab-less officer falters in his career, you can be guaranteed to hear someone say, with a tinge of pity: "Well, you know, he isn't a Ranger."

Kunk's mission was daunting. Like Ebel, he was also replacing a beloved commander, Lieutenant Colonel Del Hall, and he had only six and a half months to continue the training of 700 men spread across six companies—a headquarters company, three rifle companies (Alpha, Bravo, and Charlie), a weapons company (Delta), and a support company (Echo)—for their next deployment without a clear idea of where in Iraq they would be headed or what their mission would be.

As the battalion worked that summer, Kunk's leadership roster slowly took shape. The battalion's executive officer and second in command was thirty-seven-year-old Major Fred Wintrich. The son of an infantry officer, Wintrich had flunked out of West Point because of bad math and science grades, but he was committed to an Army career. He received his commission in 1991 after finishing a history degree at North Georgia College. Behind his back, several junior officers referred to Wintrich, with affection, as "Fast Freddie," due to his animated speaking style and wild gesticulations.

First Strike's operations officer and third in command was Major James "Rob" Salome. Bald and built like a bulldog, with a serious, almost dour demeanor, the thirty-three-year-old West Point grad was, both temperamentally and physically, an almost perfect inverse of the gangly, gregarious Wintrich. Complementing each other well, they soon developed a close working relationship.

One of the hallmarks of the modern U.S. Army is that every officer leadership position, from platoon leader and company commander all the way through brigade commander and division commander, has a parallel and complementary noncommissioned officer (NCO). Commanders are accountable for mission planning, executive decision-making, and the ultimate responsibility for everything the unit does or fails to do. Senior NCOs are responsible for helping to ensure the timely and accurate execution of the commander's orders, the care and welfare of the men, the specific tasking of personnel, and advising the commander of the enlisted man's view of things. Kunk's senior NCO was Command Sergeant Major Anthony Edwards, a native of Sanford, North Carolina, who had enlisted as an infantryman in 1980. He was known to be stern and serious about the basics, and he was also somewhat aloof, cultivating few close friends or acquaintances within the battalion.

Rounding out the rest of Kunk's leadership team were the company commanders and first sergeants of the 1-502nd's three rifle companies, weapons company, logistics company, and headquarters and headquarters company (HHC). Commanding HHC was Captain Shawn Umbrell, a former Army airborne medic who had returned as an officer upon his graduation from the University of Toledo in 1999. He had become commander of First Strike's Charlie Company in June 2004 and badly wanted to retain that position long enough to take his men into battle. To his great disappointment, that would not happen. When the HHC command slot came up in May 2005, Umbrell was, as is common for the senior company commander in a battalion, obliged to take it. HHCs may not be as hooah as infantry companies, but with nine different platoons performing functions varying from scouts and medics to supply and communications, they are bigger, more logistically intensive operations. Still, he was disappointed. Umbrell, who possesses a naturally sunny disposition and gentle manner, resolved to make the best of the situation, not to moan about the 135 men he left but to serve the 230 he now had the best that he could.

Thirty-six-year-old Captain Bill Dougherty was a flinty-eyed former infantry sergeant from Philadelphia who had served with a Ranger battalion in Afghanistan and with the 502nd Infantry Regiment during OIF1 before replacing Umbrell as Charlie's company commander in May 2005. One of Umbrell's primary pieces of advice when he handed over the reins was, "Dennis Largent is always right." Dennis Largent was Charlie's first sergeant, the company's senior enlisted soldier and right-hand man to the company commander. The son of a retired lieutenant colonel, Largent was a buzz-cutted, blunt-nosed giant. Charlie Company (nicknamed "the Cobras") had an intense esprit de corps, one of the most pronounced that many had ever seen in their entire Army careers.

Much of that Charlie pride flowed from and centered on Largent, who had been first sergeant since before the invasion. Soldiers loved Largent and they loved being in the company. He could be strict and impossibly tough on his soldiers. But there was something strange about the way Largent yelled. Even when he was jet-engine loud, Dougherty said, he was never abusive or cruel. "There was still just so much love there," Dougherty explained. "He could be dishing out the most royal ass chewing ever, but it was always clear that he was not hating on the soldier, he was trying to teach him. And there was a little bit of humor there all the time too."

There was a lot of humor in Charlie. Since they were the Cobras, they had adopted the logo of COBRA, the shadowy international bad-guy organization from *G.I. Joe* cartoons. They plastered that snake logo on everything: unauthorized unit patches, flags, T-shirts, anything they could think of. The stencil started popping up on so many flat surfaces that the line between logo and graffiti was thin.

The company also had a tribe of garden gnomes that had become mascots. Years before, a group of drunken soldiers had stolen several garden gnomes from a trailer park and, as a prank, hidden them in places that Largent would find them for weeks to come. There was a gnome in the company refrigerator, a gnome in the latrine, a gnome in every third locker. Largent turned this into a team-building opportunity. He would call the whole company into formation every time he found a gnome and pretend to be furious. The gnomes became the company's good-luck charms. Each squad was issued a gnome. Soldiers gave them names and affixed Cobra patches to their shoulders, and the company took them, these heavy stone gnomes, on deployments. It became a rule: The newest private was responsible for carrying that squad's gnome in his rucksack wherever they went.

The Cobras had come to refer to themselves as "the People's Army." Once, in garrison, the legend goes, Charlie was assigned to do some sort of community service activity like helping with a blood drive or a park cleanup project. The men were complaining, because that was definitely not something they thought soldiers should be doing. Largent was having none of this, and he launched into a long, impassioned tirade that was simultaneously tongue in cheek yet also deadly serious about how the whole reason the Army exists is to protect and serve the American people, and soldiers should consider it an honor to help with a blood drive or anything else society asks them to do.

"The Army is not a democracy," he thundered, "but we defend democracy with our lives! We are not the President's Army! We are not the Secretary of Defense's Army! Or any of the Generals' Army! We are the People's Army!" The soldiers hooted and hollered. They loved it—and suddenly they were excited and enthusiastic to go help with the blood drive.

From there, the People's Army took on a life of its own. Charlie Company was the People's Army, they told anyone and everyone. Over time, this moniker would become a source of great annoyance to the battalion's leadership, who thought the phrase sounded more than a little communist, and a lot like the battle cry of 1st Battalion secessionists. On several occasions Kunk told Largent to knock off the People's Army stuff and start promoting First Strike as his soldiers' primary rallying point. Largent replied that he didn't really think he should do that. Cracking down on the People's Army would only drive it underground, he said, and fuel its popularity, turning it into a true middle finger pointed at the battalion, rather than a funny little differentiator.

As the battalion geared up for deployment and trained throughout the summer, many of the company commanders and first sergeants determined that Kunk was not going to be the easiest boss to get along with. They knew Kunk had a reputation for being demanding and having a volcanic temper. Those characteristics were nothing special in the Army. "Demanding" and "short-fused" could, in fact, describe more commanders than not. Kunk, they realized, however, was something different. Only a few days after he took command in the spring of 2005, the whole battalion headed to the Joint Readiness Training Center (JRTC) at Fort Polk, Louisiana, where light infantry units undergo two-week, immersive "in the box" war-game exercises.

In hindsight, some point to the JRTC stint as a harbinger of everything that would go wrong in Iraq, both with Bravo's 1st Platoon and at the battalion level. On the first day of the simulation, 1st Platoon made a spectacular tactical error, and the JRTC's "enemy force" captured nineteen of their soldiers. Immediately, 1st Battalion's company commanders focused on how to rescue their men as soon as possible. So they were dismayed when they heard the brief from Kunk, that he was ordering surveillance and recon of the enemy for the next twenty-four hours. Kunk had formulated a complete plan for the next day without any input from his commanders, except to go around the room seeking affirmation that this was the right way to go. After awkward silences and halfhearted assent, Umbrell spoke up first.

"I think this plan is fucked up," he said. "We've got all these assets," he said, incredulous. "We've got Bradleys, helicopters, several companies of men ready to go, and a short time window to this whole exercise. And we're not going to go get our guys?" The rest of the commanders followed suit, saying that sitting around with men in enemy hands was a bad idea and they should start formulating a rescue now. Kunk ignored their protests and the surveillance plan remained in effect.

"That was the first big fallout between him and all the company commanders," said Alpha Company's commander, Captain Jared Bordwell. Several company leaders said they learned something that day that would be reinforced repeatedly throughout the next year: Their input was not wanted, and when Kunk was challenged, one of two things would happen. Either he demolished dissenters with an angry tirade, or he would more quietly dig in his heels. But he would not consider an alternate point of view, modify his opinion, or change the plan.

Bordwell had a particularly hard time with Kunk early on. Cocky and aggressive, he had taken command of Alpha Company in early 2005. Because he was always eager to take the next mission, his men dubbed him "Captain America." Bordwell went afoul of Kunk immediately, however, because he had not learned to adjust his style to accommodate the new boss's way of doing business. Bordwell had previously worked for a battalion commander who didn't obsess over details. When he asked his captains what they were doing and they replied, "Training my men, sir," that was all he wanted to hear. But Kunk was a demon for the minutiae: How many rifles do you have ready to go? How many of your night-vision devices need repairing? What percentage of your vehicles still need parts?

At the time, Bordwell thought a company commander didn't need this sort of information at the ready all the time. So when Kunk would ask Bordwell something like how many water cans his company had, Bordwell said not only did he not know, but he didn't really need to know; that's what his executive officer was for. This was not the kind of answer that made Kunk happy. In Kunk's world, said his subordinates, only Kunk got to employ sarcasm, and he let Bordwell have it. "Looking back, I see the whole picture now," Bordwell reflected, acknowledging that soldiers without water can't fight and a company commander should, in fact, know how many cans he has at all times. "But it was the approach he took I initially struggled with."

That approach was belittlement. The officers had a name for it: the Kunk Gun. When it swung around your way, you ducked for cover. They also called being subjected to one of his tirades Getting Kunked. It wasn't that Kunk had high standards, or yelled at them a lot, or was even mean, they said. The captains had been in the Army for six or more years. Some of the first sergeants had nearly twenty years' experience. They had all worked for difficult, even mean, bosses. This was not that. Kunk treated his subordinates with nastiness and impatience they had never seen before, where correction and coaching turned into shouted, expletive-laden humiliation and disparagement. Kunk's meetings became events to dread, more about him proving how little his underlings knew than in sharing information or solving problems. If subordinates didn't have the correct response at the ready, Kunk would humiliate them, assail their qualifications to hold command, and even fire off the sanctum sanctorum of accusations—doubt their concern for the welfare of their own soldiers.

Kunk dripped with contempt. By Army culture, superior officers may call subordinates by their first names. Some do so as an indication of familiarity or even affection. Kunk, with the venomous emphasis he applied to each name, wielded it as a weapon of disrespect. "Have you ever thought of that, *Bill*?" "Do I have to do your job for you, *John*?" He routinely ridiculed subordinate commanders in front of their own men, and he was not above threatening lieutenants with violence, telling one that he would "beat his fucking ass" if he did not follow a recently delivered order. If anyone disagreed with him or ventured an alternative idea, he took that as a personal challenge, and he would sometimes end discussions by declaring, "Trump! I win, because I'm the battalion commander."

For the few months between the JRTC and deployment, the Kunk Gun was firmly fixed on Bordwell, and it was having an effect. If, initially, Bordwell's first sergeant found his company commander a bit arrogant, though not unacceptably so, the daily drubbings by Kunk were making Bordwell indecisive and eroding his confidence. The relationship continued to deteriorate. Once, Kunk became upset because Bordwell didn't reply to some of his e-mails, but Bordwell had consciously not done so because the e-mails contained no questions, only information. Kunk interpreted the nonresponse as being ignored. Tensions came to a head: Kunk threatened to fire Bordwell, giving him another chance only after Bordwell filled out a self-analysis tool to evaluate his strengths and weaknesses and affirmed his desire to stay in command.

It wasn't just Bordwell, however. Kunk was hammering all the company commanders. The captains became timid decision-makers, avoided speaking in meetings or otherwise attracting attention, and generally steered clear of Kunk as much as they could. Several first sergeants, concerned that Kunk seemed bent on purposely embarrassing their commanders, banded together to have an intervention with Sergeant Major Edwards. You need to tell Colonel Kunk that he needs to cut it out, they told Edwards. He is undermining our commanders and they're second-guessing everything they do. In combat, that can be deadly. Edwards told them that he would see what he could do, but they never heard back from him, and they never discerned a noticeable change in Kunk's style.

Later in the summer, Bravo and Charlie and much of the battalion staff went on another war-game exercise at the National Training Center (NTC) at Fort Irwin, California. Again, there were problems and misunderstandings. First Sergeant Largent and Lieutenant Colonel Kunk got into a private conversation and, Largent thought at the time, they began talking confidentially, one old-timer to another. Largent thought, as the senior first sergeant in the battalion, he could give some honest feedback to Kunk that would be both off the record and taken to heart.

"What do you think the problem is?" Kunk asked Largent.

"Frankly, sir, you are being a dick," Largent responded. "To the men, to the commanders, to everyone," he said. "You are just angry all the time. You need to back off them a little bit." Largent later reckoned this candor was a tremendous miscalculation. Kunk, Largent concluded, did not want an honest assessment, and the conversation was not a private consultation, because for as long as the two worked together from then on, Kunk would frequently, publicly declare, "Well, that's because First Sergeant Largent thinks I'm a dick! Isn't that right, First Sergeant? I'm just a dick, so what do I know?"

As the senior company commander, Umbrell also felt a responsibility to try to be a mediator between Kunk and the captains. Once, before deployment, he tried to approach Kunk about his leadership style. He referenced a book about leadership that Colonel Ebel had assigned them to help him make his point. That book, *The Servant,* by James Hunter, uses the story of Jesus to demonstrate that leadership has nothing to do with ordering people around because you have more power than they do. True leadership, the book says, inspires people to follow you because you serve their psychological need for purpose, value, and direction. Told as a parable, there is even a drill sergeant character in the book who allows the author to tackle all the accusations that this thesis is just a bunch of feel-good mumbo-jumbo irrelevant to the tough realities of today's corporations or armed services. One passage addresses the sergeant directly, saying, "The leader has a responsibility to hold people accountable. However, there are several ways to point out deficiencies while allowing people to keep their dignity."

In private one day, Umbrell said to Kunk, "The way that you're talking to the company commanders right now is creating an environment where nobody wants to come talk to you. The book that Colonel Ebel is having us read, what that author says about leadership, you are doing the opposite." The very next morning, Kunk showed up with photocopies of material he had pulled out of another leadership manual that talked about how there were several different but effective leadership styles, including the rigid authoritarian. "So that's where we were," Umbrell recalled. "He's not changing. He's not changing. That's how it all started going bad for the command climate."

Kunk never had problems with his own staff to the degree he did with the companies. Majors Salome and Wintrich were not effusive in their praise of Kunk, but they eschewed direct criticism. "It's not an isolated leadership style," said Wintrich. "There's not just one guy in the Army who will poke you in the chest and say, 'You know what? You're not doing a good enough job right now. You need to pick it up.' It's not always a pleasant leadership style to be around, but it does often achieve results." Other subordinates not in charge of his line units, such as the medical captain and the intelligence captain, found him to be a praiseworthy, even inspiring leader. This is a discrepancy not lost on others. "For Tom Kunk, there were two types of people," said First Lieutenant Brian Lohnes, who was leader of the battalion's scout platoon and also worked in Major Salome's operations office. "There were 'his boys,' and then there were 'the other people.' And if you were one of 'the other people,' it didn't matter how great your performance was or what you did, he was going to punch you in the balls every chance that he had. Every time you sat down for a meeting, he was going to embarrass you."

Upon returning from NTC in August, the battalion staff finally got a full briefing on their mission. They were heading to the Triangle of Death. HHC commander Shawn Umbrell wrote in his diary, "6 SEP: Was briefed on battalion sector today. Looks like south of Baghdad, near Mahmudiyah. This is reportedly a rough area. We'll be going on the offensive within 24 hours of taking the sector. The enemy will be in for a wake-up call. Our boys are ready. We're prepared to take casualties, we know that's the cost."

The assignment took Kunk by surprise, but he was nothing if not certain about his own abilities. "Ebel said it was the most complex fight, dealing with people, so multifaceted," he recalled. "It was Iraqi security forces. It was building government. All the different ethnicities. The Sunnis, the Shi'ites. All those competing things. That's why he chose the 1-502nd, because he felt that I had an incredible grasp for that."

Planning was hurried. "We started having daily intel meetings," said one platoon sergeant. "It was an eye opener. We started realizing that it was time to get your game face on. I remember doing my brief to my men, saying, 'Okay, you guys wanted to get into the shit, so guess what? Here it is.' " Most of the men had never heard of the towns they were heading to, and the information they were getting from the unit already there was scant. But they did the best they could. "Open-source information is better than classified information, that's the big joke," quipped one of the company executive officers. "We did our planning off of Google Earth."

In addition to occupying their AO, First Strike had to send soldiers to fulfill two other brigade-wide tasks. Kunk chose one platoon from Charlie to become an Iron Claw team—one of several IED-hunting platoons that roamed the brigade's territory in massive, armored IED-detecting trucks with giant digging arms on the front, which inspired the teams' name.

Kunk was also required to provide 36 NCOs and officers to make a MiTT team. MiTT teams (military transition teams) were responsible for training Iraqi soldiers by living, working, and patrolling with Iraqi Army units around the clock. Kunk chose two dozen key leaders from Alpha Company to be the core of the MiTT team, shoring up the ranks with soldiers from the other companies. Bordwell interpreted this move as punishment for being Kunk's most problematic commander. "I lost my first sergeant, all three rifle platoon leaders, two out of three rifle platoon sergeants, four senior staff sergeant squad leaders, and four team leaders," Bordwell said. "They pulled the backbone out of my company."

As the wheels-up date approached, Umbrell made a final entry in his diary: "29 SEP: Said my good-byes today. One of the hardest things I have ever done. Jacob understands I will be gone for a long time. We all cried. I am happy to finally get started. I can start the countdown now for coming back. Soldiers are in high spirits. The whole outload has been smooth. I'm proud to be a part of all this. Very proud."

OCTOBER 2005

3

"This Is Now the Most Dangerous Place in Iraq"

IN THE TWO and a half years since the toppling of Saddam's regime, the rural outskirts of Baghdad known as South Baghdad had become one of the deadliest locales in the country. In one sense, this was an ignominious destiny for the cradle of civilization. It was here, in Mesopotamia, the land between two rivers, that the great Bronze Age empires of the Sumerians, the Babylonians, and the Hittites invented or solidified advances in farming, writing, astronomy, and mathematics. It was here that nameless poets assembled the legends of Gilgamesh, Hammurabi codified the first set of laws, and Nebuchadnezzar built his hanging gardens. For centuries, Babylon, the ruins of which are just fifty-five miles south of Baghdad and thirty-five miles from Mahmudiyah, would remain a leading city of the world, a place that, Herodotus wrote, "surpasses in splendor any city of the known world."

On the other hand, Mesopotamia has also been a perpetual battlefield since before history was recorded, one of the bloodiest and most frequently contested fault lines between the Eastern and Western worlds. An Arab Muslim bastion since the seventh century, when invaders from the south decisively wrested the region away from the Persians, the area also became the locus of the Sunni-Shi'ite schism that continues to this day.

All of the major events associated with the split occurred within eighty miles to the south of modern-day Mahmudiyah.

While Europe languished in the Dark Ages, the Sunni caliphate in Baghdad became the center of the greatest empire Islam ever produced until 1256, when the Mongols sacked the city. The seat of Sunni power moved to Istanbul, where the Ottoman Empire governed the region with a loose hand until the end of World War I, when Britain took control of three Ottoman governorships: Kurdish Mosul in the north, Sunni Baghdad in the middle, and Shi'ite Basra to the south. In 1920, amid widespread rebellion, the British handed sovereignty over the three provinces, now called Iraq, to a Sunni ally named Faisal from the Hashemite tribe. Monarchy was no aid to stability, however. Fifty-eight governments ruled Iraq between 1921 and 1958, until revolutionaries overthrew and executed King Faisal II.

In 1968, the Sunni-controlled socialist Baath Party returned to power for the second time in five years, led by President Ahmad Hassan al-Bakr and his right-hand man, Saddam Hussein. Saddam began eliminating opponents, and when al-Bakr resigned suddenly in 1979, citing failing health, he was sworn in within hours. He quickly initiated a series of purges and executions of anyone who threatened his grip on power, including influential Shi'ite clerics.

Saddam instituted a state that was nominally socialist and appealed to nationalism, but it was really a personality cult. In 1980 he launched a war against Iran, which would last eight years, deplete state coffers, cost a million Iraqi lives, and leave the countries' boundaries essentially where they started. Then, in 1990, Saddam invaded Kuwait, citing disputes over oil prices. The United States' response led to the Gulf War, during which Saddam was badly defeated. After years of diplomatic tussles over weapons of mass destruction (WMD) and the UN Oil-for-Food program, President George W. Bush, buoyed by then-questionable and now-discredited evidence that Saddam was pursuing WMD and aiding Al Qaeda, invaded Iraq in March 2003 and toppled the dictatorship in twenty-one days.

Saddam had realized the importance of South Baghdad as a gateway to the capital and as the fault line between the Shi'ite south and Sunni mid-

lands. Two of the country's key highways cross here, making it a transportation and logistics choke point. You cannot easily get into Baghdad
from the south without passing first though Lutufiyah, a town of 20,000,
and then Mahmudiyah, population 100,000. Likewise, Yusufiyah, a town
of 25,000 people seven miles to the west of Mahmudiyah, is a crucial con-
nector between Fallujah and the Syrian border with Iraq's south. Including all the smaller villages and farmland, population estimates for the
region as a whole range between 500,000 and 1 million people. Mahmudiyah has some apartment buildings eight or more stories high and
the densely packed atmosphere of a city many times its size. Yusufiyah
and Lutufiyah, however, with their dilapidated, low-slung tan buildings
and garbage-strewn streets with open, black-water sewers scratched into
the mostly unpaved street shoulders, feel smaller than they actually are.

Seeking a buffer of allies to balance out the Shi'ite urban popula-
tions here, early on Saddam instituted a land-grant system and other re-
wards programs for Sunni families and other political compatriots
willing to settle and farm the surrounding countryside. He made en-
ticements particularly sweet for retired military and intelligence officers
(who, in Saddam's time, were mostly Sunni) and politically connected
families of soldiers killed in the Iran-Iraq War. To this day, for example,
Iraqis call two small villages outside Yusufiyah "Al-Dhubat" and "Al-
Shuhada," which mean, respectively, "The Officers" and "The Martyrs."
Saddam improved the highways and expanded and upgraded the already extensive network of hundreds of miles of canals bringing the
water of the Euphrates to the far reaches of the area.

Some families from Sunni tribes with ancestral ties to the western
province of Anbar, such as the Janabis, Quargulis, Ghariris, and Du-
laimis, also heeded the call, becoming powerful presences in the area.
Saddam gave tribal chiefs large stretches of prime agricultural land,
money, and other favors in exchange for little more than passive loyalty.
This largesse created wide economic disparity. Many of the houses near
the Euphrates, a stronghold of the Quarguli tribe, would qualify as man-
sions in any country, with expansive, well-manicured yards and lush
palm groves, while the Qadisiyah apartments and other housing blocks
in Mahmudiyah are slums as abject as anything in poorest Baghdad. In

times of unrest, however, Saddam expected repayment. During the failed Shi'ite uprising of 1991, for example, he called upon local Sunnis, especially the Janabis, to curb the rebellion.

While the area around Yusufiyah and farther west, especially on the banks of the Euphrates, is prime farmland, Saddam turned the region around Lutufiyah into a hub of the Iraqi military-industrial complex. The Medina Division of the Republican Guard and the Hateen Weapons Munitions Complex were headquartered not far to the south, and six miles due west of Lutufiyah was the massive Al-Qaqaa State Establishment—a weapons assembly and storage depot with dozens of bunkers and buildings sprawling across twenty square miles.

Eight miles west of Yusufiyah town and right on the banks of the Euphrates is the Yusufiyah Thermal Power Plant. The Russian Technopromexport corporation started constructing a 1,680-megawatt natural-gas and fuel-oil power plant on the one-square-mile site in 1989, but work halted in 1991 before the Gulf War. Construction resumed in 2001, but the Russian, Ukrainian, and Belarusian engineers made little progress before ceasing work during the 2003 invasion, and yet again as sectarian violence escalated in 2004. By 2005, it was a wasteland of rusting water tanks and mini-mountains of rebar. Nothing on the site was close to being completed except for a five-story cement hull designed to house the turbines and the hundred-foot-tall smokestack, which was visible for miles around.

After the invasion, no Americans permanently occupied the region and the power dynamic that had existed for decades was upended. Sunni tribal leaders and other prominent men were unwilling to give up their grip on power, but their mandate, in the form of Saddam Hussein, had vanished. The Shi'ites, meanwhile, with the numbers and momentum finally on their side, were only too willing to take advantage of the power vacuum. First the government and basic services stopped functioning, and then the killing began.

In South Baghdad, civil war flared almost from the beginning. It started with a lack of law and order and a spate of revenge killings tied to anything from tribal feuds and personal vendettas to a more generalized score-settling by Shi'ites against Sunnis for decades, if not centuries, of repression. By the summer of 2003, however, the burgeoning Sunni insurgency had become more organized, allowing the outnumbered Sunnis to fight back. Two of the most powerful homegrown Sunni insurgency groups were the Islamic Army in Iraq (IAI) and the Mujahideen Army. Like virtually all Iraqi insurgent groups, both denied any fealty to Baathism or nostalgia for Saddam and his regime, even though many of their members are former party grandees, military officers, or other elements of society that were favored under his rule. Both groups' aims are distinctly political and nationalistic, and while they have become more religiously conservative over time, the roots of their sectarian hatred are not so much because they view Shi'ites as heretics but because they see them as collaborators. Sunni groups retaliated against Shi'ites but also started mounting attacks against American forces, contractors, and any element of what they believed to be a puppet Shi'ite government.

An early foreign arrival to the area was the thirty-six-year-old vagabond Jordanian terrorist Abu Musab al-Zarqawi.* After the American invasion of Iraq, Zarqawi created a group called Monotheism and Jihad and started spending most of his time in Iraq's Anbar province and South Baghdad. He didn't waste any time causing widespread carnage, developing an abiding fondness for suicide car bombings. In a one-month frenzy of violence in August 2003, he planned spectacularly lethal hits on the Jordanian embassy, the UN headquarters in Baghdad, and the Imam Ali mosque in Najaf.

Thanks to such high-profile attacks—and his gruesome habit of releasing videotaped beheadings over the Internet—Zarqawi's infamy grew, making him one of the most notorious terrorists in the world.

---

*During his February 2003 address to the United Nations outlining the United States' case for war with Iraq, U.S. secretary of state Colin Powell erroneously identified Zarqawi as a key link between Al Qaeda and Saddam Hussein. In fact, Zarqawi's ties to Al Qaeda at that time were thin and to Saddam they were nonexistent. Whether that assertion was the result of a purposeful misrepresentation or incompetent analysis is still being debated, but no link between Al Qaeda and Saddam has ever been proven.

Followers flocked to him. With each one of his well-publicized successes (or American scandals such as Abu Ghraib), more money and men from Saudi Arabia, Jordan, and Syria flowed across the Syrian border. In the fall of 2004, Zarqawi joined Al Qaeda, changing the name of Monotheism and Jihad to Al Qaeda in the Land Between Two Rivers, or Al Qaeda in Iraq (AQI), even though relations between him and Osama bin Laden had been strained ever since they met in 1999. From the start, bin Laden found Zarqawi's extreme hatred of Shi'ites to be particularly divisive. Their rift was a common one in Islamist circles. Bin Laden and Al Qaeda believed that the war against the "far enemies" (the United States, Israel, and Western unbelief in general) was the priority, while Zarqawi insisted that overcoming the "near enemies" (Shi'ites and purportedly apostate Middle East governments such as those in Jordan and Saudi Arabia) was paramount. The alliance was one of convenience for both parties, and it was deeply flawed from the beginning. Zarqawi benefited from the worldwide recognition of the Al Qaeda name and the added credibility it gave him, but he retained operational control of what targets to hit and when. Bin Laden needed a ready-made presence in the place that was quickly becoming the global epicenter of anti-American anger, and it provided an easy way to make sure Zarqawi's power and prominence did not eclipse his.

In South Baghdad the interests of Al Qaeda, local insurgencies, and pure tribalism frequently intersected. The number of nationalist insurgent groups similar to but smaller than IAI and the Mujahideen Army was legion, and they were in a constant tumult of mergers, alliances, disputes, spin-offs, and splits. But they found an early and easy ally with Al Qaeda. The Quarguli and Janabi tribes, among others, had interlinking roles in smuggling during Saddam's time, and Al Qaeda successfully co-opted and exploited those links to build a formidable recruiting and financing pipeline. Near Yusufiyah, for example, an arm of the Sunni Janabi clan had been feuding with the Shi'ite Anbari tribe for a long time. With the Janabis' help, Al Qaeda expelled dozens of Anbari families from their homes, which AQI turned into safe houses, classrooms, weapons storage areas, and torture chambers.

Sectarian violence increased. It broadened, becoming systematic, increasingly bloody, and relentless. Sunni gangs forced Shi'ites from their homes. Flyers circulated warning Sunni landowners to get rid of any Shi'ite tenants or both landlord and tenant would be killed. Kidnapping, torture, and murder became everyday events. Bands of masked thugs chased people down in the street, beat them bloody, tied their hands, and executed them. No occasions were off-limits, no tactics were taboo. One suicide bomber drove an ambulance to blow up a Shi'ite wedding party in Yusufiyah, killing four and injuring sixteen.

The Sunni groups did not limit their purges to locals. Toting AK-47s, they set up checkpoints on Highway 8, the major artery connecting Baghdad and the country's south, seizing gas tankers and cargo trucks and killing anyone they suspected of attempting to get to the Shi'ite pilgrimage centers of Najaf and Karbala. Shi'ite clerics ditched their distinctive black turbans and robes as they passed by. Insurgent groups offered $1,000 bounties for every Shi'ite killed. Gunmen checked IDs, looking for distinctively Shi'ite names, or anything else that did not meet with their liking. They quizzed passersby in theology or praxis. If the examinee failed, he would be beaten and perhaps executed and mutilated, all on the street, in broad daylight, and then left there.

Roads were littered with burned and bullet-ridden cars. Corpses festered and decayed on town streets. They became bloated, stinking, rotting masses of gooey flesh that dogs and rats fed on. Any semblance of policing stopped, because the police were frequently targets. And insurgents often impersonated the police, complete with looted squad cars and stolen uniforms.

Average citizens were forced to make unbearable choices. Caught in a kind of lawlessness that had never happened under Saddam despite all of his many crimes, they frequently had to pick a side or face kidnapping, extortion, or murder. Those who could moved away, but there was no guarantee that the neighborhood of escape would not someday be engulfed by similar violence. The hatred for Americans that the average South Baghdad resident felt, for allowing all this to happen, for removing Saddam with no plan to fill the void, was deep. Some locals quivered with rage just talking about it. It was one thing for the Americans not to be able to provide water or electricity or jobs. But safety? The basic human dignity of knowing that someone will not shoot you down like a dog at any moment? That was unforgivable. Everyone feared for their safety every minute of every day, and most Iraqis hated America, and the American soldiers they saw, with an ardor that was difficult to articulate. Some of them gladly picked up weapons to fight the Americans, some actively helped the fighters in other ways. And even those who didn't, even those who tried to stay away from conflict as much as possible, kept their mouths shut because speaking to the Americans about anything would earn them a visit from the death squads.

The area was just as dangerous for foreigners as it was for locals. More so, in a way, because they were easier to spot. Some said the bounty for a foreigner was $2,000, others claimed it was $10,000. Six Spanish intelligence officers were shot dead in November 2003. In January 2004, two Iraqis working for CNN were killed while traveling near Mahmudiyah. Four months after that, a Polish TV crew was attacked in the same area and two Japanese journalists were shot dead. Some foreigners were freed, including two French journalists as well as *Christian Science Monitor* writer Jill Carroll. Others, including Italian journalist Enzo Baldoni, the IAI murdered.

On October 3, 2004, the French newswire Agence France-Presse (AFP) was the first Western outlet to use the phrase "triangle of death," in a story, fittingly, about the discovery of two decapitated bodies in Mahmudiyah. AFP used the phrase frequently after that, noting that the term was already common among locals. AFP capitalized the coinage within a few days and it caught on with the wider press. Within sixty days, the moniker had been used more than a thousand times in newspapers across the globe.

When the U.S. Army fought to take the city of Fallujah a second time in early November 2004, thousands of fighters fell back into the Triangle of Death, making it the new heart of the insurgency. But a new American troop presence had arrived as well. As the United States accelerated the handover of sovereignty, securing enough stability to conduct credible nationwide elections became the military's priority. The United States targeted dozens of lawless towns, charging units with making them safe enough to hold January elections. For many areas, including South Baghdad, it was the first persistent U.S. military presence there had ever been.

In the fall of 2004, the 24th Marine Expeditionary Unit, a reserve group from Chicago, captured the Jurf al-Sukr Bridge, a major Euphrates crossing six miles southwest of Yusufiyah. They also set up the first U.S. bases in Mahmudiyah and Yusufiyah. A battalion commander with the 24th Marines told the UK's *Independent,* "With Fallujah over, the action has moved here. This is now the most dangerous place in Iraq." Indeed, on November 14, 120 insurgents made a full assault on the Marines' platoon-sized patrol base, a school they had commandeered on the outskirts of Yusufiyah. The attack was bold and sophisticated and the battle lasted several hours. Most of the Marines were down to their last few bullets when reinforcements finally broke through with fresh supplies. By the end of the day, one Marine and some 40 insurgents were dead.

Although the Marines attempted to establish a semblance of order, they were severely undermanned and underequipped. They lost ten men in six months and, during that time, the violence continued to escalate. Though boycotted by the Sunnis, the January 2005 elections did take place without any major incidents. The Marines decamped in February, replaced by the Army's 2-70th Armor Regiment, which nominally controlled the area until June 2005, when, with two days' notice, the 48th Infantry Brigade of the Georgia National Guard moved in. They closed up the Yusufiyah patrol base at the school and moved it to a potato-processing plant closer to the center of town.

Throughout 2005, Shi'ite partisans mounted major counterattacks against the Sunni groups. Across the country, as the Iraqi Army and Iraqi police started to reconstitute themselves, they became overwhelmingly Shi'ite-dominated institutions. Muqtada al-Sadr's Mahdi Army and the

Badr Corps, another Shi'ite militia, infiltrated them both. The police, run by the Shi'ite-controlled Interior Ministry (headed, in fact, by a former high-ranking Badr Corps member), were particularly debased. In many regions, the local police forces turned into death squads themselves, killing Sunnis without restraint. Interior Ministry–sponsored violence was so widespread that in late March 2006, Iraqi television broadcast a remarkable announcement: "The Defense Ministry advises Iraqi citizens not to obey instructions from Interior Ministry personnel unless they are accompanied by coalition forces." It was a constant point of uncertainty and frustration for American commanders working with the Iraqi police and Iraqi Army: you never knew where their first priorities lay. And average citizens? They were even harder to figure out.

4

Relief in Place, Transfer of Authority

O N September 29, 2005, at 10:00 p.m., much of 1st Battalion and the rest of 2nd Brigade left Fort Campbell, Kentucky, making a stop at Germany before arriving in Kuwait just after midnight on October 1. The bulk of the units settled in for a few weeks of last-minute training while advance parties began flying to Camp Striker, where Colonel Ebel and most of 2nd Brigade would make their headquarters. Striker was part of the Victory Base Complex, a massive U.S. military multicamp that surrounds most of Baghdad International Airport. Two and a half years into the war, Victory had become a city all its own, with hangar-sized cafeterias, fleets of SUVs, acres of air-conditioned housing trailers, and post exchanges that had Burger Kings, Subways, and Green Beans coffee shops, a fair approximation of Starbucks. Lieutenant Colonel Rob Haycock and his 2-502nd also set up its headquarters at Striker as its forces began to spread out to occupy the western half of the brigade's sector. Simultaneously, the 1-502nd's advance parties fanned out to their ultimate AOs to meet the 48th Brigade, check out their new homes, and gather intelligence before their handover. Over the next month, the 101st units would slowly add to their ranks while the

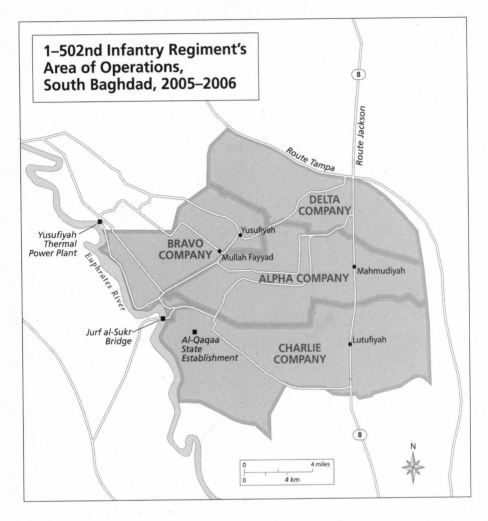

1–502nd Infantry Regiment's
Area of Operations,
South Baghdad, 2005–2006

48th drew theirs down and transferred final authority of their battle spaces at the end of October.

Lieutenant Colonel Kunk decided to split the battalion into three elements. The bulk of men, machines, and equipment would set up at FOB (Forward Operating Base) Mahmudiyah, a large former chicken-processing plant on Highway 8, which the military had renamed Route Jackson, about a mile north of the city itself. FOB Mahmudiyah became the home of battalion staff, Headquarters and Headquarters Company, Alpha Company, Delta Company, and Echo Company. Living conditions were spartan compared with those of Striker, but there was a bare minimum of support and supply amenities. The majority of the soldiers lived in five- to ten-man tents with wooden floors and air-conditioning that could bring temperatures down by 20 to 30 degrees during the summer. There were shower trailers and a chow hall serving hot meals. There was an eleven-person detachment from private contractor KBR on site with a carpenter, a plumber, a couple of supervisors, and several workers from India, Sri Lanka, and other developing countries who did maintenance and cleaning. Battalion headquarters moved into a giant three-story brick building, while the company commanders put their headquarters, staff living quarters, and other operations in the other existing structures around the site.

Delta Company took the northern slice of the battalion's area of operation, bounded by a highway the Army had renamed Route Tampa to the north and Mahmudiyah city limits to the south, while MiTT-depleted Alpha Company took charge of the central sector that included Mahmudiyah itself. Charlie Company moved south to Lutufiyah and occupied an old telephone switching station. Its territory covered Lutufiyah proper and the massive Al-Qaqaa State Establishment weapons depot. Bravo, meanwhile, headed to the town of Yusufiyah, and its terrain formed most of the 1-502nd's western boundary.

Kunk gave Charlie and Bravo the missions he judged to be the toughest because, at that time, he considered them his best companies, led by his best commanders. Both required setting up shop, in a favored Army phrase, "away from the flagpole" of battalion headquarters in the sectors where violence was the worst. This was a vote of confidence from Kunk, who was pleased with both companies' performance at NTC, but particularly Bravo's. Bravo, Kunk declared, "just did an absolutely phenomenal job. They showed the maturity, they showed the discipline, at the platoon and squad levels."

This was Bravo Company commander Captain John Goodwin's third time in the Army. Skinny, almost gaunt, with hollow, deep-set eyes, Goodwin is originally from Solon, Ohio, a well-to-do suburb of Cleveland. He enlisted in 1986, troubleshooting radio systems for the Army's signal corps. He got out in June 1990 but reenlisted two months later when Saddam Hussein invaded Kuwait. He drove a Humvee during the United States' hundred-hour push into Iraq, spent another three years in the service, got out in 1994, and moved to Pulaski, Wisconsin, with his wife and three daughters to work for a yacht builder. That career did not work out. "I don't mind hard work," he quipped, "but getting fiberglass embedded into your skin on a daily basis gets old quick." He decided to get his bachelor's degree and, upon graduation in 2000, become an officer in the National Guard. "We were looking to buy a house somewhere toward Madison," he recalled. "I was going to maybe work for the state or something. I was thirty-two and still trying to figure out what I wanted to do when I grew up."

Goodwin joined the Army this time by mistake. Rather than fill out a National Guard ROTC contract, he accidentally filled out an active-duty Army ROTC contract instead. As graduation approached, his ROTC adviser told him he was going on active duty immediately. Goodwin insisted there must be some mistake. Once he backtracked over what had happened, it took a while for the shock to wear off. His life had just been upended. Thoughts turned to his wife: he had promised her in 1994 that the second time was it. And now this. "I was dejected, we were making all these other plans," he remembered. She took the jolt surprisingly well. "If that is what we have to do," she told him, "then we will do it."

Goodwin served assignments at Fort Lewis, Washington, and Fort Benning, Georgia, but never got his Ranger Tab, washing out of the school in both 2000 and 2004. After getting promoted to captain, he arrived at Fort Campbell in June 2004 on the division staff and waited for a company command to open up. When he learned that command of Bravo Company (also called the "Bulldogs") was coming vacant in the summer of 2005, however, he hesitated: "I knew that the division was getting ready to deploy in the fall. I struggled with it. I had to do some searching. But then it was like, yeah, I want it."

Typically when a new unit arrives in Iraq, there is a several-week handoff period, known as a "Relief in Place, Transfer of Authority" (RIP-TOA), with the unit they are relieving. The outgoing unit demonstrates, via "right-seat, left-seat rides," how they have been doing business in the area, passing along lessons learned, contacts, and other inside knowledge. Many members of First Strike were astonished by what they found. They knew that Georgia's 48th Infantry Brigade was having a tough deployment. Word was, this National Guard unit was out of their depth and getting shredded. Without enough troops to actively and routinely patrol the roads, they had become easy prey for large, deeply buried IEDs that took a long time to set but produced catastrophic casualties. The 48th lost four soldiers to a single device in late July and four more from the same platoon in another, almost identical blast just one week later. Within five months of their May arrival in theater, twenty-one soldiers from the 48th were dead. It was no secret they were being reassigned to a less risky base away from direct combat missions.

Even so, First Strike's advance parties were shocked at how degraded the unit was. It is a long and not-so-noble tradition in the military to ever so slightly knock the competence of the unit you are replacing, to say, "They are a good unit, and they did the best they could, but it was probably best we showed up when we did." The put-downs are usually subtle, even artfully backhanded. That is not the case when many of the men of First Strike describe relieving the 48th.*

Many soldiers from the 1-502nd concluded that the 48th had given up. They almost never left their FOBs. They did not patrol much, and when they did, they would speed around the area in their vehicles and head back as soon as possible. They did not make eye contact with the locals, they did not stop to talk to anyone. When heading to more remote areas, they would practice "recon by fire"—preemptively shooting everywhere to announce their position and scare off anyone in the vicinity. If they were hit by an IED, or even noticed a suspicious rustling

---

*Many of the men of the 1-502nd said they would have been far more polite about the 48th if, when the 101st started making headlines in the summer of 2006, they had not read an *Atlanta Journal-Constitution* story with quotes from 48th commanders implying that they had done a better job and that the 101st was handing back the gains they had made. Feeling such comments to be a knife in the back, in addition to an outrageous aggrandizement of the 48th's accomplishments, many from First Strike acknowledged that they felt no impulse to cover for what they considered an incompetent Guard unit that they believed had surrendered its territory to the insurgency.

in the weeds, they would lay a 360-degree perimeter of fire and get out of there as fast as possible. One 101st soldier told of the time a Guardsman asked him if he wanted to buy his night-vision goggles. Another said some men from the 48th told him how to find a brothel in town and which Iraqi Army soldiers would score him booze and drugs. The 48th men in the guard towers at FOB Mahmudiyah used multiple justifications for their frequent firings at civilians. People standing up in trucks got shot at. People walking too close to the FOB got shot at. People driving too slow—or too fast—got shot at.

The living conditions on some of the 48th's outer bases, meanwhile, had turned feral. While the battalion headquarters seemed to cling to bare-bones but still recognizably human wartime living, at FOB Yusufiyah the men of the 48th were living like animals. Rather than walk the hundred or so yards to a latrine, men would urinate into empty one-liter water bottles. When Bravo Company arrived at Yusufiyah, there were hundreds of cloudy, yellowing piss bottles thrown around in lockers, on top of buildings, or simply corralled into collections on the floor. Boxes of open food from care packages were strewn about, as were rat droppings and gnawed-away panels of cardboard. Feces and other waste clogged the gutters. Discarded food, including slabs of meat, was welded by heat and sand to the floor of the chow hall, while other provisions rotted in open freezers. The insides of the shower trailers were covered in thick green mold.

In late October, the transfers of authority started nearing completion as the 48th decamped for Camp Scania, a much quieter area forty miles to the south. But it is not as if the Black Heart Brigade had enjoyed anything like a honeymoon period. Even during the right-seat, left-seat rides, soldiers from the 101st were getting mortared, IED'd, or shot at every day. Every soldier has his first combat story, and it usually took place within a day or two of arriving in theater.

First Strike's intelligence officer was frustrated by the lack of information the 48th had on the area. Since they had not been patrolling very much, they had little idea who the local power brokers were or what the current status of the eternal tribal joustings was, and no clue about what was going on anywhere west of Yusufiyah. The 48th intelligence shop had done the best it could, but it comprised only two people and was poorly resourced. They had, for example, no signal intelligence system—the monitoring of telephones and other communications—whatsoever. First Battalion's eight-man team started building a database of important people and places, times and severity of attacks, anything of interest, and interlinked it all. Within a month or two, analyses of the accumulated data started spitting out trends and probabilities of attacks.

As the battalion started to settle in and Kunk focused on his mission to fight the insurgency and support the people, he began to realize just how difficult this was going to be. "There wasn't much governance going on," Kunk said. "There wasn't any infrastructure. People wouldn't come out when it got dark." And what little governance there was could not be trusted. Mahmudiyah's mayor was believed to be corrupt and an insurgent sympathizer. During the weeks the 48th was pulling out, U.S. forces caught him in a car full of weapons and arrested him. Trying to sort out who was who, Kunk embarked on a heavy schedule of meetings with local sheikhs, strongmen, and other claimants to various seats of power. It is a role he would play throughout the deployment.

Part of Kunk's job was also to train the Iraqi security forces into competent organizations, another tall order. There was no functioning police force in the whole region. The 4th Brigade of the 6th Iraqi Army Division's area of responsibility roughly mirrored First Strike's, with a battalion in Lutufiyah, a battalion in Yusufiyah, and a battalion and headquarters in Mahmudiyah. When the 101st arrived, the Iraqi soldiers were understaffed, half of them did not have weapons, fewer had any training, and most were of dubious loyalty. Many, the Americans' interpreters noted, had slogans supporting Muqtada al-Sadr written on their rifles. Sorting through who could be trusted, let alone who was fit to fight, would prove a never-ending challenge. Kunk suspected the Iraqi brigade commander to be, if not a Mahdi Army sympathizer, then certainly prejudiced against Sunnis. Two of the battalion commanders, both Sunnis, would die under mysterious circumstances. And even though Yusufiyah was the most dangerous place, Kunk noted, the Iraqi battalion there always had the fewest resources and the weakest leaders.

The catchphrase order from Kunk to his subordinates was "Go out and get after it," and that's what they did. Delta's company commander Captain Lou Kangas divided his territory into four pieces, dealing one to each of his platoon leaders.

He told them, "You own this space now. Become the expert in absolutely everything having to do with it. Patrol every inch of it, meet every person, take a census of every house."

Within a few days of arrival, Captain Bordwell organized a full Alpha Company patrol of Mahmudiyah. "We just threw it out there," he said. "The mentality was, if this is going to get ugly, let's do it early."

Down in Lutufiyah, Captain Dougherty also started running patrols and began a census. Patrol leaders were to get names and photos of the inhabitants of every house and to develop a database. On the battalion level, operations officer Major Salome started scheduling missions into seemingly random map grid squares, to keep insurgents and townspeople off-balance and to create the impression that the U.S. forces in the area were far larger than they actually were, "that we were everywhere at the same time," he said.

As Goodwin and the rest of Bravo took over the Yusufiyah area in October, he was supremely confident in his team. Goodwin's first sergeant, Rick Skidis, would be his closest adviser, institutional memory, and overseer of the men. Rounding out Goodwin's leadership crew was his executive officer, First Lieutenant Justin Habash, and his fire support officer, another lieutenant who coordinated artillery fire into and out of Bravo territory.

The magnitude of Goodwin's task weighed on him. He had been entrusted with the safety, well-being, and fight-readiness of 135 young men. He was realistic about the dangers of war, and knew some of his men would probably not be coming home, but he was nonetheless enthusiastic about the job at hand. "I have a great bunch of guys," he thought to himself. "The ship's on course. All I have to do is keep it straight."

Goodwin's company, like most light infantry companies, consisted of his headquarters element plus three platoons of approximately thirty-five soldiers each, with each platoon led by a lieutenant who is the platoon leader and a sergeant first class who is the platoon sergeant. It also had a weapons squad, with three machine gun teams of two men each; but before deployment, Bravo's weapons squad was broken up and the machine gun teams distributed throughout the rest of the company.

Twenty-four-year-old Lieutenant Ben Britt led 1st Platoon. The son of a Texas rancher, he had propelled his high-school football team to the state finals as an all-state tackle. He was an Eagle Scout, an all-region saxophonist, and class valedictorian. He entered San Antonio's Trinity University in 1999 to play Division III football, but he transferred to West Point the next year because he wanted service and sacrifice to be a part of his life. He thrived at West Point, where he played rugby, majored in economics, and graduated in the academic top 5 percent of his class.

There is an old joke in the Army: "What is the difference between a private first class and a second lieutenant? A PFC has been promoted." That sums up the difficult task every platoon leader has establishing authority. While a second lieutenant may have a college degree and some high-class training, these officers are younger than many of the men they are leading, and they often struggle to earn their respect.

Soldiers can be ruthless in their assessment of lieutenants, but Britt's men universally said they loved him. A born leader, he was always one of the smartest guys in the room, but he never copped the superiority attitude that West Pointers are often mocked for having. He could talk about the finer points of Keynesian economics, if that was what you were into, or he could just as easily tell you why Tupac was better than Wu-Tang. He was well-read in all of his tactical handbooks, but he always weighed the input of his NCOs before making a decision. A big kid with a large round face, he was fearsome when he scowled, yet disarming when he smiled, which was often. Most of all, Britt's men respected him because he led from the front. There is no quicker way to earn a trooper's respect than to put yourself at the same risks he is forced to take. "He wanted a piece of the action," said one of his men. "Command and control? Not a problem. He did it. But he wasn't satisfied with that. He wanted to be the first guy going in."

Britt's NCO counterpart was Phil Miller, a twenty-five-year-old staff sergeant from North Huntington, Pennsylvania. Platoon sergeants are usually sergeants first class, but 1st Platoon's original platoon sergeant, Sergeant First Class Rob Gallagher, was one of the few non–Alpha Company men moved to the MiTT team, so Miller—the platoon's senior squad leader, a go-getter, and one of the only NCOs in the platoon with a Ranger Tab—took over. Despite Miller's considerable youth and inexperience, Lieutenant Colonel Kunk and Sergeant Major Edwards were impressed by what they saw of Miller at NTC and they were sure he was up to the job. He was one of the most popular NCOs in the platoon, and the guys were delighted when they heard he was taking over from Gallagher, who was widely considered a hard-ass. Small and sinewy, Miller was a strutting peacock with a loud voice. He was a tough guy when he wanted to be, but also a total cutup when he was in the mood for goofing off. Miller jumped at the added responsibility. "Right before we deployed," he said, "I pulled everyone in, and I told them, 'I'm going to do everything that I can to bring everyone home.' That's a big statement, to say, 'Hey, everyone that's standing here right now is coming home.' But I was confident. I was confident in that platoon."

While bravado can be a powerful force, 2nd and 3rd Platoons simply had more-seasoned and more-mature platoon sergeants in charge. When Second Lieutenant Mark Evans showed up at Fort Campbell in May 2005 to take over as 3rd Platoon's leader, for example, the first words of advice 1st Battalion Executive Officer Fred Wintrich gave him were: "Blaisdell's got a good platoon. Don't screw it up."

"Blaisdell" was thirty-two-year-old Sergeant First Class Phil Blaisdell, one of First Strike's fastest-rising stars and most-respected NCOs. A hard-charger and a demanding boss, Blaisdell had formidably high standards yet a surprisingly warm disposition with his men. There was something about the way he operated that made even privates feel important. People did what he said, not just because it was an order but because they wanted to please him. So effective was his charisma that when people did carp about him, they complained he was coated in Teflon. Blaisdell's position as the battalion's crown prince was so secure, they grumbled, that he was forgiven for mistakes others got crucified for. He took risks, often dramatic ones, but he was doubly charmed: most of the time his risks paid off, and even when they didn't, he suffered very few repercussions.

Unlike 1st and 3rd Platoons, 2nd Platoon was not overflowing with powerful personalities. By contrast, its platoon sergeant, Sergeant First Class Jeremy Gebhardt, had neither Blaisdell's magnetism nor Miller's brashness. If anything, the twenty-eight-year-old was a bit taciturn in a culture where leaders tend to be boisterous. But his unassuming style clearly worked for him, earning him a reputation for calm, understated excellence.

If First Strike's mission was to win South Baghdad, then Charlie and Bravo, situated on the western and southern borders of the battalion's territory, were on the frontier of the fight. Bravo's domain was a fifty-square-mile swath on the battalion's west side. On the eastern edge of the company's territory were Bravo's two anchors. To the north was the town of Yusufiyah and FOB Yusufiyah, the company headquarters that Bravo shared with soldiers from the Iraqi Army's 4th Battalion, 4th Brigade, 6th Division. The base was not large, only about 500 yards by 250 yards. American operations were almost entirely housed in one building, a gigantic corrugated-tin barn that used to be a potato-processing plant. The vast open center space had six loading bays, three on each side. Each platoon got a bay, MiTT Team 4 (a group of soldiers from the 2-502nd) took a bay, one bay was reserved for visitors such as Civilian Affairs or Combat Stress teams, and the sixth bay contained Goodwin's and his staff's living quarters. In recognition that Bravo was in the hottest area, Kunk centered the battalion's medical corps in Yusufiyah as well. Goodwin put his headquarters, which the Army calls a TOC (tactical operations center),

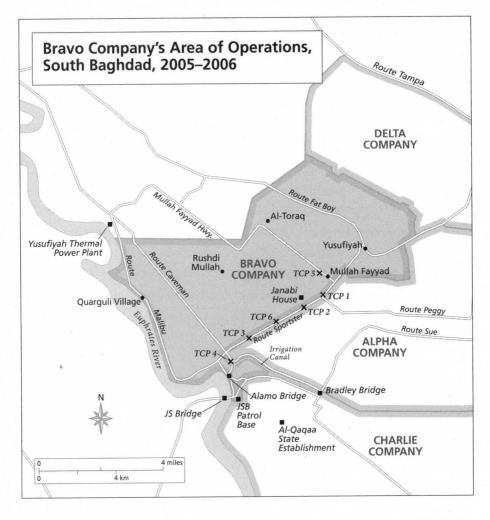

Bravo Company's Area of Operations, South Baghdad, 2005–2006

Route Tampa

DELTA COMPANY

Mullah Fayyad Hwy.

Route Fat Boy

Al-Toraq

Yusufiyah Thermal Power Plant

Yusufiyah

Rushdi Mullah

BRAVO COMPANY

Route Caveman

Route

Mullah Fayyad

TCP 5

Janabi House

TCP 1

Quarguli Village

Euphrates River

Malibu

Route Peggy

TCP 6

TCP 2

Route Sportster

Route Sue

TCP 3

ALPHA COMPANY

TCP 4

Irrigation Canal

N

Bradley Bridge

Alamo Bridge

JS Bridge

JSB Patrol Base

Al-Qaqaa State Establishment

CHARLIE COMPANY

0　　　　　　　　　4 miles
0　　　　　4 km

up in front of the potato barn, along with the interpreters and MiTT team offices. Members of the Iraqi Army's 4th Battalion occupied an identical potato barn two hundred feet away.

The southern anchor of Bravo's area was the Jurf al-Sukr Bridge (which was usually shortened to "the JS Bridge" or just "the JSB") and a smaller patrol base nearby right on the banks of the Euphrates located in a former water-treatment plant. The bridge, a large concrete span across the river, had been closed to traffic since the Marines took it over in late 2004. A six-mile-long, two-lane paved road called Route Sportster linked Bravo's two nodes. One mile south of Yusufiyah on Sportster was the smaller town that the Iraqis called Al-Shuhada ("The Martyrs") but the Americans, for reasons no one seemed to recall, had always known as Mullah Fayyad. Bravo was also in charge of a vast expanse of land to the west, which was largely terra incognita. In this area was a sprinkling of smaller hamlets that the soldiers would get to know much better over time—Rushdi Mullah, Al-Toraq, Quarguli Village. But for now, few even knew what these places were called, let alone what was lurking there.

Like much of the battalion's area, the terrain was perfect for guerrilla warfare. In the towns, the houses were densely packed, making it difficult and confusing for the Americans to find their way, especially when they were in a hurry. Outside the towns, there were acres of empty farmlands, affording ample privacy and plenty of places to hide weapons, bomb materials, equipment, and people. There were few paved roads, making it difficult for heavy vehicles to maneuver. And hundreds of interlacing irrigation canals diced up the land like a maze. It was easy to get pinned between two canals with only one avenue of escape, or to see an enemy just fifty yards away but have no way to get to him. Elephant grass and reeds ten or more feet high lined many of the roads, allowing insurgents to skulk about with unnerving ease. Thanks to the canal system, the land here was greener overall than might be expected, but there were still stark contrasts in a tightly concentrated space. Down by Quarguli Village on the banks of the Euphrates, the land is extravagantly lush, an idealized oasis. But just a half-mile in any direction are flats of crumbly brown, cracked earth.

To the north of Quarguli Village, which is strung along a route called Malibu, lay the massive, abandoned Russian Thermal Power Plant construction site. Until the last months of First Strike's deployment, however, the power plant was a no-go area for U.S. troops. "We couldn't get in the power plant under policy constraints until June of 2006," said Colonel Ebel. "We were restricted because of some diplomatic arrangement with Russia, at least that was the interpretation through the staff channels, all the way down to us." Not surprisingly, it had become a stronghold for insurgents, practically a FOB of their own.

On his early rides out around the area, Kunk saw the first glimpses of what he needed to do. Riding along with the 48th, he would hear them say, "We don't go down that road. That road? We don't go down that one either." Whenever they hit a catastrophic IED, the 48th would declare the road "black" (off-limits to military traffic) and never drive down it again. As a result, they had to take tortuous, detour-filled routes to get anywhere.

"I asked, 'Why don't you go down Sportster?' " Kunk remembered. "They said, 'That is where the bad guys are, and you'll get killed if you go out there.' They hadn't gone down there in many, many months. The enemy was dictating the fight. We had to change that. It was going to be tough, but we had to take Sportster back, and then we had to hold it."

Upon Bravo's arrival at Yusufiyah in October, Captain Goodwin split his three platoons into three duty rotations, each twenty-one days long. One platoon would go down to the JSB, secure that territory, and run patrols and missions from there. Another platoon would be responsible for holding down FOB Yusufiyah. They would pull guard and act as the company's Quick Reaction Force (QRF) if another Bravo element ran into trouble. If Goodwin spotted something on the J-Lens, the company's eye-in-the-sky camera observation system, he might send them out to investigate, and they would also run support and supply convoys up to Striker or Mahmudiyah when necessary. The third platoon would be the company's "maneuver platoon." Also operating out of FOB Yusufiyah, they would conduct ambushes, overwatches, snatch and grabs, searches, and presence patrols, as well as outreach and contact with the local populace. Every twenty-one days, the platoons would rotate.

Of course, no battle plan survives first contact with the enemy.

5

1st Platoon at the JS Bridge

GOODWIN DECIDED TO send 1st Platoon down to the JSB for the first rotation. Why? "First comes before second," he said. "No other reason than that." Following the advance teams, much of Britt and Miller's 1st Platoon helicoptered in to the JSB in early October. Living conditions were grim. The JSB patrol base was dominated by three main buildings surrounded by a ten-foot-high cement-covered cinder-block wall. A mortar team stayed in the plant itself, which is where the platoon set up its TOC. Most of the soldiers slept in a dingy basement of one of the other main buildings, a place they called the Bat Cave. And leaders stayed in a third, smaller building.

There was no chow hall or any kitchen to cook meals. All the food was either the Army's cook-in-pouch combat rations called MREs (meals, ready to eat) or hamburger patties or steaks they would grill themselves. Their first barbecue was made from a storm drain—they had cleaned it by burning it with diesel fuel—placed on top of an oil drum. There were no dishes or cutlery, so if they grilled, they either saved the MRE plasticware or gnawed on hamburger patties with their bare hands. There was no electricity, no lighting that wasn't battery-operated, no air-conditioning during the day and no heaters at night.

There were no showers, no toilets, and no Porta-Johns. There was no running water of any kind—ironic, they noted, considering the place was a water-treatment plant. Soldiers defecated in "WAG Bags," small green garbage bags with solvents inside that were tied off and then thrown in a pit and burned once a day. Often the smoke would blow back into the guard areas, bathing the men in odors of smoldering plastic, feces, urine, and trash.

Besides holding down the JSB patrol base itself, their other major duty was to secure something called an Armored Vehicle–Launched Bridge (AVLB), a metal span that Army engineers had placed over a bend in a canal that joined the JSB frontage road to Route Sportster and provided access to both north and west. The bridge was narrow and the banks of the canal it crossed were steep. It was a lonely outpost, three-quarters of a mile from the JSB. There would be frequent controversy over the best way to secure it—and what the word "secure" meant—but generally, 1st Platoon adopted the staffing rotation that the 48th employed: three to four soldiers parked in a Humvee off to the side of the road, near the canal, twenty-four hours a day. During the daytime, it was not uncommon for the bridge to be guarded by just two soldiers in a truck. Everyone who looked at it knew it was a dangerous position. There were angles of attack from virtually every direction but bad defense sight lines, and virtually no barriers, man-made or natural, to slow any approaching vehicle. It could not be directly defended by the JSB base because it was barely within that outpost's visible range and well beyond effective rifle range. Most of the men started calling the AVLB what the 48th had called it: the Alamo.

Besides guard duties at the JSB and the Alamo, 1st Platoon kept patrols to a minimum early on because building up the site's defenses was unquestionably the priority. The 48th had stationed only about a squad of men out there and they hadn't fortified the place. There was no high gun position and there were big holes—literally blasted-out gaps—in the perimeter wall that anyone could have walked through.

"From the moment those guys hit the ground down there, it was, 'What the hell is this trash heap? How are you supposed to defend this place?' " said Bravo's executive officer, First Lieutenant Justin Habash. "The duration of 1st Platoon's first rotation was work. Manual labor." First Platoon filled sandbags, from sunup to sundown. It was dirty, demoralizing physical labor that quickly devolved into sheer exhaustion. To build a rooftop gun perch, soldiers would load rucksacks with as many sandbags as they could carry and trudge up several flights of stairs. There was a profound lack of equipment. They had only two hammers. They had only two pairs of gloves to string concertina wire. They had no saws. They had to use their Gerber hand tools, essentially high-end Swiss Army knives, to cut two-by-fours and planks of plywood.

Staff Sergeant Miller had no doubts about 1st Platoon's abilities, but there was no denying they were a young and inexperienced group. There had been a lot of turnover after Operation Iraqi Freedom 1 (OIF1). Many of the NCOs were in leadership positions for the first time. Obviously, many of the youngest soldiers were hardly men at all— eighteen-, nineteen-, and twenty-year-olds. But in this platoon, even some of the older guys with ample time in the military had had little time in the infantry.

Forty-one years old, 1st Squad's leader Staff Sergeant Travis Nelson enlisted in the Army before some of his soldiers were born, but he'd been an infantryman only since he re-entered active duty just over a year before this deployment. Born in Cullman, Alabama, he entered the service in 1982 and served twelve years as a tanker. During the Gulf War, absolutely everyone who talks about Nelson will tell you, he was part of the longest tank-to-tank kill in history. Men in the platoon lovingly called Nelson "Gramps" or "Old Man River." Old as he was, Nelson never dogged it during a run or PT (physical training). He always hung in there and sometimes bested kids half his age.

Nelson's wife, Shelly, was always amazed when a young soldier mentioned to her that Travis was a tough boss. To her, at home, he was as cuddly as a puppy dog. She mailed him a steady stream of care packages, filled with Marlboro Lights and Red Diamond single-serve coffee sachets. Nelson was willing to endure many hardships, but he was not willing to forgo freshly brewed coffee. Back home, Shelly and he had become especially good friends with Miller and his wife. The two couples would spend long nights playing Spades and the men would go fishing all the time. Not long before the division headed out, Shelly was sitting out on the front porch of her home and she told Miller to bring Travis home safe to her.

"The old man will be home," Miller said. "I promise."

Nelson's Alpha Team leader, and thus the squad's second in command, was Sergeant Kenith Casica. A thirty-two-year-old native of the Philippines, Casica grew up in Virginia Beach, Virginia. He met his wife, Renee, in high school when he was seventeen and she was fourteen. She got pregnant and they got married two years later. He worked at McDonald's, delivered papers, and poured concrete. Sick of dead-end jobs, he joined the Army in 1996 to give his family a better life. Ken and Renee ultimately had three kids. While he enjoyed the Army, he was looking beyond it. He ran an Amway business and wanted to go to college, become a registered nurse, and someday get his U.S. citizenship. Casica was, everybody says, the nicest guy they had ever met. A lean six foot three and handsome, with a big, broad smile, he made his home one of the unofficial clubhouses for the platoon, especially for the younger unmarried guys. They were always welcome to come over, hang out, and have a beer.

Casica's unflappable friendliness extended to Iraqis. When he was in OIF1, also with Bravo Company, he was always the most outgoing to the Hadjis (or simply Hadj), as soldiers universally called Iraqis. He learned an impressive amount of Arabic during his first deployment. He had mastered the common Middle Eastern and Asian resting position back on one's haunches that soldiers called "the Hadji squat," and he had even bought a dishdasha, the white flowing Middle Eastern garb that soldiers call a "man dress." Because of his dark complexion, Iraqis often thought he was an Arab and locals warmed to him instantly. He didn't just talk about helping Iraqis, he actually did it. He'd use his own money to buy extra cases of soft drinks, or sometimes he'd "find" a few extra during a resupply mission, which he would give to a couple of Mosul boys who had a roadside beverage business. He helped them build their stand out of broken-up shipping pallets and other street jetsam. It looked just like Lucy van Pelt's psychiatry office from *Peanuts*. The hand-lettered sign he helped paint declared the name of the watering hole: "The Thirsty Goat." He retained his optimism about the Iraqis even after he was injured by an RPG (rocket-propelled grenade) blast in OIF1 that sank shrapnel fragments deep into his shoulder blade. His platoon mates frequently ribbed him about just how buddy-buddy he was with the Iraqis. They called him a Hadji Hugger or Hadji Fucker, but he didn't care. If the point of being here was to help the people, he said to anyone who gave him a hard time (which was often goodnatured, but sometimes not), then let's help them. Because otherwise, what the hell are we doing here?

A kid desperate for a father figure, Private First Class Jesse Spielman was exactly the sort of 1st Squad trooper to flock to Casica's house. The twenty-one-year-old was born in Chambersburg, Pennsylvania, to a teenage mom. Spielman's grandmother was concerned that her own daughter was not fit to raise the child and, after some ugly legal wranglings, she assumed custody of the boy when he was seven. Beyond that rocky beginning, Spielman's grandmother remembered him as a sweet child who was eager to please. One of Spielman's uncles gave him an Army camouflage outfit when he was eight or nine years old and from then on all he would do was play Army man outside. Sometimes his grandmother had trouble getting that getup off of him long enough for her to wash it. He joined the Army in March 2005 and became a member of the 101st in August. He married just before deploying, his bride wearing a T-shirt that said, "I love my soldier." His superiors found Spielman to be a quiet kid, hard to draw out, but a competent trooper who was easy to lead and eager to advance. If there was a cleanup call or some other random task to accomplish and his squad mates were resting, he'd just do it himself. When an NCO would tell him to wake his buddies up and spread the work, he'd say, "Naw, let 'em sleep."

Private Steven Green was one of those squad mates Spielman would let sleep. Growing up in Midland, Texas, Green was always the odd kid, the outsider, the strange child on the margins always picked last for kickball. Though highly intelligent, he was bowlegged and uncoordinated. He bumped into things, and he had a drooling problem that lasted well into the 8th grade. According to court records, he was an unwanted child, his mother did not hesitate to tell him. She simply never bonded with him, never grew to love him. She called him "demon spawn" and constantly compared him unfavorably with his brother, Doug, who was three years his senior. Working nights at a bar, she was a neglectful mother who let her children fend for themselves. Doug was, not surprisingly, unable to cope with the responsibility of being a surrogate parent from as young as age seven or eight. He subjected Steven and their little sister to frequent, brutal beatings, sometimes requiring trips to the hospital and once breaking several of the girl's fingers.

Green's parents divorced when he was eight and he lived with his mother until she kicked him out of the house at age fourteen. Diagnosed with ADHD and low-grade depression as an adolescent, he bounced around various family members' homes for the next few years. Desperate for attention, he did win a few friends in high school by being the class clown. He would entertain at pep rallies by doing a spastic chicken dance and smash dozens of soda cans on his forehead during lunch. After he dropped out of high school in the 10th grade, trouble followed him wherever he went. Smoking cigarettes, drinking booze, and walking around with marijuana are fairly common activities for teenagers, but Green managed to get caught, arrested, and convicted for each of those things by the time he was nineteen, spending a few weeks in juvenile detention for one and a few days in jail for another.

Along the way, he had developed some pointed ideas about society, culture, religion, and race. He decided to join the Army in early 2005, not just as a way out of his rut but as a means to participate in what he saw as the latest flare-up of a centuries-long struggle between Western civilization and Eastern barbarism. "This is almost like a race war, like a cultural war," he said about 9/11, the March 2004 Madrid train bombings, and the now lengthening conflicts in Iraq and Afghanistan. "And anyone who is my age who is not going to go fight in it is a coward. They can say it's about this or that, but it's really about religion. It's about not even which culture is going to rule the Middle East, but which culture is going to rule the West. I felt like Islam is, was, and always will be like fascism."

Green spent several months obtaining a high-school correspondence diploma and the Army granted him a "moral waiver" for his prior convictions. With the Army strapped for personnel, it granted such waivers to almost one in five recruits in 2005, an increase of 44 percent over prewar levels. After graduating from basic training, he headed to Fort Campbell in July 2005. Green was not a terrible soldier—in fact, he would be promoted to private first class relativly quickly, in November— but here, as in school, he developed a reputation for not being quite right in the head. There was no doubt he was smart, and he read far more widely than is typical for a soldier. One lieutenant was surprised to find Rousseau's *Social Contract* on his bookshelf. But he was a racist, a white supremacist, and a misanthrope. He remained socially awkward and unable to control his emotions or impulses. He was also an incessant monologuist, with no internal editor, who launched into the most ridiculous and offensive tirades about "niggers," about Jews, about northerners, about foreigners, about anyone. He did have some friends, but much of the platoon viewed him less as a class clown and more as the village idiot—occasionally entertaining as spectacle, but best kept at arm's length.

Second Squad was a much more low-key operation than Bravo's other squads, and that suited squad leader Staff Sergeant Chris Payne just fine. To the best of his ability, Payne pursued a no-drama policy in his personal and professional life. It was part of the reason, the twenty-four-year-old said, he had advanced fairly quickly in his career: he tried not to get bothered by the things that other people wasted their time getting upset about. The politics, the power games, the backbiting—he just blocked them all out and did his job. Some of his men said that this remote and detached attitude sometimes lapsed into inattention that put outsized responsibility on his subordinates. Payne countered that training his team leaders to step up was part of a squad leader's job.

The team leader whom Payne relied upon most was Sergeant John Diem. By most other soldiers' definition, Diem would appear to be a textbook dork. He was not physically imposing and he did not have a commanding voice. He had thick glasses and reddish curly hair. He played a lot of Xbox, read Japanese comic books, and was a role-playing-game enthusiast. But Diem had fought in OIF1 and he had ascended to a leadership role by virtue of hard work, accomplished technical proficiency, and an obvious, overwhelming intelligence. He always got the job done, and he also had a steely will. Easy to underestimate, he was impossible to intimidate, and he was not afraid to tell subordinates and superiors alike truths they did not want to hear.

Upon taking leadership of 3rd Squad, thirty-four-year-old Sergeant Eric Lauzier resolved to turn his crew into the toughest, hardest, tightest squad in the company, if not the whole battalion. Lauzier was aggressive, manic, task-driven. He was Sergeant Miller's go-to guy. Captain Goodwin came to think of him as his Clydesdale, who would just pull and pull and pull until he reached the goal, or broke down trying. Whether it was his maps or his green, cloth-covered notebook that every Army NCO and officer carries around, or even his underwear, Lauzier signed almost everything he owned with his name followed by the initials "BMF"—Bad Motherfucker.

This was his second stint in the military. He'd been a Marine in the 1990s. Dissatisfied with civilian life, he sought to reenlist in 2001. The Marines wanted him to complete boot camp again as a private, but the Army said he could keep his rank and head straight to Fort Campbell. He was a specialist with Bravo during the invasion (and he would be promoted to staff sergeant in December 2005), making him the only squad leader in 1st Platoon with OIF1 experience.

That campaign, especially the invasion, felt like everything Lauzier thought war would be: entire companies of men following slow-moving tanks as they advanced on a defined enemy. He remembered his first kill, the pink mist of impact, the way the man's body dropped—instantly—drained of all vitality, hitting the ground with a thud. Lauzier remembered the electric, elemental frisson of realization that he was still alive, and that other guy, that guy was now dead because of him. He remembered all of them, five confirmed kills, including one rare hand-to-hand kill in Mosul. He still thought a lot about those five men, often when he didn't want to.

Lauzier did not head out on his second tour to make friends with Iraqis. He was going to Iraq to put the hurt on the enemy. And don't let anybody lie to you, he cautioned: All throughout the deployment, nobody was talking about counterinsurgency the way they might be now. That suited him just fine. Hearts and minds didn't work in Vietnam, he often said, and it wasn't going to work here.

Lauzier was emphatic in wanting his men to be the best and he rode them hard. He made his guys do extra PT, extra drills, extra book study. He rarely slept and he consumed almost a case of energy drinks a day. After OIF1, he had washed out of Special Forces selection because he botched a land-navigation test, a failure that irked him. From then on, he made map and compass skills a priority for himself and his squad.

Despite the French half of his ancestry that contributed his last name, he identified much more with the Italian side of his heritage. Woe to the smart aleck who asked, "How you doing, Sergeant Lo-zjay?" because that kid was going to be doing push-ups for hours. Some of the senior NCOs called him Lolo, but the younger guys were strictly forbidden from calling him that too. He had several tattoos, including the face of the Joker on his left forearm, the phrase "Laugh Now, Cry Later" on his left calf, a memorial to a fallen friend from OIF1 around his right wrist, and "Machine 0311" around his left ("0311" is the Marine designation for infantryman and "Machine" an expression of his indefatigability). Lauzier looked around at his squad and he liked what he saw. He had more OIF1 veterans than anyone in the platoon, and they were some pretty tough customers.

The toughest customer of them all was Sergeant Tony Yribe, a walking, talking G.I. Joe action figure and Lauzier's Alpha Team leader. He'd joined the Army just eight days after 9/11 and had already served tours in Germany, Kosovo, and Iraq during OIF1 with the 1st Infantry Division before transferring to the 101st in January 2005. Though only a team leader, he radiated a powerful charisma that made him by far one of the dominant personalities of the platoon. Some say he surpassed the squad leaders and the platoon sergeants as the real seat of power in the platoon. The younger guys flocked to him, wanted to be like him, idolized him. He could be brusque and intolerant of those he did not like or respect, and extraordinarily loyal and kind to those he did, which made being a member of his inner circle particularly sweet.

No small part of Yribe's persona was his fearlessness in combat. If the situation was getting dicey, he was not afraid to pull the trigger. He saw a lot of fighting during his first deployment, and that experience had hardened him greatly. He had a tattoo of a Glock 9mm pistol on his right hip and the word "Warrior" in a semicircle around his stomach. Lauzier called Yribe his linebacker because of the way he would just blow through doors and lay dudes flat. Yribe had an uncanny knack for being where the action was. "I would joke with him that if something bad was going to happen, I could count on him being there," said Goodwin. Yribe saw no need to apologize for this. He just refused to take any shit, especially from Hadj. If you had to use force to get their attention or win their compliance, he argued, then that was what you had to do. And if anyone thought it could be any other way, well, then, he was quite certain they hadn't spent very much time on the line.

One of the guys most completely under Yribe's spell was Specialist Paul Cortez, who had recently transferred to the Deuce from the 4th Infantry Division. With wide-wingspan ears and a pronounced widow's peak, he resembled a postadolescent Eddie Munster. Living in motel rooms around Barstow, California, with his drug-addict mother for most of his childhood, Cortez was taken in by the parents of a school friend around the age of fourteen. Under his foster parents' care, he flourished, pulling his grades up and finishing high school. When he turned eighteen, they discussed his options. College wasn't realistic, and technical schools were expensive, so Cortez joined the Army.

Cortez had driven a Bradley Fighting Vehicle with the 4th Infantry Division during OIF1, and when he arrived at the 101st Airborne, he was originally assigned to Payne's squad. But Payne couldn't deal with him.

Cortez had potential, Payne thought, but his work was inconsistent. For two, three weeks, even a month, he could be a good soldier with real leadership potential, and then he'd mess things up again, get into a fight, get busted for weed, or drink himself into the hospital. He had a nasty streak, too, and a chip on his shoulder. He was obsessed with proving himself better than others, but he was rarely more than average at anything he did. When given a challenge, sometimes he would rise to meet it, but just as often he would quit in a heap of complaints and sulks.

"You take him," Payne told Lauzier. "See if you can do something with him." Lauzier could and did, finding him to be a classic "field soldier"—someone who doesn't do well in garrison but excels on the front line. In a lot of ways, he was exactly what Lauzier wanted.

Specialist James Barker was an even better example of a field soldier. Just five foot six, Barker was a natural outside the wire, one of the best combat soldiers Lauzier had ever seen. Childhood friends from Fresno, California, described Barker as a mischievous, lovable dork nicknamed Bunky who hung out mostly with girls. But as he grew older, darker traits emerged. His father died when he was fifteen and Barker fell into a depression. He joined a gang, drank, did drugs, and dropped out of school. He finished high school in 2001 at a continuing education program and had a son with a girl he met there.

He married and joined the Army in March 2003, he said, because he couldn't hold down a job. Almost immediately, his marriage started to sour. As he was relocating to Fort Campbell, an NCO helping with the move reported Barker for being abusive to his wife and child. Barker said he grabbed his son to prevent him from falling down the stairs, but all the NCO saw was rough treatment. Barker was forced to go to anger management classes, which delayed his first deployment to Iraq by several months. After spending October 2003 to February 2004 in Mosul, he returned home, where his marriage continued to unravel even though his wife was having their second son.

Rounding out 3rd Squad were a handful of younger soldiers whom Lauzier and Yribe worked mercilessly. Being in 3rd Squad, they declared, was a privilege, and they hazed the hell out of new privates before accepting them. Twenty-two-year-old Private Justin Watt, from Tucson, Arizona, was among the newest arrivals. He had dropped out of high school to take a job with a dot-com during the Internet boom, but it went under in eighteen months. He got his GED and tried a few semesters at a technical college in Tempe, but that didn't work out so well. He was struggling to find his role. He was a computer enthusiast who wasn't a geek; the smart kid who wasn't a student; the athlete who wasn't an all-star.

He just wasn't inspired, so he took a job as a blackjack dealer at a casino in Tucson. The money was good and, around the same time, he'd fallen in love with a girl. They were going to get married and they had a plan. He'd go back to school, get a degree, and pursue a career in casinos. No doubt it was a growth industry, but he was conflicted. At its root, gambling is a shady, depressing business. As he was questioning whether he really wanted to be a part of all that ugliness, his girlfriend dumped him, causing a total reappraisal of his priorities. He'd always admired his father, who was an Army airborne combat engineer during the late 1970s. The war in Iraq did not look like it would be ending soon. Joining the Army, especially now, he decided, would be a chance to test himself, to take the harder route for once, to be a part of something big.

Yribe and Lauzier had months of fun tormenting the small new private. But Watt never quit. He had made a promise to himself that this was the one time in his life he wasn't going to wuss out, and, after thousands of push-ups, miles of running in place, and hours of repeating some stupid phrase or self-insult—"I am the fucking new guy, and I am gay"—it wasn't long before he was a fully accepted member of the squad. They never stopped teasing him, but the tone had changed. It wasn't a tryout anymore, it was just good-natured ribbing, and Watt was as proud as he had ever been.

6

Contact

A S 1ST PLATOON moved into the JSB sector, the insurgents
didn't waste any time testing their new neighbors. Only two or
three days after 1st Platoon's arrival, Yribe and two other men
were guarding the Alamo in a gun truck. It was dark and quiet, almost
one-thirty in the morning, when Yribe heard rustling in the reeds. Animals? People? There was no good reason for a man to be out here at
night. He looked around nervously, but he couldn't see anything. Then
his vision sharpened, and silhouettes of crouched men skittered against
the night sky. Jesus Christ! Two, maybe three shadows, definitely people.
They were trying to sneak up on him. He opened fire. His two soldiers
followed suit.

Soldiers on guard at the JSB heard a volley of fire and several
grenade explosions.

"That's the Alamo!" Platoon Sergeant Miller yelled. "Get up! Get up!
Get the fuck up!" Men started piling their gear on. There was no offi-
cially designated Quick Reaction Force (QRF) yet, so everybody scrambled into the armored personnel carrier. When about a squad's worth
of men had loaded, it took off, with Cortez driving. Roughly halfway
there, the shooting stopped. They arrived, unloaded, and assessed. All

of Yribe's men were fine. The insurgents had beaten a hasty retreat. Miller took Lauzier and half of 3rd Squad to search the nearby hamlet that the shooters would have had to pass through. The soldiers kicked in doors and questioned the locals, but they all professed ignorance.

First Platoon was usually up and working by 6:00 or 6:30 a.m., filling sandbags or fortifying other positions until sundown. Between those duties, patrols, and guard rotations, soldiers were lucky to get more than four hours of sleep a night. Miller was appalled at the lack of equipment and lack of support 1st Platoon received from the very first day. They were dependent on airdrops for everything. He would get on the radio every few minutes to request new supplies. You name it, they called for it: sandbags, food, ice and coolers. Two minutes later it was cots, wood, water, charcoal, and lighter fluid. Two minutes after that, shovels, pickaxes, hammers, and hoes. Finally, Goodwin said no more calls. Keep a list, for chrissake. For weeks afterward, it became a running joke. Anytime Goodwin saw Miller, he'd say, "Need anything? Need anything? Need anything?" Miller didn't find it funny. He was annoyed that getting his guys even the bare minimum of equipment seemed to be such a low priority.

Working like coal miners and just as dirty, most of the men stripped down to their T-shirts while they were filling sandbags or doing other manual labor. Being "away from the flagpole" had its benefits. Britt and Miller didn't sweat the finer points of uniform discipline. They were familiar with the theory why strict adherence to uniform regulations is important at all times: If you get the little things right, it shows an attention to detail, a seriousness, and a vigilance that results in greater self-respect, situational awareness, and, ultimately, safety and combat effectiveness. That's all well and good, they reasoned, but with all the work they were doing on such little sleep and having so few of the necessities like, say, enough water to drink, if a soldier didn't feel like shaving for a day or two, that was fine with them.

But it was not fine with battalion command. Senior leaders started circulating First Strike's territory within the first few days of arrival and Kunk or Edwards began visiting the JSB every few days. They did not like what they saw. "Supposedly they weren't fortifying their positions fast enough," said Bravo Executive Officer Habash. "The Colonel came to the FOB and just destroyed Captain Goodwin over the conditions of the JSB. They're working their asses off to fortify this place, and to have your battalion commander come down and destroy you over not doing enough was frustrating."

But Kunk wasn't just annoyed at what he perceived to be lack of progress. Hard work or not, he and Edwards concluded 1st Platoon was awfully quick to decide that the rules didn't apply to them. The men looked like slobs and were sauntering around not just in their T-shirts but in T-shirts with the sleeves cut off! And flip-flops?! There was trash everywhere. They told Miller and the other NCOs to get their acts together and knock their men into line. Miller and the squad leaders tried to explain that if they had seen what the place looked like before, they'd understand how clean it actually was, how many improvements they had made, and how they were doing it all without any equipment or support. In fact, they thought they were doing a hell of a job. "I wasn't concerned about the small shit," said Miller. "Your boot's unbloused? Who the fuck cares? Last time I checked, that fucker ain't gonna stop you from getting shot in the face. But me putting up nine hundred fucking strands of wire is. The guys had their sleeves rolled up. Whoopie. It's a hundred and twenty fucking degrees out here. Maybe they saw that as lack of leadership because I didn't make them keep their sleeves rolled down."

That's precisely the way Kunk and Edwards saw it. Being far away was no excuse to let standards slip. If anything, they insisted, it made enforcing standards even more important. What really made Kunk mad was the feeling that he wasn't being taken seriously. "There was always a reason why they couldn't do something," he said. "I would put out instructions, I would be gone for a day, get back out there, and they wouldn't be doing what we had talked about. Sergeant Miller and different people wouldn't write stuff down. And I'm like, 'Look man, I'm not saying this for my health. I'm saying this for a reason.'"

But to Miller, there was a very good reason they couldn't do things as quickly as Kunk wanted: Battalion was not providing the tools they needed to do the job right. "I asked for engineer support," he said. "Couldn't get it. Couldn't get any backhoes or any of that stuff down there. My big question was, 'I know they're here, so what's the issue?' And I didn't get any clarification on that."

A few days after the first attack on the Alamo, it got hit again, from the same direction, but this time in the late afternoon and with a rocket-propelled grenade (RPG). The RPG didn't hit anything, but 1st Platoon was better prepared to react. They had a QRF ready to go, which found an IED made of three 155mm artillery rounds on the road leading to the Alamo from the other side. (One 155mm shell weighs about a hundred pounds and, when fired conventionally, has enough destructive force to severely damage a tank.) A squad moved into Quarguli Village. They started kicking in doors, searching houses, looking for the men or man who just shot at them and laid that IED. In a chicken shack out back of one of the houses, they found a man with an AK-47, detonation cord, and what looked like an IED trigger. They zip-tied his hands, put a sandbag over his head, roughed him up a little, and brought him back to the JSB to be picked up.

Watt remembered everybody standing around the man nonplussed. He was a skinny little wretch, 150 pounds tops, with muddy feet and no shoes. This was the enemy? How disappointing. But finding a clear suspect like this proved to be a rarity. Most of the time, they wouldn't find anything. They would receive fire, return fire, and by the time they could get a search party together, the insurgents would be gone, and the locals would claim ignorance, not just about where the bad guys might be, but often that they had even heard shots. The men started calling their enemy "the ghosts."

Up at FOB Yusufiyah, Goodwin and the rest of the company were also trying to settle in. The battle rhythm, it quickly became clear, was going to be unrelenting. It was a rare day when no member of Bravo got attacked by the enemy in some way. This was true throughout the entire brigade's sector (four 2-502nd soldiers died in an IED strike on the unit's first full day in charge of the area), but, over the year, Bravo always had a little bit more, sometimes a lot more, going on than everyone else in First Strike. Days with multiple, even ten or more, significant violent events were commonplace.

From the start, Kunk was unsympathetic to the notion that Bravo should be given any special treatment. Captain Goodwin, First Lieutenant Habash, and First Sergeant Skidis attempted to explain that their environment was more chaotic than Mahmudiyah's, but that got no play. "Don't think you have it any worse than anyone else" was one of Kunk's common refrains. Bravo's leadership couldn't figure out if this was a motivation technique or if Kunk really thought it was true. "If Kunk really believed that, then he had to be crazy. Or supremely out of touch," said Habash. "When we tried to say that we weren't like Alpha and Delta, with all our troops inside the wire, sleeping peacefully at night, Battalion reacted like we were just making excuses."

Kunk railed that Bravo was not getting the job done. Even the way they filed their daily reports was deficient. Battalion wanted highly detailed updates every day about everything that happened in each company's sector. Alpha and Delta platoons at Mahmudiyah could go on patrols and then debrief company leadership in detail, in person, down to the color of every car they had searched. It wasn't that simple for Bravo. "When you're spread out and half of your reports are coming via the radio, the transmissions are unavoidably less complete," commented Habash. "I understand what Battalion was trying to do. But there was a certain level of reality we needed to confront." But every time he attempted to explain why Bravo's reports were more fragmented, he said, "they thought I was blowing smoke up their ass."

Those reports should have been the company commander's job, but Habash started doing them because almost immediately, Goodwin seemed overwhelmed. It wasn't more than a week or two into the deployment that the officers and NCOs around FOB Yusufiyah noticed something odd, and disconcerting: Goodwin never left the TOC. Twenty, twenty-two, even twenty-four hours a day, you could find him by the radios trying to keep tabs on the entire company's operations. Sometimes he would skip meals. Often, soldiers would find him passed out, in the middle of the TOC, sitting in a folding director's chair he liked to use, with a poncho liner pulled over his head. "I just thought it was the growing pains of starting up," said 3rd Platoon's Second Lieutenant Mark Evans. "I thought surely as we got more settled, he'd start to go to sleep. You'd just say to the guy, 'Sir, you look like hell. You've been here for four days.' "

Beyond the relentless pace and the incessant violence, working with the Iraqis was maddening. "Take whoever was supposedly the mayor," said Goodwin. "The locals tell you, 'This is where he lives.' So you go to the house. 'Where is he?' 'He's not here.' 'Well, does he live here?' 'No.' 'So where is he?' 'I don't know.' You know, you could be talking to the guy's brother. Hell, you could be talking to the guy himself. One of the big questions: 'Where's so-and-so?' 'He's in Baghdad.' 'What's he doing in Baghdad?' 'He's looking for work.' That happens all the time. Or, asking somebody: 'Do you speak English?' There are two answers. Either 'No' or 'A little bit.' Sometimes 'No' means they are fluent, while 'A little bit' means that 'A little bit' is the only thing they know how to say. You never know what the real answers are. I would send squads out, saying, 'You need to go find this guy.' They would come back. 'Where is he?' 'He's in Baghdad looking for work.' It became a running joke. One of the things I was trying to work on, and one of the things that I didn't accomplish, I was trying to find out where everybody lived. Basically trying to build a phone book. But in a town that size it's kind of hard, especially when half the people were squatters."

Men up and down the ranks echoed similar frustrations. First Platoon's Tony Yribe, who had been deployed before, didn't trust the Iraqis at all. The ones who were insurgents would lie, the ones who supported insurgents would lie, and even the ones who didn't also lied, all the time, for seemingly no purpose or gain. He described a common scene: "We went to a house because they had a boat, and there were supposed to be no boats along the river. And I was like, 'Whose boat is that?' And he's like, 'Oh, it's my brother's.' And I'm like, 'All right. Who lives on the other side of this house here?' He's like, 'Oh, I don't know.' So we go over there, and we're like, 'Hey, whose boat is that?' 'Oh, that's my brother's.' 'Where does he live?' 'Right over there.' Where we just came from. There's a big pile of hay nearby. And I said, 'Hey, what's in the haystack?' And he said, 'Nothing.' And I was like, 'Lieutenant Britt, you see what I'm saying? This is exactly what I'm saying. That guy lied to you. And now this guy is lying, too.' Of course, we pulled out an AK and some rounds hidden in the haystack. I ended up grabbing the Hadji over my head and I threw him down. We kept searching and there was a fucking mortar pit behind his house. It had a baseplate, it had defilade. You could see the white line measuring marks. And guess what they were aiming at? The JSB. Wherever you're from in the United States, if your neighbor's up to something, you're going to know. And that's how they are. Everybody that you see knows or has participated in some kind of insurgency, or if they haven't participated, then they've supported it in some way. And I told Britt, 'You've got to think that way.' "

The Iraqi Army (IA) was as frustrating as the locals. It was well known around the battalion that Yusufiyah's IA unit was the weakest in the sector. To many of the men, they were worse than useless: they were dangerous. In a diary entry, a squad leader in 2nd Platoon wrote about his frustration at being sent out on patrol with a squad of Iraqi soldiers on a particularly dangerous stretch of road. "The Iraqis were weak, they were tired and wanted to quit about two clicks into it," he wrote. "I told them to suck it up and continue to walk or I'm gonna throw them into the canal. I told my interpreter to tell them that they need to learn to fight for themselves or they are gonna get whacked when the Americans leave. One of the IAs even took out his bulletproof plate and threw it in the canal because he said it was heavy and it hurt his back. Then an Iraqi sergeant gave his weapon to the interpreter and told him to carry it because it was too heavy. I will request to never go on another patrol with them."

The biggest concern of the deployment quickly became apparent, however: the perfect terror instrument that is the IED. In their vernacular, "getting blown up," say many of the soldiers, is by far the craziest and scariest experience of their lives. They dare you to imagine what it is like: You are driving along, handing out Beanie Babies or patrolling a road or bringing water to people, and then, boom, a violent jolt of heat, light, and force up-ends your universe. There is no warning and there is nothing you can do except hope you don't die. And it doesn't happen once, it happens over and over and over again. So, obviously, it doesn't take long before every time you roll outside the wire, you are terrified, truly terrified that you are going to get hit. And which is worse? Getting hit or the anticipation of get-ting hit, the pain and damage being done to your body or the feelings of inevitability and helplessness that come before? Because that uncertainty is as pure a torture as has ever been invented.

"It's like someone has a gun to your head and you don't know whether they're going to kill you or let you live," remembered one sol-dier. Even in a firefight, as scary as those can be, at least you feel like you have some control over your destiny, which is why, let's be honest, they can also be exhilarating. You can fight back, there are people to engage, and even though some Americans might get shot or even die, an unde-niable confidence remains because you seriously doubt that a bunch of insurgents, even a large group of them, will beat a group of Americans in a straight-up firefight. But IEDs? They are inescapable, they are fright-ening in an almost unimaginable way and they begin to weigh on you.

Every ride in a Humvee, every one, is an exercise in terror. You're riding, with your butt cheeks and fists clenched, doing deep breathing to get control of your heart rate and your nausea the whole time, wait-ing for it, waiting for it, waiting for it. And still, when it happens, it is still the most surprising thing in the world. One fraction of a second, every-thing is normal, and the next, well, it depends, but it is definitely not normal. Depending on the size of the bomb and how closely it deto-nates, any combination of light, heat, pressure, dirt, fire, metal, wind, and noise will hit you in a way your body can never be prepared for. Sometimes you remember every millisecond of the thwomp of that ele-mental combination blast. Other times you black out for those crucial few seconds, come to with your body in any number of surprising con-tortions, and wonder, what, what happened? How long ago did it hap-pen? Am I okay? Is that other guy okay? Are we all okay? And if you are not cut and bleeding, you're probably still hurt in some way. You might not be able to hear for hours, and you might not hear right for days. Your vision might be blurry. And the headaches, there will be headaches, because you can't knock around your brain like that without there being some aftereffects. And if you are not injured but the vehicle is undrivable, you should settle in, because you have to cordon off the area and there's a good chance the wrecker is not going to show up for several hours. And while you are sitting there, the anger builds as you review what just happened. Somebody, not far from this spot, someone right around here—it could be him, or him, or him—just tried to kill you. Who of these motherfuckers just tried to kill you? If you conduct a search and are a combination of lucky and good, you might find a guy or two who have incriminating evidence on them. And then you can lay into them, have a momentary lick or two of revenge. But otherwise? Nothing. There is nothing you can do. There is no release for the anger and the adrenaline coursing through your veins. And look around. There's a man on a cell phone, a lady putting out some washing, a kid walking down the road, and you just cannot figure it. How can none of these people know anything about what just happened here? All of them said they have no idea. How could they not know? Of course they know. Somebody tried to kill you, he got away, and all of these people know something, yet they aren't saying anything. How could you not want to kill them, too, for protecting the person who just tried to kill you? How would you contain that rage?

On October 25, less than a month into its deployment, Bravo took its first serious IED casualty. Led by Second Lieutenant Mark Evans, 3rd Platoon was running a heavy schedule, at least three or four separate patrols that day. They had already been on a 3:00 a.m. patrol when, at 11:00 a.m., they headed back outside the wire from FOB Yusufiyah. Evans was in the first of four Humvees in an eighteen-man patrol, driving down Mullah Fayyad highway when, out of the corner of his eye, he saw a rag tied to a power line that he had never seen before. Great, he thought, that's a marker for an IED. Before he had time to complete the realization, an IED exploded near the No. 2 truck. Everybody got on the radio as they checked men and machines. You good? You good? they asked one another. Okay, we're all good. Everybody was fine, except for the gunner. His bell was rung a little, but he'd be okay, so they pressed on. The patrol headed back to the FOB.

Later in the day, Evans got assigned to inspect a site where insurgents had previously fired mortars at the FOB. He generally regarded these as a waste of time. Sometimes there was evidence, or it really was someone's backyard, but most of the time the enemy mortar teams were good about cleaning up all of their equipment or any other trace that they had been there. More often than not, Evans and his men would go out, look at an empty field, and return, which is what happened this time. But driving back, Evans saw a guy on Route Peggy, just hanging out around his car. As soon as the convoy slowed down, the Iraqi got into his car and sped away. Evans had his gunner fire a warning shot, and the man stopped. He spoke excellent English and his car was clean. Both of these facts were out of the ordinary, but not exactly suspicious, either, so Evans let him go. As the convoy started up again and turned at the next intersection, 3rd Platoon's second IED of the day went off. Again, after a quick check of everyone, there were no injuries. Evans decided to dismount everyone and search the area. The men fanned out, looking for wires, blast fragments, witnesses, anything. Walking up to the crater in the center of the road, which was about twelve feet wide and four feet deep, he saw some wires, which he figured must lead to the trigger position. He had removed his protective eye shields to get a better look at them, and he was getting ready to call some men over to help him investigate, when he had the distinct sensation he was being watched. He stood up to find who might be looking at him. There was another IED still buried next to the crater he was inspecting, and he was standing on top of it. The triggerman closed the connection and Evans's third IED of the day exploded.

He felt no pain. Just the sensation of wind on his face, and then what felt like a bad sunburn. Evans couldn't tell at first if he was standing anymore (he had been knocked off of his feet, several feet in the air, and was now lying on his back), but, to himself, his thought process was calm and rational.

"As long as I have all my fingers and toes," he told himself, "everything's going to be okay." He couldn't see a thing, but he was much more concerned about accounting for his digits than the fact that he had been blinded. He counted his fingers and wiggled his toes. "All right, I'm good," he thought and sank serenely into a kind of catatonia. For some time, his sightlessness did not bother him very much. The medic ran over and started applying an IV to Evans, telling him he was going to be okay.

"Am I burned, Doc?"

"Oh no, sir, you're fine," said the medic, lying. In fact, he was badly discolored, his neck was bleeding, his eyes were swollen shut, and he had several broken bones in his face—he looked much more like he'd smashed his face on a car windshield than he'd been hit by an IED. Another soldier had been knocked off of his feet by the blast, too, but he did not have a scratch on him.

Evans had entered a very placid state of shock. His primary thought was that tonight he was guaranteed a good night's sleep, a prospect that pleased him very much. When they returned to the FOB and prepared for the medevac helicopter, Evans still wasn't registering just how seriously he had been injured. Probably because he couldn't see how disturbing his bloody and disfigured face was, he wasn't grasping why everyone was freaking out. In his mind, everybody just needed to chill out.

When they loaded him into the helicopter, the medevac guys were all business. They kept asking him his Social Security number, his birth date, his hometown. He was pretty sure he was speaking coherently, so what was this all about? he wondered. Was this supposed to keep him from falling into shock?

"My birthday is the same as the last time you asked," he finally said. They put a heart-rate clip on his finger. He held his breath, and the thing started beeping.

The paramedic started rattling around in his bag and yelling, "Come on, buddy! I need you to breathe, buddy! Come on!"

"Hey dude," Evans said, "I'm just messing with you. I'm fine." The medic was not amused. Evans was flown back to the States.* Bravo Company had just lost its first platoon leader.

While Kunk and the rest of the battalion leadership already had their concerns about Bravo's 1st Platoon, an early major noncombatant injury ensured that the unit registered quickly in brigade commander Ebel's mind as well. As a part of routine hygiene and maintenance down at the JSB, some unlucky private would have to burn the platoon's WAG Bags and other accumulated garbage in a large pit every day. It was common practice to use diesel fuel to speed the process. Diesel is ideal because it burns slowly and is less volatile than other types of fuel. On October 28, the private in charge of the pit-burning detail did not douse the waste with diesel but used JP-8, the Army's standard kerosene-based vehicle fuel, which, like gasoline, is highly combustible.

He leaned over the open pit, looking down as he threw a match. Whoomph! A geyser of flame and green and black and brown debris shooting thirty feet high engulfed him. Soldiers scrambled out of the way of the incoming shit as burnt, runny plastic remnants cascaded down like a fecal fountain. When the flame died down, the private was still standing there, blackened and crusted like Wile E. Coyote when one of his inventions blows up. His shirt was gone—it had been blasted off of him—and his hair and eyebrows were burned off. His skin was literally smoking. And he was in tremendous pain.

Paul Cortez, who was out on patrol a mile or two away, called back on the radio, "Hey, did you guys get hit? We saw an explosion." Several soldiers, already laughing their asses off, found Cortez's call utterly hilarious. Others, however, realized the seriousness of the situation, that the soldier was covered in second- and third-degree burns. He was so badly

---

*Back in the United States, doctors determined that his corneas were so scratched and one retina was so badly detached that it took three weeks and scores of experts' consultations before anyone was sure he would be able to see again. After surgeries to both eyes and six months' recuperation, Evans made a full recovery and is still serving in the Army.

hurt, in fact, that he had to be medevaced out and ultimately sent home. Kunk and Edwards were apoplectic. The first major casualty that 1st Platoon suffered was not just a completely preventable noncombat injury but a humiliating one at that: a soldier blew himself up with a pile of shit.

Once Ebel learned what had injured the Bravo soldier he was visiting in the Camp Striker hospital burn unit, he was dismayed as well. And when Ebel saw Miller after the accident, which was the first time the two had ever met, the initial impression he had was that the young platoon sergeant was immature and overconfident and had failed to appreciate the enormity of what had just happened: a classic case of a poorly led, poorly supervised soldier.

Miller was not aware that opinion of him was already turning. He readily accepted his reamings from Kunk and Edwards, and a letter of reprimand from Ebel, over the burned soldier because, no question, there was a lapse of discipline. But he also said he got a lot of praise and left his first JSB rotation believing everybody thought he had done a good job. "I'd probably personally talked to Colonel Kunk four times, including the ass chewing for the accident and one other time he was unhappy about us being sloppy," he recalled. "But the other two times he stopped by, he said we were doing great things, telling us, 'You guys are doing a good job. Keep it up.' So I felt comfortable at that point. I felt real comfortable."

NOVEMBER 2005

7

Route Sportster and Bradley Bridge

ON OCTOBER 29, a 3rd Platoon Bravo patrol was heading down Route Peggy on the way back to FOB Yusufiyah. Only a few hundred yards from the intersection with Sportster, one of the Humvees hit an IED that blew the front of the vehicle clean off. The triggerman miscalculated by a split second. If the blast had been a belly shot, everyone in the vehicle would have been vaporized. The truck's chassis skidded to a stop and everyone checked themselves over. Amazingly, no one was hurt.

After toying with the Sportster problem since the moment they got there, Goodwin and Kunk decided the time had come to secure it for good. On October 30, 2nd Platoon, which had been sent out as the original Quick Reaction Force (QRF) for the IED hit, took over a house on the northwest corner of Sportster and Peggy. It was a large, square, two-story home on the southeast corner of Mullah Fayyad with storefronts on the two street-facing sides and living areas in the back and on the second floor. This house would come to be known as TCP (traffic control point) 1.

A day or two after that, with the help of an Iron Claw IED-sniffing team, Bravo mounted an all-day clearing mission of Sportster. But everybody already knew that once you cleared something, if you turned your back, insurgents could reseed a road in a matter of hours. In order to keep Sportster clear, they had to hold it. So Goodwin started dropping Humvees with fire teams at one- or two-mile intervals down the stretch.

"We just started parking vehicles on the road, telling them, 'Stay here until properly relieved,' " said Goodwin. But the ideal relief, in the form of Iraqi soldiers manning the checkpoints, never came. Kunk intended the TCPs to be a way for the Iraqi Army to take more responsibility for this sector, but, especially this early in the deployment, they simply refused to operate in so dangerous an area. In Mahmudiyah and Lutufiyah, Kunk had more success persuading the Iraqi Army to participate, but, he says, "anything on the west side, Yusufiyah, Mullah Fayyad, Sportster, they would say, 'Ali Baba is there. The bad guy is there.' " Kunk's idea thus became to use the TCPs as a stairstep. Build them with U.S. forces and then, as the IA gained confidence, slowly hand them over.

The vehicle drop positions, over time, would evolve and harden into TCP positions 2, 3, and 4. "We thought it was going to be a seventy-two-hour mission," said 3rd Platoon's platoon sergeant, Phil Blaisdell. "Seventy-two hours turned into like six days. I had a beard. And all of a sudden it was permanent. We started getting concertina wire down there. And I'm like, 'Good God, what are we doing?' " The numerical designations and configurations of the TCPs would vary slightly throughout the year. A fifth TCP would open on the northwest corner of Mullah Fayyad, and a TCP6 would ultimately open between TCP2 and TCP3. Bravo Company was now in the road checkpoint business, and by the end of the deployment, the stairstep strategy had resulted in the Iraqi Army claiming full control of only one checkpoint on Sportster.

Across the battalion, the TCPs were controversial. It was far from unanimous that they were a good idea. The TCPs were static positions, and they were not well defended. They were not patrol bases, but outposts in true enemy territory with no more—and usually far less—than a squad manning each one. TCP1 and TCP4 had buildings where troops could eat and have some form of downtime, while TCP3 had not so much a building but, as Goodwin put it, "a bunch of cinder blocks piled together in an organized manner."

In the first incarnation of TCP2, troops lived out of two Humvees, including trying to sleep in them, for days at a time. Early on, there were no HESCO Barriers, large six-foot cubed mesh baskets that when filled with dirt by a backhoe provided admirable protection from gunfire but when empty were no better than a chain-link fence. When HESCOs did arrive, there was no heavy equipment to fill them.

Even with each one so thinly manned, the TCPs were also a drain on the company's combat power. Manning the TCPs consumed a whole platoon. Bravo's initial staffing philosophy—one platoon at the JSB and two platoons at Yusufiyah, with one to be home guard and one to run maneuver operations—was out the window. Goodwin worried about the staffing pressures the TCPs were putting on his company. Between guard rotations, scheduled and unscheduled patrols, and sleep, the "troops-to-task" math was already not adding up. "The first time I requested more men in November, I was, I don't want to say joking, but we'd sit down at a Commanders' Update Brief, and it would be like, 'What do you need?' And I would say, 'I need a platoon,'" Goodwin remembered. "'No, really, what do you need?' 'Well, I need water, and I need this, and I need that. And a platoon would be nice.' I know the battalion is short on manpower. The brigade is short. But I need another squad or four to keep doing what I'm doing, to give my guys a break."

This frustration was echoed at every level. "Before," said 2nd Platoon's platoon sergeant, Jeremy Gebhardt, "if you were a platoon back at the FOB, you rotated with another platoon, so when they patrolled, you got some downtime to catch your breath. Once a platoon's on TCPs, you've lost that completely. You look at it on paper, and you're like, 'Okay, this can work.' But even when guys are just sitting at the TCP, there's several hours per day just doing patrols around your area that aren't factored into what's on paper. Then, at that point, you start seeing guys getting strung out, and you start getting concerned for how they are holding up. That was a yearlong struggle trying to convince the battalion level of this. But it all came back to, 'Hey, you've got this many guys. It takes this many to do this.' And that was it."

Second Platoon's platoon leader, Lieutenant Jerry Eidson, said his faith in his superiors evaporated once he took stock of the TCP mission. "It was ridiculous," he said. "We were a company spread out trying to operate like we were a battalion. Nobody in my platoon had any confidence in our command structure at all after that."

Kunk maintained that the strategic importance of Sportster left him no choice. "It had become a superhighway for the insurgents to get into Baghdad, so we had to take it back," he proclaimed. In that regard, the Sportster plan fit with Ebel's strategy for the brigade as well. Sportster, in Ebel's words, became "the base of the anvil" upon which the rest of the brigade, and special operations forces, would continue to hammer the insurgent hideouts to the west. "The risk was, if we gave that up, we would have released an avenue where the enemy would skirt around," he said.

But many others dismiss the idea that Sportster, when open, was an insurgent superhighway or, when occupied, acted as a barrier to infiltration. They point to a number of routes on a map that circumvent Sportster on the way to Baghdad or Mahmudiyah. "It was obvious they were still coming into my AO across Sportster," said Alpha commander Jared Bordwell. "They just didn't have T-shirts that said 'Insurgent' on them when they did. I don't think we needed to own Sportster. It didn't do anything except give the insurgents a static target and allow soldiers to get complacent and do stupid things."

Others maintain that even if securing Sportster as a resupply route to the JSB was important, it could not be done with so few men. Charlie Company First Sergeant Dennis Largent believed this was obvious from the beginning. "Bravo couldn't do shit in their own sector because they were tied down to those TCPs," he said. "As early as November we saw that Bravo Company was getting attrited. They needed some help. That's where the fucking fight was. It wasn't in Mahmudiyah with the sewer project or whatever. The focus of that battalion sector should have been clearing out Yusufiyah. Cleaning house in there so that that company would stop getting attrited."

A major component of the Sportster effort was psychological, an affirmation that the enemy never tells the U.S. Army where it can and cannot go. "The taking of Sportster was a big moment, because that sent a clear message to the enemy that we were not going away," Kunk explained. "We said early on, 'We are taking it back and we are keeping it. And we are going to own it. And not only are we going to own that, we are going to go anywhere we want to go because we are going to dictate everything.'"

But some officers wondered if this idea of freedom became too much of a priority for its own sake than one that served a larger mission. "Colonel Kunk put his name out there by saying 'We will own that road,'" explained Bordwell. "Well, in Iraq when you say 'I am going to own something,' that means your feet are on it ninety-nine percent of the time. So he bought something by saying that. And no one did the math on what it was going to take and what we were going to sacrifice in order to own that piece of property."

On November 2, Sergeant Major Edwards was making a routine battlefield circulation. First Strike had been in theater just over a month. One of Edwards's priority stops, on the orders of Ebel, was to go to the JSB and impress upon Miller the seriousness of the burn-pit incident. The Personal Security Detachment (PSD), the convoy unit that escorted Kunk or Edwards wherever they went, was another battalion-wide tasking, and each company had to provide a handful of soldiers for the effort. Bravo had detailed several, including Specialist Josh Munger and Private First Class Tyler MacKenzie.

As Edwards was chewing out Miller, the guys from 1st Platoon had a chance to catch up with Munger and MacKenzie and the rest of the PSD hanging out at the motor pool, just to gab and get the scoop on what life was like for the rest of the battalion. MacKenzie was Justin Watt's roommate back in the barracks at Fort Campbell and one of his best friends. Once, before deployment, MacKenzie told Watt that he was confident he wouldn't die in Iraq because he had never won anything in his life, even a raffle, so why should he win the biggest, baddest, anti-lottery of them all? Nah, he assured Watt, he'd be fine.

Heading back to Mahmudiyah, the PSD traveled along Route Temple in Charlie's area. Around 12:45 p.m., the lead vehicle of the four-truck convoy crossed a large earthen bridge known as Bradley Bridge, so named because it was where a catastrophic IED had hit a Bradley Fighting Vehicle during a previous unit's deployment. Here, the lead Humvee met the same fate. An intelligence report later said that insurgents had posed as contractors and dug in a gigantic IED with heavy construction equipment months before. The explosion was enormous, completely obliterating the Humvee, leaving it a smoking and twisted heap of metal.

First Lieutenant Tim Norton was on patrol with a group of Charlie Company soldiers when they heard the explosion. Norton was assigned to the Lutufiyah MiTT team, but before deployment he had been a Charlie platoon leader. Since Charlie was based out of Lutufiyah, and Norton was a devoted child of the People's Army, he would hang out with, and patrol with, his old Charlie guys every chance he got.

The twenty-three-year-old from Mansfield, Massachussetts, was the Distinguished Military Graduate ROTC cadet at Providence College in 2004, a history buff, and a proficient violinist who could identify most songs on a classical radio station within a few seconds. Straight out of Ranger School, he headed to Charlie, where he benefited enormously from the mentoring of his platoon sergeant, Sergeant First Class Lonnie Hayes, one of the best NCOs in the battalion. Norton was assigned to the MiTT team when somebody discovered he had studied Arabic in college. He had vigorously resisted being moved away from his men on the eve of battle, but it was futile. He was making the best of the MiTT beat, but he far preferred what he was doing now, out patrolling with the Cobras, and he did it every chance he got.

With the explosion only a few miles away, the Charlie soldiers got a call to head straight there. Reports from the scene were fragmented, but it was clear there were dead and wounded, and medevac choppers started spinning up. Munger, along with Specialist Benjamin Smith, had been thrown more than twenty feet from the vehicle and were likely killed instantly. Sergeant Cory Collins was injured but MacKenzie was missing: he was simply gone.

Norton and the Charlie guys arrived about ten minutes later. This was Norton's first experience of combat, and he was surprised at how disorienting it was. The Humvee was obliterated. The entire engine block had been detached and thrown clear of the rest of the assembly. The chassis looked like a scale model of a roller coaster that had been set ablaze. A door had been tossed more than three hundred feet. The roof and gun turret landed in the canal and there were no tires left, just fist-sized scraps of rubber.

Most of the men in the other three vehicles had taken up defensive positions, while the medic and a few others ran to the canal to try to find their men and treat any survivors. Some seemed to be walking around almost aimlessly in a state of shock. Sergeant Major Edwards himself was in a daze. Several men were firing on suspected trigger locations to the north and west. A .50-caliber machine gun, which fires rounds several inches long that can rip through solid concrete, started banging away at the houses from atop one of the intact Humvees. Its barrage lasted probably only a minute or two but it seemed like an hour, with soldiers tearing through ammo. Once the fire stopped, Norton coordinated with the PSD leaders and sent some patrols out, sweeping the area. Soldiers started picking up smaller pieces of remains and searching for MacKenzie.

Other soldiers followed the IED's still-intact command wires back to a chicken coop about three hundred yards away. In the coop was a sand-table model of the area for the triggerman to plan his detonation. In a nearby house, they found four Iraqis and they sprayed their hands with Expray, an aerosol-based field test that diagnoses a range of explosives chemicals depending on what color the spray turns upon contact with a surface. Two of the men "popped," in the soldiers' parlance, for a positive reading. (Later, there would be serious doubts about Expray's reliability in some contexts. Specifically, the spray turns pink in the presence of nitrates, which are a common ingredient in explosives. But in Iraq, fertilizer also has a heavy nitrate content. So, getting caught literally "red-handed" here might mean that a person had been working on a bomb—or was an innocent farmer. The margin of error is so large, for example, that Expray test results are not admissible in U.S. courts. At the time, however, "popping" during an Expray test was considered ironclad proof of being an insurgent.)

Using the PSD's interpreter, a couple of NCOs began to question the suspects. The Charlie guys had to pull one of the PSD soldiers away from the detainees. He was shouting, hysterically upset, going for his pistol, screaming and swearing at them about his dead friends. Whoa, dude, you gotta back up, they told him. All you guys gotta back up, or you're gonna do something you regret. A wrecker convoy and QRF that had been dispatched to recover the Humvee carcass hit a pressure-plate-triggered IED just fifty feet from the original blast site around 3:00 p.m. The explosion lifted the thirty-ton wrecker's rear end several feet into the air. This time, a gun battle erupted as the Americans started taking fire from several buildings to the west. Two fire teams headed out to flank the new shooting positions, and Norton and Hayes and a couple of other soldiers, trapped just off the bridge and out in the open, started unloading their weapons in counterfire.

Time slowed down drastically for Norton. While he was fighting, he had time to contemplate the bullets landing all around him. Each one kicked up a pool of dust just like a raindrop did. If he didn't know any better, he mused, he would swear it was raining. And then he thought that this was a moment they tell you only happens in Hollywood, but here they were, and it was happening. Norton and Hayes were standing back to back and completely exposed, blazing away with their guns like they were Butch and Sundance, taking fire from three, maybe four shooters—and they weren't getting hit. It was surreal. The combined firepower of their position and the flanking soldiers ran the shooters off.

Ebel and Kunk and a variety of relief elements arrived shortly after, not that anyone was happy to see them. It is a universal complaint: No matter how much soldiers and junior officers lament the lack of senior leadership presence on the ground during day-to-day operations, the one time when they are uniformly not wanted is the one time they can be guaranteed to show up—in the aftermath of a catastrophic loss. The search for MacKenzie continued. It was Ebel, chest high in the canal water, who pointed to the culvert where his body had likely gotten caught and pulled underwater. At about 6:00 p.m., they finally recovered his remains.

With many relief units now in place or on their way, Charlie and the PSD got sent back to their bases. Norton's adrenaline flush was receding, and it was a hollowing experience, a bottomless pit of exhaustion. Not despair or sadness, elation, relief, or any other emotion, just exhaustion. He had a shower and headed to the chow hall. They were serving chicken wings. He had never looked, really looked, at them before. Flesh. Bones. Red sauce. All in a pile. He stared at them, dozens of heaped little carcasses. He decided to have a granola bar instead.

After the cleanup was finished, Charlie commander Captain Dougherty was ordered to guard that intersection. The insurgents, Kunk maintained, were counting on the 101st to do what the 48th would do—withdraw. It's great to make that kind of stand, Dougherty replied, but who's going to provide the men to staff it safely? He and Kunk fought hard about this position. Dougherty believed in force demonstration as a deterrent. He put fifteen men in three trucks on it. "It's the difference between looking like a chuck wagon and a war wagon," Dougherty said. When he then complained that he did not have enough soldiers for regular missions, and battalion leadership told him to pull some men off the bridge, he and First Sergeant Largent dug through the thousands of regulations from division headquarters and pointed to the one saying that all convoys had to have three vehicles. "That was the last we heard about it for a while," recalled Largent. This impasse was laid to rest within a few months without a full confrontation, however, because the Iraqi soldiers in Lutufiyah were more competent than any in the rest of the region, and they were able to take over the Bradley Bridge position fairly early.

Since the Personal Security Detachment had been pulled from every company, the deaths of Bravo's MacKenzie and Munger and Alpha Company's Smith hit the entire battalion hard. Most soldiers can pinpoint three times when their war began. The first is the day they arrived in theater, the second is the day when the enemy first did violence to them, and the third is the day they lost their first comrade. For many in 1st Battalion, November 2 was their entrée to the third and most painful day of war's stutter-step beginning. "It affected everybody differently," said Private First Class Chris Barnes. "I was pretty angry. It scared a lot of people. Some people were mad. Some people were in tears."

Two days later, Charlie was dealt a blow. At about 8:45 p.m. on November 4, Charlie's executive officer, First Lieutenant Matt Shoaf, was leading a three-truck convoy from MacKenzie, Munger, and Smith's memorial service on FOB Mahmudiyah back to Lutufiyah along Route Jackson. He was in the front passenger seat and Staff Sergeant Jason Fegler was driving. Most of the soldiers were having trouble seeing; their night-vision goggles were whiting out due to the oncoming headlights.

Shoaf saw a spotlight flicked on up ahead and Fegler flashed his back. One of the trucks behind him reported receiving small-arms fire from the right. Others would later say the fire was coming from the left. In sworn statements, several men were very specific about the color of the tracer rounds or the angle of fire they witnessed from rooftops on both sides of them. Shoaf's gunner saw some flashes to the left and fired at the rooftops. Shoaf was waiting for a report back, leaning down to grab something off the floor or adjust a dial, when rounds, big ones, started hitting his truck from straight ahead. Even though Humvee windshields have bulletproof glass, these large-caliber rounds smashed straight through. Shoaf, already leaning over, ducked under the windshield as best he could as the bullets riddled the truck's interior, shredding metal, glass, and canvas. Shoaf's gunner dove into the belly of the truck as bullets penetrated the turret shield. One bullet nicked the lip of the chest plate of Fegler's body armor but kept going straight to his heart. The two Humvees behind Shoaf's got hit as well. One bullet hit the gunner of a rear Humvee and he slumped over. Another soldier, Sergeant Juan Hernandez, pulled the hit gunner down and took his place. Hernandez got one burst of rounds off before he too was hit in the left shoulder. The lead truck, pocked with no fewer than three dozen bullet holes, rolled to a stop off the side of the road. Fegler managed to put the truck into park before he fell face-first unconscious into the steering wheel. Shoaf was wounded and in shock. He had been hit in the shoulder and his face had been torn up by flying glass.

In a mad blur to get out of the kill zone, the back Humvees didn't realize that their lead truck had pulled off. They floored it, speeding the final few miles to get to FOB Lutufiyah. The two Humvees pulled into the FOB. Both gunners were badly hurt, bleeding profusely. Captain Dougherty called in a medevac to the FOB and tried to figure out what was going on. Where was Shoaf? Where was the lead vehicle? The men in the Humvees didn't know.

Left out on Route Jackson, Shoaf and the other soldiers in the truck were having trouble piecing together what had happened to them and what they were going to do. Four of them were slightly or seriously injured, but Fegler was in critical condition. They tried to treat him, but they didn't have anything but a small first aid kit and though he still had a pulse, Fegler was completely nonresponsive and quickly bleeding to death. Their Humvee didn't work, the radio was out, it was pitch-black, and they were injured and alone on the side of a large but lightly traveled highway due to a nighttime curfew. Shoaf spotted an Iraqi checkpoint two hundred yards away and started running for it.

The leader of an Iron Claw platoon from the 2-502nd was listening to the radio network, which had just erupted with chatter. His crew had come south from Camp Striker several hours ago and was checking Jackson for IEDs. It was weird, though, they had just had a very close call not a minute or two ago. The gunner of his rear vehicle had spotted a couple of pairs of headlights coming up fast on him and he tried to elicit a friendly response by signaling with a flashlight twice. When he got no response, he fired a warning burst with his M249 machine gun. When the headlights still kept coming, he switched to his heavier .50-cal machine gun. He aired one more burst of warning shots and then opened fire with shots to kill right between the headlights, tearing through all of his .50-cal ammo. The headlights receded, the threat was neutralized, and they kept driving.

There was a rush of confusing cross talk on the various radio networks. A Charlie Company Humvee had hit an IED, one transmission said. There is a disabled Iraqi vehicle on the side of the road, said another. An Iraqi checkpoint was protesting that coalition forces were firing on them, said a third. It took a while for people in company and battalion headquarters to work out what one soldier from the Iron Claw convoy had been telling his truck commander from the beginning: They had just shot up an American Humvee.

"The two Humvees that just sped past us," he said. "They were part of the U.S. convoy we just fired on."

Shoaf ran toward the Iraqi Army checkpoint, yelling in English as he approached, hoping that he wouldn't get shot. In pidgin Arabic and hand gestures, Shoaf, soaked in Fegler's blood, convinced the Iraqis to load up a truck and return with him to pick up Fegler. Bleeding himself, and struggling to remain lucid, Shoaf somehow got the radio working again long enough to contact Charlie headquarters. An air medevac to the site of the shooting was denied because they did not have a precise location, so Dougherty launched a Quick Reaction Force to go find them. Shoaf and Dougherty decided they should get the Iraqis to drive to Mahmudiyah instead of Lutufiyah because the two bases were almost equidistant and the larger FOB had better medical care.

But they could not leave without an American escort. "It was one of the hardest things I've ever had to do," said Shoaf. "If I sent an unmarked Iraqi civilian truck with no radio to the gates of Mahmudiyah, it would've been destroyed. I had to sit there and wait and watch Sergeant Fegler bleed more while our guys came to get us." After what seemed like an eternity, but was really only fifteen or twenty minutes, the QRF unit rolled up. Fegler no longer had a pulse. In the meantime, Dougherty called Mahmudiyah to tell them that a U.S.-Iraqi convoy was going to be barreling up to the gate soon.

"One truck is an IA truck," he told Mahmudiyah. "It has multiple litter-urgent [critical] U.S. pax [passengers] aboard. Do not, repeat, do not shoot that truck." The good news was that no one tried to shoot up the evacuation convoy. The bad news was there was no one to escort them to the aid station. There was no one manning the front gate whatsoever. The lead evacuation vehicle drove around the FOB for a few minutes trying to figure out where to go. Finally, the driver stopped to ask for directions. Thinking that they had arrived at the aid station, the soldiers in the back vehicle began unloading Fegler. Not knowing what the rear vehicle was doing, and with accurate directions in hand, the lead truck then drove off, leaving the soldiers in the rear to carry Fegler the final seventy-five yards to the medics. Although an autopsy ruled that no amount of medical attention could have saved Fegler's life, it took, in all, about forty minutes to get him the four miles from the accident site to Mahmudiyah.

Around this time, the Iron Claw convoy arrived at FOB Lutufiyah. Word was circulating at all levels about what had happened, and some of the Charlie men were getting heated.

"They fucking shot up our guys!" some of them yelled. "They killed our own dudes!"

Dougherty called the Iron Claw platoon leader into his office and said to him between deep breaths, "I know this was an accident, but there is a lot of anger here right now. So you and all of your guys need to be out of here and out of the way. You guys need to go to your trucks and stay there."

In all, six Charlie Company soldiers were hurt and Staff Sergeant Jason Fegler died. Extensive investigations followed. The Iron Claw gunner was exonerated for following proper escalation of force procedures even though there was no standard, brigade-wide night recognition signal in place at that time. If anything, the reports found areas of fault with the Charlie convoy for using closed radio frequencies and because they had taped their Humvees' headlights square to look more like Iraqi vehicles—a tactic that has obvious benefits and drawbacks. The investigating officer found only U.S. shell casings along the route and did not find any bullet holes on the vehicles' sides and rear, concluding that there had not been any insurgent fire that night. Kunk refused to recommend any of the Charlie men for Bronze Stars with Valor medals or any other awards for their actions because he concurred that there was no enemy fire at all that night—something that the Charlie men involved in that incident passionately claim there was. "All the written reports saying there were no enemies involved? That's bullshit," said Shoaf. "We started shooting because there were some dudes shooting in our direction before any of this occurred."

Fegler's memorial was held on November 11 at FOB Mahmudiyah. The battalion typically held a memorial service within a week after a soldier died. They were simple but emotional affairs. Kunk would say a few words, the company commander would say a few words, there would be a few Bible readings, a few hymns, a friend would give a remembrance, and the chaplain would give a homily. Soldiers, two by two, would pay their respects to the classic soldier memorial erected on a dais—the soldier's helmet perched atop his rifle, its barrel stuck to the ground, with his dog tags hanging from it and his boots in front. The hardest part for most soldiers was the final roll call, when the first sergeant would call the names of the platoon's soldiers and they would shout back, "Here, Sergeant!" Until he got to "Fegler! . . . Staff Sergeant Fegler! . . . Staff Sergeant Jason Fegler!" Anyone who had resisted crying until now was usually in tears.

Transportation from MacKenzie, Munger, and Smith's memorial had been the occasion of Fegler's death. And, like a daisy chain of carnage, transportation from Fegler's memorial became the setting for another major casualty. As the Bravo Company convoy mounted up following the memorial, Executive Officer Habash asked First Sergeant Skidis if his truck had an extra slot. Sure, get in, Skidis said. Habash headed for the front right passenger seat, the customary place for the man with the highest rank. But the left rear door on this truck didn't open, he remembered, so he climbed across the truck's interior to that seat. Skidis took the front right spot.

Just before 10:00 p.m., the Humvee hit an IED on Route Fat Boy just north of Yusufiyah. There was heat, flash, and confusion. Habash remembers everything going white and then black, and, for a moment, none of his senses were working. Unable to process any data, he asked himself, "Am I dead?" Reality reasserted itself within seconds, however, as he saw and smelled the cab, which was filled with smoke.

The driver was yelling, "What do I do? What do I do?"

Between his screams of pain, Skidis yelled, "Just go! Go! Just drive!" Safely past the kill zone, they assessed quickly that no one was mortally wounded, but the truck was on fire. They stopped and extinguished the flames, pulled security, and a QRF from Yusufiyah came to relieve them. One soldier had a sprained wrist, but the blast had pulverized Skidis's calf. He was in excruciating pain. The explosion had not penetrated the door, but the concussive force of the shock wave was so powerful, the door wall hit Skidis's leg like a hammer, and now his lower leg was swelling fast. The head medic diagnosed it as compartment syndrome, a serious condition in which so much blood is pouring into the relatively inelastic leg muscles that surgery is required to relieve the pressure. Skidis was medevaced to Baghdad and then home, where he would endure seven surgeries to regain almost 100 percent use of his leg. Less than three weeks after Bravo had lost one of its platoon leaders, its senior enlisted man was out of the fight too.

8

Communication Breakdowns

THE MOUNTING PRESSURES of combat made encounters with Kunk even more stressful than they had been in garrison. Kunk had three meetings with company leadership every week, one each with the company commanders, company first sergeants, and company executive officers. Many attendees loathed them since so much of them involved Kunk yelling erratically at various people for a variety of reasons. "His reaction to everything was the same," remarked Charlie's first sergeant, Dennis Largent. "If you lost a soldier, or if you had cigarette butts on the FOB, it was the same reaction. He would explode on you. He would just lose his mind, which made his whole leadership style just totally ineffective."

The meetings frequently started with the tedious but necessary minutiae of war fighting: How many trucks were running? How many suspected insurgents had been detained? How many weapons caches had been found? But something along the way would set Kunk off. The company commanders would joke among themselves before the meetings started: Did you hear that sound? Who's the Kunk Gun traversing on today? Everybody got Kunked once in a while, but early on a pattern was established: Goodwin and Dougherty got Kunked all the time. It was very direct and very negative. Kunk yelled that they were shitbags; everything they did was fucked up. Sometimes, after the meeting, he would haul one or the other of them into his office to yell at them privately, although it wasn't really private because the whole episode could be heard down the hall. Bordwell, who started the deployment on such shaky ground, had quickly rehabilitated himself into the battalion star, while the predeployment favorites suddenly became the problem cases. The company commanders routinely had small debriefing sessions among themselves afterward, just to decompress and assess what had happened in there. "We would sit down with Goodwin and just let him vent, the guy was just beat down," remembered Bordwell. "Every time he went up there, it was a public whipping session."

Many of the company commanders and first sergeants didn't see Sergeant Major Edwards as any help in turning the battalion into a well-run unit. In many battalions, intentionally or not, the lieutenant colonel and the sergeant major usually assume a good cop/bad cop act. One half of the duo is the hard guy, and the other balances as the more approachable one. In this battalion, however, both were bad cops. "Both assumed the negative role," explained Bordwell. Many of the lower-ranking soldiers found Edwards to be an ineffectual yes-man. "The battalion sergeant major is supposed to be the guy that when I have a problem, and my first sergeant can't fix it, I can go to the sergeant major, and he will go to the commander and say, 'This is a problem. This needs to be fixed,' " said Bravo 1st Platoon's Chris Payne. "And that did not happen. Or, if it did happen, he wasn't any good at it."

Kunk threatened to fire both Dougherty and Goodwin within the first few months of arrival and several times before the year was through. These were not idle, motivational threats. He made moves. He passed the recommendations up to Ebel, but Ebel would always say no, there was no reason to fire them, and there were no captains in reserve anyway, so you had to work with what you had. When Kunk made his first serious attempt to fire Goodwin, because he perceived that the captain was not moving fast enough to install a piece of radio-relay equipment at the JSB, Goodwin decided he now had three enemies on his hands. "I had Al Qaeda, and I had the Iraqis. Not so much as an enemy, but I had to deal with them on a daily basis," he said. "And I had Battalion. That's who my enemies were."

Many company-level leaders were concerned about the command climate, and Headquarters and Headquarters Company commander Shawn Umbrell continued to try to mediate between the captains and Kunk, but those efforts were frustrating. "I couldn't understand why a battalion commander would have such a hard time building a team," he said. "If you continuously crush their spirit, they are going to be timid, wondering if everything they do will earn them another ass chewing. It had an impact on the way those guys operated."

But Kunk did not see any problem with the battalion atmosphere. "I believe it was an open, honest command climate where you could come if you needed help. I thought there was an open and honest dialogue back and forth. I mean, could it be contentious? Yes. But trying to understand the whole environment there and the complexities of it was very challenging."

Delta commander Lou Kangas felt that was true—for him, anyway. "I personally felt like I had support. I would go to the boss with bad news and tell him what I was doing about it, and I was treated positively," he said. "Colonel Kunk and the sergeant major supported me and my first sergeant for the most part. Now, other companies are guaranteed to say something dramatically different."

Umbrell tried to convince Kunk to reconsider some of his perceptions of his other subordinates, but Kunk frequently ended discussions with one of his favorite phrases: "Sometimes perception is reality, Shawn." Umbrell found there wasn't much he could say once Kunk had rested on that position; the way Kunk saw things equaled reality.

As the battalion's operations officer, the man who actually wrote the orders, Major Rob Salome contended that Kunk's intentions were clear; Charlie and Bravo simply failed to meet them, and that was the problem. "Everyone got a Task and Purpose," he explained. "Some people can look at the Mission Statement and the Commander's Intent, and then the Task and Purpose, and tie all those things together to see how it achieves the mission. Some guys didn't have the ability to make those critical links. One thing that you learn in Ranger School is how it all ties together. And John didn't have that experience to lean on, so I had to become more and more descriptive as we went through the year. To the point where I was writing extremely descriptive Mission Statements where I put not only Task and Purpose, but a full Who, What, When, Where, and Why so there was no misunderstanding about what I was trying to say."

As he tried to manage both Goodwin and Dougherty, however, Salome discerned a distinct difference between them. "If I saw that John had done something that I thought was just wrong, and I said, 'John, what were you thinking, man? That's just dumb,' he'd reply, 'Sir, I know. I'm screwed up. I shouldn't have done it that way. What can I do to fix it?' Very apologetic and very submissive. But if I called Bill and had the same discussion, it was, 'No, sir. We are not screwed up. We've never been screwed up. We did the right thing and I'll tell you why.' "

With this pressure bearing down on him, Goodwin became increasingly filled with self-doubt. He was not the most confident leader to begin with. According to Salome, Goodwin needed to have his every decision validated, which was fine when everyone shared a headquarters. But being physically removed from the battalion, and with battalion-Bravo relations going poorly from day one, Goodwin frequently seemed at a loss, without initiative, or even a firm grasp of what was going on in his sector.

First Sergeant Skidis and First Lieutenant Habash had supported Goodwin the best they could. They not only had run a big portion of the company's affairs, they had become his sounding board and confidants. Now, however, with Skidis hurt, Goodwin was even more at sea. Sergeant First Class Andrew Laskoski, who had been the battalion's scout platoon sergeant, came in to replace Skidis, but it was hard to match the degree to which Skidis had run things and the degree to which Goodwin had relied upon him.

Soldiers loathed the traffic control points for a variety of reasons. They hated the very idea of them because they despised being tied down to a fixed position. Everything they had ever been trained to do, every piece of Army doctrine they had internalized, told them that the key to the Army's lethality was its ability to maneuver and fire, maneuver and fire. If this was the heart of bad-guy country, they wanted to actually go hunt bad guys, not play crossing guard. As Squad Leader Eric Lauzier put it, "If we were supposed to control the area, we said let's go seize control of it, not sit around waiting to get hit. Let's do patrols, set up ambushes and observation positions, do recon, control the tempo. Let's put the pressure on them, instead of the reverse."

But not only were the TCPs static, they were undermanned. There was never any consensus about just how many men there should be at each position. Before late June 2006, Kunk issued no written guidance to the companies on staffing requirements at the TCPs, and Goodwin never issued written guidance to the platoons. Recollections of what the verbal guidance was varies widely. A squad at each position was the preference, but with four or five TCPs to cover, and with the company depleted through casualties and mandatory midtour leaves, that almost never happened. Add in missions that spontaneously arose—whether BDAs (battle damage assessments), Quick Reaction Forces, or investigating something suspicious that somebody at Bravo's headquarters had seen on the J-Lens—and it was not uncommon for a TCP to have just three or four soldiers for an extended period of time.

Squad leaders routinely received ad hoc mission assignments over the radio. The sergeant would frequently radio back to say that he only had five, or six, or seven guys total, and that he was the only NCO there. He would ask: Do you really want me to leave three guys at the TCP, and none of them a sergeant? Affirmative, would come the response. Do the mission. "Now you are going a click and a half to two clicks out in the bush with four guys," Lauzier said. "You need four guys just to carry one casualty. What am I going to do if we get hit out there? Or the TCP gets hit and there are three guys there? You are screwed."

The TCPs were also shockingly underfortified. After 1st Platoon's initial several-day rotation at the TCPs, platoon sergeant Phil Miller went to Goodwin to complain. Specifically, he wanted to get rid of TCP2, which he thought was a death trap. "I told Captain Goodwin that it's in the open, there's no cover, it's only a click from TCP1," he recalled. "So what do I gotta do? What would you like to see happen at that TCP to get rid of it?" Goodwin told Miller that he was worried about the canal running under the TCP. If it was undefended, insurgents could lay an IED big enough to make the road completely impassable. "So, the next time we went out to the TCPs, I took seventy-five strands of wire down there and told Sergeant Nelson, 'You need to make sure no one can get anywhere near this canal.' "

Nelson and his squad did as they were told. "We got it all done, and I told Goodwin, TCP2's good to go. You can't get anywhere near that fucking canal now, that bitch is locked down." But TCP2 stayed. "Well, then I was pissed," Miller said. "Because I was told one thing, and now I'm being told another. I don't know whose call it was, but my big thing is if you're fighting on the ground, it should be your decision."

The overwhelming majority of interactions with locals at the TCPs were routine, just men and women and kids trying to get wherever they were going and be on their way. But there were enough odd or disconcerting interchanges from the start to make the whole experience tense and unnerving, all the time. Sometimes it was like the Iraqis were testing them. Sometimes it seemed like a car would pass the stop signs or disobey a stop order from a soldier just to see how fast the soldier would resort to a warning shot. When they were back at the FOB, the soldiers loved reading in the news about how Iraqis were being terrorized at checkpoints because they were unfamiliar with how roadblocks worked or, since so many Iraqis were illiterate, they couldn't read the warning signs. What utter bullshit, they would exclaim. After two and a half years, every single fucking Iraqi knows exactly what a checkpoint is, they would shout, and exactly how they work. Ninety-nine times out of a hundred, they said, if there was a car speeding for the no-go line, that Iraqi was doing it on purpose.

Iraqi men would loiter around the TCPs. It was obvious to the soldiers that they were doing recon on how the checkpoint operated. If you sent someone out to go talk to them, they would slink away, or if you happened to sidle up to them before they could get away, they would turn as friendly as could be.

"Oh, hello, Meester. Very good. USA, number one!" they would say, all smiles. Likewise, it was common for a car or truck that had been waiting in line to pull out of the queue and speed away as soon as the driver could verify that full searches were in effect. That is exactly the kind of car that sergeants would love to send a team to follow, but there were rarely enough guys at a TCP to do that, so they just had to let them drive off. Other times, the soldiers would get scowls and get into scuffles with men pulled from cars, obviously humiliated, obviously pissed off, either about the rough way they were being handled or perhaps about the fact that their women were being looked at, commented on, talked to, ogled. Sometimes an Iraqi man would actually push a soldier. Sometimes there would be an interpreter to try to smooth emotions on each side, but often not. Soldiers couldn't figure out why they got any resistance at all. The power dynamic at that moment was not exactly equal. But when they did get attitude, many soldiers found that a swift and solid jab to the kidney was very useful in extracting maximum compliance.

By far the biggest complaint the men had with the Sportster TCPs was the way they were forced to look for IEDs. Every morning around dawn, soldiers had to conduct "dismounted IED sweeps," essentially walking from their post to the next TCP and back looking for makeshift bombs. The policy was to walk in a V formation, with the tips of the V well off of the road looking inward, but Sportster was so narrow, with built-up areas or other features such as reeds or canals coming all the way up to the shoulder, that soldiers had to do the sweeps basically walking on top of the street. For many, this was almost unbearably stressful. "Every morning before conducting an IED sweep, you truly felt that this was the day that you were going to die," Lauzier once wrote. The fear and the mental stress were cumulative. It was not so much that the men were asked to do something hazardous, it was the daily, grinding awareness that tomorrow they would have to do it all over again.

"Let me put it to you this way," explained Private Justin Watt. "Take something you do every day, like go to the mailbox. Every day, you go to the mailbox. Now say that every time you go to the mailbox, there was, say, a 25 percent chance that the mailbox was going to blow up in your face. The explosion might not be big enough to kill you. But it could be.

You just don't know. Either way, you do know that there was a one-in-four chance that it was going to blow right the fuck up in your face. But you have to go to the mailbox. There is no way you cannot go to the mailbox. So, I ask you: How many times do you think you could go to the mailbox before you started going crazy?"

The strain, for some, was debilitating. "How many times can you wake up in the morning knowing you have to do this death walk?" wondered Private Justin Cross, an eighteen-year-old from Richmond, Virginia. "How many times can you walk down the road saying, 'I might die this time' before you're like, 'Fuck it, I hope the next one does just fucking kill me, because I'm tired of this shit'?"

Lauzier, as one of the leaders, did his best to keep his fear hidden, but he could not understand why the Army would make him do this. They found a lot of IEDs this way, no doubt, but they also got blown up a lot too. "Men would be engulfed by the smoke and you would lose visual," Lauzier wrote. "Debris from the explosion would be hitting you." Once the postexplosion fear subsided, the headaches, ringing ears, or deafness might last for hours or into the next day. But no matter how fatalistic Lauzier and his men became, and how convinced that the battalion and the brigade valued their Humvees more than their men, he took pride in the fact that they kept getting up in the morning and kept doing what they were told. "It is amazing that these men, mostly boys, did their duty and conducted themselves with such courage and constantly put themselves in harm's way to preserve the lives of their fellow soldiers, with total disregard for their own personal safety," he wrote.

Ebel understood that the men disliked the TCPs, but he mistook the primary emotion they inspired, and he argued that it really wasn't that bad out there anyway. "The thing is that it gets boring," he said. "That's the reality. And it doesn't matter how effective you are, for the individual soldier he's just seeing his job as 'I'm in the Humvee, I'm in this hut, I don't have the best food, my other guys are out there on base camps. They don't have to live like that.' "

The NCOs would constantly ask to do IED sweeps using the Humvees, but the requests were always denied because the human eyeball is, in fact, one of the best IED-finding devices on Earth. Some of the squad leaders devised workarounds. Lauzier would study a map and plot a route the morning before. On the morning of the patrol, his men would take over a house, head to the roof, scout a stretch of road with their binoculars, and then move forward. Scout, move forward to the next building. Scout, move forward to the next building. It was a completely unauthorized way of doing business, but it was effective.

The TCPs never eliminated IEDs on Sportster. People still got blown up all the time, though the IEDs did decrease in deadliness over the year. With American eyes on the road fairly regularly, insurgents could not lay in hundred-pound bombs anymore. But they could drop small package bombs out of a hole cut in a car's floorboard or quickly bury one while pretending to change a tire. Even so, the staffing rotations were exhausting the men. "My vehicle got hit on Sportster once," related Alpha commander Bordwell, "and I could see the eyes of the dude in the tower from where I got hit with the IED. I went to that tower, and I looked back and I could see the hole, nothing obscuring it. So I asked the soldier, 'What the hell, man?' He was like, 'Ah, sir, I've been on guard for eight hours.' So, you can't really yell at the soldier. Well, you can. But how does anybody stay sharp for that long a time when there's no one to replace him?"

Staffing became a constant and contentious topic of discussion at battalion-wide meetings as well as during one-on-one consultations between battalion staff officers and company-level leaders. These discussions rarely deviated from this: The companies routinely declared they did not have enough men, and Battalion countered that they did, but they weren't using them efficiently. Kunk always sneered at claims of overtaxed duty rosters.

"Bullshit!" he would shout. "Do I have to show you how to do it? Do I have to draw it out for you myself?" When presented with compelling shortfalls, he would ask, "What are your cooks and mechanics doing?" When told that they were cooking and working on vehicles, he insisted that every specialist in the Army is a rifleman first, and they could soldier too.

"That was always his big thing, to use them on missions," said First Lieutenant Tim Norton. "Sure, sounds great. So they come with us for a huge operation. And once we come back, everybody is saying 'Man, I can't wait for some fried chicken.' Oh, but whoops, the cooks are racked out. Can you really tell them, thanks for coming on that mission with us, and now that we are all taking a break, you need to get cooking?"

Operations Officer Salome believed troops-to-task calculations were straightforward mathematics. "I would take the task that we had assigned each of the company commanders, and then I would say, 'Okay, this is what they have.' I had been a commander of two companies by that point, and I'd say to myself, 'If I had the resources that they have, could I accomplish the mission that they have?' And, you know, we always felt like they had what they needed." Executive Officer Fred Wintrich concurred. "If you had a combat power problem, you always had a sympathetic, attentive audience, but it had to start with a cogent argument. If your math sucked, you got told to pound sand."

Salome conceded that sometimes it took a little creativity to solve an apparent staffing scarcity, but he found Goodwin the least adept at this kind of thinking. "If a unit from 3rd Platoon was going out to recon a certain area in their Humvees, and 1st Platoon needed chow at TCP1, then why can't 3rd Platoon take the chow out to TCP1 on their way to the other mission?" he asked. "That is a simplified example, but I don't think that John ever really looked at it like that. He looked at those tasks as discrete things. He didn't multitask anybody. And if you don't multitask everyone, then you're never going to get it done." Sometimes, Salome said, Goodwin would send three separate patrols to Mahmudiyah in one day, each for a reason as mundane as picking up a spare part, even though a scheduled supply run the next day could have accommodated all four trips.

"Hey, man," Salome would say. "You just wasted a patrol, and you didn't get the mission done that I had given you because you were running supplies back and forth all day long. Help me help you, okay?"

But others maintain that 1st Battalion's quests for efficiencies didn't just stretch the staffing models to their limits; they started violating them. "Several times, Kunk tried to tell me I could do something when my troop-to-task roster said I couldn't," asserted one of the companies' first sergeants. "He said, 'You got this amount, and you can do this.' I said that was possible only if I plan on letting this guy who just came in from a twenty-four-hour mission sleep for five hours before rolling him out for another twenty-four-hour mission. And you can do that—for a day or two. But for a week or longer? To have that be the normal duty rotation? No. Someone's going to get hurt."

Charlie's First Sergeant Largent asserted that not only was the math not working, the battalion was playing loose on their reports to brigade. "They would call three guys a squad," he said. "But you can't turn three guys into nine unless you are lying. They were bullshitting brigade. They were sending up reports saying this checkpoint is manned, but if the guidance is you got to have at least a squad out there with two vehicles, and if you're not doing that, then you are bullshitting them."

Charlie's Executive Officer Shoaf had similar convictions that information was getting distorted as it got passed up. "I saw reports that I had written myself misquoted by the time they got up just to the brigade level," he said. "It's not like that one little piece of information is going to lose the war, but when you see the cumulative effect of information becoming washed in order to tell a story that a battalion or brigade commander wants to tell to their highers, then you got real problems. That's the more sinister side of it."

9

The Mean Squad

IN THE EARLY days of the deployment, whenever Bravo's 1st Platoon was on a TCP rotation, Lauzier's 3rd Squad usually volunteered to occupy TCP3, because that's where shootouts were most likely. They preferred to be out hunting bad guys rather than sitting on their butts waving through cars all day. Whenever they had enough men, they would do patrols, search houses, see if they could draw fire. The Army phrase for this is "moving to contact," and, until they got sick of absolutely every- thing about the war, including killing, that is what 3rd Squad liked to do best. They were always up for a mission—especially if the answer to their questions "Will we get to shoot something? Will we get to kill people?" was yes. Lieutenant Britt called 3rd Squad "Task Force Lauzier." It was a designation Lauzier loved.

The Arabic interpreters (called "terps" by the soldiers) who worked with the company told them that the locals knew who everybody was. It did not take the locals long, they said, to know which platoons were which. And if the locals knew you all, they told the men, it was an easy bet that the insurgents knew you guys too. One interpreter told them that the locals even knew which squads were which, and that 3rd Squad was known as the Mean Squad. Third Squad did not mind this at all. They took a kind of pride in it.

They ran their checkpoints ruthlessly. If they were stopping and checking cars, it could be a slow process, with only one car allowed through the barbed-wire serpentine at a time. Long traffic jams were common, and the soldiers were impatient with Iraqi impatience. "They'll push your buttons," Watt said. "They will play a game of chicken with you. They'd get impatient, pull out of line, and gun the engine to the front of the line. We'd say, 'Stop!' and, bang, put a shot through their engine block. I don't know who they are. I'm not going to let a VBIED [vehicle-borne IED] roll up on me."

When the battlion put out orders to stop firing warning shots at the cars themselves, they would fire into the dirt and find other ways to teach a lesson. "You didn't come in our wire without my okay," said Lauzier. "Because once they are inside your wire, you have already lost. If you came in our wire without my say-so, you got thumped. We would pull them out and rough them up. Check them against the vehicle. Give them a kidney shot, tell them, 'I'm not fucking around. Do not come in my perimeter. I own this shit. I'm the sheriff here.' "

Sometimes the soldiers would sit the offenders in the sun for three or four hours. Not do anything else to them, just sit them in the sun. "I would drink my water in front of them, and go, 'Mmmmm, so good,' " said Watt. " 'Are you fucking hot, you dumbass? You want to be stupid? If you keep being stupid, I'm going to treat you like an idiot.' "

Occasionally, one or the other of the lieutenants would pull Lauzier aside and tell him that he was being too aggressive, that he should tone down the physicality. He would, respectfully, tell the young lieutenant that he didn't know what he was talking about.

"I've been here before," he told them. "I know how these fuckers are. You can't show them any kindness, because kindness is weakness. You gotta let them know you're in charge." If there was an error in judgment regarding the use of force, he'd rather use too much than too little. He'd rather absorb the second-guessing consequences than have more Americans dead.

Yribe and Lauzier were in absolute agreement on this, and they formed a unified front on how the squad conducted itself despite their vastly different personal styles. Lauzier was a bundle of manic energy, excitable, almost hyper, while Yribe was Mr. Chill, self-possessed and laid-back, even when in a firefight.

The constant gunplay bred an intense hostility. "It is well in excess of a hundred and twenty degrees, you had just been out on a six-hour patrol, and some sort of bug you just caught made you vomit and shit yourself with watery diarrhea all at the same time," described Lauzier. "You have finally gotten back to the TCP, and you are just starting to clean yourself up, and then somebody starts shooting at you. All you can think after that is 'All right, motherfucker. You want to shoot me? I'm going to fucking kill you.' So you head to the house where you know the shots came from, and you are going to put a lot of hate and discontent out there. We would patrol in there, toss their house, throw their shit around and go, 'Who the fuck fired at us? They were from your house. And we know you know. So I'm going to be a pain in your ass until you tell me.' "

On November 11, Yribe and members of 3rd Squad went out on their first-ever patrol with Civilian Affairs, the community outreach arm of the Army, to hand out Beanie Babies or pencils or soccer balls. They left FOB Yusufiyah and hadn't walked more than three hundred yards when Yribe noticed a car speeding toward them too fast for his liking.

He shouted, "Stop!" and got no response, so he fired a warning shot into the dirt. Still getting no response, he fired two more shots until the car finally slowed down. One of those shots had ricocheted and hit a teenage boy standing nearby. From the front, it looked like he just had a pinhole wound, but the bullet had blown a crater the size of a grapefruit out his back. The Civilian Affairs patrol was over before it started. "You can't really go hand out Beanie Babies after you shoot a fucking kid," said Watt.

Since Watt had taken an advanced first aid class, he was frequently the designated medic whenever Specialist Collin Sharpness, the platoon's real medic, wasn't on patrol. Watt started patching the boy up. It was his first major injury and it was an odd one. On the one hand, much of the kid's back was missing, and Watt had to quickly go through a series of complex procedures: sealing the wound off, deflating the boy's lung. On the other hand, the boy was conscious and alert, it didn't seem like he was in too much pain, and there wasn't a lot of blood.

"You're doing it all wrong!" Lauzier shouted.

"I'm nervous. I've never done this shit before!" Watt yelled back. They sent the boy to the local hospital. Back at the FOB, Yribe got yelled at for about thirty minutes but it was ultimately deemed a clean shot.

Six days later, 1st Platoon headed back out to the TCPs to relieve 3rd Platoon, with 3rd Squad taking over TCP3. The next morning, Lauzier woke up Yribe to tell him that somebody had found an IED farther north on Sportster and that he and Miller were going to go check it out. Lauzier was leaving Yribe in charge of Cortez, Barker, Watt, and several other soldiers. Bravo halted all traffic on Sportster until the IED threat was resolved. When Yribe got onto the road, there was a line of cars stacked up, honking, trying to get through, trying to figure out why the traffic was stopped.

Tension was escalating, and Yribe was nervous that he was losing control of the situation. He decided to fire a warning shot to get the locals to disperse. He passed by Cortez and Watt, walked over to the front of the wire, and aimed his rifle into the ground near the line of vehicles. He fired one shot but it ricocheted off of a tractor rather than hitting the ground, and pierced the windshield of a pickup truck. There was much commotion. All the other cars that were waiting in line peeled out and sped off. The driver of the pickup started pulling a woman out of the cab.

"You fucking shot her in the head," Cortez said. Yribe yelled to the medic, who was at the other end of the TCP. The medic started running as Watt got his first aid bag and ran over as well. By the time they arrived, the woman was on the ground, her head oozing blood. Watt knelt down and stopped cold. Her brains were coming out of her skull, white and gelatinous, and she was making shallow, rattling breaths, which the medic said meant she was "expectant"—medic-speak for "about to die."

The other woman in the truck had been injured by flying glass, and the medic started treating her.

Watt did not move. He was watching a woman die and there was nothing he could do about it. A third woman from the truck knelt down next to him, grabbed his hands, and pushed them toward the first aid bag, as if to say, "Do something, do something to save her life." It was always this way, Watt thought. Sometimes Iraqis seemed not to believe that Americans did not have magical powers. They seemed to think that the Americans were capable of fixing every problem—generate their electricity, make their water run clean, bring their sisters back to life—but just chose not to.

Watt didn't know what to do except say to the woman, "I am sorry. I am so sorry."

Yribe called Lauzier on the radio: "Dude, you should get down here right away."

"Why?"

"I just killed a woman."

Yribe and Cortez conferred briefly, and Cortez started moving the concertina wire and the stop signs farther out, so that it looked like the truck had driven into the TCP's kill zone. Although the shot had been an accident, the men were scared that no one would believe them. Yribe had been involved in an accidental shooting just days before. By simply moving the wires and fabricating aggressiveness on the part of the driver, it would be far easier to convince the inevitable Army investigator that the death was justifiable.

Within an hour and a half, a lieutenant from one of the battalion's other companies had been assigned to conduct the AR 15-6. Common investigations in the Army, AR 15-6s are routinely ordered up by a commander in the aftermath of a death or other major event. They are usually informal, with an officer assigned to gather evidence, conduct interviews, formulate an analysis, and offer findings and recommendations. While merely fact-finding reports, they are frequently used to determine whether to proceed with a legal investigation, and they can be presented as evidence later because they include sworn statements from participants and witnesses. By the time the lieutenant showed up that afternoon, most of the men at the TCP had already written sworn statements about what had transpired.

The statements filed by Cortez, Barker, and Watt, the only soldiers who claimed to have seen what had happened (Yribe either never wrote a statement or it has been lost—he does not recall writing one), are as consistent as they are inaccurate. They lied that Cortez was pulling a strand of concertina wire across the street when a fast-moving truck approached and did not stop, forcing Yribe to shoot before the vehicle hit Cortez. With no reason to suspect that the sworn statements were bogus, the investigating officer found no wrongdoing on Yribe's part.

_____

10

"Soldiers Are Not Stupid"

OFTEN, THE BRAVO platoons received missions that they viewed as recklessly dangerous or a waste of time, or both. One of the most hated types became known as "Chasing the J-Lens." The J-Lens was a high-powered video aerial observation system with remote-controllable camera mounts attached to a high tower, so a technician could search wide swaths of the company's sector from FOB Yusufiyah's tactical operations center. When the company headquarters saw something on the screen it deemed suspect, it would often send a fire team or two to check it out.

After the first JSB rotation, parts of 1st Platoon were ordered to investigate some suspicious-looking crates in a field. They mounted up and headed to the coordinates, but the J-Lens had not been properly calibrated, so they were perhaps miles off course. For hours, Bravo headquarters had them crisscrossing the area looking for the crates.

"Bulldog Main, this is 1-7. We just gave you our grids, and now we have our infrared strobe on. Can you see us, over?" Miller asked at several points.

"Negative" came the response from the TOC (tactical operations center). The calibrations were so far off, they weren't even looking in the right zone.

"Well, I don't know what else to do, because we are where we are," Miller said. "And the crates aren't here. Over." When they finally found suspicious boxes, they were full of eggplants.

Even when the J-Lens was properly calibrated, these were still unpopular missions. Bravo headquarters would routinely send J-Lens chase missions straight to the TCPs to investigate a suspicious vehicle, say, or check out a guy who was digging a hole in the middle of the night. And again, a squad leader would be forced to split an already small unit into two smaller elements.

"You know we only have six dudes, right?" the squad leader would ask. Usually by the time they walked out to the grid location, whatever they were trying to check out would be gone.

Another despised mission company-wide was the "gravel run"—escorting convoys of gravel from Camp Striker to FOB Mahmudiyah. The fractured relations between Bravo and 1st Battalion were already trickling down to every level of the company. Word was getting out that Kunk had it in for Bravo, so it did not take much prompting for Bravo to view all of the battalion's moves with suspicion. A major source of resentment was the notion that Bravo, with all that was going on in their sector, had to assist in the beautification of FOB Mahmudiyah, especially when that FOB had Alpha, Delta, Echo, and HHC on site. "Colonel Kunk wanted gravel on the battalion FOB," said 2nd Platoon Leader Jerry Eidson. "He wanted rocks, I guess, because it was muddy. I don't know why. But I do know I routinely had to give up half of my platoon to Colonel Kunk so he could have gravel on his FOB. I'm not sure if Colonel Kunk's intent was malicious, but facts are facts. My guys spent a lot of time pulling security for gravel trucks, not fighting the insurgency."

"Area Denial" was a third type of mission that raised hackles throughout the battalion. The idea was to lay an ambush in a zone that someone in division or brigade headquarters had calculated to be an ideal place from which to launch a rocket or mortar at the Green

Zone. It was irrelevant that no rocket had ever been fired from that area before or that local commanders had no intelligence that rocket teams ever operated in the area. Company commanders had long lists of places where they wanted to set ambushes based on actual enemy behavior, and they resented having to send a platoon to stare at an empty field for eight hours based on hypotheticals. These kinds of missions took their toll on the men's confidence. "Soldiers are not stupid," said Lauzier. "They know when the chain of command does not know what it is doing."

It wasn't just the soldiers, either. Soldiers complain, all the time, about everything. To complain is part of the soldier's very essence. But one of the most valuable functions a platoon leader serves is to explain to a bunch of complaining soldiers why a mission is not stupid, a time waste, or a death trap. He helps the soldiers understand the often nonobvious logic of unpopular missions. But 2nd Platoon's Lieutenant Jerry Eidson found he had trouble rationalizing missions to his men, because he didn't understand them himself.

Bravo's platoon leaders frequently received missions they had to saddle up for immediately, even though Goodwin knew about them the night before or several days before. Often the missions were delayed for hours because men were either taking showers, sleeping, or otherwise unavailable, simply because they did not know they were on deck. And once the missions were assigned, the instructions were vague and incomplete. "The orders we got didn't make sense at all," Eidson recalled. "They were 'Go here and do this' and that's all. There was no purpose why. I had a hard time dealing with that. I needed more information about why we were doing things. I would call up to get Task and Purpose and some of those were just retarded. Some of the missions I just wouldn't do. Is that wrong? Yes, it's probably wrong. But I was not going to risk the lives of my men for something that didn't make sense."

Charlie's relationship with the battalion brass was no better than Bravo's. In many ways, it was worse. Dougherty and Largent were by far the most combative of the company leadership teams with Kunk. Like Bravo,

Charlie was away from the flagpole, so seemingly simple things, such as communications connectivity, were difficult, especially during the early days. Battalion and brigade headquarters wanted immediate, accurate, and complete reporting for every event, and they were impatient with the excuse that some time delay and errors were an inevitable part of any information relay system. "If I were up in Mahmudiyah," said Largent, "I could walk over and explain everything in detail and answer all of your goddamn questions, and everything would be fine. Instead, you've got questions about my reporting, and you're not going to see me in person for another three or four days. And that shit just festers and causes a rift." Like Bravo, Charlie also had an early, dumb accident—a soldier fell out of a guard tower—that earned them unwanted attention and created lots of second-guessing.

But unlike Goodwin, Dougherty and Largent did not silently absorb Kunk's vitriol. Dougherty and Largent consciously decided, painful as it was, that they would not let Kunk bully them, and they would object, every step of the way, to his insistence that he knew how to run their company better than they did. When Kunk told Dougherty he was fucked up, Dougherty would respond, "No, sir, we are not fucked up," and try to explain why. Sometimes he would rebuff Kunk's abuse with a tenacity and vehemence that would elicit knowing smirks and glances that said "Here we go again" from the other commanders. He and Kunk got into loud, long fights on every topic imaginable. "They would argue about the color of an orange if they could," as Goodwin put it.

And during the first sergeants' meetings, Largent's interactions with Kunk were just as fractious. "I can only assume that it was because of our personal dislike for each other," said Largent. "I hated him. I grew to hate him as a leader. And I'm sure that came across in some of those meetings. I tried to keep my mouth shut, but I just couldn't do that sometimes."

The best way to hunt for IEDs was a constant source of tension. Early on, for example, Bordwell's Alpha Company was having great success in their area doing dismounted IED searches with the V formation. Because many of the roads he hunted on allowed his men to spread out, and most of the IEDs were command-wire-detonated with two hundred or more yards of wire, his guys would frequently jump the triggerman in the bush or find the wire. Based on that success, Kunk enforced this method of IED hunting throughout all areas of operations.

"Well," said Bordwell, "different AO, different terrain, different IED cell." In other areas, remote-detonated or pressure-plate IEDs were more common; there was no wire to intercept. Likewise, some roads were bounded by canals, making it impossible to search a road on foot unless you were standing on it. "So it's ignorance saying this or that technique works for everybody," said Bordwell. "That was one of the fights we were fighting as company commanders. To say, 'Hey, don't tell me how to do that. Because it doesn't work in my AO. Or, it might have worked last week, but it doesn't work this week, because that guy has a brain, and he's watching me respond, so he's changing his techniques.' "

Increasingly frustrated by Kunk's micromanagement, Largent and Dougherty focused on the concept of "commander's intent" instead. They aimed to fulfill what the battalion wanted accomplished, and ignored its proscriptions on how to do it if they disagreed with them. "The battalion commander's job is not to tell you how to suck the egg," Largent quipped. "But he was just terrible about telling you exactly how to hold the egg, and on and on. We refused to let them tell us how to suck the egg."

More galling to Largent was that Kunk would explode if he figured out they had deviated from his instructions, even if they had been successful. "Why would you direct us to do the most tactically unsound method of clearing that route for the type of terrain we had? And then, when we didn't do it your way but were successful anyway, you still got angry? But he'd get off-the-charts pissed if we didn't use the technique, the exact technique, that he had specified. It came across like he was angry that we didn't get blown up. That's how silly it was. But we weren't going to put our guys at undue risk if there was another way to do it safer, and we would get yelled at about it later." Sometimes they told Kunk, "If you want me to do it that way, you'll have to issue an order, because then it is on you."

The battalion leadership didn't see it that way and came to believe that soldier safety was taking precedence over mission accomplishment. So they generated even more detailed instructions. Those, in turn, increased Charlie's perception that they were being babysat. "If I gave Dougherty a mission, I would tell him, 'Your task is to interdict along this route,' " explained Operations Officer Salome. "Well, if I just said that, he would take the fastest method he could to get what I said done to keep his guys from getting hurt. They'd go out and do that mission in an hour, which, in my mind, should take four to six hours. That does not achieve the commander's intent. So I had to write, 'You'll take a platoon. You'll leave no later than this time. And you'll return no earlier than this time. And you'll go in this area from here to here.' It wasn't necessarily that they were blatantly not doing what we said. It was that they were being less than honest with the way they accomplished it. They were doing the task, but they weren't achieving the intent, so they weren't accomplishing the mission."

Largent had little patience for Salome's lectures. "Major Salome?" he exclaimed. "He might have left the FOB three or four times. None of those guys had a clue. The reality of what was going on out there, they were blind to it." In Charlie's opinion, the battalion did not understand that the operations tempo they were asking the company to perform outstripped the limits of long-run human endurance. "I'm going to be honest about this: we intentionally pulled the patrols sometimes," revealed Matt Shoaf, Charlie's executive officer. "We definitely walked the border of not obeying orders from time to time. And we'd just take the heat for it."

First Strike's second month in theater ended with a spike in violence that hit both U.S. forces and Iraqi locals. On November 23, Sergeant Yribe, a group of IAs, and a MiTT team took a patrol down Caveman, a dirt road that ran from Sportster northwest all the way to the Russian power plant. During this patrol they discovered a shallow grave with a body that had been there for a while. Yribe called it up, providing grid locations. "We were real lackadaisical," he confessed. "If we had known at that time how dangerous Caveman was, we wouldn't have been there. We were just ignorant enough not to be scared."

At about 1:40 p.m. the next day, some military police from the 170th MP Company, 3rd Infantry Division, traveled out there to retrieve the body. Near the gravesite, they hit an IED big enough to blow the Humvee upside down and into the canal, killing four. Earlier that day, a suicide car bomber, whose hands were wired to the steering wheel, drove into the southern gate of the Mahmudiyah Hospital, killing at least two dozen locals, injuring thirty more, and wounding several soldiers who were on a Civilian Affairs visit. And, after weeks of constant shelling, a mortar round finally slammed home at FOB Yusufiyah on the afternoon of the 24th, injuring three soldiers. Five days later, a 120mm round crashed right through FOB Mahmudiyah's headquarters. No one was injured because much of the staff was at the chow hall for lunch. If the headquarters had been fully staffed, much of the leadership of First Strike would have been wiped out.

DECEMBER 2005

11

Nelson and Casica

A FTER FIRST STRIKE took back Sportster, Lieutenant Colonel
Kunk turned his attention to other initiatives throughout the
battalion's area of operations, including doing more community outreach, bolstering water and electricity capacity, establishing better relations with the locals, and helping to build government institutions
that had both power and credibility. Within Bravo's area, specifically, he
saw the next priority as pushing out to terra incognita in the west and
making overtures to the Quarguli sheikhs who lived along Route Malibu
on the banks of the Euphrates.

Some sub-clans of the Quargulis, along with certain arms of the
Janabis, were among the tribal groupings most deeply entrenched in
the insurgency. But at least in official, daytime, face-to-face meetings,
Kunk built a fast rapport with them. "The Quarguli would guarantee
my life the whole time I was there," Kunk said. "I could move up and
down Malibu freely. I was known as the Sheikh of Peace. I felt secure
when I would go meet the Quarguli sheikhs." Sheikhs, with ties to various factions of the insurgencies or organized crime, were similar to
Mafia bosses. They may have had their hands in all sorts of shady dealings, but they were smart enough that it was difficult, if not impossible,

to tie them directly to anything illegal. And, like syndicate kingpins, they invested great energy in maintaining a veneer of respectability. A particular sheikh might be an essential ally in keeping a specific stretch of road free of IEDs. But his underlings might have been just as active in funding an IED cell that focused on a different geography or in running guns the whole time he was talking to the Americans about a weapons turn-in program. The military had no choice but to work with the sheikhs even when they were of questionable character and loyalty.

It was from these and other sheikhs that Kunk got the idea of how he would take control of Caveman, the road about a mile or so to the northeast of Route Malibu and the Euphrates River, where Quarguli Village was located. Caveman was a gravel road split down the center by one of the larger canals in the area. The canal was concrete-lined, sixty feet across and twenty feet deep. Since neither side of the road was paved, it was very easy to plant large, deeply buried IEDs there. The key value of Caveman, according to what the sheikhs told Kunk, was the bridges that spanned the canal, which made north-south travel easier.

"The sheikhs would say, 'How dumb are you, Coalition?'" Kunk remembered. "'Why don't you drop the bridges along the canal, then the insurgents can't move across them?' So that is what we did." But before those bridges could be blown up or dismantled Caveman had to be cleared, and Caveman was a beast.

Others considered Caveman unimportant, because it ran parallel between Route Malibu and Mullah Fayyad Highway and perpendicular to Sportster, all of which were hard-topped roads and fairly well controlled by the Army. Throughout November, Bravo had done some sporadic patrolling of Caveman, but in early December it began dedicated clearance missions. The IEDs were so densely packed that the road was more of a minefield than a thoroughfare. Once, they found twenty-six IEDs in one three-mile stretch. But because the insurgents could reseed the dirt-topped Caveman so easily the moment U.S. forces left, it had to be recleared every single time. "The first time we went down there, we just turned around and came back," remembered Goodwin. "No intentions of setting TCPs up there or staying in any way. So why are we doing this?"

The Caveman missions were likewise baffling to the soldiers. "Battalion's idea was 'It's our piece of land, and we want to go down it,' " explained Chris Payne, Bravo 1st Platoon's 2nd Squad leader. " 'We will not be denied using a piece of land in our area.' Okay. Good job. But there was no tactical advantage to having that land. We weren't going to use it. We weren't going to keep it. We weren't patrolling anything on the road other than the road itself. There weren't any houses. There weren't any villages. It was just a dirt road."

In early December, 1st Platoon began another multiday rotation out at the traffic control points. First Squad, with Staff Sergeant Travis Nelson in charge, headed down to TCP2, which was on the intersection of Sportster and a smaller east-west canal road. There was a small structure on the northeast corner that was empty, but the men, at that time, were told not to occupy it. So, for three to five days at a time, the squad lived at the TCP itself, by the side of the road on a few cots protected by strands of concertina wire. When soldiers wanted to sleep, take refuge from the elements, or just come off of a combat footing even for a minute or two, they had to do so either on the cots or in—or under—their Humvees. They were supposed to keep their helmets and body armor on at all times, whether they were on guard or not. Even when they were off guard, there was nowhere for them to go that was safe. For twenty-four hours a day, uninterrupted for days on end, even when shaving or brushing their teeth, in the heat and the dust and the wind, they had to keep forty pounds of gear on. The men found it virtually impossible to do this without going crazy.

December 10 started off as a beautiful morning. Watt, Yribe, and others from 3rd Squad not pulling guard or patrolling out of TCP1 were playing Spades. Watt remembered turning his face to the sun and letting the not-yet-too-hot rays wash over him. "You know," he thought, "we have been here for a couple of months now. This might not be so bad after all."

Platoon Sergeant Phil Miller, who was at TCP3 with other men of 3rd Squad, began a mission to get some more concertina wire from Yusufiyah as well as a resupply of food and other necessities. He grabbed

Lauzier and a couple of other soldiers for the trip north, and stopped to pick up another Humvee and three more soldiers from TCP2 around 10:30 a.m. Nelson and Sergeant Kenith Casica had just come off of several hours of guard duty. They were sitting on the cots in the open, central area. They had removed their helmets to brush their teeth and shave.

Private First Class Jesse Spielman and Specialist David Babineau had relieved them, with Spielman in the Humvee's gun turret looking south and Babineau pulling guard on foot nearby, on the east side of the Humvee, the opposite side of Nelson and Casica. Every company has a guy like Babineau. The twenty-five-year-old had been a specialist for years and was happy to stay that way. He was a solid soldier, was well-liked, and had leadership potential. Every once in a while, he would catch the eye of a lieutenant or a senior NCO who would say, hey, Babs, what's your deal? You wanna move up? We could send you to the promotion board, make you a sergeant? He would always say, no, thanks, sir, who needs the headache? I'm good where I am. The other members of the squad were manning the serpentines to the north and south.

Pulling up to TCP2, Miller asked Nelson and Casica what was new. They told him that the night before, they had received a tip about an attack. According to their informant—a guy who had passed along solid info in the past—four guys with guns and RPGs were going to roll up around noon in a black Opel sedan from the southeast.

"If you say there is going to be an attack, why don't you have your shit on?" Miller demanded.

Will do, one of them said, and asked Miller when he would be back. About an hour later, Miller responded. He figured he could finish his run to the FOB and still be back in plenty of time in case anything did happen. When he returned, he would pull the guys in close and be ready for anything. In the meantime, three 1st Squad soldiers loaded up one of TCP2's Humvees and left with Miller.

Not long after Miller pulled out, a handful of kids walked through the TCP. This was a twice-daily event, as the TCP was on their route to school. Casica, as he always did, passed out candy and pencils as they walked by. He would give high fives and banter with them in intermediate Arabic and they would respond in broken English.

At almost 11:00 a.m. exactly, Spielman noticed a man wearing track-suit bottoms and a white button-down shirt walking along the canal road from the west. They had all seen him around here before. He had given them some info in the past and he'd always been friendly, so he did not arouse much suspicion. As the man approached, Casica walked over and, as was his way, even seemed glad to see him. Nelson stayed sitting on a field stool, smoking a cigarette, looking in the other direction. Casica started talking to the man, in a mixture of Arabic and English.

"Hey, man, what's up?" he asked. "How are you doing? Where you going? You getting a taxi? Meeting someone?" The whole time, all the man said was "La, la, la," the Arabic word for "No." Spielman began to think this guy was acting funny after all. But before that thought could take hold, and just as Casica began to tell the man that he couldn't just hang out here, the man pulled a 9mm pistol from his waistband. Taking aim quickly, he shot Casica in the neck. Casica dropped, with a thud, an instantly inert mass. Nelson did not even have time to react. The man pointed the pistol at the back of Nelson's head and pulled the trigger. The bullet slammed through the base of Nelson's skull. His body barely moved, except to slump.

The man turned to Babineau and fired three or four shots, trying to find an angle around the Humvee that separated them. Babineau ducked behind the driver-side wheel well of the Humvee, trying to get as much steel between him and the bullets as possible. As Babineau dove for the tire, Spielman cranked the Humvee's turret around toward the gunman. When the gunman saw the truck's M240B machine gun swinging his way, he aimed up at Spielman and squeezed off three or four more shots. Spielman ducked in the turret as some shots pinged off the gun's shield and some zipped overhead. While down, he flipped the safety off on the machine gun. Sensing the man had stopped shooting for a moment, Spielman popped up, leveled his gun, and fired a three-round burst. From his eyes up, the man's head exploded into a pink cloud as the 7.62mm bullets blasted his skull apart. His body fell to the ground, brains and blood spilling to the dirt.

Babineau popped back up and Spielman was already on the radio, calling to TCP1 and Yusufiyah declaring, "This is TCP2. We have two men down. We need immediate medevac." Most of the guys playing cards at TCP1 heard whoever was on the radio yelling, "TCP2 has casualties, TCP2 has casualties!" but they were confused. They hadn't heard any shots or explosions, so at first they couldn't fathom it.

"Casualties?" Yribe thought. "They had been putting up some concertina wire there, so maybe somebody cut their hand?" Nobody was in all that big of a hurry until a second, clearly more emotional and urgent call was relayed only a few seconds later. "TCP2 has two soldiers down, two soldiers shot. They need help. Now!"

Yribe, Britt, Watt, and another soldier grabbed their gear and piled into a Humvee. Since 1st Platoon's medic, Doc Sharpness, was on the FOB run with Miller, Yribe reminded Watt, coolly and quickly, to grab his first aid bag. Up at Yusufiyah, Miller was finishing up loading his Humvee when someone ran out of the TOC to say that there had been casualties at TCP2. Miller and Lauzier and the rest of that contingent dropped everything, unhooked their equipment trailer, and sped back down Sportster.

Yribe, driving down from TCP1, made the three-quarter-mile trip in under a minute. He hit the brakes hard, the wheels kicking up sand and rock. He got out of the truck and the first thing he saw was Nelson, on his stool, a cigarette burning in his hand. "If the squad leader is sitting down and having a smoke, it can't be that bad," he thought. But then he noticed a massive bump on Nelson's forehead. He turned around and saw a nearly headless local and, nearby, Casica, facedown, a black pool of blood welling underneath him. He looked around at the others. Everybody seemed dazed and was moving slowly. Spielman was still in the turret; Babineau was over with Casica; and Specialist James Gregory and a couple of others, who were at the other end of the traffic control point when the shooting occurred, were standing nearby.

"Gregory, what is going on?" Yribe asked. Gregory was pointing, trying to explain: one neck wound, one head wound, local national shooter, handgun. Watt got out of the Humvee, looked around, and dropped his first aid bag. He didn't even know where to start.

Yribe ran over to Casica and turned him over. Casica's wound was gurgling blood. Yribe picked him up, body armor and all, and threw him on the hood of the Humvee. Watt tried to pressure-dress Nelson's wound, but he could not even find it on the first pat-down; he started giving him CPR. Britt was still in the passenger seat of the Humvee. He was on the radio, but Yribe needed help.

"Britt! Sir!" he yelled. "You have to get out! We have got to move!" Yribe yelled. This seemed to jolt everyone into action. Britt got out of the truck and helped to cut away Casica's gear as others trundled Nelson into the backseat of the Humvee. Private First Class Steven Green, who had been in the truck from Yusufiyah, got on the hood to hold down Casica as Yribe drove back down toward TCP1. In the back, Watt tried to give Nelson CPR, but he was not responding.

Yribe's and Miller's Humvees converged at TCP1. They both pulled aside TCP1 and men poured out of the trucks. Doc Sharpness got on top of the Humvee hood and began putting a C-collar and respirator bag on Casica. Soldiers from TCP1 were out front, wanting to get a look, trying to help. Miller got on the radio to Yusufiyah and tried to call in a medevac helicopter.

"Negative" came the response. "It will be faster to drive the casualties to Yusufiyah and medevac from here." Miller took over the driver's seat and Yribe moved to the back, where Watt was still trying to get a response from Nelson. Miller peeled out, hurtling down the road at fifty miles an hour with three men on the hood as Sharpness worked on Casica, trying to get an IV started, and Green tried to hold the dying man steady. Green was talking to Casica, and listening for a heartbeat. He looked at Casica's arm. It was tattooed with his daughter's name. Green, as he was shouting at Casica, drooled on him a bit. He worried about that, wiped it off, and then thought it was a weird thing to be worried about.

In the back, Watt and Yribe traded turns giving Nelson CPR, but they suspected Old Man River was already gone. The bulge on Nelson's forehead was growing and no one could find an exit wound. His eyes were rolled back and glazed over. He was making gurgling noises, but they could not tell if they were respirations or death rattles. Yribe began punching Nelson as hard as he could in the groin, to get some sort of pain response, any reaction at all. Nothing. The Humvee pulled into Yusufiyah around 11:15 a.m. and multiple medics were waiting. People crowded around. The medics began working on both men, but neither had any vital signs when they arrived. Casica's mouth and throat were filled with blood. The chief medic still ordered them both intubated, hooked up to IVs, and administered with CPR. Nobody wanted to let them go and, hoping for a miracle, they worked long beyond the point it was clear they were dead. The medevac helicopter landed a few minutes before the chief medic pronounced them deceased at 11:35. Miller had to be physically pried off of and pulled away from Nelson as they loaded the body bags into the helicopter.

Once Nelson and Casica were pronounced dead, 1st Platoon was yanked back to FOB Yusufiyah for a Critical Incident Debrief, a standard post-casualty session. A Combat Stress team from FOB Mahmudiyah, headed by psychiatric nurse practitioner Lieutenant Colonel Karen Marrs, traveled to Yusufiyah to conduct the group therapy meeting.

"The focus of the intervention," in cases like this, explained an Army memo, "is returning the soldier to duty using nonclinical, simple techniques in a safe environment. The goal is to prevent the soldier from assuming the sick role, so no psychiatric diagnosis is given and interventions are aimed at reassuring the soldier that s/he is capable of fulfilling his/her mission." The men, overall, were skeptical that Critical Incident Debriefs did any good. Lauzier likened them to a mechanic who fixes a flat tire when it's really the engine he should be looking at. "All they would do is hand out Ambien," said another soldier. "Go sleep it off? Well, guess what? I got to wake up here tomorrow with the same shit."

First Platoon was back on the TCPs that night. "They wanted to go," said Miller. "They wanted to show the enemy that you cannot knock us down." Miller made Yribe, the senior sergeant in the platoon, 1st Squad's new squad leader. Upon the squad's return to the TCP, the gunman's body was still there. Often family members would retrieve a corpse, but since this man had just shot U.S. soldiers, that wasn't likely. And the Iraqi medics, local hospital staff, or other parties who picked up bodies in cases like this didn't arrive until at least the next day. Yribe carried him off to the trash pit, his brains spilling onto the street, where dogs feasted on them in the middle of the night. As some of the men kicked the body in frustration, Green noticed that the dead man's teeth were loose. He reached down, pulled several out, and put them in his pocket.

In the aftermath of the shooting, there was speculation about the gunman's motives. Some were convinced that it was a revenge killing for the woman Yribe had shot three weeks before, as it was so unlike any other kind of attack they'd seen to that point. But the gunman, since he was missing most of his head, was never identified. Other soldiers were just as convinced that revenge wasn't the reason. Yribe's shooting happened at TCP3, they said. Why wouldn't the shooter have targeted that TCP, or why wouldn't he have targeted 3rd Squad, or even Yribe, more specifically? These soldiers contended that this guy was pissed off for any number of unknowable reasons, saw an opportunity to capitalize on a weakness, and took advantage of it.

Regardless, the platoon was galvanized by the feeling of Iraqi betrayal. "That was the point where I just didn't care about Hadjis anymore," revealed one 1st Platoon soldier. "As far as I was concerned, any military-aged male in Iraq, they could all die. I just wanted to kill as many of those motherfuckers as I possibly could." For many, the shooting proved that no Iraqi could be trusted. If there had been a philosophical dispute in parts of 1st Platoon—some thought the Iraqis were worth helping, others thought they were all the enemy—the deaths of Nelson and Casica strongly bolstered the confrontationalists' claims. "That's when things started to turn," observed Staff Sergeant Chris Payne, 2nd Squad's leader.

Just a few days after Nelson's and Casica's deaths, Green and some parts of 1st Platoon were up at Mahmudiyah and Lieutenant Colonel Kunk and Sergeant Major Edwards walked by. Edwards corrected some element of Green's bearing, and Green mouthed off.

"Why're you in such a bad mood, Green?" Kunk asked. "You're talking to a sergeant major here."

"Why do you think I'm in a bad mood?" Green sneered, noting that Casica's blood was still stippling his boots. Kunk told him that he had to pick himself up and drive on as good soldiers must.

"I just want to get out there and get some revenge on those mother-fuckers," Green responded. "They all deserve to die."

"Goddamn it, that's not true," Kunk responded testily. "Ninety to ninety-five percent of the Iraqi people are good people and they want the same thing that we have in the United States: democracy. Yes, there are five percent of them that might be bad, and those are the terrorists. Those are the bad guys that we're going after."

"Fuck the Hadjis," Green declared.

"Calling them that is like calling me a nigger," said Edwards. "This sounds like you hate a whole race of people."

"That's about it right there," Green said. "You just about summed it up."

The officer who conducted the AR 15-6 investigation of the December 10 shooting concluded, "The deaths of Sergeant Casica and Staff Sergeant Nelson could not have been prevented either by their actions or the actions of the other two soldiers at TCP2." He acknowledged that there was a degree of complacency at the TCP that day. The men were not wearing their helmets and the shooter got too close without being searched, but the investigator did not find that either fact cost the men their lives. He noted that Casica was shot in the throat and Nelson at the base of the skull, neither of which is covered by a helmet. Likewise, he found Casica's trust unfortunate but not culpable and resisted second-guessing it. "In order to maintain positive relations within the local population," he wrote, "it is necessary for soldiers to, on occasion, when they feel it prudent, lessen their readiness posture. In this case, Sergeant Casica approaching the assailant with his M4 oriented toward him (possibly the only measure which would have prevented this incident) would have been wholly inappropriate."

Brigade commander Colonel Todd Ebel rejected this conclusion. On the cover sheet of the report, he scribbled, "I determine that SSG Nelson and SGT Casica were killed because each failed to maintain discipline at the TCP. . . . While hard to accept, I believe these soldiers' deaths were preventable. . . . Each failed to follow instructions and it cost them their lives."

Kunk concurred with this sentiment completely, and did not resist telling the men of every rank, on numerous occasions, that Nelson and Casica were responsible for their own deaths. The blame that Ebel and Kunk placed on the dead incensed the men of 1st Platoon. "The real fault, the real blame, belongs to the chain of command for not securing that house and giving soldiers proper cover," declared Watt. "The real blame belongs to them for not putting up HESCO baskets around that checkpoint, for not providing someplace where you can take off your helmet for five minutes in seventy-two hours. Kunk and the chain of command cannot face the fact that they failed us, so they pushed 100 percent of the blame onto the soldier."

Any argument that anyone made to Kunk that there were other factors at play was met with a fusillade of abuse about making excuses, being a whiner, or not coming to terms with the reality of the situation.

He lectured the men of 1st Platoon directly, booming, "When are you going to face up to why Staff Sergeant Nelson and Sergeant Casica are dead? Because they weren't doing the *right* things, the *harder* right. Leaders were not enforcing standards and discipline."

The more Kunk pounded this message home, the more the soldiers resented it. "If you are the battalion commander, you don't have to tell every last Joe, 'The reason that your team leader and your squad leader died is because they were pieces of shit,' " observed Yribe. "And that's what we were getting from him."

Nelson and Casica's memorial was held a few days after their deaths. During the memorial, Green spoke simply but movingly about both men: "Staff Sergeant Nelson, Old Man River, was a fine leader with an outstanding career behind him. We all knew no matter how much he yelled, or how many packs of cigarettes he took from us, or how many times he smoked us, that he would do anything for any of us," he said. "Sergeant Casica was probably the kindest man in Bravo Company and one of the best people I have ever known."

A lieutenant from another company who attended the memorial wrote in his journal, "I could see the pain of the loss on every soldier's face in Bulldog Company. Their commander, CPT Goodwin, looked worn, wounded, emotionally tired. The service was the same as the others. The toughest part is the roll call. The gunfire from the salute caught me even though I was anticipating it. The platoon sergeant, SSG Miller, broke down as people started to go up to the tributes of the two. As I was watching all of the soldiers begin to file up to the tribute by twos, 1LT Britt, the platoon leader of the two soldiers, moved to the back corner of the maintenance bay behind me. His eyes were already welled up before he tried to move out of sight. I felt very sorry for him. I imagine it's a huge burden that you will carry around for the rest of your life. He's the one who's responsible for those men, in good times and bad. I walked back to him and shook his hand. I stood there for a moment and just looked at him. He looked back, tears running down his face. I wanted to say something but I couldn't, I just didn't know what to say. I gripped his hand tightly and nodded my head in consolation."

Already displeased with Miller's performance and convinced these deaths were more evidence of lax leadership, Lieutenant Colonel Kunk had written Captain Goodwin a performance warning the day after the shooting, and now he and Sergeant Major Edwards decided to remove Miller. They had already talked about reinstating Sergeant First Class Rob Gallagher, the previous platoon sergeant who was currently on a MiTT team in Lutufiyah, and now they decided to act. Miller heard about the move from a back channel as Kunk and Edwards drove to Yusufiyah to fire him, and he was furious. He felt he was being unfairly punished for the deaths of Nelson and Casica. No matter how often you tell a grown adult squad leader and a grown adult team leader to put on their helmets, he maintained, they are ultimately going to make their own decisions. He didn't see what more he could have done. He went to the potato bays and began packing his stuff. Lieutenant Britt stopped by and asked what was going on.

"I'm out of here, man," Miller said. "They are coming to get me." Word spread, and 1st Platoon rallied. The squad leaders and Lieutenant Britt asked to talk to Kunk. They lobbied for Miller to stay. Britt spoke with Kunk and acknowledged that he, and Miller, and all of 1st Platoon, were having some trouble, but he assured Kunk that they could turn things around and that Miller was the right man for the job. Kunk relented and gave Britt some more time to get Miller and the rest of his platoon squared away. Britt returned to tell Miller that he and the squad leaders had been successful. Miller was staying. But, Britt said, they were on a short leash and they needed to work some things out. Battalion thought that 1st Platoon's standards were low.

"Shaving, uniforms, discipline. We need to improve those things," Britt said, "or they are going to make this change."

12

"It Is Fucking Pointless"

ISOLATED PHYSICALLY AND with limited links to the outside world, Bravo soldiers frequently had no knowledge of how their efforts were fitting into the broader strategy of the war, let alone what that strategy might be. Indeed, the very notion of strategy, and whether America's strategy was sound, was simply not a concern for many of them. All that mattered was what was happening in and around the ground they were occupying.

News of anything occurring beyond the FOB, the traffic control points, and the JS Bridge was hard to come by, and even major events about Iraq making headlines around the world seemed to have little impact on their lives. In the two and a half months since their arrival, for example, Iraq had ratified its constitution, the trial of Saddam Hussein had gotten under way, and Democratic congressman from Pennsylvania John Murtha had begun calling for a U.S. troop withdrawal from Iraq. None of these got much notice from men on the ground. Far more important to them was staying alive until the next morning and whether there would be hot food for dinner that night.

One exception to the company's odd remove from national affairs was its activities in support of Iraq's December 15 nationwide parliamentary elections. Polling-day safety became a priority for American forces throughout Iraq, and, hoping to entice Sunnis (who had largely boycotted a round of elections in January), U.S. commanders put particular emphasis on safeguarding Sunni areas such as Yusufiyah.

Shortly after coming off of a full day of patrolling on December 13, Eric Lauzier was ordered to take a 3rd Squad fire team out for an overnight ambush at a site where mortars had been launched at Yusufiyah several times before. He protested, because his squad was supposed to be off. They had just put in an eighteen-hour day. His guys hadn't slept that day. They needed some rack time, he insisted.

Arguing was futile. He was ordered to move out. So he and five other men walked about three or four miles into the bush and settled into their overwatch positions, on the inclined banks of a canal. Winter nights in Iraq can get cold, with temperatures plunging to the 40s, and the guys were freezing. Soldiers got an hour or two of sleep when they could, but most of them were up at any given time pulling 360-degree security. When the sun rose, they expected to stay in position and, if they made no contact, they'd return after nightfall. About 4:00 p.m., they got a radio call. Their mission was changing.

"Uh, you know we're in an ambush right now, over?" Lauzier asked. Roger, came the response. Scratch that mission. Do the new one. They were now to walk another five miles to do a battle damage assessment on some mortars that an element of 2nd Brigade had fired. Lauzier was pissed. Things come up, yes, but to be forced to abort an ambush for a nonessential mission, to have nobody else to send, is either bad planning or bad priorities. They got the grid coordinates, popped up from their hiding position, and started walking. The coordinates were off, however, so they spent another several hours crisscrossing the fields trying to find the impact site. They were starting to run low on water. Trying to keep his men's morale up, Lauzier told them that when they got back, he guaranteed they would get some hot chow and several hours of uninterrupted rack. He would make sure nobody messed with them. They were doing a hell of a job, he told them, and they'd be rewarded for sucking it up and driving on.

A few hours later, they found the place. There was nothing there except a few large smears of blood, like someone had been dragged, and a child-sized bloody flip-flop. Now Lauzier was pissed and disgusted. He called it in.

"Hey, you wanna know what you hit? You fucking blew up a kid. Good job, over." Night fell as they humped the several miles back to the FOB. Third Squad had just started to unload their equipment when Miller called Lauzier over.

"Sorry to dump this on you, but you need to go out and patrol Fat Boy overnight," Miller said.

"What do you mean 'patrol Fat Boy overnight'?" Lauzier asked.

"I need you to go out with two Humvees, and drive up and down the road."

"Drive up and down the road?"

"Yeah."

"In two trucks?"

"Yup."

"Just us, driving up and down the road, all night."

"Yes, that's what I'm saying."

"That is fucking retarded."

"I know. I tried to tell them that, but that's the mission."

"Bullshit. No. We're not doing it. Get someone else."

"There is no one else. Everybody else is out. 'Cause of the elections, doing the same stuff."

"So our mission is to drive up and down Fat Boy drawing out IEDs—with no medic and no QRF and no air support—so they don't bomb the civilians tomorrow? Our mission is to get blown up?"

"Yup, pretty much."

"But my guys haven't slept. They haven't eaten. I promised them."

"Dude, I'm sorry, but you know how it is."

Lauzier could not bear going back to his men and telling them what they had to do after he had promised them they would get a break. He knew what got soldiers through the nights, the hard times, the exhaustion, or the stone-cold conviction that the commanders either were incompetent or didn't give a damn about them. What got them through the night was the next moderately pleasant experience: the next hot meal, the next time they could sleep for five or six hours, the next time they could just be left alone, for just an hour or two with an iPod, a movie on the laptop, or a book. He had just dangled that in front of them, and now he was going to snatch it away. He went back to look at them, exhausted, dirty, hollow-eyed. They knew bad news was coming, and he delivered it. They all sat silent for several seconds as the mission sank in.

"Fuck it," said Private First Class Chris Barnes, raising his hand. "Let's do it. This sounds like a great fucking idea. Who wants to get blown up?" They started laughing. Watt, Barker, Cortez, and Private First Class Shane Hoeck all raised their hands. They did not give a damn anymore. It was all so absurd to them, that they were going to drive up and down a road for the next eight hours as bomb magnets. The only thing that they could do was laugh. "Hooray! We're going out to get blown up!" they sang. "Who's on board? Hey, who wants to come get blown up? Woohoo! Yeah, dude, I am ready to go fucking die! We are all going to fucking die!" Lauzier, at that moment, was prouder of them than he ever had been, and he loved them more than he ever thought possible.

The six men went out, and until well past sunrise they zipped up and down Fat Boy, dozens of times. They did not, in fact, get blown up, although one of the trucks did hit a dog, which scared the hell out of them. Once they returned to the FOB, fifty-six hours since their last downtime, their mission was still not over. They had to turn around and escort Captain Goodwin for ten more hours to all the polling locations so he could shake the hands of voters and meet with local officials. By late afternoon of the third day, there was no one who could drive the Humvee longer than a minute or two without falling asleep. The man in the passenger seat had to hit the driver in the arm every twenty or thirty seconds. As they walked back into the FOB, dirty, delirious, strung out, and aching for sleep, First Sergeant Andrew Laskoski took a hard look at them and asked, "Did you men shave today?"

On that election day, about 70 percent of Iraq's eligible voters, including a broad turnout from Sunnis, went to the polls on a generally peaceful day. The Sunnis' strong participation indicated that rifts between the native Sunni tribes and Zarqawi's Al Qaeda in Iraq (AQI), which had started small, were widening. To Abu Musab al-Zarqawi, cooperation with the U.S. and Iraqi governments, or voting in the elections, was intolerable. But the Sunni sheikhs were becoming disillusioned by the barbarity of Zarqawi's extreme and violent policies, and they had begun to explore other alliances, including with the Americans and the Iraqi government. Al Qaeda, some Arab papers said, was starting to get expelled from Sunni strongholds in Anbar. This trend would very slowly build nationwide throughout the rest of the winter and the following year. Zarqawi would find himself in far smaller regions to operate with far fewer allies. But while the west and north of Iraq led the turning away from Zarqawi, the Triangle of Death remained a holdout area of support.

Al Qaeda's senior leadership was concerned about this rift and thought Zarqawi's heavy hand was threatening the entire movement in the country. In December, a senior Al Qaeda leader sent Zarqawi a blunt and rebuke-filled letter. It exhorted Zarqawi to spend more time on winning over the people and to be more compassionate and tolerant of other Muslims, even those with whom he disagreed. A month after the elections, in a move widely interpreted as an attempt by Al Qaeda to combat the impression that it was an anti-Iraqi hyperviolent nihilistic band of exterminators, it actively sought allies among Iraqi insurgent groups and declared itself subservient to this coalition of its own making, which it called the Mujahideen Shura Council (MSC). Along with the creation of this new group was a purported shift away from wanton attacks on civilians. AQI stopped taking credit for some of the most violent strikes against Shi'ites. Even so, many of the most prominent native insurgencies, such as the Islamic Army in Iraq, Ansar Al-Sunnah, and the Mujahideen Army, refused to join, leaving the MSC open to the charge that it was really just AQI by another name.

On December 19, Bravo's 2nd Platoon was operating in two different sectors. Platoon Sergeant Jeremy Gebhardt had one squad up in Mahmudiyah, assisting with the much-loathed gravel runs from Camp Striker to FOB Mahmudiyah. Platoon Leader Jerry Eidson and the rest of the platoon were chasing the J-Lens. Upon Eidson's return to Yusufiyah, he was sent out to Mahmudiyah to pick up Gebhardt. Gebhardt had only two trucks. He had hopped a larger convoy out there, but because higher command was enforcing a regulation they didn't enforce, for example, on election night, and enforced only selectively—that all convoys must be at least three vehicles—he was now stuck. Cursing the inefficiency of it all, Eidson grabbed eight volunteers to form a three-vehicle task force and headed out to retrieve their platoon mates.

Eidson was in the lead truck when the convoy left Yusufiyah just after 9:00 p.m., Specialist Noah Galloway drove, and Private First Class Ryan Davis was in the gun. They left the wire and turned the corner, heading north on Fat Boy. A minute or two down this road, they hit a trip-wire-triggered IED that struck the truck's front-right quadrant, tossing it like a matchbox onto its right side and into a canal. The bright blast kicked up a cloud of dirt, dust, and debris that blocked out the night-vision goggles of the drivers of the two trailing vehicles, so they gunned their engines to get past the kill zone. The occupants of one of the trucks thought they saw the taillights of the lead Humvee ahead, so they kept rolling, trying to catch up to it, until they realized they were mistaken. They started calling Eidson on the radio, but there was no response.

"Hey," said one of the soldiers, "we need to turn around, we need to go back." When Eidson came to, sideways in a truck filled with water, he asked if everybody was all right. Davis said he was fine, just that his leg hurt. Galloway did not respond.

"Noah, Noah, are you okay?" No response. Eidson could not open his door, so he followed Davis out of the gunner's hatch, jumped out, and landed in chest-deep water. He made his way back over to Galloway, who was mangled. His limbs were going in the wrong direction, and he was not responding to Eidson's yells and slaps. But he was breathing and he had a pulse. Eidson pulled himself out of the ditch and stood in the middle of the road. He had no weapon or helmet, his other trucks were gone, Davis was limping around, and Galloway was unconscious. He did not notice that his arm was broken and the bone was sticking out of his flesh until he tried to pick up the shredded remnants of Galloway's helmet. It was at that moment that Eidson expected to die.

Insurgents frequently followed an IED strike with small-arms fire, so they should be opening fire any second, Eidson thought. He was scared, terrified of death. He waited a beat or two for the shots to come, but they didn't. And then a few more seconds. Still not really believing that he was getting this reprieve, he headed back to check on Galloway. He jumped back into the canal, assessed Galloway's condition, evaluated his weight versus the steepness of the canal banks, and concluded there was no way he could pull him out.

He heard two trucks coming from the north and he signaled with his flashlight. His men had arrived.

Tearful and shell-shocked, Eidson approached Staff Sergeant Les Fuller and said, "We have to get Noah out."

Fuller, a devout Christian who tried never to swear, looked down, saw what had become of the Humvee and Galloway, and exclaimed, "Oh, fuck!" The entire engine block and driver-side door had been blown off. Fuller and another soldier jumped down and started trying to pull Galloway out of the seat. Fuller grabbed him by the body armor while the other soldier hugged his torso. Fuller noticed that Galloway's left leg was pinned under the seat. He grabbed it to try to free it, and the leg twisted loose in his hand. They decided that Galloway would be easier to pull out if they took off his body armor. But as Fuller grabbed Galloway's left arm to pull it through his body armor's armhole, that limb came off in his hands as well.

Eidson was now thinking clearly enough that he was doing platoon leader math. He had nine guys and two operating trucks. He had one critical case stuck in a Humvee with two severed limbs who needed to be extracted from a ten-foot-deep ditch with muddy, slippery, steep-angled walls. He needed at least two men on the guns to pull security. Two men, including himself, were too badly hurt to help with the rescue. That left four men to try to lift Galloway out of the ditch, practically straight up. It was not going to happen. He called up to FOB Yusufiyah requesting more manpower. Goodwin told him there was no one at the FOB to send. There was no Quick Reaction Force, there were no extra men on the entire base whatsoever, and the medevac was not responding yet. Goodwin told Eidson that he had to get himself to the FOB.

"There is no way we can do that with Galloway," Eidson responded.

"You have to," said Goodwin. "There is no one—repeat, no one—who can come get you." Luckily, a convoy of U.S. and Iraqi platoons happened to be passing by. They stopped and formed a chain of about a dozen Americans and Iraqis to yank Galloway from his seat. They reloaded everybody into the Humvees to catch the medevac that was now en route to Yusufiyah.*

It was not lost on anyone: The casualties just kept mounting. Every week or two, they were losing someone, or multiple people—frequently leaders—to injuries or death. The average was about one a week. Lieutenant Ben Britt was the only platoon leader left in Bravo Company, and while he hid it from the lower-enlisted soldiers, Eidson's injury shook Britt badly.

"I just know I'm next," he told Yribe and Lauzier that night. "It's bad juju to be a lieutenant," he said. "My number is up." They told him that you can't talk like that, but they viewed Britt's pessimism as a significant change. He had always been the one to tell the most depressed, fatalistic, negative soldiers to always look at the odds—even in a war zone, he would often counsel them, the numbers are always with you. Far more

---

*Galloway survived but lost both his left limbs, and Eidson, the third Bravo leader to be injured in less than three months, was sent back to the States, where he underwent several surgeries that restored function to his arm.

people come back than ever get killed, and it almost always is the other guy who gets it.

The feeling that death was certain was becoming pervasive throughout the platoon, and it was spreading like a panic. More and more men started to believe that they simply weren't coming home. Some of the men say drinking in the ranks was becoming fairly common around late December. It is difficult to judge just how pervasive the drinking was, but it was common enough that just about everyone in 1st Platoon under the position of squad leader acknowledged that it was happening, even if they denied taking part. More than a few soldiers were sneaking drinks to cope with the stress, to take the edge off, to fall asleep, to calm their nerves.

Booze was always on offer in Iraq, even in the Triangle of Death. There were plenty of IAs or interpreters who were happy to procure bottles of whiskey or gin or even pills or hash for any soldier who wanted them. A lot of Iraqis were users themselves, often on the job. In addition to their drinking and smoking habits, IA soldiers were also enthusiastic consumers of pornography. Anyone who thinks that Iraq is a Muslim puritan stronghold where nobody drinks or does drugs is sorely mistaken. Many Iraqis enjoy a stiff drink (or several), and it is not outlandish to speculate that part of the reason Iraqi society ultimately rejected Al Qaeda was because they were simply not going to live by its teetotaler code.

While many men within 1st Platoon were having trouble adjusting to the casualties the unit incurred, the incessant operations tempo, and the constant threat of violence, Private First Class Steven Green was reacting particularly badly. He had always been a loudmouth, a malcontent, a racist, and a misogynist. He was fond of quoting a line by Nathan Bedford Forrest, Confederate general and first Grand Wizard of the Ku Klux Klan: "To me, war means fighting, and fighting means killing."

But the day Nelson and Casica died he had snapped. That was when he gave up even pretending to support any notion of peacekeeping, society-building, or being nice to Iraqis. From then on out, all he cared about was killing them. This was well known, and not something he attempted to hide, even from superiors.

That, in itself, was not necessarily exceptional. Many of the men by this point hated Iraqis and many would offhandedly opine that the whole country needed to be leveled, or the only good Iraqi was a dead Iraqi. But only Green talked about killing Iraqis all the time, incessantly, obsessively. Only Green talked about wanting to capture Hadjis, flay them, and hang them from telephone wires. Only he talked about burning them alive so they had to smell their own flesh cooking. Everybody was frustrated that the enemy was cowardly, but Green had a harder time accepting that this was simply the nature of this war: U.S. soldiers had to behave more honorably than the enemy. Why, he sincerely wanted to know, did Americans have to restrain themselves when the insurgents did not?

At the prodding of Staff Sergeant Miller, Green went to see Lieutenant Colonel Marrs from the Combat Stress team, who was visiting from FOB Mahmudiyah on December 21. The intake evaluation form she filled out while talking to him that day is a horror show of ailments and dysfunctions. In the entry marked "Chief Complaint," she quoted him: "It is fucking pointless." Green told Marrs he was a victim of mental and physical childhood abuse by his mother and brother, he was an adolescent drug and alcohol abuser who drank every day between 8th and 10th grade, and he had been arrested several times. He told Marrs he had been suffering from symptoms of instability, extreme moods, and angry outbursts, including punching walls, ever since the deaths of MacKenzie and Munger. (Her notations indicate he said their deaths happened about a month before, but it was actually seven weeks.) Green told Marrs he was experiencing all of the following: sadness, difficulty falling asleep, nightmares involving violence and the death of his friends, anxiety, worry, increased heart rate, tightness in his chest, shortness of breath, feelings of helplessness, being easily startled, being quick to anger, and thoughts that he would not make it out of combat alive.

In her own observations, Marrs noted that Green had abnormal eye contact, including staring, and that his mood was angry. Green told Marrs he was having suicidal and homicidal ideations, especially thoughts about killing Iraqi civilians. On his one-page intake sheet,

Marrs noted his wanting to kill Iraqis four separate times. One entry states, "Interests: None other than killing Iraqis."

She diagnosed him with Combat and Operational Stress Reaction (COSR), an Army term to describe typical and transient reactions to the stresses of warfare. COSR is not a condition recognized by the *Diagnostic and Statistical Manual of Mental Disorders-IV,* the bible of the psychiatry profession, something the Army is well aware of, since it doesn't even consider COSR an ailment. As one Army journal article puts it, "Those with COSR are not referred to as 'patients,' but are described as having 'normal reactions to an abnormal event.' " Thus believing Green's psychological state to be normal, Marrs prescribed him a small course of Seroquel, an antipsychotic drug that also treats insomnia, and recommended that he follow up with another visit (though she didn't specify when), and she sent him back to his unit.

"I told her, 'My main preoccupation in life is wanting to kill Iraqis, whoever they are, wherever they are,' " Green recalled. "She said, 'Okay, here's these pills that will help you sleep, and we'll probably be around.' I don't think she thought I was serious, even though I was going out of my way to be like, 'Look, I'm serious about this.' "

According to Goodwin, Marrs reported back to him that Green "needed a little bit more counseling." Goodwin, like most of Green's superiors, thought Green's problems were manageable anger issues that could be dealt with, he said, "through time, through grief counseling, if necessary, medication, through Combat Stress, and supervision." When Staff Sergeant Bob Davis, a Combat Stress technician with a reserve unit out of Boston, arrived in January 2006 as part of the team to relieve Marrs's team, she told them about Green. "She warned us that, given his experiences and the things that he's done, he might be someone we'd want to follow up with." Despite this warning, they would not see Green until March 20, 2006.

While Sergeant First Class Phil Blaisdell and his 3rd Platoon suffered countless frustrations with Iraqis who would lie and stonewall, he always tried to put himself in their shoes, and he tried to get his men to think that way too. One day, a local told him that the traffic control points were particularly onerous in the mornings because people were trying to get to work in Baghdad. He had never thought of that before, that people were commuting. But from then on, he tried to get the checkpoints open by 6:00 a.m. to handle what he quickly noticed was, yes, a morning rush north. On particularly hot days, when the backups were long, he'd have his men hand out bottles of water to the waiting cars. He tried to talk to the people and explain to them what was going on to the best of his ability. Whenever he was at the JSB, he would run up and down Malibu as much as possible, talking to the Quarguli sheikhs, trying to solve their problems, even if they were small ones. If the roads were closed but they had a harvest of apples they wanted to get to Baghdad, they would call Blaisdell. "I'd say, 'Okay, but I got to search the cars, though. Is that okay?' They'd be like, 'That's fine.' We worked together on shit. It made all the difference in the world."

Getting his guys to not give in to hate no matter how frustrated they were, or how badly some of their friends got hurt, was by far his biggest challenge. "Soldiers can turn negative in a heartbeat," he remarked. " 'Fuck this! Fuck these people!' People would get mad that they were not telling us information. But you know what? If I was them, I wouldn't tell an American anything either!" He tried to make his men understand that the main reason Iraqis were uncooperative was that they were scared to death for their own lives and they did not believe that the United States was capable of protecting them. When a squad of Americans rolled up at a house and asked for info, and if an insurgent then got nabbed, every single other insurgent in town knew who had squealed, and there would be reprisals. Blaisdell started getting informants to text him, or to drop notes out of car windows at TCPs, rather than risk talking to him in person. He told his men not to tear apart people's houses, not because he was a softy but because Iraqis are not stupid: they knew houses were getting searched regularly now, so the ones who happened to be insurgents pretty much stopped hiding incriminating materials in their homes months ago. This was another reason he told his men to be careful when they found a cache of weapons in someone's yard. Some Iraqis had started framing neighbors they had grudges against. And then, once that started happening, others figured out that by saying they had been framed, they could still stash guns in their own backyard. See? It was all a mind game, he explained, and it was dizzying. But the worst mistake you could make was to think that the Iraqis were not several steps ahead of you.

Blaisdell had the same lack of patience for soldiers slapping people around. "There's a twelve-, thirteen-year-old kid in the house, and if I saw a soldier slap the father around, I'd ask that soldier, 'Hey, what would you do if some guy came in your home and slapped your dad around?' He'd always say, 'I'd fucking kill him.' Okay, so what makes you any different than that kid right there? And you know what he's going to do now? He's going to go plant an IED. And it might not be you that gets killed. But some other soldier is dead because you had to be a tough guy."

Second Platoon's Sergeant First Class Jeremy Gebhardt was quieter than Blaisdell and did not have quite the local politician in him that his counterpart did. He did not glad-hand the locals as much, but he believed in and worked on some of the larger infrastructure missions, such as getting schools reopened and water treatment plants up and running. But he, like Blaisdell, considered managing the attitudes and morals of his men to be the biggest part of his job. Anytime he heard complaints about the Iraqis—or about superior officers, for that matter—he snuffed it out quick.

"You need to shut the fuck up and focus," he would say.

13

Britt and Lopez

TWO DAYS AFTER Eidson and Galloway got hit by an IED, Britt was still in a melancholy mood.

"I just have a feeling that I'm not going to make it back from here," he said.

"Sir, you can't think like that," Yribe responded.

"It just doesn't seem like I'm going to be able to make it back with all the people that are dying."

"If it's your time, it's your time," Yribe said. "There's nothing anybody can do about it."

One of the day's major missions was another clearance of Caveman. Bravo First Sergeant Andrew Laskoski, Britt, and a mixture of 1st Platoon's 3rd and 1st Squads were assigned to accompany an Iron Claw team. In the medic area of FOB Yusufiyah, there was a dry erase board where all the medics were supposed to write their whereabouts. Since he knew they were going on Caveman that day, Specialist Collin Sharpness wrote, "Getting Blown Up."

They started around 8:00 a.m. Following Iron Claw's big rigs as they slowly inched west on the north side of Caveman, the men walked behind, looking for IED triggerman hides or caches along the side of the

road, walking cloverleaf patterns for five hours straight in the drench-
ing heat. The Humvees, each with a driver and a gunner pulling security, followed behind them. Around 1:30 p.m.—whoosh!—an RPG
screamed past them and narrowly missed one of the Iron Claw vehicles.
A few soldiers tracked the flight path across the canal, over the south
side of the road, to where they saw an assembly of some type, a tube
from which it looked like the RPG had been fired remotely. As Lieutenant Britt and the Iron Claw lieutenant were discussing their next
move, three mortar rounds landed nearby in quick succession, one hitting the right rear quadrant of the lead Iron Claw vehicle, disabling it.
The Iron Claw lieutenant said his crew needed to go back to Yusufiyah
for repairs before they could do any more clearing.

Everybody started turning around as Britt called the situation up to
the TOC. The Iron Claw convoy was long gone, and the Bravo vehicles
were almost back at TCP4 when Goodwin told Britt to go get the mount.
But that wasn't feasible, Britt responded, because it was on the other
side of the canal. Go get it, said Goodwin. That is a no-go, said Britt, it
is on the other side of the second road as well, and that road had not
been cleared. Britt asked if it was okay for them to backtrack all the way
from the beginning and clear the south side of Caveman up to the
mount. They had already been out there six hours, Goodwin calculated,
and one Iron Claw vehicle was now damaged. To get more clearance vehicles out there could take well past nightfall. Goodwin refused. Find
the closest bridge, get in there, get the thing, and get out, Goodwin said.

"I don't care if you have to swim across the fucking canal," he insisted, "but you will get me that tube."

"Yes, sir," Britt responded.

The men saw a small footbridge about two hundred yards northwest
of the spot where they first turned around. Britt assembled a team of
about eight men, including Laskoski and Yribe. They'd have to walk
across the bridge, track back southeast another three hundred and fifty
yards, pick up the mount, and return. They headed out. Just as they
crossed the canal, they saw a blue Kia Bongo, a kind of small, high-cab
pickup truck that is ubiquitous in Iraq, driving toward them from the

southeast on the south side of Caveman. The soldiers wanted the Bongo to stop well in advance of where the RPG mount was, so they started yelling and making hand gestures to stop. The Bongo would not stop. Now it was approaching the RPG's kill area. Laskoski ordered one of the soldiers to fire a warning shot. He did, but the Bongo still didn't stop. The soldier fired another. With the truck about to enter the area, and still defying the warning shots, Laskoski ordered the men to open fire on the truck. They sprayed it with dozens of bullets, yet it continued to drive all the way through the RPG tube's area, while under fire, until it rolled to a stop fifty yards past it.

Laskoski said, "We're going to have some dead bodies in that truck." The group headed down to check it out. Astonishingly, there were no dead bodies, just an older man in the passenger seat, with a gunshot wound to his right calf, and a younger man, the driver, who was completely unscathed. The older guy was some sort of Quarguli sheikh, carrying an ID card that Kunk had distributed to local grandees.

Britt said, "All right, let's go get this thing." Laskoski and some other soldiers hung back to deal with the men in the Bongo, while Britt, Yribe, and Sergeant Roman Diaz headed out to get the RPG tube. Thirty-three-year-old Specialist William Lopez-Feliciano from Quebradillas, Puerto Rico, who had arrived at Bravo only three weeks earlier, was standing there, tentative, not knowing which way to go. They were already fifty or sixty yards on their way, but Yribe turned back and yelled, "Yo, Lopez, let's go," and he scrambled to catch up.

The four men walked closely together. They were bunching up, which wasn't safe. Yribe was up front, but Britt, with several feet of antenna sticking out of his backpack, was almost on top of him.

Yribe turned around and said to all of them, "Hey, back off me. Get separated." He turned around again, and said to Britt, "Back off me, sir." Britt fell in behind Yribe and Diaz, with Lopez bringing up the rear.

Then everything went black. A deeply buried IED with several hundreds pounds of explosives exploded directly under where Britt and Lopez were standing. The blast was so massive that soldiers heard the explosion in Lutufiyah ten miles away. Britt was thrown fifty feet into the air, cartwheeling "like a rag doll," remembered one soldier. Within a second or two, his body had plummeted back to Earth and into the canal. The blast ripped Lopez into two pieces, bisecting him at the waist. The pressure wave sucked the earplugs out of Yribe's ears and covered him and Diaz in dirt, smoke, and human tissue. The bomb was so big that all four of them should have been dead, but something about how the IED was set focused almost all of its energy straight up rather than out. Diaz and Yribe were relatively unharmed, but they didn't know that yet. At first they were just trying to figure out if they were still alive.

When Yribe shook himself awake, he couldn't tell how long he had been out. It must have been only a couple of seconds. Diaz was on one knee, right behind him.

He grabbed Diaz and yelled, "Are you okay?" Diaz said yes. They started to run back west where Laskoski was heading toward them. Laskoski gripped Yribe by the vest, but Yribe couldn't make out what he was saying. Yribe was trying to talk, but his mouth was full of dirt, so he started spitting it out, right into Laskoski's face.

Finally, he started to understand Laskoski: "You gotta get ahold of yourself, you gotta get composure."

"Composure," Yribe thought. "How can I get composure when I don't even know what is going on?" By then, the dust was starting to settle. Diaz and Yribe patted each other down for injuries. Diaz had a faceful of superficial shrapnel wounds, and something had hit or twisted Yribe's gut hard enough that he'd ripped his abdomen's muscle wall. But they were both okay. Laskoski told two soldiers to fire into some treetops about a hundred yards away, since that seemed like the most likely trigger spot. They called in the IED hit to Bravo's TOC (Tactical Operations Center). Looking around, the men tried to figure out if there was another blast coming or if insurgents were going to follow with a small-arms attack. But it was quiet, completely still. After such violence, it was amazing how quickly mundanity reasserted itself.

Goodwin had hoped that his order was the correct one. He was tense when he overruled Britt's wishes. He was nervous, and he was still weighing the pros and cons when the call came over the radio at 2:37 p.m.

The patrol had hit an IED, the transmission said. They couldn't find Britt and Lopez, but it was likely they were dead. Goodwin reeled. He felt nauseated. He thought only one thing: "I just sent them to their death."

"Britt! Lopez! Britt! Lopez!" the men who had been walking shouted. They didn't know where they were. The two had effectively vanished. But the soldiers in the Humvees across the canal had seen the whole thing. Private First Class Chris Barnes, in one of the Humvee gun turrets, yelled and pointed that Britt was in the water. He'd seen the canal go crimson with blood, but the current had carried the stain away almost instantly.

Yribe turned and said to Laskoski, "Hey, First Sergeant, I'm going in." He ripped his vest and helmet off and jumped in. Almost immediately, he realized that this was a mistake. The canal's water temperature was about 55 degrees, its depth was twenty feet, and the current was moving so fast that Yribe was as much trying not to drown as trying to find Britt. Soon exhausted, he barely reached the other bank, where soldiers from the trucks helped him to dry ground.

After a minute or two, as the shock wore off and the permanence set in, Goodwin realized he was about to have a breakdown. He needed to get out of the TOC. He couldn't let his men see him in that state. Laskoski was running the recovery mission down at the site, helicopters were already in the air, and QRFs were already either en route or being staged from both the JSB and Mahmudiyah. So at least for a little while, the wheels were turning and Goodwin was not needed. Which was fortunate, because he was suddenly, massively, uncontrollably incapacitated by grief and guilt. He told First Lieutenant Habash, "Hey, you're in charge. I need to step outside."

Goodwin sought out Combat Stress nurse Lieutenant Colonel Marrs, who was still on the FOB. He broke down in sobs and self-recrimination. "You tell a guy to go across a bridge, and within five minutes he's dead," Goodwin said. "With everything that had been going on, I just snapped." The two talked for about an hour. The session helped. By the end of it, Goodwin was at least able to project a composed demeanor and go back out and do his job. But he wasn't sure how. "At this point, how do you manage this debacle?" he wondered.

Phil Miller also sought out Marrs later that day. During their discussion, he told her that he thought 1st Platoon had become combat ineffective. "It's one of the most embarrassing things for a leader to do," Miller admitted, "to call your platoon combat ineffective, but I told Captain Goodwin, too, that they are not in the fight. Their soul, everything, is gone right now."

Goodwin went down to TCP4. People there were doing math problems. He couldn't believe how morbid and mundane it was, but they were trying to figure out how far and how fast Britt's body might flow through in the canal system. If the canal's water is traveling X miles per hour, they scribbled, and object A at start point Y has a mass of B, how fast would object A travel to position Z? "We were throwing sticks into the canal to determine how fast the water was running, so we could figure out where the body was," he said. "It was ridiculous, ungodly, inhuman."

Multiple relief teams, including the original Iron Claw team, Bravo's 3rd Platoon, Army dive teams, Edwards and Kunk, and Ebel and a general from division headquarters would eventually converge upon the site, but it was up to the squad on the ground to begin the recovery effort.

The carnage in front of them was difficult to process. There was a jawbone, stripped clean and shiny white, lying in the dirt. There was a large internal organ that Yribe could only think was a liver, Lopez's liver. Flack vests, or parts of them, were lying on the ground, ripped to shreds as if they were made of paper. They found ID cards, tatters of money, a wedding ring. Lopez's torso had been thrown two hundred yards from the blast site. His arms were gone from the bicep down and his eyes were wide open. The men put his upper body in a poncho because they didn't have any body bags. Yribe carried him over to one of the Iron Claw vehicles and handed him off to another soldier. They didn't know each other, and there was nothing to say. They just nodded to each other.

Captain Jared Bordwell showed up with a team of Alpha soldiers to relieve the shaken 1st Platoon men. Alpha started jumping into the canal and dragging it with grappling hooks. As usual after a catastrophic event, the men on the ground found the senior officers who had flocked there disruptive. Bordwell thought the men could have used a kind word from Ebel about how crappy it was to have to look for a dismembered comrade, but Ebel wanted to know why they weren't wearing eye protection. Bordwell said that the men in the canal weren't even wearing their body armor so he didn't really see what difference eye shields made at this point. Later, the general from division called Bordwell over and inquired what that was that he had found sticking out of the road.

"That is det cord, sir. That is an IED," Bordwell responded. "You need to back away from that." The general sent his aide, a captain, to mark it by setting an oilcan on top of it. Bordwell looked at him and said, "Sir, you're fucking nuts." The Alpha guys shook their heads in disbelief.

By 4:50 p.m., the medevac took off with Yribe and Diaz to get treatment at FOB Mahmudiyah. That night, they had part of a tent to themselves, and they talked about what they were going to do now, how they were going to survive.

"I don't even know what to tell these guys anymore," Yribe said to Diaz. "Because I can't tell them it's going to be all right. What do I tell them?" Diaz said he didn't know—all they could do was get back out there and be with the rest of the men as soon as possible. They both caught the first convoy to Yusufiyah the next morning.

Lieutenant Colonel Marrs agreed with Miller's and Goodwin's assessments of 1st Platoon. Later that night at FOB Yusufiyah, she told Kunk that "hostility and vengeance seem prominent in 1st Platoon." She advised him that the platoon's mental health status was "red"—non-mission capable—and they should be given respite from their current operations tempo to recover from their losses.

Kunk and Edwards approached Goodwin that same night. They asked him how he was doing and what he needed. This time, there was no joking around, no sheepishness about how unlikely the request was.

Goodwin said, "I need another platoon." They asked him how he thought 1st Platoon was doing. Goodwin replied, "They are not mission capable, and I don't know when they will be. They are done."

Kunk looked Goodwin in the eye, said, "Okay," and got into his truck. Goodwin was confident that something would be done to reduce the pressure on 1st Platoon. He was sure, now, that some sort of relief was coming.

Later that night, the word came down. First Platoon was being pulled out of the fight for forty-eight hours, after which they would resume their normal duties.

When asked about staffing, Kunk sometimes said that he tried to get more troops down in the AO, but there were none to be had. "If I needed more manpower," he explained, "then I would ask for more manpower. I would lay it out to the best of my ability. If the resources aren't there, then my brigade has to rob Peter to pay Paul, and they weren't willing to do that." Other times, he asserted that he rejected Goodwin's requests for more men because he didn't think that Bravo needed them. He thought the company had enough troops to complete the job. The problem was that 1st Platoon could not get their act together and Goodwin was not using what he had efficiently.

Goodwin insisted on going through and boxing up Britt's and Lopez's personal items that night. He didn't want to put any of his men through that. Everything was shredded and mangled—Kevlar, ammo magazines, pieces of uniform—and soaking wet, whether from water or blood or both. The smells were ripe, the textures magnified, either extraordinarily rough or extraordinarily smooth. Goodwin tried to separate the stuff as best he could. The wedding ring was obviously Lopez's. The watch, probably Britt's. He made two piles, trying to get back to each family as much stuff as possible, so maybe they could feel more connected to their father and husband, or son and brother. The whole time, Goodwin was thinking to himself, "This is what you did. You killed them."

Around-the-clock dive teams did not find Britt until the middle of the next day. HHC commander Shawn Umbrell was there as Britt's body was pulled out of the canal, and the sight took his breath away. With the water running so fast and so cold over him for so long, Britt had been thoroughly washed and preserved. He was perfectly white and clean. He was immaculate.

Caveman was declared black (closed to military traffic) after the incident and, with few rare exceptions, it remained black for years afterward. First Strike units patrolled the road periodically, but not in any concerted way ever again. And even though there was still one large concrete span over the canal that his own chain of command would not let him blow up, and all the other bridges could be easily rebuilt, Kunk considered the Caveman missions a success. "If you are stopping the freedom of movement of the bad guy, now you are controlling and dictating where he can move and can't move. We did go in there and drop a lot of the bridges. And it paid huge dividends. It got to the point where I didn't need Caveman, but the reason why I didn't need it was because I took it away. We took Caveman and the use of Caveman away from the enemy."

Others disagreed. "I don't know what the hell we were thinking," Goodwin volunteered. "Seriously. It poses absolutely no significance to anything. And I hate to say that for as many hours as I spent on that fucking road, for nothing. There was no reason for us to go down there. None. It served no purpose. Insurgents could maneuver in there, but they couldn't get out. There was nowhere for them to go. They were going to run into us or the IAs somewhere. So what did we need this road for?"

14

Leadership Shake-up

WHEN THE PLATOON assembled at FOB Yusufiyah for another Critical Incident Debrief, Colonel Ebel came down too. He was in the potato barn talking to Goodwin and Laskoski when Miller walked up. They talked for a while and Miller mentioned Green, saying that Green was having a particularly hard time dealing with these deaths. Ebel and Green met privately for about thirty minutes, an extraordinary occurrence. Although Ebel spoke briefly with a wide variety of soldiers every day, frequently consoling them during times of loss, he cannot remember another occasion when he met one-on-one with a private for half an hour.

During the meeting, Green told Ebel that he hated Iraqis and wanted to kill them all. Ebel thought that this was a normal reaction to what he had just been through. When you watch a comrade destroyed by the enemy, Ebel felt, everybody goes through a full range of emotions.

Green asked about the rules of engagement, wanting to know, "Why can't we just go shoot them all?"

Ebel responded, "Because that is not what American soldiers do."

"I'll be all right," Green told Ebel. "I'm just frustrated." Ebel was re-assured by the conversation and told Green's immediate supervisors to keep looking after him.

Green said Ebel's high rank made it just the most noteworthy ex-ample of a fairly common occurrence: he'd simply agree to what a su-perior officer was asserting about treating Iraqis humanely, and the officer would think he had fixed him. "I would tell them right from the get-go how I was," he recalled. "And then they would tell me, 'No, this is how you're supposed to look at it.' And I would say, 'All right.' They outranked me by so many levels, it's not like I'm going to get into a big argument with them."

The debilitating effects of warfare have likely been known to humankind since warfare existed, at least since Homer described Achilles' rampage and desecration of Hector in the *Iliad*. But scientists have been studying the topic in earnest only since World War II. And that work, though con-stantly growing and being revised, is conclusive on several major points. Primary among them: A soldier can endure combat for only so long be-fore he begins to break down. In *The Face of Battle*, military historian John Keegan wrote that early studies concluded that a soldier "reached his peak of effectiveness in the first 90 days of combat, and after that his efficiency began to fall off, and that he became steadily less valuable thereafter until he was completely useless."

It is tempting to contrast the great battles of Normandy and the Bat-tle of the Bulge and even the Tet Offensive—massive waves of tens of thousands of soldiers clashing against one another as gunfire rained down for days and thousands of men died—with Bravo Company's fight and say the two don't even compare. And that is true in certain re-spects. Bravo faced no force-on-force battles that lasted more than a few hours, and these were rarely larger than a squad fighting a hand-ful of insurgents. But to then conclude that Bravo's struggles were somehow less significant or more bearable does a disservice to the way that warfare has changed in the last few decades and glosses over the psychological effects—still largely uncharted—that these changes have wrought. During World War II, units would be thrown into major battles that could last a day, a week, perhaps a month or even two—but then they would be withdrawn from the front lines for weeks, sometimes for several months, before being sent into battle again. American policy during WWII was to never leave troops on the front lines longer than eighty days.

The men of Bravo stayed in a combat zone, went "outside the wire"—onto the front lines—every single day for eleven months straight. In the case of the TCPs, they lived outside the wire twenty-four hours a day. And they experienced some form of enemy contact almost every single day. Deployments where every day is a combat day are a fairly new phenomenon in the U.S. Army. As former lieutenant colonel and psychological researcher Dave Grossman writes in his 1996 book *On Killing*, "Spending *months of continuous* [emphasis his] exposure to the stresses of combat is a phenomenon found only on the battlefields of this century . . . it is only in this century that our physical and logistical capability to support combat has completely outstripped our psychological capacity to endure it."

Even pushed to the limits this way, the vast majority of Bravo did not crack. But all men start any endeavor with different capacities to cope, and in this environment, with so little support from superiors, it is not surprising that some were overwhelmed. After Britt and Lopez died, an already fraying platoon began to unravel more quickly. Its psychological separation from the company and the battalion became more pronounced. The platoon began falling in on itself. In the turmoil of combat and stress, violence and death, they started to redraw moral and social codes that they believed applied only to them. Foremost among their rationalizations was their conviction that no one else had experienced what they had, and no one else could possibly understand it. "We didn't want to hear anything from anybody, because nobody knew what we were going through," explained Sergeant John Diem. "That's the leitmotif: 'Nobody knows what we're going through.'"

They became isolated in every sense; the Pygmalion effect was in full swing. After being continuously told that they were screwups and outcasts, 1st Platoon consciously or subconsciously decided to live up to their outcast status. This "shrinkage of the social and moral horizon," as psychologist Jonathan Shay puts it in *Achilles in Vietnam,* is a common phenomenon for small groups of soldiers in prolonged combat settings. Such soldiers, Shay writes, "sometimes lose responsiveness to the claims of any bonds, ideals or loyalties outside a tiny circle of immediate comrades. An us-against-them mentality severs all other attachments or commitments."

Extreme hatred of Iraqis was now common, widespread, and openly discussed. Paul Cortez rated his hatred of Iraqis as a 5 on a scale of 10 when he first deployed. By December, he said, it had hit 20. The platoon became more aggressive. Suspects were routinely beaten before being brought back onto the FOBs. There was a hierarchy that governed who got to punch or kick a detainee—new men were not allowed to participate until they had experienced a sufficient amount of combat. There were insiders and outsiders and you had to earn your way in. "If you weren't there the whole time," said one soldier, "new guys would get told, 'Who the fuck do you think you are?' 'Stay away from me. I don't even want to know you.' " Many of the men suffered from other well-documented symptoms of extended combat exposure, including fatigue, anxiety and panic attacks, increasing irritability, and obsessive-compulsive tendencies. Drinking increased, became more open, and was not limited to the lower-enlisted. Some NCOs not only allowed their soldiers to drink, they were drinking themselves. A common attitude was: Everything's fine as long as it doesn't get out of hand.

"The platoon rejected anything that wasn't tailored to the reality that they had crafted to protect them from what was really happening," explained Sergeant Diem. "And what was happening is they were debasing themselves as individuals. I'm not coming down on these guys any harder than I come down on myself. Because I can church it up and say, 'I was doing the best I could. We were doing the best we could.'

I allowed myself to feel overwhelmed and I allowed myself to misinterpret reality, allowed myself to basically become insane in order to make it as easy on myself as possible."

The whole brigade was aware that Bravo was depleted, and that it would be a challenge to fix it. "Having to reseed the leadership of virtually an entire rifle company while in combat is a very difficult thing to do," commented battalion executive officer Fred Wintrich. The answer, battalion leadership decided, was not to rotate units but to rotate leaders. "Maybe we should have put a whole new company in there," reflected Ebel. "But I don't know—the model was that a company builds credibility with the populace by having some tenure there. Tom Kunk's strategy was sound. He was rotating his leaders, his platoon sergeants, thinking that's the catalyst."

In reality, everyone understood that there was no real issue with 2nd or 3rd Platoon. Sergeants First Class Gebhardt and Blaisdell and their men were performing exceptionally well even without lieutenants. The real focus of the leadership shake-up was 1st Platoon.

Enough with the false starts and second chances, Kunk and Edwards decided. Miller had to go. They started lining up Rob Gallagher, the former 1st Platoon sergeant now on one of the MiTT teams, to take over the platoon immediately.

"The exact words I received from the sergeant major were 'You need to fix things quick, fast, and in a hurry,' " Gallagher said. Beyond that, he didn't receive a lot of guidance on what was wrong or instructions on how to correct it. He knew that there were problems with morale, discipline, and coping with the loss of four comrades in a short amount of time. And, as Gallagher understood it, Miller would continue as platoon sergeant. He was being installed as platoon leader, in the same way that Blaisdell now ran 3rd Platoon and Gebhardt ran 2nd. He loved his old unit and he was immensely honored to be handed the task.

Gallagher was a surprising choice for many in the battalion. Before this deployment, he had been Bravo's platoon sergeant for nine months, and before that he had taken over as 3rd Platoon's sergeant three months into OIF1. But Battalion moved him to the MiTT team, it is widely acknowledged, as a graceful way to reassign a platoon sergeant who was not jelling with his men. Before deployment, he'd had some close friends in 1st Platoon, including Nelson and Miller ("Nelson" is Gallagher's son's middle name), but his opinion of the junior soldiers in the platoon was low. Among the biggest complaints from peers and superiors about Gallagher in garrison was that he was too critical and dismissive of his own men. He was quick to declare them beyond hope. He would vent inappropriately at meetings that his men were a bunch of losers and dimwits who couldn't do anything right. Both Blaisdell and Gebhardt liked Gallagher personally, and both resisted offering an opinion on whether he was the right man for the job, but they agreed on this: If the chain of command did not have confidence in him in garrison, which was no secret, they did not understand why they would bring him back now.

Gallagher arrived on December 26. Although he was excited to be asked to take charge of his old platoon again, there was not exactly a receiving line waiting for him. "The company commander didn't even know that I was coming," Gallagher said. "The first sergeant didn't even know who I was. So I don't know at what level I was directed to go back to the unit, but I got the impression that no one really knew what the purpose of it was." Nonetheless, after showing up and introducing himself around the TOC, he dropped his gear and headed out to the TCPs to be with the platoon.

The men of 1st Platoon were not happy to see him. At best, he was tolerated. To a degree, this was the inevitable by-product of Gallagher's conscious decisions. His friendships with Miller and Nelson notwithstanding, he rarely cultivated relationships, with either subordinates or superiors. He came to the job with an old-school mentality that being overly familiar clouded one's judgment and ability to perform the tough tasks that both leading men and taking orders required. He was disdainful of "Joe lovers," leaders who sought approval or friendship from those many ranks below them. He thought the informal and relaxed dealings between enlisted men and senior NCOs and junior officers that was increasingly becoming the standard in the Army was a disgrace. Nor did he develop mentors. "I am never the type to cultivate close relationships with a person regardless of their rank," he said. "So I was never in Sergeant Major's tight circle. I did not arbitrarily strike up a conversation with him just to have a conversation." While principled, his taciturn, standoffish, and tetchy demeanor meant that he had few friends, no allies, and no base of support.

Arriving at the TCPs, Gallagher was stunned by how 1st Platoon had changed in just three months. "I don't think he was prepared for what he was walking into," said one 1st Platoon soldier. They looked nothing like the happy, eager, optimistic troops he had said good-bye to. They were dirty, haggard, exhausted, pale, and dead-eyed. Many were alternately angry or despairing. Some of them would tear up on routine missions or cry into their lunches. "I have been in the Army a long time," Gallagher said. "And I was overwhelmed by the amount of despair." Asked about morale, he said, "On a scale of 1 to 10, it would probably be 1, the lowest possible."

Miller was among those hurting the worst. After losing four men so quickly, he was having doubts about himself, but he also knew, with the arrival of Gallagher, that Battalion had lost its faith in him as well. Although he still retained the title of platoon sergeant, the move felt to Miller like a demotion and he did not subordinate himself to Gallagher gracefully. His relationship with Gallagher, once strong, was now strained, and would soon break down completely. He undermined Gallagher's authority. Squad leaders and soldiers exacerbated the power struggle. They would frequently look at Miller after Gallagher issued an order, as if to ask, "Is it okay to do what he says?"

Gallagher spent his first few days trying to restore order and discipline to the unmoored platoon. He emphasized proper uniforms, grooming, and hygiene. The men were unimpressed. According to Lauzier, Gallagher's fatal flaw, in their eyes, was his inability to filter out the pressures coming down from higher-ups, one of the widely acknowledged but unofficial jobs of a senior platoon NCO. Ideally, the men should have no idea how hard they are being leaned on. Gallagher would not just pass along the stress, Lauzier said, but magnify it. "He'd get the lash, and then he'd come back and explode on you," explained Lauzier. "And you can't do that. He put a lot of stress on everybody."

Unbeknownst to Gallagher or Miller, however, there was another leadership shake-up in the works. Kunk planned to bring in First Lieutenant Tim Norton, who was also serving on a MiTT team in Lutufiyah, as 1st Platoon's platoon leader. Norton was the senior lieutenant in the battalion, he had received high praise from everyone he'd worked with, and he was considered one of First Strike's most promising young officers. Kunk called Norton to his office shortly before the New Year to tell him of his new assignment. Norton got only the shortest of briefings on what to expect and what was expected of him. Kunk told him that the platoon was having some morale and discipline issues and that he wanted Norton to help get them on their feet.

Kunk mentioned that Miller had declared the platoon combat ineffective, but added, "The platoon sergeant doesn't get to do that. Only I get to do that." Get them to work through their losses, focus on the basics, and start being soldiers again, Kunk said.

Norton was wary, but willing. Bravo, and 1st Platoon especially, had developed a reputation throughout the battalion. Depending on how charitable the person relating the info was, around the battalion you could hear anything from "Bravo is in a fight to the death down there," to "Bravo is having a tough time," to "Bravo is seriously dicked up." Norton was confident in his abilities, and excited to lead a platoon again, but he was well aware that he was not inheriting a custodial role. He was being brought in to fix something no one had been taught to fix. As he noted, "There is no manual that says, 'Here's how to take a war-torn platoon and train it back up to a fully operational level while still in combat.' "

Norton caught a ride to Yusufiyah on New Year's Day. He arrived at about 10:30 p.m. to report in to Goodwin, whom he had never met. He found Goodwin sitting in the TOC, in flannel pajama bottoms and a T-shirt with a poncho liner over his head. He was asleep. Norton said hello to the rest of the TOC and headed out to meet the platoon. Not surprisingly, he got the cold shoulder from them. "Who the fuck are you?" some soldiers ranking as low as private challenged him. Others barely acknowledged his existence, hardly responding when he spoke to them, until he explained that he was not some cherry lieutenant straight from Officers' Basic. He had been in Lutufiyah the whole time, and before that he was with Charlie, so it was not like he just fell off the turnip truck. That, at least, prevented outright insubordination, but it still took a while for him to be taken seriously because, as the soldiers never ceased to remind him, "Lutufiyah sure as shit ain't Yusufiyah."

Norton's leadership philosophy was based on a quote he picked up somewhere: "Leadership is 90 percent people skills and 20 percent motivation." He didn't see any point in being aloof, or in pretending that he wasn't the same age as most of his soldiers. He thought it was possible to maintain a command separation, but the line could be drawn in chalk, it didn't have to be etched in stone. "You have to feel people's emotional states, their wants and needs," he explained. "It's not like I have to be their best friend. But if I know some dude likes fishing, then I'll start the conversation with fishing."

Given how closed off 1st Platoon had become, Norton did break down their walls very quickly. Soldiers grew to like him because he had an infectiously upbeat attitude, even in that environment. He didn't demand a salute and he insisted on being called not "Lieutenant Norton," or even "Tim," but "Timmy." He was not happy unless other people were laughing and, unusual for a lieutenant, he was not afraid to make a fool of himself to do it. He did a wicked Harry Caray impression. He was also an enthusiastic soldier who always volunteered to patrol, who always offered to ride along into the field. Frequently, he wouldn't wait for orders to come down, he'd just draft up a mission and go. "He merged with the platoon like he had been there the whole time," remarked one soldier. "To take over a platoon that smoothly, never mind just join one? You've got to be doing something right. He fit right in with us, no problems whatsoever."

That's not exactly true. Taken by surprise, Gallagher and Miller both had a big problem with Norton's arrival. They both felt lied to. As Gallagher understood his initial brief, he was coming in as the platoon leader, so for Norton to arrive just a couple of days later, with no communication, no warning, no nothing, did not start things off well. And as Gallagher slotted back to platoon sergeant, that relegated Miller back to being a squad leader, which incensed him. If Miller had felt as if he was being demoted before, now he explicitly was.

"At that point," Miller said, "I was like, 'You know what? You can fucking kiss my ass. I'm not going to be part of this bullshit anymore.' " He would have had no problem taking a squad with a different platoon or a different company—he was still a staff sergeant, after all—but to be relieved yet forced to remain in the platoon was a double humiliation. "I was bitter. And I was fucking pissed. To be lied to like that, to be told that I was staying on as platoon sergeant, and then moving me down to squad leader after I had run this shit for four months without a word to me? That's when I started thinking, 'I am not going to be a party to this abortion anymore.' "

After the Britt and Lopez memorial, a general asked the 1-502nd's executive officer, Major Wintrich, "Where are you getting your replacement lieutenants?"

Wintrich told him, "We aren't. We don't have any infantry lieutenants sitting on their hands saying, 'Put me in, Coach.' "

Actually, there was one sitting on the bench up at Striker: twenty-three-year-old Lieutenant Paul Fisher. And soon after that memorial, he started as Bravo Company's 2nd Platoon leader. Fisher entered the Army on an officer candidate contract in February 2004. Basic Training, Officer Candidate School, Infantry Officer Basic Course, Airborne School, and Ranger School kept him in training until August 2005, when he got to Fort Campbell. He arrived just as the brigade was making its last push toward deployment. He was excited to get a platoon and "live the dream," as infantry officers in on-the-ground leadership positions like to say. Then he received his assignment: in the Brigade Public Affairs Office. He was not happy. "So my first job as a lieutenant who did absolutely everything correctly, all the right schools, everything to a T? I got fucked."

He spent two and a half months up at Striker with Brigade Head-quarters, and he was frustrated. "I was living on this little Fort Campbell in the desert," he said, "where I could not have felt safer than in my own bed at home." The sound of gunfire in the distance especially irritated him because that's where he should be. The idleness of his job drove him crazy. Among his tasks was delivering the morning newspapers to brigade senior command. Desperate, he started pulling guard at the front desk of the TOC checking IDs—ordinarily an enlisted man's job—hoping someone from an infantry unit would notice his lieutenant's bar and his Ranger Tab. It worked. Lieutenant Colonel Rob Haycock, com-mander of the 2-502nd, passed him one day and asked him what the hell he was doing there, and told him to come work for him. Fisher was ready to head down to 2nd Battalion, but on December 29, he got the word: 1st Battalion needed him more. He was going to Yusufiyah. "You're going down to the Wild West," one of the brigade staff officers told him.

Fisher caught a MiTT convoy down to Mahmudiyah carrying a ridicu-lous amount of equipment: two footlockers of stuff in addition to his rucksack. "Little did I know what a brigade puke I had turned into," he admitted. "I didn't even know how soft I had become." He had a quick briefing with Kunk and Salome.

"You need to get your shit together, Lieutenant," they told him, "be-cause you're about to go where things are life or death. It ain't DVD Night every night around here, so get your head screwed on straight and you might be okay." He caught another convoy to Yusufiyah about an hour later.

Halfway to Yusufiyah, at the exact same spot that Specialist Galloway and 2nd Platoon's previous platoon leader, Jerry Eidson, had been hit ten days earlier, Fisher's Humvee triggered a trip-wire IED, setting off three 120mm rounds strung together. The entire truck was lifted off the ground, and it landed with a thud. He heard screaming and checked himself. He was unhurt. Sitting in the rear left seat, he could tell the guy next to him, the gunner, and the driver were all wounded. He got out and started trying to treat the driver. The driver had a two-inch hole through his leg that was gushing blood, soaking Fisher's uniform as he tried to stanch the bleeding. Other members of the convoy took over, started applying tourniquets, and managed to save all of the injured soldiers' lives. The three other occupants of the Humvee were later evacuated back to the United States. But at that moment Fisher stood in disbelief at what he had just witnessed. Just hours earlier he was naively ensconced up at Striker and now he had narrowly escaped death his first time on the road.

Once all the blast debris was cleaned up, the convoy completed its journey to Yusufiyah. Fisher headed to the TOC. He thought it odd to find Captain Goodwin asleep in the middle of the headquarters. First Sergeant Laskoski gave him the thirty-second tour, introduced him around, and pointed him toward his platoon sergeant, Jeremy Gebhardt, in the potato bays and told him to introduce himself.

At no time did anyone at Yusufiyah seem to find it strange or feel the need to mention to Fisher that his uniform was covered with fresh, wet blood. "So I can only conclude that this is completely normal, to get blown up out there like this," he said. "I was freaked."

He met Gebhardt and they had coffee while Gebhardt tried to bring Fisher up to speed. There was a midnight mission heading out soon, but Gebhardt suggested Fisher skip this one, grab some shut-eye, and get ready for tomorrow. Fisher noticed that 2nd Platoon's bay had a wall where soldiers marked down each time they got hit by an IED or a mortar. They were running out of room for their hash marks and they had only been there three months.

JANUARY 2006

15

Gallagher

WITHIN A COUPLE of days of his arrival, Sergeant First Class Rob Gallagher was deeply concerned about what he was seeing in 1st Platoon. The whole setup was insane, he thought. Bravo's mission was clearly flawed by design. "There were three rotations," Gallagher said. "There was the JSB rotation, there was the TCP rotation, and there was the mission rotation. But there are only three platoons. There was no downtime. Everything was a constant on. The guys lived outside the wire three hundred and sixty-five days a year, and in my eighteen and a half years of experience, I just didn't envision a soldier being able to handle that tempo without some sort of consequence on the back end."

He considered FOB Yusufiyah outside the wire because, to him, it could not be called a forward operating base at all. A FOB, in his mind, provided a degree of comfort and rest, a measure of safety and security. But after eight months of that potato factory being occupied by U.S. forces, including three months by the 101st, Gallagher could not understand how the place had none of the basics that most people would consider essential to maintaining the long-term morale and welfare of combat soldiers. He could not believe that they were still living in the potato bays, with no more overhead protection than the building's corrugated tin roofing.

"I addressed that with First Sergeant Ski [Laskoski]," he said. "I explained to him that in my opinion morale is terrible and immediate steps needed to be taken to correct this, otherwise we were going to have major problems. Simple things in regard to the living conditions, which were abysmal in my mind."

When he voiced such concerns, he was told that he was whining. Laskoski, for his part, had quickly decided that Gallagher was incompetent and noted deficiencies of not just discipline but combat readiness. "It was the rainy season," Laskoski said. "Arms and ammunition, you've got to keep that maintained twice daily, three times, it doesn't matter how many times, daily. I looked at some of his vehicles and they were just trashed out. Ammo rusted, commo [communications] gear just not working. That's unacceptable."

Looking more closely at the assignments at the TCPs, Gallagher concluded that he did not have enough men to meet minimum staffing requirements. "When you talk about an Army guard rotation, you are talking about three reliefs," he explained. And when he arrived, each TCP typically had six, seven, or eight troops. Guard detail alone required three people, with three in relief for every guard position. "So, right there, there are not enough people."

And at the TCPs, time not on guard was not really downtime. Soldiers not on guard had to search vehicles and people passing through the checkpoints, do IED sweeps, supervise IAs, and be ready for any ad hoc tasks or emergencies that arose. "You are burning the candle at both ends," Gallagher admonished. "You can't ask a guy to pull guard for six hours and then as soon as he gets off guard to go on a six-hour IED sweep." Similarly, because everyone was already doing something else at the TCPs, it was impossible to reinforce the positions' pitiful defenses.

He likewise thought that searching for IEDs on foot was crazy and dangerous and demonstrated contempt for the soldiers' safety. "You are looking for a large-caliber artillery round that is designed not to be found, and the blast radius of that round exceeds your visual radius," Gallagher said. Gallagher would clear Sportster using Humvees until he had to be specifically ordered not to. He began butting heads with Sergeant Major Edwards immediately over the issue. "It was a death march," he asserted. "I told them the way we were doing business was absolutely ridiculous. The exact words I received from the sergeant major were 'Who are you to question brigade policy?' "

Even Gallagher's critics among the soldiers acknowledge that he always led from the front. He never asked his soldiers to do something that he didn't do. Frequently, he would pull guard himself, just to buy another soldier an hour or two of rest. "He was the only platoon sergeant that would pull guard," said one. "He'd be like, 'Yeah, put me up for two night shifts. You guys need to rest too.' "

And despite how foolhardy he thought the policy was, he led every IED sweep he could. "I was the point man," he said. "I felt if anyone should be blown up it should be me. I was not going to put soldiers in danger." He also ranged 1st Platoon's positions randomly. It was his way to stay connected to every facet of the platoon and keep his soldiers on their toes. "I have been in the Army a long time," he explained. "I know soldiers act out when there is no leadership. I would try not to let the soldiers know where I was going. I was the variable that nobody knew. It was deliberately built that way so that the soldiers don't plan on doing things that they are not supposed to do."

Once he had fully evaluated the situation, Gallagher became convinced, like many of the others in 1st Platoon, that he was going to die. "My survivability as well as the soldiers' was very suspect on any given day," he acknowledged. "My wife asked me the likelihood of my, based on my experience, making it out. I said it was not very good. It's probably not going to happen."

Gallagher had little time at the helm of 1st Platoon before Battalion deemed his tenure a failure. Not a week had gone by before Kunk and Edwards regretted their decision. "Gallagher was not getting his job done,"

Kunk said. "Gallagher was falling under the same trap that Miller had. There was an excuse why they were not in uniform, why they didn't have security." Circling the battlefield, Kunk and Edwards would see that, again, 1st Platoon didn't have their helmets on, or were failing in some other way. "So we took corrective actions, we did some teaching, coaching, mentoring," Kunk said. "We followed up about three days later, and it was worse." Kunk repeatedly pointed to the success that 2nd and 3rd Platoons were having as proof of Gallagher's deficiencies. "The other two platoons never had any trouble doing the three missions they had to do," Kunk said.

Many members of 1st Platoon insist that if uniform discipline, let alone other more serious discipline breaches, was really an issue, then the sparkle of Blaisdell's and Gebhardt's halos had become so strong that Kunk, Edwards, and the rest of the battalion were simply blinded by them. Second and 3rd Platoons, they claimed, dumped their ACU (Army combat uniform) tops when it was too hot or went several days without shaving when it suited them just as often as 1st Platoon did. To the men of 1st Platoon, the battalion's conviction that they were incompetent now just seemed like a grudge. "Everything that ever went wrong in that entire area was our platoon's fault," said 2nd Squad Leader Chris Payne. "We were the *only* ones ever out of uniform. We were the *only* ones who took our Kevlars off outside the wire. We were the *only* ones who did this and the *only* ones who did that."

Compounding Gallagher's problems was the fact that he and Lieutenant Norton did not get along. Gallagher thought Norton was young and callow, the epitome of the "Joe lover" he despised. He found Norton unprofessional, even treacherous, going behind his back to discuss important matters with Miller or the other squad leaders before he discussed them with him. "I do not know why I was X'ed out of the loop in a very early period," Gallagher said. "I felt the relationship was sort of doomed from the beginning. I just think Norton's demeanor, his character, was very immature."

Norton didn't have a huge problem with Gallagher, aside from the fact that he was not impressed with his intelligence, his tactical skills, or his relationship with his men. Coming from Charlie, where he bene-fited from First Sergeant Largent's and Sergeant First Class Hayes's men-toring, he found Gallagher wanting. Norton thought Gallagher was clueless when it came to managing relationships. It is one thing not to want to be a political hustler, Norton observed, but it is another when your sour disposition starts working against your own goals.

Norton felt he had been put in this position to fix things, not to de-clare 1st Platoon unfixable, as Gallagher was doing. Emotionally, 1st Pla-toon was frayed, there was no question about it. But tactically, Norton felt, they were not that bad. They still got up every morning and they went on patrols and they completed their missions. They needed a huge attitude readjustment, obviously. Norton was trying to get the guys to focus more on the Iraqis as people, to consider that man over there as not just another fucking Hadji but as Ali, who owns a falafel shop and loves his kids and has problems because he needs to get to Baghdad and back every week to buy restaurant supplies.

"I really had to work to convince them, 'Dude, not everybody out here needs to be killed. Not everybody needs to get the crap kicked out of him. In fact, beating the crap out of people is wrong, you know? Geneva Conventions? Look it up. It's a concept.' " Norton thought that getting the men to change their focus was an achievable goal, but he was certain that if Gallagher really wanted to get 1st Platoon yanked to the rear, he wasn't going about it the right way. "Gallagher vocalized it too emotionally and not tactfully at all," Norton explained, "so it was easy for them to say, 'Oh, he's just throwing fuel on their fire.' "

Around this time, Miller headed up to Striker for a week or so to get a chipped tooth fixed. While there, he started looking for a new job without telling Kunk or Edwards. He bumped into Staff Sergeant Chaz Allen, who was in Battalion's liaison office with Brigade and was itching to see more action. "I told him that it was rough down there," Miller re-called. "I asked him what his plans were. He said he was trying to get down there. I asked him did he want to swap?" Allen was all for it. He had been to Kosovo, but he hadn't deployed for OIF1, so he was eager to get back down on the line.

Second Brigade's Command Sergeant Major Brian Stall called Edwards to say, Miller is up here wanting to know if I have a job for him. This was not a move Kunk took kindly. "Instead of looking us in the eye, like a leader should, and being honest and straightforward, and telling your command sergeant major and your battalion commander that you can't do the job, or that you're burned out, or that you might be under stress, he went fishing for a job," he said.

Miller didn't see it that way. "I wasn't going to let someone determine my fate," he stated. "I wasn't going to be held responsible for my guys dying if I wasn't getting the support I needed to prevent it from happening. I think I had the leadership ability to get them through, after all the casualties we were taking. Maybe not. But if they had said you're the platoon sergeant and you're staying the platoon sergeant, then, roger that, I would have Charlie Miked," he said, using Army slang for "Continued Mission." "I will take the responsibility for every casualty when I was in charge. If they want to blame me, then so be it. Those were my guys. And they still are, whether they're here today or six feet below. But to blame me, and make me a squad leader, and still keep me around in the same platoon? No, that ain't gonna cut it."

After rotating down to the JSB for the first time, Gallagher assessed the Alamo bridge as even more dangerous a position than the TCPs, and he pulled his men off of it. How to properly treat the AVLB had been a controversial issue throughout the year and would continue to be so for the rest of the deployment. The battalion's order was to "secure" it. According to the U.S. Army's *Field Manual 3-90: Tactics*, "secure" means to prevent a unit or facility from being damaged or destroyed by the enemy. Obviously, there are a number of ways to secure something, a point that Operations Officer Rob Salome said he consistently tried to impress upon Captain Goodwin. "I don't have to physically have my hand on something to secure it," he pointed out. "I can secure it by fire or overwatch or with a patrol, not necessarily by occupation. John didn't understand those critical pieces of those definitions, so he couldn't articulate those to his NCOs either."

Kunk asserted that it was possible to see the Alamo from the JSB patrol base's crow's nest and thus it was securable from there. Everyone else disputed this. The bridge may have been technically visible, but sight lines were not clear enough to make it securable, especially at night, especially since there were recessed routes to the bridge via the canal banks that could be checked only from very close distances. Before late June 2006 the battalion never issued written guidance to Goodwin on how the position should be manned, rationalizing that squad-level staffing decisions are customarily a company commander's job. Goodwin, for his part, never issued any kind of guidance to the platoons. "I let the platoons figure out their staffing down there," Goodwin said.

So it is unclear who ordered Gallagher back out to the bridge, and it is unclear whether he received instructions that he had to have men literally on top of it, but he was under the impression he had no choice. "I had to send people back out there," he explained. "So I sat my best NCOs down and told them these are dangerous missions. I told them what could happen if they go out and not do the right thing. 'You need to be on your guys' ass. You need to not be fucking around, or these will be the implications if you do not obey,' I told them. 'You will be on Al Jazeera getting your head chopped off.' "

Second and 3rd Platoons found other ways of securing the bridge without always having men standing next to it. Sometimes 2nd Platoon would run patrols down there, or they would overwatch it from an ambush spot, or they would just run a Humvee back and forth from TCP4 to the AVLB to the JSB and back at irregular intervals. Blaisdell would employ all of these tactics as well, saying that he never put a Humvee down there in exactly the same location twice. He used the truck, he said, "like a roving TCP."

Regardless of how they varied the detail, it was still common for there to be just two to four men and a truck guarding the AVLB. No one passing by, from Brigade on down, ever corrected them. Captain Shawn Umbrell and other company commanders said the staffing down there was common knowledge. "Sometime in November or December, I remember in a meeting being briefed that the truck at the

AVLB took some small-arms fire," Umbrell recalled. "And I think they said there were like four guys at that position with one truck. And that was the first I heard of it. And I remember thinking, 'Holy cow! We're manning a TCP that shorthanded? Four guys in one truck?' I'm looking around and trying to gauge the looks on other people's faces, and I don't recall Colonel Kunk ever saying, 'That's unsatisfactory. You need to up the numbers down there.' But I remember hearing Colonel Kunk talking later, 'I never knew we had three or four guys!' And I'm thinking, 'What do you mean, you never knew? We all knew.' "

Their relationship already strained, Sergeant Major Edwards and Sergeant First Class Gallagher almost came to blows in January. An Iraqi base was being constructed adjacent to the JSB, which required earthmovers, bulldozers, dump trucks, and other heavy support machinery. On the day Edwards came to visit, it had also been raining. There was not enough room at the JSB to harbor all this equipment and the terrain was messy, so the place was sloppy.

"I think what upset him the most was when his PSD came in—because he had a large entourage, there was not enough room for him to move around," Gallagher said. "His discomfort getting in prompted much of this." Edwards sought out Gallagher and began to berate him about how messy the JSB was. He was especially irritated that he had also seen some soldiers relaxing, playing a video game. This was not the first time that Gallagher had heard Edwards's concerns about tidiness, but he frankly thought they were misplaced and mistimed, and, given everything that was going on, he had less patience for Edwards's yelling than ever before.

"I am not really worried about trash right now, Sergeant Major," Gallagher replied. "I am worried about my guys getting some rest." Edwards did not like that response and started to yell some more, so Gallagher volunteered to go pick up the trash himself rather than disturb the men. He started walking around plucking cigarette butts out of the mud. This response was also not acceptable. The discussion, according to Gallagher, went downhill quickly, turning personal and almost degenerating into a physical altercation. "The conversation was very volatile, and I took some offense to the fact that the conversation degraded to a nonprofessional basis," Gallagher said.

Not long after Gallagher's run-in with Edwards, he tangled with Green, who had continued his downward slide. No one thought he was an exceptional soldier, but he was not terrible. While not extraordinarily brave, Green was no coward, either. He never ducked a combat mission or froze under fire. But his performance and his attitude, even his hygiene, were declining rapidly. Many in the platoon, when they thought about him at all, were split on whether he was just a little messed up or a turd through and through. Some could not countenance all his talk about blacks or Jews or his increasingly frequent assertions that they should lay waste to the entire country. Others admit to having an odd kind of affection for him, like a disturbed, runty little brother they wanted to protect.

Lieutenant Norton remembered having a couple of late-night bull sessions with him as he made the rounds checking on guard positions. "He was very mad with everything that happened," Norton said, "but the more you talked to him, the more you realized just how demented his thinking was. Pretty much everybody besides himself was bad. Democrats were bad. Republicans were bad. JFK was an idiot. Abraham Lincoln was a dumb ass. Everybody outside of his town in Texas was an idiot. But then, all the people inside of his town were idiots too. 'If we just killed everybody in Iraq,' he'd say, 'we could go home.' In conversation, he'd come around and see that, no, we can't kill everyone. In fact, we need to be nicer to Iraqis than they are to us. But it was like *Groundhog Day*. The next day, it was back to 'Everybody's a dumb ass. Everybody deserves to die.' "

Gallagher could not figure out why the NCOs allowed Green to coast by on lower standards than those applied to everyone else. On this particular day in late January, when the whole platoon was back in Yusufiyah, Gallagher was especially high-strung. He was getting in everybody's face about rolling down their sleeves, cleaning their area, making sure stuff was picked up. Lauzier grabbed a toothbrush and started scrubbing away on a doorjamb or a piece of equipment in elaborate and mocking protest against Gallagher being so fussy. Green walked by, with sunglasses atop his off-kilter cap, his ACU top unzipped, and his trousers slung low, almost falling off his butt. Gallagher could not believe what he was seeing. The lack of discipline, the insolence, the completely unsoldierly bearing were simply dumbfounding to him. The final outrage: The crotch of Green's pants was ripped and his genitals were exposed.

"Green, get the fuck over here!" Gallagher bellowed. "What is your motherfucking problem, son? You had better get your uniform straight or I will kick your ass." He told Green to hit the floor and start doing push-ups. Green grudgingly did so as Gallagher continued to upbraid him for his slovenly appearance. "You are a fucking scumbag, Green, you know that?" Gallagher yelled. The word "scumbag" hit a nerve. Green popped up and stepped to Gallagher.

"I'm a scumbag?" he screamed. "Fuck you, you fucking bitch!" Incensed and eyes wide at this insubordination, Gallagher squared his chest to Green, whom he outweighed by at least sixty pounds, and shook his pointed finger to the side of his face, in the classic drill-sergeant pose. He yelled every syllable ponderously.

"Stand down, Private. Get yourself squared away, Green, or you will regret it."

"Oh yeah? Let's go, right now!" Green yelled. "You want to make it personal? Well, come on, motherfucker, let's go." Gallagher was again dumbfounded. He had never experienced anything remotely like this. "I seriously contemplated, after eighteen years in the Army, throwing away my career to physically abuse him," Gallagher later recalled. They stepped up to each other even closer, chest to chest, a ridiculous picture because Gallagher outsized Green in every way.

"Do it, motherfucker!" Green continued to yell. "Come on, motherfucker, do it!" Squad leaders and others leapt to separate the two. As soldiers pulled Green away and led him off, he shouted behind him, "You are driving me crazy! You are driving us all fucking crazy!" Green pushed his rescuers away and stormed off, hurling expletives as he went. Before leaving the room, he swung a kick at a pallet of one-liter water bottles, but he missed completely, the momentum of his leg throwing him up and over, and he landed on his back with a thud. "Goddammit!" he shouted as he pulled himself up and continued to curse as he sulked off. Some soldiers rushed off to console Green, while others talked to Gallagher, trying to convince him that Green was a unique case who needed special handling.

Gallagher had tried to be tolerant considering everything 1st Platoon had seen, but this was way over the line. He went to First Sergeant Laskoski to get Green removed from the platoon. "I required him to take all of his belongings and all of his gear and get it out of our platoon area, because I didn't want him associating with any of my soldiers," said Gallagher. After hearing about the altercation, Laskoski gave Green an administrative job up at the TOC where he didn't have much contact with the rest of 1st Platoon.

As part of a broader battalion strategy, Bravo started running more frequent missions to the west, toward a small town called Rushdi Mullah. Lieutenant Norton and Captain Goodwin planned a platoonwide mission into the nearby town of Al-Toraq, which is about three miles northwest of Yusufiyah. Norton and Goodwin would go with the main effort and Gallagher would stay behind with the support and relief element. They would push out from TCP5 and head down Mullah Fayyad Highway. The main element was to move into town while the support element would pull off and wait until the mission was over.

Reviewing the map, Goodwin told Gallagher, "You are good up to this point on Mullah Fayyad Highway. But at this intersection, turn right and stay off the road. We will call you. Head east and we will link up with you there." He lost count, he said, of how many times he told Gallagher: "Do not drive on Mullah Fayyad Highway past this point. If you go past this point, you're going to die."

They headed out after nightfall and a firefight took place. Some insurgents shot at them. They returned fire. Nobody hit anybody, but the platoon searched several houses and detained three men. As they were leaving, Norton called Gallagher to meet at the linkup point. Through his night-vision goggles, however, Goodwin could see vehicles way past the no-go line and headed in the wrong direction. A soldier in Gallagher's convoy said, "He took us down this road, up to these fields, and everywhere in the world. We're driving Humvees through fields in the middle of the night like a bunch of morons. It was a mess."

"Rob," Goodwin called over the radio, "where you at?"

"I don't know," Gallagher responded. "I'm lost." Goodwin couldn't tell which road, if any, Gallagher was on either, but he could see the convoy crawling back and forth. Goodwin was getting worried, and angry. They were overdue for the pickup, and now the men were just sitting there, a juicy, stationary target. A mosque's speaker system crackled to life.

Goodwin's translator listened and said, "That is not a call to prayer. It is telling people that we are here. They know we are here." Goodwin radioed some Apache helicopters that he had on call.

"Hey, can you see my Humvees?" he asked.

"Roger," came the reply.

"Can you direct them to our linkup point?" Goodwin gave the Apaches the grid coordinates, and over the next couple of minutes, the helicopters guided Gallagher back to Goodwin.

As they were waiting, Goodwin said to Norton, "Were we not perfectly clear?" Both Goodwin and Norton had seen enough. They knew that Edwards had been displeased with Gallagher from the start, but after a potentially life-endangering operational screwup like that, Goodwin decided he was not taking any chances.

Goodwin told Laskoski, "Hey, go talk to Sergeant Major. I need another platoon sergeant." Laskoski responded that that would not be a problem, since Edwards had wanted Gallagher gone within the first three days.

Even before Goodwin demanded a new sergeant, Edwards had been telling Brigade Sergeant Major Stall that things were still not clicking with 1st Platoon. Edwards wondered who else was available. Stall had an idea. How about Fenlason? Jeff Fenlason was a thirty-seven-year-old sergeant first class from Springfield, Massachusetts, who had just moved from the brigade MiTT office to its Civilian Affairs shop up at Striker. How about him? He'd just had a little problem with his previous boss, which is what facilitated his most recent move, but overall he had a reputation as a good logistician, an organized administrator, and a meticulous planner. He was Ranger qualified and he had been a drill instructor, so he knew a thing or two about discipline. And he'd done a good job in 2004 and 2005 as first sergeant setting up Echo Company, First Strike's support company, so he was already a known entity to the rest of the battalion. Kunk, in fact, had known Fenlason since 1993 and considered him very much what Kunk liked to call "an engaged leader."

Blaisdell and Gebhardt thought 2nd and 3rd Platoons had a couple of strong staff sergeants who could step up, but after Miller, Edwards felt 1st Platoon needed a sergeant first class. Blaisdell even volunteered to take the platoon, which might have happened, Edwards told him, if he wasn't running 3rd Platoon without a lieutenant.

Several times throughout the winter, First Sergeant Laskoski had also offered to take over 1st Platoon. In several regards, he seemed like an ideal candidate. He had been with this deployment from the beginning, so he had extensive combat experience, and he had seen firsthand all of the losses that 1st Platoon had suffered. But as an outsider, he also maintained a certain psychological distance that Gallagher and Miller didn't have. He felt the losses that they had suffered, but he did not dwell on them. The men may not have loved Laskoski, but they respected him. "I tried my damnedest to take that damn platoon," he recalled. "I don't think any of the platoon sergeants that they had made them understand what the hell they were doing there, and how important it was. They just needed the right frigging dude in there." The higher ranks discussed the merits of Laskoski versus Fenlason, but they decided to keep Laskoski where he was and put Fenlason, who had never been a platoon sergeant before, down with 1st Platoon.

Second Squad leader Chris Payne had gotten to know Fenlason when they were stationed at Fort Campbell together during OIF1 and found him to be a canny careerist, always aware of résumé gaps and how best to fill them. Payne had just arrived on base in August 2003, and even though it was late in the 101st Airborne Division's first rotation of the war, he was eager to get to Iraq.

"Whoa, slow down," Fenlason said. "What's your situation?" Payne, then a sergeant, told him that he had just gotten married and he had a child at home, but he had talked to his wife and she supported his desire to deploy. Fenlason wanted to know if Payne had been to Primary Leadership Development Course (PLDC), a school he needed to attend to get promoted again. Payne hadn't. Fenlason told him, "You need to go to PLDC now so that you have the chance to get promoted if the opportunity comes about." And that, said Payne, taught him a lot about Fenlason's perspective. "He's very much, 'I'm going to make sure that I have my ducks in a row, so that if the opportunity for me to advance comes along, I will be ready for it.'"

Fenlason's briefing from Stall was short but direct. Stall told him his charter was to fix a platoon that had been hit by several leaders' deaths and was now suffering from low morale and bad discipline.

"Go down there and just do the basics," Stall told Fenlason. "Don't pull anything special, don't try any heroics, just get the platoon back on its feet."

"What's the issue with the platoon sergeant down there now?" Fenlason asked.

"Sergeant Gallagher is all about Sergeant Gallagher, and not necessarily taking care of the platoon," Stall replied. "Go do what you do." Fenlason, who never betrayed any doubts about his own abilities, leadership style, or decisions, knew he was up to the job. "I knew what I needed to do and I knew how to do it," he said. "It wasn't difficult. I knew exactly where we needed to go and exactly how we were going to get there."

If the battalion's decision to plug Gallagher back into 1st Platoon had raised eyebrows, the brigade's decision to tap Fenlason was downright shocking. The Army tries to cultivate a culture of universal proficiency, but the fact remains that not every officer or NCO is good at

every task. Among the most persistent skills split is that between "line
guys" and "staff guys." Fenlason was the consummate staff guy. He had
spent most of his career in support positions and did not have any combat experience. Before this deployment, his only foreign posting during
his fifteen-year career had been a one-year tour to South Korea in the
late 1990s. He'd spent all of OIF1 at Fort Campbell as 2nd Brigade's
rear detachment NCO in charge and the four months of this deployment up at Striker.

"He helped stand up Echo Company as their first sergeant," commented HHC commander Shawn Umbrell. "But he didn't have a platoon for very specific reasons. Some guys are not platoon sergeants for
a reason. And now we're sticking him in there, in combat? It didn't
make any sense." Charlie's First Sergeant Largent, as usual, was blunter.
"The reason we take NCOs and put them in jobs away from soldiers is
generally because they can't lead soldiers," he said. "You can type fast,
you can do your computer stuff, you can follow orders, and that's great.
But following orders and being an effective leader of men in combat
are so far apart it's not even funny. Fenlason should never, ever, have
been put in charge of soldiers in combat."

Some members of 1st Platoon said the ongoing shuffle of platoon
sergeants was just proof that the chain of command was not taking 1st
Platoon's problems seriously. "I'm just a sergeant," remarked John
Diem, "but I would say this: If we had really gotten what the Army calls
'inspired leadership,' if someone had honestly taken the time to seriously fix 1st Platoon, they wouldn't have just sent a sergeant first class
with a gun to his head to do it without any support. They wouldn't have
just sent a lone lieutenant to make the impossible happen. They have a
lot of tools and a lot of flexibility up there that they did not use. Because
the 'basics' shit wasn't working. And when soldiers start to feel isolated,
throwing a new platoon sergeant down there is just going to isolate them
more. And if every time you go down to see your soldiers, you tell them
that they're fucked up, then guess what? They don't want to see you anymore. And they will do just enough to not get your attention. But they
aren't going to trust in you as a commander, and as a leader you have

no influence. And when the formal chain of command breaks down, the informal command steps up, and then you are entering dangerous territory, because nobody has any idea where the informal leaders will take the group."

Gallagher knew that his superiors didn't think he was getting off to a strong start. He knew that something needed to be done, and he was entertaining several different ideas about how to fix the situation. On February 1, 2006, a little over a month since Gallagher had returned to 1st Platoon, First Sergeant Laskoski called him into his office. Gallagher was expecting a frank discussion about how to knock things back on course. But when he entered, Sergeant Major Edwards and Staff Sergeant Miller were both there already as well. Obviously, something was afoot. Edwards and Laskoski got straight to the point: Miller and Gallagher were being moved to new jobs, effective immediately.

In his final analysis, Gallagher felt he, and the platoon, were being punished because he wouldn't stop telling his superiors things they didn't want to hear.

"Essentially," he concluded, "it was easier to move me than to satisfy me."

Traffic Control Point 1. Bravo Company seized this house on the corner of Routes Sportster and Peggy in November 2005 and turned it into a patrol base. *(Courtesy of Christopher Thielenhaus)*

A Bravo Company soldier on the way from Yusufiyah to Rushdi Mullah, walking across a pipe spanning a dry, overgrown canal bed. *(Courtesy of Phil Blaisdell)*

Specialist James Barker embraces Sergeant Kenith Casica at the JSB Patrol Base, October 2005. The grill was the only kitchen the platoon had. *(Courtesy of Eric Lauzier)*

Lieutenant Benjamin Britt, leader of Bravo Company's 1st Platoon. Behind Britt is Staff Sergeant Travis Nelson.
(Courtesy of Eric Lauzier)

An Iraqi boy placing an IED—several small artillery shells in a yellow plastic bag—into a cardboard box. The boy was unaware that a U.S. soldier was in the vehicle behind him photographing the act.
(Courtesy of Phil Blaisdell)

Wreckage of a 2nd Platoon Humvee that hit an IED on December 19, 2005, driven by Specialist Noah Galloway.
(Courtesy of Christopher Thielenhaus)

Captain John Goodwin, Bravo
Company Commander, outside
at FOB Yusufiyah.
*(Courtesy of Christopher Thielen-
haus)*

Lieutenant Colonel Thomas Kunk, commander of the 1-502nd Infantry Regiment
during its 2005–2006 deployment to Iraq,
arriving for the trial of Steven Green in
Paducah, Kentucky, in April 2009. *(AP)*

Staff Sergeant Phil Miller, 1st Platoon's platoon
sergeant from the beginning of deployment in
October 2005 until early February 2006.
(Courtesy of Eric Lauzier)

Sergeant First Class Rob Gallagher was brought on board in late December 2005 to put the ailing 1st Platoon back on course. He lasted barely thirty days. *(Courtesy of Eric Lauzier)*

Sergeant First Class Phil Blaisdell (left), platoon sergeant for Bravo Company's 3rd Platoon, and Staff Sergeant Christopher Arnold, a 3rd Platoon squad leader. Both Blaisdell and Arnold fought in the February 1 firefight at Rushdi Mullah, a skirmish that brought new attention to Bravo's western territory. *(Courtesy of Phil Blaisdell)*

Staff Sergeant Eric Lauzier, leader of 3rd Squad, 1st Platoon, Bravo Company. *(Courtesy of Eric Lauzier)*

Sergeant Anthony Yribe at Fort Campbell before deployment. *(Courtesy of Eric Lauzier)*

Sergeant John Diem, Alpha Team leader of 2nd Squad, 1st Platoon, Bravo Company. *(Courtesy of Eric Lauzier)*

Private Justin Watt on patrol with 3rd Squad. *(Courtesy of Eric Lauzier)*

First Lieutenant Tim Norton (left) and Sergeant First Class Jeffrey Fenlason, 1st Platoon's platoon leader and platoon sergeant. *(Courtesy of Eric Lauzier)*

Private First Class Christopher Barnes (left) and Private First Class Steven Green. *(Courtesy of Eric Lauzier)*

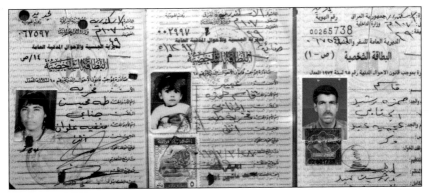

Identification cards issued by the Iraqi government show Fakhriah Taha Mahsin al-Janabi (left), Qassim Hamzah Rashid al-Janabi (right), and their elder daughter, Abeer, who were all murdered by U.S. soldiers on March 12, 2006. No ID card of the fourth family member killed, six-year-old Hadeel, is known to exist. *(Reuters)*

A photo taken by U.S. Army investigators of the living room of the Janabi house, where Abeer was raped and murdered. Although the house was deserted by July 2006, the scorch marks where Abeer was burned remained. *(Courtesy of Steven Green defense team)*

Abeer Qassim al-Janabi, in an undated photo, who was raped and murdered by U.S. soldiers on March 12, 2006, when she was fourteen years old. *(AP)*

Specialist Paul Cortez's mugshot.
(Courtesy of Steven Green defense team)

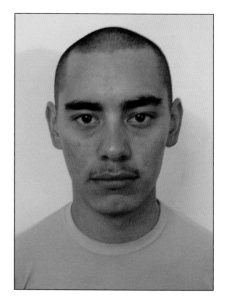

Specialist James Barker's mugshot.
(Courtesy of Steven Green defense team)

Private First Class Jesse Spielman's
mugshot. *(Courtesy of Steven Green
defense team)*

Former Private First Class Steven
Green's mugshot at the Mecklenburg
County jail in Charlotte, North Car-
olina, July 3, 2006. *(AP)*

FEBRUARY 2006

16

February 1

WORD ABOUT GOODWIN'S office habits was getting around the battalion. He rarely left the TOC. Almost daily, he would fall asleep in his chair.

When one of the other captains visited, they would say, "Hey, man, you need to get to your hooch. You need to get out of here at least a little bit."

"But I can't leave the radio," he'd say. "What if someone calls?"

"John, your rack is right there," they'd reply. "They will come and get you if they need you. That's the way it works." Usually passing out just before dawn, sometimes he wouldn't wake up until 10:00 a.m. He looked unhealthy. He said he didn't have time to eat. His eyes were vacant, hollowed out. His own men, ranks as low as private, were worried about him.

Kunk saw that Goodwin had the famous battle-fatigued "thousand-yard stare." Kunk had already tried to remove Goodwin from command several times, but Ebel wouldn't sign off on it. Keep working with him, Ebel told Kunk. Work with what you have.

"I think you need a break, John," Kunk told Goodwin. "I am sending you up to Freedom Rest for a few days." During Vietnam, soldiers on

R&R got to go to Saigon, or even Hong Kong. These days, however, they went to a former Iraqi Army officers' club in the Green Zone called Freedom Rest. The complex could accommodate 135 soldiers on four-day passes in the closest thing Baghdad had to four-star-hotel standards. There was still no alcohol, but the food was good, the cotton sheets were clean, the climate control always worked, and a giant, immaculately chlorinated pool featured an array of Olympic-standard diving boards.

"Thanks very much, sir, but I don't want to go," Goodwin responded. "I'd rather stay here with my men."

"I am not giving you the option to decline, John."

On the evening of January 29, Goodwin caught a Black Hawk to LZ (landing zone) Washington in the center of the Green Zone and got a ride to Freedom Rest. He could not believe his eyes. Although the perimeters of the Green Zone were well defended, the interior of the heart of Baghdad was not. It was the only place in the country that even approximated normal city life anywhere else in the world. People, even Western civilians, were just walking around, unarmed, as if it were nothing. Goodwin's Yusufiyah alert system was still firing. "Where is the security?" he wondered. Most of the vehicles were soft-skinned cars and SUVs. He looked around and saw undefended lines of sight, ideal perches for snipers, and innumerable points on the roadside that would be perfect places to hide an IED. "This place is a death trap," he thought. "Oh my God, I am gonna die here."

Goodwin checked in and, as was standard, left all of his gear at the front desk. He went to his room and fell asleep immediately, but only fitfully, waking at 3:00 a.m., again at 4:00, again at 5:00. With morning finally arriving, he headed off for breakfast. Every time a helicopter passed overhead, he'd tense up, waiting for it to take fire. Every time he heard a shot, no matter how far off, he'd jolt. But after going for a swim, talking to his wife over IM, and reading a little, he was, by the end of his first full day, starting to unwind, actually starting to relax. By the second day, he was feeling even better. Hanging out, eating good food, not worrying so much for the first time in months. On the third day, February 1, he woke up refreshed and in a good mood, looking forward to the day. "Maybe things are looking up," he thought.

At 8:45 a.m., 3rd Platoon's Sergeant Daniel Carrick was leading his fire team on an IED sweep down Sportster when they spotted a suspicious object. They called it in to Explosive Ordnance Disposal (EOD) to do a controlled detonation. EOD said they needed confirmation that it was really an IED before heading out there. Carrick knew what was going to happen. He and another soldier walked up to it to get a better look, and it blew up on them. Carrick broke his finger and the other soldier suffered a herniated left calf.

A 1st Platoon convoy was nearby. Carrick's finger needed an X-ray at Mahmudiyah, so the 1st Platoon men ferried him over. After Carrick got his knuckle looked at, 1st Platoon was hurrying-up-and-waiting around the motor pool to drive back to Yusufiyah. Kunk walked by.

"How you all doing?" Kunk asked. There were inconclusive, unhappy mutterings.

"Except for getting blown up twenty-four/seven, we're just fine," went one response.

"Pretty shitty, sir," went another.

Kunk was not in the mood for bad attitudes. Surprisingly often, Kunk would discipline lower-ranked soldiers directly, and even more surprisingly, those sessions would frequently turn into profanity-laced arguments with entire squads or platoons that disintegrated into wide-ranging castigations of all the soldiers' faults. This was one of those times.

"You are getting blown up because you are not following the proper tactics and procedures," he declared. He upbraided Bravo Company for not doing their IED clearances as well as Alpha Company. He invoked the deaths of Britt and Lopez, saying they were dead because they hadn't cleared the route well. The men responded with a furious outpouring of ire, shouting that Britt had wanted to clear the route but he had been denied. Kunk pronounced this claim to be bullshit. He looked at Carrick. "What the fuck happened to you today?" he demanded. "What the fuck were you doing? Probably just walking down the fucking street not paying attention."

Carrick flushed with anger. "I did everything by the book, sir," he said. "EOD told me to get closer."

"Bullshit!" Kunk yelled. "You were not following the proper tactics, the proper methods."

"Fuck you, sir," Carrick said, walking off as the men from 1st Platoon continued the row.

Sergeant First Class Blaisdell was at Yusufiyah trying to get a mission under way. A few days earlier, they had caught some suspicious types driving around and found several weapons in their truck, boxes of propaganda, a few artillery shells, and a handheld GPS device. Today, Blaisdell and parts of 3rd Platoon were planning on investigating some of the coordinates they had pulled off that GPS, a couple of spots in and around Rushdi Mullah. But the IED that took out Carrick had left him shorthanded a fire team. He spotted Lieutenant Norton.

"Oh, hey, sir, how you doing?" he said.

"Hey, Blaisdell, what's up? I heard what happened. Your guys okay?"

"Just a few scrapes. Everybody will be fine. Hey, you ever been to Rushdi?"

"Never been."

"You wanna come?"

"Yeah, sure."

"Dude, I need a favor. Can you get like five guys? Because we're strapped with all those guys back at Mahmudiyah getting checked out."

"Yeah, I think I can work it." Norton found his platoon. "Hey, I need a fire team to do this joint mission with 3rd Platoon."

"Why?" some of them muttered. "They never help us. Fuck them." Jesus, Norton thought, typical.

"Look, I am not playing this game," Norton said. "We're not rolling like that anymore. Bravo is Bravo, period, and we help each other out. So, who's with me?"

Sergeant Roman Diaz volunteered, along with Specialist David Babineau, Specialist Thomas Doss, and Specialist James Gregory. They talked to Bravo and battalion commands and wrote up the order. Everybody headed to TCP1 to stage. They prepped their gear and checked the maps and Blaisdell briefed the men.

"You like it?" he asked Norton about the plan.

"Love it," Norton said. Norton held the superior rank, but this mission was Blaisdell's show. Norton would be overseeing Diaz's fire team, but Blaisdell was calling the shots.

Leaving at around 3:00 p.m., they started walking the three miles toward town. Norton's five-man fire team split off and veered to the west to investigate one set of coordinates, toward what the map suggested was a farmhouse. They would inspect the scene, a suspected cache site, and also lie in wait and support two 3rd Platoon fire teams, led by Staff Sergeant Chris Arnold and Staff Sergeant Joe Whelchel, who all continued toward the other grid closer to town. Rounding out Blaisdell's crew were a handful of IAs and an interpreter. In a decision that would be second-guessed later, Blaisdell did not bring a medic.

Norton arrived at the farmhouse quickly. As his team approached, two men jumped into a blue hatchback, peeled out of the driveway, and sped off. Diaz asked if they should shoot.

Norton told him to hold fire, "but let's get to that house, call Blais, and tell him that car might be coming his way." They half knocked on, half barged in the door and, typically, the only person there was an older woman. She was flustered and upset. Norton had studied Arabic in college, and after spending four months in country, he knew how to say most of the important questions. And while he couldn't follow the paragraph-long answers he frequently received, he could usually get the gist.

"Who just left in that car?" he asked.

The woman started talking and did not stop: "Car? . . . What car? . . . I don't know what you're talking about. . . ."

"The car we just saw leave. Where's the man of the house?"

"He's not here . . . gone . . . long time. . . ." Her favorite phrase was "maku," which means "there's isn't any." She repeated it often. Norton told the men to search the house. They found a CD hidden in some blankets, but they had no idea what was on it, and an AK-47, which was not incriminating because U.S. policy allowed every family to have one rifle. Then they uncovered some propaganda leaflets, a laminating machine, and other ID-making equipment. All of which was more suspicious, but not worth arresting a fifty-year-old woman over.

Norton ordered Gregory and Diaz to dismantle the weapon, take the ammo, and start searching the field out back while he continued to talk to the woman. Don't go far, he told them, no more than seventy-five meters out. They went outside and less than a minute later—dit, dit, dit—rounds from what sounded like a machine gun started hitting around the house.

"Jesus Christ!" Norton exclaimed. "Babineau," he said, "get Blaisdell on the radio and see what is going on," and he headed out the back door to find Gregory and Diaz.

As Babineau was trying to call Blaisdell, Blaisdell and the men of 3rd Platoon were diving for cover. Insurgents had set up at least two firing positions with multiple men each. They had pinpointed both U.S. elements and had opened fire on them simultaneously. This was a sophisticated group. Minutes ago, 3rd Platoon had reached their target house and taken it down flawlessly. Whelchel and his fire team kicked in the door and secured the family inside, some women and an old man, quickly and with no violence, while Arnold and his fire team secured the perimeter. As Arnold set up a hasty traffic control point on the road about a hundred and fifty yards from the house, he noticed a woman walking with a couple of her cows. A few moments later, he watched her split off from her cattle, leaving them in the road as she ducked into a house's courtyard. Uh-oh, Arnold thought.

The rest of Blaisdell's men had searched the house and were digging around the yard and scanning it with a metal detector, but they weren't finding anything. "We were getting ready to go," said Blaisdell, "when the world just fucking erupted with machine gun fire." Some soldiers ran up to the roof to see where the shots were coming from. The shooters were northwest a couple of hundred yards. "I think we stumbled upon some kind of meeting, and they got scared thinking we were there to raid them," Blaisdell said. "We weren't even planning to go anywhere past those two objectives. My guys by the road said a bunch of cars started taking off when the firing started. I think they left a fire team back just to deal with us, pretty much to die in place if we decided to fight them." There were several gunmen, perhaps many gunmen, on the move and shooting straight down the street.

Whelchel, Specialist Kirk Reilly, Specialist Anthony "Chad" Owens, and Specialist Jay Strobino started to maneuver to the shooters, who seemed to be consolidating at a house farther up the road. Whelchel's fire team headed out of the house and met up with Arnold and his men, who were behind a berm. From that position, Arnold had been able to set up a base of return fire. As they were talking about next moves, they saw a heavily armed fighter run across the street toward the house. Several of them opened fire, but the man successfully scampered to his destination.

With Arnold's guys laying down more covering fire, Whelchel, Strobino, and Reilly crossed the street and headed toward the new target house. Blaisdell and the rest of his men joined Arnold's support position. Sneaking down a back alley, Whelchel's team stumbled upon an old man cowering behind the external staircase of his house. Trembling, he gestured one house over. They approached that house, which had a large hedgerow too thick to bowl through, so Strobino flung himself over the top. Landing in the corner of the yard, he could see two insurgents milling around a Toyota pickup, no more than fifty yards away. They were walking arsenals, wearing suicide vests and carrying AKs. There was another insurgent in the pickup bed loading it with mortars, RPGs, and packs of explosives. Past them was the side of the house. Reilly and Whelchel were trying to make it over the hedge, while Strobino's mind went into overdrive. "My guys are making too much noise," he thought. "But I can't tell them to shut up, 'cause these Hadjis will hear me. But it'll take too many shots to get them all before one of them gets me." All he could do, he decided, was to try to catch one of his buddies' eyes, while also hoping one of them got over the hedge quickly and quietly.

Outside the farmhouse, Norton found Diaz and Gregory, prone and returning fire toward multiple muzzle flashes a few hundred yards away. Norton wanted to flank them to the west. He told Diaz and Gregory to keep occupying the shooters.

"We don't know where Blais is," Norton yelled, "so watch where you're shooting! Only shoot at targets you can hit!" He grabbed Doss, planning to head west to the back of the field and then hook hard north and open another position of fire on them. Doss and Norton started running through the farm, which was like an open manger. Within a few strides, they were covered in manure from a variety of species. Rounds started zinging around their heads, too. "Shit," thought Norton, "more gunmen than I thought!" Norton changed course and doubled back to where Diaz and Gregory were. Just as he approached them—fwomp, kaboom—a rifle-mounted grenade shell exploded right behind them, knocking Norton and Doss off their feet. Norton didn't like this at all. The four of them were exposed in an open field and they had accurate fire bearing down on them.

"Get back, get back to the house!" he yelled. "Break contact, break contact!" They withdrew in twos, with Diaz and Gregory laying fire while Norton and Doss headed back to the house, and then Norton and Doss firing as Diaz and Gregory backed up. "Babineau! You got Blaisdell yet?" Norton asked. They could hear multiple explosions, more than several distinct rifles and machine guns firing in the distance.

"I ain't got shit," said Babineau.

The two insurgents outside the pickup turned to talk to each other, and something Strobino's way caught their attention. Just as they turned, Strobino opened fire on them both. Both men went down, just as Whelchel dropped down beside Strobino and opened fire on the man in the truck's flatbed. One of the downed men was still going, reaching for his weapon. Whelchel shot him several more times. As Reilly heaved over the hedge, Whelchel and Strobino saw an AK muzzle and two hands poke around the corner of the house and spray them with fire. They all hit the ground.

Whelchel said, "I'm going to throw a grenade."

Strobino said, "I'll follow." Whelchel untaped it, pulled the pin, and lobbed it over to the front of the house. The moment after it exploded, Strobino sprinted to the wall of the house flush with them, while Whelchel and Reilly ran as far as the truck. His back against the wall, Strobino could see Whelchel and Reilly in front of him, behind the truck. Peeking around the corner to the front of the house, he could see a small piece of the insurgent's muzzle poking out the front door. He thought for a second that he could sneak along the front wall and grab the muzzle while shooting the guy by holding his own rifle like a pistol. But there was a large front window between the corner and the door that the insurgent could see him through. He snapped back around the corner to think.

Whelchel yelled, "Is he there?"

Strobino gave him a shut-the-fuck-up face and whisper-yelled, "Yeah, he's right fucking there!" Strobino's split-second plan: Speed. He'd jump around the corner as fast as he could, never mind the window, and maybe he'd have time to slap the barrel out of the way long enough to get a shot off. He put his M4 on its three-round-burst setting and flung himself around the corner. He almost bumped into the insurgent, who had also decided on a bold frontal attack. Strobino got his shots off first, and the three rounds knocked the man backward. As the man fell away, he pulled his own trigger, spraying Strobino with bullets. Strobino caught one bullet in the forearm and his hand involuntarily flung his weapon away. He took another bullet to his leg that snapped his femur, so the very next step he took backwards, his momentum carried him around the corner, but he fell to the ground, landing on top of one of the insurgents they had killed a minute earlier.

From behind the truck, Whelchel yelled, "What happened?"

"I hit him but he's still going," said Strobino.

"Are you hit?"

"Yeah, I'm hit. I can't move my arm or my leg."

"Give me your grenade," Whelchel said as Reilly started moving forward to "pie the corner" as Strobino had just done. While trying to open
his grenade pouch with his one good arm, Strobino saw a grenade come
flying from the front of the house over the top of the truck. Whelchel
dropped down behind the truck, where fuel was pouring out of a punc-
tured gas tank. Whelchel caught sight of the fighter's foot stepping out
from the corner and popped a three-round burst from underneath the
pickup, hitting just above a pair of black tennis shoes.

Strobino heard the grenade go off and Reilly scream. And he heard
nothing from Whelchel. "They're both dead," he thought. Then the insurgent came flying around the corner. "This is it, I'm dead too,"
Strobino thought. The emotions that washed over him were more anger
and depression than fear. "How come I have to die in this horrible country?" he thought. But either the man was surprised to see Strobino lying
there, or he was recoiling in pain from Whelchel's shots, because he
jumped back around the corner, pointed his weapon down, and started
pouring more bullets into Strobino. Strobino rolled into the dead man
he was lying on top of, taking four bullets in the front of his vest, two in
his side, two to the back of his vest, two more in the leg, and a tracer
round to the neck. Having been shot a total of seven times in the flesh
and six times in the vest, he did not feel much pain. His bigger worry was
whether the insurgent was coming back. He was more afraid of getting
captured alive and being tortured than dying, so he pretended to be
dead. After a few seconds, it became clear the insurgent must have re-
treated again. Whelchel started calling him again.

"Bino! Bino! Are you alive?" Strobino felt a wave of euphoria wash
over him. "Not only am I alive, but Whelchel is alive too!" he thought,
suddenly in a deliriously good mood.

"Yeah, I'm here," he replied.

"Do you still have that grenade?" It had fallen out of Strobino's
pouch when he got shot, so he rolled over, picked it up with his left arm,
and tried to throw it to Whelchel. But being a natural righty and severely injured, he could only flip it halfway. The look of disappointment

on Whelchel's face as it plopped between them was heartbreaking and comical to Strobino all at once. Reilly, who had taken shrapnel in his legs and groin from the grenade, ran up to Strobino, grabbed him by the loop of his vest, and started pulling him toward the back of the house. "Oh, wow," Strobino thought, "Reilly's still alive too. This is great! We're all alive!" As he got dragged, however, the pain came on hard. Every inch he was dragged, his leg, gushing blood and oozing flesh, hurt worse than anything he'd ever experienced.

"Somebody get down here! I need more guys," Whelchel screamed into his radio. He had taken some shrapnel near his eye, and blood was running down his face. Blaisdell and several soldiers moved forward to help Whelchel. Whelchel lobbed the grenade at the front of the house and then pulled back to pull security on Reilly as he gave Strobino first aid. Reilly wrapped the leg, applied a tourniquet, and asked Strobino if he was ready. Strobino had seen the movies. He knew what was going to happen. Reilly would crank the tourniquet, the pain would be so unbearable that he would pass out, and then he'd wake up in a few days in a nice hospital in Germany with pretty nurses and strawberry ice cream.

"Yeah, I'm ready," Strobino said. Reilly cranked, Strobino screamed. And screamed, and screamed, fully conscious of excruciating pain.

Blaisdell responded to Babineau's hails. "I need you guys up here now. I got multiple wounded." Ordinarily, that would be bad news, but all Norton could think was, "Thank Christ. They're not all dead."

"Okay. Where you at?" he asked.

"Just head up the center road and you'll see us." Since the fire to their farmhouse had petered away as soon as they took cover inside, Norton grabbed the bolt from the dismantled AK-47, which rendered it useless even if the woman could reassemble it, left her there, and took his guys to meet 3rd Platoon. Blaisdell radioed for a medevac and sent several guys to prep a landing zone and several more to secure the perimeter of the house.

This was far from the only emergency that the battalion was dealing with that day, however. At almost exactly the same time that Blaisdell was calling for a medevac, soldiers in Delta Company were facing a catastrophe themselves. Just before 5:00 p.m., a two-vehicle convoy hit a massive IED on a road parallel to Route Tampa. The IED's location was chosen well and the explosives were perfectly concealed. Made of two or three 155mm artillery shells, the bomb rested in a sharp dip and curve in the road. Even traveling slowly, soldiers in Humvees would have had a hard time spotting it before they were practically on top of it. The detonation was perfectly timed, ripping the center of the truck apart and leaving the front and the back relatively untouched. Platoon leader First Lieutenant Garrison Avery, gunner Specialist Marlon Bustamante, and driver Private First Class Caesar Viglienzone were all killed instantly, their bodies ripped to flaming pieces and thrown, along with massive hunks of the truck, as far as seventy-five yards by the blast.

The 1st Platoon fire team spotted Whelchel, who waved them forward. The medevac chopper, which had just come from the Delta IED site, started its approach toward the landing zone about two hundred yards away. Because Strobino could not move his leg and was in agonizing pain, it took about six people to carry him to the bird. Blaisdell supported one of Strobino's arms while members of 1st Platoon took his other arm and legs. Reilly ran alongside pushing up on his hips. As they loaded him into the chopper and Reilly hopped in as well, Blaisdell looked Strobino in the eyes and then kissed him on the forehead. Fully loaded, the medevac lifted off at 5:40 p.m.*

Back at Freedom Rest, Goodwin was feeling better than he had in months. Since it was getting to be a reasonable hour in the morning back in the States, he had just logged on to IM and pinged his wife.

"Did you hear?" she typed.

"Hear what?" he responded.

"There is a communications blackout down in Yusufiyah. I was talking

---

*Strobino would undergo dozens of reconstructive surgeries over the next year, but he would retain both limbs and make an almost 100 percent recovery. He would also receive the Silver Star, the military's third-highest award for valor.

to Justin and all of a sudden the line went dead." It is not uncommon in the information age for the company commander's wife or some other representative of the family support group back home to get daily updates on the unit's goings-on. In this case, Goodwin's wife just happened to be getting an update from Bravo's executive officer, Justin Habash, at exactly the moment things started getting hairy.

"No," Goodwin typed. "I gotta go. I'll talk to you later." Goodwin's heart began to race and blood rushed to his head. He was having trouble thinking. "This is exactly why I didn't want to go," he thought, "if something happened when I wasn't there. And now it has. Phone. Need a phone." Goodwin rushed to the front desk and said, "I need a phone, I need a phone. Now." He dialed through to Habash. "Hey, Justin, what's going on?"

"We've been in a firefight. Third platoon. Rushdi Mullah. Looks bad."

"Freedom Rest is over," Goodwin thought. He started calling around, trying to get on a Black Hawk back to Yusufiyah.

"Sorry," he was told, "there are none available until the morning."

There was a lull. A long lull. The helicopter had evacuated the wounded, but there was still one fighter inside the house. They couldn't tell if he was dead or wounded. Maybe he had booby-trapped the house, maybe he was just lying in ambush. Whatever he was doing, he wasn't firing anymore. The 3rd Platoon and 1st Platoon men conferred. An Apache Longbow combat helicopter buzzed overhead.

"How do you want to go about this?" Blaisdell asked Norton. After floating several options, they decided to do a "mad minute," shooting rounds into every window and lobbing rifle-fired grenades in there as well, hoping to kill the insurgent or, if he survived, enrage or frighten him into shooting back. They shot hundreds of rounds and several grenades into the house. The grenades ignited something in the house. Smoke began to leak out of one window. When they ceased fire, nothing. No response from the house.

"Now what?" asked Blaisdell.

"Air strike?" Norton offered.

"Just what I was thinking."

"Requesting destroy," Blaisdell radioed to the pilot.

"Roger," replied the Apache. But, the pilot followed up, "We're not sure which house it is. Can you confirm?" Blaisdell and Norton looked at each other.

"Um, it's the one that's on fire, over."

"Sorry, still can't make it out. Can't see a fire."

"Okay, we'll point some lasers at it." Everybody had a PEC2 laser-pointing device, which can be seen only with infrared optics. Blaisdell called the men around and had them lay a beam on the house. They had more than a dozen targeting the house.

Sorry, came the word from the Apache, can't make anything out. We can't read PEC2s.

"Seriously, what the fuck," Norton said to Blaisdell as Blaisdell radioed the pilot.

"Um, how about a Phoenix?" A Phoenix is also an infrared signaling system, but it's a throwable beacon about the size of a baseball, powered by a nine-volt battery.

"Roger, that'd be good," said the pilot.

Norton turned to the men. "Who wants to go throw this on the house? Anyone? Anyone?"

"Fuck it," responded Diaz, "I'll do it."

"Be careful," Norton said, "that guy might have set up a shooting position by now." Diaz grabbed the Phoenix, ran out about a hundred yards into the street, and heaved it. It landed short of the house, bounced in front of a car out front, and, in a one-in-a-million throw, flew into the car's open window. Diaz returned out of breath.

"Strobe is activated, can you read?"

"Negative" came the call.

"Motherfucker!" Blaisdell shouted. The roof of the car might be blocking the signal, the guys hypothesized. Maybe it broke. Diaz shook his head, swore, rousted himself, and sprinted back out, all the way to the car, where he reached inside, pulled out the strobe, and put it on top of the car, then hauled back.

"How about now?" Blaisdell asked the pilot.

"Roger," he replied.

"Thank God," they exclaimed.

"Request destroy," Blaisdell said.

"I am not approved for Hellfire," the pilot said, referring to the rockets that are the Apaches' main weapons system.

"What is the point of being out here, then?" one of the guys muttered.

"We are approving you," said Blaisdell, looking at Norton, who nodded. "We are the on-ground commanders."

"Negative," said the pilot. "That is a no-go. I need clearance from my chain of command." Another round of "what the fuck" mutterings from all the men. The pilot came back a moment or two later and said, "Hellfires denied." The men let loose with a long and committed round of profanities.

"But I can do a gun run," said the pilot. Apaches have a 30mm cannon for strafing.

"Roger, do it," said Blaisdell. Apaches are like hovering tanks. They are designed to move slowly, rise up out of the tree line, unleash a hellacious Hellfire barrage on big targets such as bunkers, armored vehicles, and artillery batteries, and then recede. Unlike nimbler helicopters, Apaches are not particularly good at close-quarters combat or strafing. "You're gonna need to push your cordon out," the pilot said.

"Roger." The men moved about fifty yards farther back from the house, finding refuge in a stable filled with livestock.

"Okay, we are coming in," said the Apache. "Guns are hot, and we are cleared." The Apache came in drastically short, hitting very close to the stable where the men had taken refuge. Doss was sitting near a mudwall berm when the first of the Apache's rounds impacted twenty to thirty yards away from him, blowing that part of the berm to particles. Doss, taken totally by surprise, was blown off his seat and accidentally squeezed a burst from the light machine gun he was carrying. The first run completely missed the target house, shooting up the livestock field between them and the house. One of the cows got hit and started moaning in a sickening and nerve-racking wail.

"Describe effects," said the pilot.

"Describe effects?!" shouted Blaisdell. "You almost hit us, you jackass! That shit is danger close! You did not, repeat not, hit the target!"

After a minute or two of the cow caterwauling and writhing in pain, Norton said, "I can't fucking stand this," stood up, and shot the cow in the head. It gave a final moo-gasp and fell to the ground. Sheep and goats and chickens scurried around the men in various states of distress. The Apache swung around and returned, this time moving much more slowly. It almost hovered above the house and fired six to eight rounds that blew some sizable holes into and through the house, but the structure remained standing.

"Okay, you're good," said the pilot, who pulled back to circling distance. This was not at all what they had had in mind.

"What in the fuck do I have to do to get a house blown up around here?!" Blaisdell yelled. "Seriously," he asked Norton, "what do I have to do?"

"I don't know, man, I don't know," replied Norton. "We told him everything."

Blaisdell and Norton conferred between themselves and talked to the TOC and they decided to breach the house. Arnold took the lead, with Specialist Owens and Specialist David Shockey behind. They threw a frag grenade into the foyer and piled through the front door. They did not have a floor plan, and they had discussed how they had no idea what the layout of the house would be, but Arnold found the entryway even more confusing than expected. It was a tiny vestibule with four doors leading off of it, each covered with a sheet, and the house was filled with a haze of smoke. Moving clockwise, they cleared the first two rooms. They had all just regrouped back in the foyer and Arnold had started moving into the third room when the insurgent, in the fourth room, started firing into the foyer. Owens got hit with multiple rounds, slumped, and started screaming. Shockey, the number-three man, tripping up on Owens, took several bullets too. Arnold, whose momentum had carried him out of the line of fire, stepped to the side of the doorway and pumped rounds through the sheet covering the fourth door as Shockey pulled Owens out. Arnold followed them both.

Norton, Diaz, and Gregory rushed forward to pull Owens out of the front yard, and Blaisdell called in another medevac. Arnold prepped a grenade and threw it into the house. Norton, Diaz, and Gregory started working on Owens. He'd been shot several times and his breathing was labored. He could not speak and was barely responsive. Shockey had been hit in the leg. He was in pain, but he would be fine. By 6:25 p.m., the second medevac had arrived, taking Owens and Shockey. Shockey did not want to leave the battlefield and had to be ordered onto the bird. Owens's injuries looked serious, but the men were optimistic. Everybody had seen worse, and they were getting him to the hospital well within the golden hour. He was not speaking, but he squeezed Blaisdell's hand as they loaded him aboard.

Goodwin was still trying to get on a flight, but nothing was opening up. He called Habash back and found out that the situation had deteriorated. Owens, Habash told him, was dead. He died from massive internal bleeding forty minutes after the medevac picked him up. Goodwin headed straight to the front desk of the hotel.

"When you guys checked us in, you said we could talk to Combat Stress," Goodwin said. "I need them now. Right now. I don't care where they're at. I don't care if they're at frigging chow. I need to talk to them right now." Goodwin spent three hours talking to two different members of Combat Stress. Topics ranged from the responsibility he felt when soldiers under his command died, to his relationship with Kunk, to his constant sensation that he was barely keeping his head above water. After he finished with them, he made more calls about finding a helicopter back to Yusufiyah. Actually, came the answer, if you get down to LZ Washington, we might be able to get you a flight tonight. Goodwin walked back to the front desk. "I need my gear," he said. "I need to get out of here."

Owens was dead, another soldier had been injured, and the men in Rushdi Mullah were right back where they were several hours ago. There was an insurgent in the house and they did not know if he was alive or dead. Blaisdell got back on the radio to request Hellfire destruction of the house. He was tired of putting his men at risk when there were multimillion-dollar choppers out there that could end this with one missile. This time, Blaisdell's request was approved. "Another scenario where somebody has to die in order to get what you want," Norton later observed.

It was 9:00 p.m. The bird came back in. Again, it could not acquire the target house. It's the same house you guys already fired on, Blaisdell said, incredulous. It has dead insurgents in front of it, and it is on fire—what more do you need? Negative, came the response from the helicopter, we can't see it. Again, they shined lasers and threw beacons at it and, again, nothing worked. Finally, Blaisdell ran up to the house so he could capture an eight-digit grid location of it, and he passed the exact coordinates up to the helicopter.

With the grid in hand, the helicopter fired one rocket. It missed.

"I think I'm going to hit it again," said the pilot. The men looked at each other: *Again?* He circled around and fired two more missiles, both of which slammed home, finally reducing the house to smoking rubble. A patrol to the house confirmed that the final insurgent was finally dead. That night, Blaisdell's and Norton's men took over a house nearby to wait for EOD to show up the next day to deal with the suicide vests and to make sure more insurgents didn't try to retrieve the bodies. First Sergeant Laskoski and a Bravo relief patrol showed up bringing food, water, and more ammo.

Back at LZ Washington, Goodwin spotted two of his men, Shockey and Reilly.

"What are you guys doing here?" Goodwin asked.

"We got tore up, sir." Medevaced out, they had been treated and released. Now they were looking for rides back to Yusufiyah themselves.

Third Platoon left the next morning as elements from Headquarters and Headquarters Company, Explosive Ordnance Disposal, and more relief units arrived. EOD retrieved the insurgents' explosives and, after photographing and analyzing the vests, blew them up. Passports found on the fighters indicated one was Yemeni, one was Lebanese, and two were Syrians. The mission was not over, however. Word came down that Brigade wanted to air-evacuate the insurgents' bodies out. This was not unheard of, but after a daylong battle and an overnight away from the FOB, most of the men were not excited about babysitting and playing taxi service to a bunch of dead enemies.

The helicopters never arrived. The delays were various: The birds had to refuel, so they sent another tandem from another base. But they got diverted into another mission, so the original copters were back on the job. But one had a mechanical malfunction, so they headed back again. One hour stretched into three and then five.

Norton called up to ask if photos of the insurgents were good enough, distinguishing marks, scars? Negative, came the call, higher headquarters wants the bodies. Kunk was getting involved on the radio chatter too, and he was getting heated. He wanted his men out of there, but Ebel or somebody higher than him was insisting on retrieving the bodies. Sitting in the same position for hours on end, the men started taking mortar fire and sporadic small-arms fire. Bravo was getting more and more irritated. Norton called in to see if they could get some mortars to counterfire on the insurgents' mortar positions.

"Negative" came the word. "There are high-tension power wires in the area, and there is collateral damage risk."

"Okay, when one of their mortars hits us, I will let you know," Norton snapped back. "And if you don't hear from us, it's because we're dead."

They were still waiting for the helicopters when some men pulling guard on the roof noticed lots of women and children fleeing Rushdi Mullah. More than a hundred of them, in an orderly evacuation. They had donkeys, carts, and shopping bags filled with clothes and goods. Soon after that, three or four Bongo trucks drove up from the power plant and parked on the outskirts of town, at different points, like they were cordoning off the town from the west, just as the Army had done from the east the night before. This was not looking good.

HHC commander Shawn Umbrell had been dismayed that the Bravo relief group had not arrived with as much weaponry and supplies as he would have expected. Now he was downright alarmed and frustrated. "I was thinking we were not ready for a fight here," he said. "We needed to get the hell out of there." The officers and NCOs conferred. This is a fight we're dying to have, they told each other, but we're just not prepared for it.

"Where are the birds?" they asked the higher command.

"Still an hour, hour and a half out."

"That is not doable," Norton said. "We cannot stay here any longer. We have multiple Bongos cordoning the town, women and children fleeing, and we are taking fire. We need to get out of here."

"The order is to hold your position" came the response. Norton just about lost it. He threw the mic to his radioman, because he did not trust himself to remain civil on the radio.

"You tell those motherfuckers, if they want to goddamn identify these people, I will gladly cut off their fucking heads, put them in my bag, and fucking throw them right on top of Ebel and Kunk's desks."

The radioman translated like a pro: "Uh, Bulldog 1-6 says it is getting pretty hairy out here, and he is in favor of, uh, *alternative* means of identifying these bodies. And, uh, I don't think anyone is going to be thrilled with what he's come up with, over."

Umbrell got on the radio. Laskoski got on the radio. Minutes of heated discussion ensued. Finally, word came down. Kunk was putting an end to this, regardless of what Brigade or Division wanted.

"You're good to go," they were told. "You're cleared to walk out. Just leave the bodies there."

17

Fenlason Arrives

IN THE AFTERMATH of the February 1 firefight, Rushdi Mullah took on a new importance in the battalion's battle plan. While First Strike always knew that the area was an insurgent stronghold, they were now slowly mapping that terrain, piecing together the intelligence. As Alpha and Delta Companies were having measurable success in Mahmudiyah itself, the battalion was able to focus more on pushing farther and farther west. Air assaults and patrols to the town became more frequent, with platoons being sent out there for three or four days to set up a hasty patrol base, make some trouble for insurgents, and then withdraw as another platoon arrived either immediately or a few days later. Any trip up there, soldiers knew, guaranteed a firefight.

On February 4, Goodwin headed to Mahmudiyah for the memorial for Specialist Owens and the three other soldiers from Delta who had died in the IED strike. Sergeant First Class Jeff Fenlason had just arrived, so Goodwin met his new platoon sergeant. Over an hour-and-a-half conversation, Goodwin gave him as full a brief as he could.

"Second and Third Platoons are running on cruise control at this point," Goodwin told Fenlason. "They have firm leadership in place and have been running smoothly for some time. But First Platoon has been beaten up pretty bad. They need some tough love, but don't be afraid to hug them once in a while. In the morning, we'll get out after it."

Before dawn the next day, someone shook Goodwin awake.

"Hey, sir, are you awake?"

"I am now. What's up?"

"Hey, sir, your TOC's on fire."

"What?"

"Sir, your TOC is on fire."

"They're in contact?"

"No, sir, not taking fire. On fire. In flames. Your TOC is on fire."

"Okay." Goodwin paused to take it all in.

"Sir, are you okay?"

"Yeah, why?"

"Sir, your TOC's on fire."

"Right. I got it. Roger."

Goodwin threw his top on and hustled up to the Battalion TOC. He went over to the J-Lens that was focusing in on Yusufiyah, and sure enough, there was a big cloud of black smoke. Goodwin called over and tried to figure out what was happening, but he could get only bits and pieces. After a couple of minutes, he realized this was futile. He sent someone to get Fenlason and everybody from Bravo to get a convoy together as soon as possible.

First Platoon's 3rd Squad was at TCP5. Specialist James Barker had just woken up for an early morning guard shift. He got his gear on and went to the roof. The sun was not completely up yet, just enough for him to be able to see without night-vision goggles. He asked the guy he was relieving if there was anything going on. The guy said he wasn't sure, but he thought FOB Yusufiyah might be on fire. Over to the north there was a dark column of smoke that looked about where the FOB would be. Calls were passed over the radio. Yes, Yusufiyah confirmed, we are on fire. Barker called everybody out to the roof to take a look. All they could do at this point was laugh.

"Look, there goes my laptop."

"Do iPods go to heaven?"

"Which is worse? Losing all my photos of my family, or my porn? Family, porn? Porn, family?"

Everybody had known the FOB was a firetrap, that something like this was not a matter of if but of when. A short had caused an overloaded set of outlets in the MiTT team bay to catch fire and the blaze quickly spread throughout the barn. The structure was engulfed in flames in thirty minutes. Battalion had requested a full complement of fire extinguishers at FOBs Lutufiyah and Yusufiyah and the JS Bridge in December, but defense contractor KBR responded that it was obligated to provide such support only on Camp Striker. Battalion repeatedly sought assistance from both KBR and Army engineers on Striker, but they got little attention. Two KBR electricians had come down to FOB Yusufiyah to inspect the wiring a few weeks before, but their repairs were minimal. Just nine days earlier, soldiers fighting a fire in the Iraqi area of the FOB had nearly expended all twenty-nine of the FOB's extinguishers. First Sergeant Laskoski sent most of them to Mahmudiyah for an emergency refill, and on January 30 he filed a dire written assessment of the FOB's fire-readiness, plaintively requesting fire extinguishers, fire axes, and crowbars.

Six days later, the inevitable happened. No one was killed, or even injured, as Laskoski walked through the nascent inferno yelling, "Get up, get up, get up! We are on fire. Out, out, out. Just take what you are wearing. Don't grab anything, don't stop. Out, out, out. Move, move, move." In the MiTT bay itself, some of the men barely escaped with their lives, gulping down large swallows of acrid smoke as the fire spread fast. Others directed what few sputtering extinguishers were left on the FOB at the flames. One soldier said it was less than a minute from the time he was awakened by the blaze to the time he was pushed out of the room by the spreading smoke and heat.

The loss was devastating to morale. Men snatched what handfuls of personal stuff they could as they left, but almost everything the men owned was gone: clothing, equipment, weapons, pictures, letters, journals, photos, movies, DVDs, music, laptops. Goodwin lost his wedding ring. Goodwin's wife had sent every man in the company a Valentine's

Day present, but those were burned before they could be distributed. Norton lost a rosary given to him by his favorite, and recently deceased, uncle.

Most of 2nd Platoon and Bravo Company's headquarters staff were milling around. Some were wearing T-shirts and ACU bottoms, others had their PT uniforms on, and a couple of guys were wearing just towels and flip-flops. Almost nobody had their vests or helmets. Goodwin thought to himself, "I have a platoon that is not mission capable with a new platoon sergeant, I have thirty-five guys without equipment or weapons, and two more platoons who just lost all of their personal possessions. At least no one is dead, but what else could go wrong?"

That's when the mortars started coming in. A column of smoke makes a great target beacon for long-range weapons, and insurgents took advantage of it. In addition, the company's own ammunition stores started to cook off. First the small-caliber rounds began to go. They sound like popcorn, but then the .50-cals started to discharge, and their sound was deafening. Finally, all the big stuff—white phosphorus rounds, grenades, and AT-4 rockets—ignited in big thunderous booms and showers of sparks.

Battalion Operations Officer Rob Salome arrived on one of the many convoys the battalion started sending in to ferry whatever supplies they could scrape together on short notice, though the complete refitting of the company would be a months-long process. Brigade and division headquarters tried to push down as much new equipment and clothing as they could, but shortages lasted for weeks, if not months. A box of socks would come in, for example, but they would all be size small. One soldier says he wore the same uniform for seventy days in a row before he got issued a spare. Until housing tents showed up a few weeks later, Bravo lived with the IAs in their barn "hot bunking"—sleeping in whatever cot was open, when it was open, regardless of who supposedly owned it.

Blaisdell had been out on an overnight patrol with most of 3rd Platoon. He walked into the FOB midmorning.

"Hey, sir," he said to Salome. "Looks like our building burned down."

"Yep," said Salome.

"Anything we can do?"

"Nope, not really. I think we got it all covered."

"No help at all?"

"Really, I'd tell you. There's nothing to do at the moment."

"Well, in that case, we'll just go back out on patrol." Third Platoon turned around and headed back into Yusufiyah.

After the immediate emergency of the fire was taken care of, Fenlason headed to TCP6 and made that the staging area for 1st Platoon to sift through what they did and did not have. It did not take him long to formulate an opinion of his men. "My initial impression of that platoon was that they were a joke," he said. The first time he got the whole platoon in one place, he addressed them as a group. "The first words out of my mouth when I addressed this platoon that night, I said, 'Okay, I'm Sergeant Fenlason. I'm the new platoon sergeant. There are no more victims in this platoon.' "

He found 1st Platoon to be undisciplined, disrespectful, and defiant. They were wallowing in self-pity. They were unprofessional. They talked back. When he first arrived and began issuing orders, they would frequently buck against them, saying, "We don't do it that way."

"Excuse me, soldier?" he would reply. "This ain't a democracy, bud." The platoon had gotten the impression that they could run things by committee, that they were a voting body, a notion Fenlason intended to curtail immediately. He instituted boot camp–style routine and discipline. "We started with basic stuff, like first call is at five-thirty a.m.," Fenlason said. "Shaved and dressed by six-fifteen." They had morning formations and uniform inspections, which the men thought was idiotic: one mortar round hits right now, they said, looking around nervously, and the whole platoon is dead.

Fenlason told Blaisdell, "You gotta break them down before you build them back up." To Blaisdell, talk about breaking guys down in the middle of a combat zone sounded insane.

The men pushed back immediately. In their eyes, Fenlason may have had rank, but he had no authority. He may have had a Ranger Tab, but he had zero combat experience. To them, no combat experience meant he didn't know anything. "So, who the fuck is this asshole?" said medic Specialist Collin Sharpness. "This is his first combat tour? He's been in staff the whole time? And he's coming in here fucking pumping his chest?"

Fenlason knew that the men did not hold his career in high esteem, but he didn't care, because he was none too impressed with their supposed battle-hardening either. "I'm not going to pay a whole hell of a lot of attention to that anyway," he rejoined. "You know, Private Snuffle-upagus, who has been in a firefight, that doesn't necessarily make him Johnny Rambo. So his experience level is still somewhat small."

Fenlason knew that it would take a while for 1st Platoon to come around, but that was okay. Unlike the other platoon sergeants, he wasn't going anywhere. Early on, he hit upon the idea of the immovable object—he was the immovable object. "The resentments were already beginning," he said. "The men didn't like the idea of being told when they were going to do certain things and when they weren't."

Since Fenlason knew 2nd Squad's squad leader, Chris Payne, from Fort Campbell in 2003, he drew him close to help him get up to speed on the platoon. Payne tried to preemptively play the peacemaker, advising Fenlason on how to talk to Lauzier. "I tried to say, 'Look, he's wild and he's unpredictable and he shoots a lot, but he's a good leader,' " recalled Payne. Payne saw the clash coming. Lauzier was tempermental and very particular about the kinds of leaders he esteemed, while Fenlason was blunt to the point of being tactless and convinced there was his way to do something, or the wrong way. "I said, 'You need to be careful with Lauzier or you'll lose him,' " Payne remembered. "And he did. It didn't take long."

"I heard you like to shoot a lot," were the first words Fenlason spoke to Lauzier. The relationship went downhill from there. Fenlason came to see Lauzier as a loud, immature bully who constantly abused, needled, and micromanaged his men and overcompensated for battlefield risk with excessive force and firepower. Lauzier thought Fenlason was a tactically incompetent desk jockey who hid out in his office at

TCP1 all day long. Lauzier took offense at Fenlason's insinuation that he was some sort of loose cannon. How could Fenlason assess battlefield risk, Lauzier wanted to know, if Fenlason never put himself on the battlefield? "I would say, 'Hey, you're out of touch here, pal,' but he wouldn't listen to me," Lauzier lamented. "He thought I was a cowboy."

Lauzier was not the only soldier Fenlason formulated a quick opinion on. It wasn't long before he'd identified several soldiers he felt were particularly problematic cases. He was the one who had put Barker in anger management classes back in 2003, and he didn't see anything in Barker out here to change his opinion that he was a punk. Cortez, he concluded, was a pout and a borderline malingerer who routinely declared he wanted out of the platoon whenever anything didn't go his way. And he quickly learned all about Green and his extreme hatred of Iraqis. Green had recently rejoined the platoon after a few well-behaved weeks working at the FOB following his altercation with Gallagher. But of all the soldiers who dwelled on the past, who simply could not get over the deaths of Nelson and Casica, Green was, in Fenlason's estimation, the worst. All day long from Green, it was Nelson and Casica this, Nelson and Casica that.

Throughout the rest of the deployment, Payne tried to be the translator and peacemaker between Fenlason and the rest of the platoon; he felt that he understood both parties better than anyone else. It was a role he thought was important even if it made him less popular. "Everybody hated Fenlason," said Payne, "and I don't think that the guys can understand why I always defended him. But the way I saw it, I needed to be able to go to Lauzier and Yribe and say, 'This is what he said. This is what he wants,' as opposed to them having to hear it from Fenlason, who didn't know how to talk to everybody. He has a condescending way of talking, like, 'I know more than everybody in this whole company. I know more than everybody in this platoon. You guys are fucked up, and I'm here to fix it.' "

Staff Sergeant Chaz Allen, who replaced Phil Miller, joined 1st Platoon the same time Fenlason did. He was surprised not just at how divorced the platoon was from the rest of the company, but even at how disorganized it was from within. There was very little cooperation between squads. "There was no distribution plan for water and chow," he said. "It was every dog for himself. Each squad, in their own little TCP, they would get in their vehicles and drive up to Yusufiyah, get what they needed, and come back." And combat credibility for the new guy, regardless of rank, was always an issue. "I received so much flak, like borderline mutiny," Allen recalled. Men would throw down their weapons, refusing to take orders from him because, they declared, he had never been in combat before. But he had been shot at, he had been blown up before. "So it was them not understanding who I am, and me not understanding who they are."

Allen tried to undo the bad habits the squad had acquired. The men, for example, did not keep guard rotation schedules, telling Allen that whoever was able to stay awake took guard. Once, when he asked who was going to relieve a soldier who'd been on guard for six hours, several troopers shouted, "Not it!" as if they were in grade school.

During one of his first days on the job, Fenlason was at TCP1. Some of the men were giving him a tour of the house. They were on the roof when an insurgent shot a rocket at the TCP from a broad field to the southeast. It did not reach the TCP, and did not even detonate. But the gunner on the roof thought he spotted a puff of smoke, so he began banging away on the machine gun. Before long, several soldiers had joined him at the walled edge of the roof, shooting at the field with their M4s. Within a few seconds, almost the entire checkpoint was up there, eleven or twelve guys and several IAs, slamming rounds into the field. Fenlason couldn't believe what he was seeing. He yelled for them to stop shooting.

"What the fuck are you shooting at?" he yelled. "Stop shooting!"

"No, Sergeant, no!"

"Yeah, stop! I'm telling you to fucking stop now. Hold your fire! Hold your fire!" He threw a soda can at one soldier who wasn't stopping.

"What?" One by one, the soldiers ceased firing and turned toward Fenlason.

"What in the fuck are you shooting at? Do you have a target?"

"It's a suspected enemy location."

"The whole frigging country is a suspected enemy location. What are you shooting at?"

"There's a probable . . ." someone started. Fenlason was livid.

"No. I will tell you what you are shooting at. You are shooting at nothing. When you just go up here and start shooting at everything in sight, that's not doctrine. It is not correct. It never has been the answer. You got a target, you got a sector of fire. In that target area, you engage your sector of fire. You control the rate and distribution of fire. But you don't just shoot just for shits and grins. You are wasting ammunition. You want to put a patrol together and go try to find the bad guy? Let's do that. Let's go find evidence of the launch. Let's do something. But you just wasted five minutes and hundreds of rounds of ammunition up here fucking around shooting at nothing."

Soon after that altercation Fenlason told somebody over the radio, "Well, I guess I got my CIB!" The CIB is the Combat Infantryman's Badge and it is one of the most prestigious medals in the Army because it indicates that you weren't simply an infantryman in a war zone but that you took direct enemy fire. Guys from real combat units had nothing but contempt for the rear-echelon types up at Striker who would go running in the direction of a mortar impact that landed harmlessly two hundred yards away so they could try to convince their superiors that they were "under fire" and get their CIB, or its non-infantry equivalent, the Combat Action Badge. And now, 1st Platoon sneered, they were being led by one of these pogues. Fenlason later said he had no recollection of saying such a thing and doubted he would have. "It's not the kind of thing I would have cared about one way or another," he stated.

Norton and Fenlason had no problems getting along. While no platoon sergeant would probably ever live up to Norton's idealization of Lonnie Hayes in Charlie Company, Fenlason was, in Norton's eyes, an improvement over Gallagher. Though Fenlason usually did most of the talking, Norton felt he could have real conversations with him about goals and progress for the unit and the area. Fenlason thought they should be doing a lot more community outreach, more counterinsurgency. That sort of stuff was a high priority up at Brigade, and other companies were moving far ahead of them in that regard. Bravo wasn't even trying in Fenlason's eyes. Part of the problem was that these platoons were moving around too much, especially in and out of the TCPs. The people of

Mullah Fayyad and surrounding villages could hardly get to know, much less trust, any of the soldiers if they were always just passing through. There should be more ownership, Fenlason thought.

Norton definitely agreed, at least in theory. He was wary of doing anything drastic, however, because he did believe that Bravo's sector was hotter than the other companies'. Maybe this area wasn't quite ready to make the big transition to community building yet, Norton wondered. Or maybe it was. Maybe it was something to try, or at least think about, but Norton reminded Fenlason that he was going on leave on February 22. He assumed they would pick up the discussions after he returned in about a month.

As Fenlason settled in, the men determined another thing they could hate him for: He almost never left the wire. He rarely patrolled. He never went on IED sweeps. He seemed never to ride along on a Quick Reaction Force when anyone got into a scrape. And the thought of Fenlason pulling guard the way Gallagher had made the soldiers laugh out loud. Fenlason always made sure to get a full night's sleep, they said. "Sergeant Fenlason didn't do anything," said Sergeant Daniel Carrick, one of the battalion's young stars, who was transferred from 3rd Platoon to give 1st Platoon better junior NCO leadership. "He sat around smoking cigarettes, drinking coffee, and that's it. He'd do patrols once a month to go talk to some leaders."

Fenlason conceded that he did not get out very often. "I did one IED sweep my first few days there," he said. "I did a half a dozen walks in Mullah Fayyad. And I did the two walks out and back to Rushdi Mullah." But he does not see this as a failing. "Iraq in 2006 was a squad-level fight. The patrols were squad-level patrols, or fire-team-level patrols. I don't go on fire-team-level patrols. Why would I? I never considered the perception of the soldiers or even the junior leaders. It never occurred to me to look at it through their eyes."

In the early morning of February 22, about a dozen men, possibly dressed as policemen, entered the venerated Shi'ite Askariya mosque in the city of Samarra, wired it with some five hundred pounds of explosives, withdrew, and detonated it remotely. Zarqawi was among the suspected masterminds, and AQI's umbrella organization, the Mujahideen Shura Council, issued a statement celebrating the Shi'ite outrage that followed. AQI never explicitly took credit for the attack, however, and several of the bombing's characteristics were atypical of an AQI hit. Regardless, it was spectacularly provocative and successfully ushered in a new escalation in the civil war between Shi'ites and Sunnis, throughout Iraq and in the Triangle of Death.

The Samarra bombing galvanized and remotivated Muqtada al-Sadr and his Mahdi Army (also known as Jaish al-Mahdi, or JAM) to push into locales they had not been operating extensively in for months, including Mahmudiyah. More Iraqi civilians were killed in Baghdad during the first three months of 2006 than at any time since the end of the Saddam regime. Sectarian killings now claimed nine times more lives than car bombings, and executions had increased 86 percent in the nine weeks after the February mosque bombing.

According to Captain Leo Barron, the 1-502nd's intelligence officer, this trend played out much the same way in Mahmudiyah. Ethnic tensions erupted anew and violence spiked past all previous levels. Less than a week after the bombing, Alpha Company witnessed the first open gun battle in Mahmudiyah they had ever seen between the Mahdi militia and a local Sunni tribe. Alpha did not get involved. "I don't want to get in the middle of that," Alpha company commander Bordwell told *Stars and Stripes* at the time, but added, "If that were to continue, that would be a real concern."

It did continue. In fact, an all-but-government-mandated Shi'ite counterattack was already beginning before the Samarra bombing. On February 7, seven masked men in IA uniforms and one in all-black clothing carrying AK-47s and 9mm handguns had "arrested" the Sunni mayor of Mahmudiyah, who had been elected by a council of elders Kunk had organized several weeks before. Four men pulled security outside his office and told anyone who asked that they were working "for Baghdad." Inside, the other team presented the mayor with an arrest warrant that appeared to have been issued by the previous mayor, the same one who had been arrested just as First Strike was taking over this area. That first mayor, is, today, the mayor of Mahmudiyah, and the second mayor has never been heard from again.

Prior to the Samarra bombing, Barron said, violence in the area was dominated by Sunni locals planting IEDs for money. AQI or other Sunni insurgent groups paid up to several hundred dollars to locals to lay an IED. But after the Samarra bombing, Barron saw an increase in violence committed by Shi'ites and then a counterreaction from Sunnis who started fighting back, not for money but out of hate. In this spiral of violence and battle for control, JAM became even more brazen. "Shi'ites took over many of the city council positions in Mahmudiyah, they were pushing Sunnis out of their neighborhoods," Barron said. "What started as threats and propaganda turned into intimidation and then murder and assassination. Over time, the demographics of the city changed completely. It flipped from being a mixed city to one with an overwhelming Shi'ite majority."

First Strike was not powerless to stop this ethnic cleansing: they were ordered not to. "We had a massive amount of intelligence on JAM," said Barron. "We knew JAM's hierarchy inside and out. But the orders were very explicit: Go after Al Qaeda. Do not worry about JAM." A reluctance by U.S. commanders to antagonize the Shi'ite-dominated Iraqi government, many of whose highest-ranking members had long-established ties to the militias, drove such decisions, but it badly damaged U.S. forces' credibility among Sunnis in places like Mahmudiyah. "It was very frustrating," Barron admitted. "Sunni sheikhs came in and asked, 'So how many Shi'ites are in your jail?' And the answer was, not a lot. Part of the reason the Sunni insurgencies were having so much success, especially in Bravo's AO, was because the locals, Sunni locals, did not see us as evenhanded."

On February 28, almost five months to the day since the deployment started, Lauzier was scheduled to go on a month's leave. He didn't want to go. He was afraid of what would happen if he left his men. Not every squad leader went on a lot of patrols, but Lauzier went on every one he could. "He would try to take point on every mission, and it got to where it bothered me because I would be like, no, man, I got it, you know?" Specialist James Barker recalled. But Lauzier couldn't bear the thought of sending somebody out and them not coming back. If that happened, how could you live with not having been there? Now that he was going on leave, who would lead in his place? He would have been confident leaving Sergeant Tony Yribe in charge, but Yribe had been moved to 1st Squad after Nelson and Casica got shot. Specialist Paul Cortez and Specialist Anthony Hernandez were his team leaders, but they weren't even sergeants yet. He loved his guys, but without him, he was worried they were going to get killed.

The truth was, for all his bluster, this deployment was wearing Lauzier down. Under Lieutenant Britt and Platoon Sergeant Miller, Lauzier had been far and away the favored squad leader, but with Fenlason in charge, Lauzier had lost status fast. He felt marginalized. The new golden-boy squad leader was Payne, which made Lauzier bitter.

"Sergeant Fenlason and I didn't talk too much because he wasn't around," said Lauzier. "But when we did talk, it never went well. Whenever I offered a suggestion, Fenlason would shoot it down straightaway. 'Oh, did you read a book?' he would say. I called Norton, Fenlason, and Payne the Circle of Three. I was not included in their little club."

Lauzier's fall from favor was obvious to most in the platoon, and many thought it was unfair. "Lauzier was very, very tactically sound and very tactically minded," opined Sergeant Roman Diaz, who served in both 1st and 3rd Squads. "Weapons were always clean, night vision and optics were always functioning. Lauzier took his responsibilities very seriously. Things like noise and light discipline were very important to him. Third Squad had this reputation for being cowboys, but we jumped when we had to jump, and we ran when we had to run, and we operated like an infantry squad."

Halfway into his second deployment Lauzier was rapidly losing his taste for combat. "Killing AIF is useless beause there are ten more to replace each one," he said. "It is a pointless fight. When you first get here it's like, yeah, let's go kick butt. But that ends real quick. It gets to the point where you hear a gunshot and all the strength zaps out of your legs." His body was breaking down, too. He was suffering from painful back problems, and a worsening bone spur was making it difficult for him to walk.

Increasingly alienated, Lauzier started falling back on the men from his squad for support, especially Barker. "The Army would probably say I'm a shitbag soldier for that because I'm confiding in one of my subordinates. But I had no one to talk to," he confessed. "What am I going to do? I'm human. You get real close out there, closer than a mother's bond with her child. That's how it was for me. Those men were my responsibility. I'm their mother, I'm their father, their counselor, police officer, principal—whatever you want to call it, that's what I am."

The affection was reciprocal. "He would have done anything for us and we would have done anything for him," said Barker. When asked what kind of leader Lauzier was, Cortez said, "By the book, led from the front, took care of his guys first, looked up to by everybody. Loved. Respected."

But outsiders to the 3rd Squad dynamic said Lauzier was, in fact, losing control of his men. "They were a bunch of loose cannons," pronounced Sergeant Carrick. "He was either babysitting one guy or he was trying to stop that guy from kicking in some girl's face, just because he could." This was the difference between control and influence. "Yes, he had control if he was there watching them all the time," said Sergeant Diem. "But nobody supervises their subordinates that much. He had no influence over his squad. He had no power over their behavior when he wasn't there." And even though Lauzier thought highly of his men, many of the other guys in 1st Platoon thought some of the characters in 3rd Squad, especially Barker and Cortez, were just hoodlums who happened to be wearing uniforms.

Cortez was particularly tweaked these days. Just before Lauzier's leave, 3rd Squad got the call to go fill in some IED holes off of Fat Boy. It was, the men thought, a typically dipshit mission. "That was the order: Go out there to fill holes, so that the insurgents could put bombs back in them and blow the fuck out of us again," said Lauzier. "If you wanted to fill the holes with concrete and do an overwatch until it was all dry, that's one thing, but this was just dumb—and we got ordered to do stuff like this all the time."

It was common for soldiers to complain, even vehemently, when sent on these types of missions. A soldier screaming, "This is fucking bullshit!"

and then throwing something across the room was a normal occurrence, but it would always be followed by his picking up his helmet and continuing to suit up. He might be grumbling to himself the whole time about how he didn't sign up for this shit, this was the dumbest fucking thing he'd ever done, this is the dumbest fucking idea in the motherfucking history of warfare and he can't wait to get out of the Army so he can go to the White House himself and shove an IED so far up George Bush's ass that they are going to have to pry his teeth out of the walls. But he would continue to suit up and be ready to go when it was showtime.

With Cortez, this time, it was different. He was teary-eyed, sometimes blubbering, sometimes shouting, hysterical about how he was sick of it, he couldn't do this anymore.

"They don't give a shit about us!" he shrieked. "They don't fucking care if we die, they don't fucking care. This is suicide, every day is another suicide mission, day after day after day! I'm not doing it!"

Lauzier tried to talk him down for a minute or two, but that wasn't working. He tried to get him into a separate room, away from the other men, because Cortez's losing his mind was now freaking them out. Either freaking them out or, for the guys who didn't like Cortez, confirming that he was a little bitch after all. Lauzier wanted to punch him.

"You're a specialist, for chrissake!" Lauzier yelled once he had gotten him into a semiprivate corner. "You're about to get promoted. Everybody feels the stress. Go ahead, have a breakdown! But you can't do it in front of the men." Cortez continued to spout hysterics. Lauzier decided he really didn't have time for this, so he got angry. "Fuck it, Cortez, then stay back!" he yelled. "If you don't want to go, then don't go. Just stay the fuck back, okay? We got it covered. You're good, all right? You're good. Don't worry about it."

Lauzier and his squad-sized patrol headed out. Lauzier stewed on it during the patrol, and when he got back he happened to pass Norton and Fenlason while he was still fuming. They asked him what was wrong, and he vented. Fenlason called Cortez in. This was not what Lauzier wanted to have happen. He should have held his tongue. He did not want Fenlason involved. Fenlason chewed Cortez's ass.

"I will bust you a rank and make you a SAW [squad automatic weapon] gunner if you pull shit like that again!" Fenlason yelled. Lauzier took Cortez aside and apologized for losing his temper, and apologized for getting Fenlason involved.

"But," Lauzier told Cortez, "you can't pull that shit in front of the guys. If you are freaking out, you need to talk to me in private. I am going on leave soon and Fenlason has it in for all of us. He is gunning for us, waiting for us to fuck up. So when I am gone, you have got to be shit hot and wire tight, you hear me?"

"I hear you," said Cortez.

MARCH 2006

18

Back to the TCPs

BEGINNING MARCH 1, 1st Platoon rotated back out to the TCPs. Norton had gone on midtour leave in the third week of February, so Fenlason had sole control of 1st Platoon. Goodwin was aware that morale had not come around, but he was optimistic, and he had expected the adjustment to Fenlason to be rocky at first. "About thirty days into it, they're at the lowest point," he recalled. "This is when everybody is just fed up. They hate each other. The guys just are pushing back. It's what happens. New guy comes in. There is always a downturn. Then the body adapts." He was hoping the body would adapt soon.

But 1st Platoon was at a far lower point than even those who were supposed to monitor it realized. The psychological isolation that 1st Platoon had been experiencing throughout the deployment was becoming nearly total. "First Platoon had become insane," declared Sergeant Diem flatly. "What does an infantry rifle platoon do? It destroys. That's what it's trained to do. Now turn that ninety degrees to the left, and let slip the leash, and it becomes something monstrous. First Platoon became monstrous. It was not even aware of what it was doing."

Some of the mental states that the men describe are well documented by psychologists studying the effect of combat on soldiers. The men spoke about desensitization, how numbed they were to the violence. They passed around short, graphic computer video compilations of collected combat kills and corpses found in Iraq. One, with a title card dedicated to "Mr. Squishy Head"—a dead body whose skull had been smashed in—was set to the track of Rage Against the Machine's "How I Could Just Kill a Man." It was a horror parade of stills and short clips of gore and carnage.

Justin Cross, who had been promoted to private first class in March, admitted he talked with some of the other men about how the social breakdown and the extreme Iraqi-on-Iraqi violence around them would be a perfect cover for murder. "I was on guard one day and they radioed in to be extra alert because people were rioting," he said. "At that point in time, in that state of mind, I had this bright idea. I said, 'You know what's funny, man? Go behind the TCP, kill anybody. Kill anybody. And fucking blame it on the riots. And we'd get away with it.' After saying that shit, everybody looked up and was like just looking at each other. Barker and Cortez were just staring at each other. It was like, 'That's a damn good idea.' "

Iraqis were not seen as humans. Many soldiers actively cultivated the dehumanization of locals as a secret to survival. "You can't think of these people as people," opined Yribe. "If I see this old lady and say, 'Ah, she reminds me of my grandmother,' but then she pulls out a fucking bomb, I'm not going to react right. So me, I don't see them as people." Children were considered insurgents or future insurgents, and women were little more than insurgent factories.

Some began hoping they would die. "I don't know if you have ever honestly prayed for death, but there were times we would just fucking take our helmets off," remarked Private First Class Justin Watt (who had also been recently promoted). "We'd be sitting in a guard tower and be like, "Please, please put me out of my fucking misery." Cross described an almost identical experience: "I had my first breakdown right there, where I was like, 'Fuck this shit.' I took off my helmet, threw it down, and just sat there. I stood up on top of the turret and started yelling, 'Fuck this shit. You want to fucking kill me, just kill me, please.

Somebody, sniper, come on, shoot me!' " Charlie Company's First Sergeant Dennis Largent said, "My soldiers passing through Bravo's AO would tell me about their soldiers saying, 'It would be easier if I got shot or blown up. At least this shit would be over.' "

Specialist James Barker described the paradoxical yet typical swings that combat-weary soldiers have between thinking they are doomed and thinking they are invincible. "I knew I was going to die, it was just a matter of time, so I just didn't care. I would run straight at somebody shooting at me instead of taking cover. That was my mentality: I'm already dead so, fuck it, what can anybody do to me? I'd gotten shot at so many times and blown up so many times and hadn't taken a scratch that it's like, 'Oh fuck, I'm untouchable. I am a bad ass and nobody can fuck with me.' "

Second Platoon and 3rd Platoon survived, stayed sane, and arguably even thrived in the exact same environment in great part due to their outstanding platoon sergeants and their daily, active effort to combat the hate 1st Platoon had given in to. But 1st Platoon did lose more men, including three leaders killed in a two-week period, which they did not. The disarray caused by those losses was compounded by a consistent leadership vacuum. And emergent dysfunctions were magnified further by the higher command's constant unfavorable comparison of 1st Platoon with Bravo's better-functioning platoons. "You can see what happens when the pressure on a set of leaders—junior leaders—becomes so great that men's decision-making processes start to break down," observed the battalion's executive officer, Major Fred Wintrich. "Moral decision-making processes. And that's what leadership is supposed to mitigate."

House searches turned extremely violent. "A lot of people got dragged out of their house by their hair and beat down," recalled Diem. "I want you to imagine just for a second that you and your wife are watching TV one day, and then the door gets kicked in and some soldiers come in and drag your wife out by the hair and smack the piss out of you in your living room, asking you questions in a language you've never heard, holding guns to your head." Most of the time, this violence was not strictly random. Usually there was a shred of evidence or a whiff of suspicion before such force was employed. But the trip wire was thin. "It's not like we did it for no reason," Diem said. "We worked off suspicion. It was sort of like Puritan witch-hunters."

Suspected insurgents were beaten as a matter of course, with the full blessings and, in fact, insistence of some team leaders and squad leaders. Sergeants would egg the younger soldiers on, making fun of privates who didn't hit detainees hard enough.

During patrols, Green frequently volunteered to kill anyone his NCOs wanted him to. "I was always saying, 'Anytime you all are ready, you all are the ones in charge of me. Anytime you all say the word "go," it's on,' " he recalled. "One time, we pulled these guys off the road and took them in this house and we were hitting them and trying to make them tell us what they were up to, and Yribe was talking about shooting them. And I was like, 'I'll do it! I'll take them out right now and shoot them. All you gotta do is tell me to.' And Yribe started talking to Babineau, like, 'Oh, Babs, but you wanted to shoot them, right?' " That's when Green realized Yribe had been pulling his leg the whole time.

Many of the men say the beatings began in earnest when they watched the men they had detained get released by higher headquarters. The way they saw it, they were just taking justice into their own hands because the battalion or the brigade could not be trusted to keep the men trying to kill them behind bars. Brigade commander Colonel Todd Ebel countered that 85 percent of the brigade's detainees went to prison, a statistic he points to as proof that raids were well targeted and backed up by a judicial system that worked. The men of 1st Platoon say that number does not come close to their experience. "We would turn them in to Mahmudiyah and what happens?" said one. "They're released. Not enough evidence. It came to the point where we had to have criminal investigation packets thicker than a book to send these assholes to jail. We couldn't rely on Army intelligence to put these guys in jail, so we had to let that town know that we were in charge."

Many men believed it to be a fact that the battalion and brigade not only did not care if they lived or died but probably even conspired against them. Their disenfranchisement and their apathy would get them into more trouble, which in turn would then further convince them that they were being singled out.

"I probably didn't help it sometimes with my platoons, since our AOs bordered each other," said Alpha Company commander Jared Bordwell. "One of my platoons would be in contact and would send a report up, or an explosion would happen in B Company's area and we would send up a report of 'We just heard an explosion 600 meters this degrees.' And they would ping Bravo. 'What the hell is going on in your AO?' And the TCPs were like, 'Oh, yeah. There was an IED that just went off.' Those guys had gotten to the point where they were like, 'Whatever.' "

At the beginning of the March TCP rotation, Fenlason sent 2nd Squad to TCP5. He, the headquarters element, and 1st Squad went to TCP1. And he sent 3rd Squad to cover both TCP2 and TCP6. Fenlason said that there was no difference in the dangers between TCP1 and TCP2, that the TCPs were equally dangerous, but this is not true. By March, TCP1 had been running continuously as the TCP mission headquarters for four months. It was a sturdy two-story house with working, generator-driven electricity, good sight lines in every direction, and defenses that were still crude but that had been improving steadily. This TCP was also the most heavily staffed, usually with a full squad plus the medic, radioman, platoon sergeant, and a squad of Iraqi soldiers.

Fenlason would not have known about the relative safety of TCP2 anyway, because he had never been to TCP2, either before this rotation or at any time during it. TCP2 had just been reopened for the first time since it had been shut down in mid-December. This time, at least, the men were allowed to take over a house on the northwest corner of Sportster and the small, unnamed canal road. It was a hovel, more a collection of rooms than a home, each no bigger than 150 square feet, laid in an end-to-end, almost serpentine arrangement. Many of the rooms did not have windows, and of those which did, the windows were just small, paneless holes a foot or two square. There was no electricity, no running water, and no furniture except for cots, plastic patio chairs, and tables fashioned from sheets of plywood laid atop cardboard boxes. The latrine was a plastic chair with the seat cut out where soldiers would defecate into a WAG Bag. There was a wall along the Sportster side and about ten feet of wall on the canal road side. The rest of the house's yard was exposed. To mitigate this danger, there were several HESCO Barriers, but not having been filled with dirt, they were useless.

With Lauzier on leave, Fenlason gave 3rd Squad the job of manning TCP2 and TCP6 because he believed it to be the easiest. Unlike Blaisdell and Gebhardt, who preferred switching up guard rotations every few hours, Fenlason ran TCP2 and TCP6 as static positions. The men would live out there the whole time. Even though Fenlason once declared that he would not have sent Specialist Cortez to the promotion board to become a sergeant if he had been platoon sergeant at the time, he maintained that this duty was an appropriate tasking for Cortez. "Cortez was going to go to TCP2," he explained, "because all I wanted him to do was pull guard. That's it. IED sweeps and pull guard. Which is tactically and technically well within the realm of someone of his experience and pay grade."

Fenlason had a fondness for static positions, seeming to think they were easier to man than dynamic positions. It was an infantry philosophy that many of his men could not fathom, and one that the other platoons did not subscribe to. Fixed positions invite attack. Said one squad leader from a different platoon: "A static position like a TCP was a no-go for us. In order to keep them from attacking us, we had a constantly roving patrol out there." When they are boring, static positions breed complacency, and when they are dangerous, they are mind-rackingly stressful.

Indeed, Cortez was not coping well with the added responsibility. He was focusing intently on the dangers around him and becoming increasingly bitter about his sense of abandonment. "A lot of time you couldn't sleep," Cortez said. "There were windows where somebody could walk right up and just drop a grenade and you wouldn't even know it." Fenlason maintained that no one ever expressed anxiety to him about the dangerous conditions at TCP2, but several soldiers contradict this assertion. "I kept asking to get the HESCO baskets filled," said Cortez. "I asked for more concertina wire, more sandbags to fortify the position. All they kept telling me was 'No, don't worry about it. We will get it later on. We don't need it right now.' So basically we were just told to just sit there and wait to get killed, that's the way I took it."

In *Achilles in Vietnam,* psychologist Jonathan Shay describes how the long-term debilitating effects of combat are exacerbated exponentially when a soldier's sense of "what's right" is violated by his leaders. "The mortal dependence of the modern soldier on the military organization for everything he needs to survive is as great as that of a small child on his or her parents," he writes. During his clinical treatment of Vietnam veterans, one of the most persistent causes of stress soldiers described was the perception that risk was not evenly distributed. Shay continues: "Shortages of all sorts—food, water, ammunition, clothing, shelter from the elements, medical care—are intrinsic to prolonged combat. . . . However, when deprivation is perceived as the outcome of indifference or disrespect by superiors, it arouses *menis* [the Greek word for 'indignant rage'] as an unbearable offense." This rage, Shay writes, is instrumental in the soldiers' own "undoing of character" and "loss of humanity" essential to the commission of war crimes.

Even though TCP2 was only three-quarters of a mile from TCP1, Fenlason never went to evaluate TCP2's defenses or to see how his soldiers were performing there over the next three weeks. With Platoon Leader Norton and 3rd Squad Leader Lauzier both on leave, and with 3rd Squad headed by a soldier Fenlason knew to be a poor leader, not once did he go to TCP2 in the next twenty-one days to assess how Cortez was enforcing standards or fortifying a brand-new battle position.

Fenlason justified his absenteeism as a reflection of the degree of trust he suddenly had in his men—whom he had originally assessed as a "fucking bucket of crap"—after just a month of leading them. The men down at the TCP didn't know why Fenlason did not come down, but by this point that suited them just fine. He was the last person they wanted to see. "Fenlason was reliable, I will give him that," said Specialist

James Barker, one of the soldiers stationed at TCP2 with Cortez. "We knew he would never, ever come check on us, so we could do whatever we wanted."

While 1st Platoon's attention was focused on the TCPs, Kunk and the rest of the battalion, in fact all of 2nd Brigade, were looking west, to the Yusufiyah Power Plant. On March 2, a brigade-wide effort called Operation Glory Light kicked off. A weeklong initiative, it was one of the largest missions of the war since the invasion. It began with joint air assaults by U.S. and Iraqi troops into the town of Sadr-Yusufiyah, just north of the power plant, by troopers from both infantry battalions of the Deuce. Though the effort was spearheaded by the 2-502nd, the 1-502nd's Charlie Company and Alpha Company both contributed a platoon or two, flushing terrorists from one of the most lawless areas of the brigade's AO. "This could be the final crushing blow for the anti-Iraqi forces in the Baghdad area," Kunk told *Stars and Stripes* at the time, something he could not possibly have believed.

Parts of Bravo's 2nd Platoon moved with Captain Goodwin into Rushdi Mullah as a blocking element to prevent insurgents who were fleeing the main thrust from coming their way. They rolled in first thing on the morning of March 4 and cleared the entire village. Then they took over a house and laid in for several days of overwatch. They suffered intermittent fire in various forms, including mortars and small arms. They had a sniper dogging them, who was particularly aggravating because he was extraordinarily patient, firing perhaps as few as ten shots in thirty-six hours, from as far away as three-quarters of a mile, and he moved after every shot. They sent some snipers of their own to lie in wait for him, but they never found him. They tried making a "Scare Joe," a helmet on a stick that they would pop just above the rim of the walled roof, but he never fell for that. Goodwin also sent out patrols into town every few hours to maintain a presence and keep the townspeople on their toes.

Just after 4:00 p.m. on March 5, twenty-one-year-old Specialist Ethan Biggers got out of one of the Humvees parked in front of the house and went inside and up to the second-floor balcony, which had a protective four-foot wall running around its perimeter. He needed to stretch his legs, get a change of scenery. He was Bravo's radioman, the communication link between Goodwin, the rest of the company, and higher command, so he had been practically living inside the truck for two days straight to be near the radios. Some people were always up on the balcony, either getting some air or as part of the guard rotation. Because of his job, everybody in Bravo knew Biggers, and because of his personality, everybody loved him. He was the entire company's little brother, who never had a sour word about anyone. He and his fiancée, Britni, were expecting their first child.

Goodwin was up there too, inside one of the two rooms on the second floor, and so was Platoon Sergeant Jeremy Gebhardt. Gebhardt had his vest on but his helmet off, and others, even those on the balcony, were in similar states of disrobe. It was against regulations to have anything but "full battle rattle" on when outside, but on days-long missions like this, even leaders thought that was not really realistic. Gebhardt allowed soldiers to remove some of their protective gear as long as they kept their heads below the lip of the wall, because this was the tallest house in the neighborhood. Goodwin knew about this and tacitly approved the relaxation of the rules.

Upstairs, Biggers sat down on the outdoor stairwell leading up to the third floor with his head still below the outer wall, took off his helmet, and started talking to one of the medics. Several minutes later, first one shot rang out, from far away. But it was quickly followed by a second, perhaps as close as a hundred yards. This one hit the wall behind the stairwell, ricocheted, struck Biggers above his left eyebrow, and exited out the back of his head, each hole about an inch wide.

Jesus, that was close, some of the soldiers exclaimed. But then the unit's interpreter noticed that Biggers was not moving. "He's hit, he's hit!" he shouted. Soldiers dragged Biggers inside and started first aid, but blood and brains were spilling out of his skull. There was so much blood, a bandage would not stay on his head. A medevac bird arrived quickly and rushed him out, but he had lost a substantial amount of his brain and was in a coma.*

Another arguably avoidable casualty was a further blow to Goodwin's status. "That shooting became a huge thing," remarked Alpha commander Jared Bordwell. "Diagrams, trying to figure out the trajectory and all that stuff. They were trying to figure out not only how it happened but who they could blame. Who can we blame for this happening?"

The first lieutenant who investigated the event found Biggers's head shot preventable, and Colonel Ebel agreed. Ebel recommended that letters of reprimand be issued to Goodwin and Gebhardt. He chastised the commander and the NCO for "failure to ensure a climate of leadership that *demands* strict adherence to published standards. . . . In this case the commander bears the responsibility for enforcing policy." As with Nelson's and Casica's deaths, however, the men who were there insisted that a helmet would not have stopped the shot. "If you were there and actually saw where the bullet was, it wouldn't have even hit his helmet," said one of 2nd Platoon's squad leaders.

While far from the final crushing blow to the insurgency in the Baghdad area, Operation Glory Light was declared a success. U.S. soldiers cleared significant amounts of new territory, found nearly two dozen IEDs, uncovered two weapons caches, and detained seven suspects.

On the morning of March 8, Kunk's convoy was returning from the area of the power plant as Glory Light was winding down. "We had to come down Sportster," he said. "Stopped at every one of those battle positions. Talked to every one of the soldiers. Everything was going good." His convoy headed up Fat Boy, where it hit an IED but no one suffered any casualties. Twenty minutes later and three hundred yards up the road, the convoy got hit again. This time Kunk suffered a puncture wound to his left calf. The wound got infected and he was relegated to bed rest from March 12 to March 19.

---

*Shortly after his injury, after he had been sent back to the United States, Biggers and his fiancée were married by proxy, and a few months later she gave birth to their son. Biggers would remain in a coma for nearly a year, until his family took him off of life support. He died on February 24, 2007.

19

The Mayor of Mullah Fayyad

DURING THIS TCP rotation, Fenlason decided to begin a community-building initiative he had been mulling over for several weeks. Having most recently been assigned to the brigade's community affairs office, Fenlason was in tune with the counterinsurgency ideas that were gaining traction around this time. And upon his moving into this AO, the town of Mullah Fayyad had caught his attention. A cluster of a couple of hundred houses and other buildings in a compact area that bordered Sportster and was the home of TCP1 and TCP5, Mullah Fayyad seemed to him the perfect target to begin a serious effort to help locals get better control of sewerage, water, electricity, education, and other basics of civilized life. "I went to Goodwin with the idea of changing the focus," he said. "Let's do the CMO—the civil-military operations stuff. We are not finding insurgents in Mullah Fayyad, we're not getting anywhere with these IED sweeps, except finding IEDs, because we're not really establishing ourselves in Mullah Fayyad in any way that makes sense."

They were already five months into this deployment and Mullah Fayyad was still only a town in the sense that it was a dense collection of houses. There was no government, and due to vagaries of demographics and tribal dynamics, the town was so mixed that there was no dominant sheikh or local strongman there. Fenlason wanted to jump-start a campaign that would put the town on its feet, or at least start to. He believed he could do this by providing the Iraqis continuity, familiar faces. Rotating soldiers through every three to five days was not enough time to get anything done. "Every patrol that went out, my guidance to them was to engage people, talk to them, find out what is going on," he said. He told 1st Squad to make contacts and ask them what they needed and what they thought the Army might be able to do for them.

Alpha and some of the other companies throughout the battalion were successfully beginning such programs, and some were quite advanced, but Bravo, because of its restive area, lagged. Blaisdell was adept at achieving a rapport with the locals and had developed an extensive network of Iraqis who liked him and worked with him, but Fenlason had grand plans to bring a whole town to a higher level of healthy functioning. Encouraged by the progress he said he saw in just a week, and believing stability to be paramount, he lobbied Goodwin to let 1st Platoon stay in place while he tried to get something going.

Goodwin was encouraged. "They started doing minor patrols outside of the TCPs," Goodwin said. "They're starting to improve, starting to clean things up." Fenlason told him he wanted to stay a month, Goodwin remembered, but Goodwin responded, "Let's see how it goes."

Fenlason got this extension without speaking to Blaisdell or Gebhardt, which irritated them immensely; each move a platoon makes—or does not make—impacts the other two. "I was fucking pissed," Blaisdell admitted. "We had shit going on in Mullah Fayyad too. We could have shared that shit. I remember yelling at him on the radio, 'Who in the fuck put you in charge of the goddamn company?' "

Gebhardt, as usual, was more understated. "It was a unilateral call by one platoon sergeant. There was no discussion. I think that's what upset people more than anything." He acknowledged that one reason he wasn't as upset as Blaisdell was because his platoon was down at the JSB, which was the choicest of the three missions, and he certainly wasn't dying to have 2nd Platoon cover the TCPs. "If there is one position that the privates hated, it was the TCPs," he said. "But it was bearable because you did it seventy-two hours or so. But weeks at a time? That would drive me crazy."

The impact the extended TCP rotation was having on 1st Platoon was manifest, said Gebhardt. "A lot of his guys were upset by that. And that was obvious, just as you drove through. If you ever drive through the TCPs, platoon passing another platoon, there's friendly waves and chitchat as you go through. But they wanted none of that. They didn't want to talk to anybody. They were just mad. Not that I blame them. I'd be mad too."

Charlie Company's First Sergeant Largent remembered driving through Bravo's sector and looking at the soldiers manning the checkpoints. "You know, you see guys in the movies, and they've been in combat for months and they're just ragged and dirty and filthy and they got that thousand-yard stare and they're just burnt out?" he says. "And they're not all there mentally? That was Bravo Company. Those guys were strung the fuck out."

Fenlason was operating in a cocoon. He wasn't talking to the other platoon sergeants, nor was he communicating the mission, the importance of it, or the success he was having to any of the TCPs but his. Those not stationed at TCP1 had no idea what was going on when they radioed about when they were rotating back to the FOB. Fenlason said he couldn't tell, because he himself didn't know: the mission was results-dependent and could end at any moment.

Private First Class Justin Cross had one of a couple breakdowns around this time. "My brain was overheating. I started sweating, got really light-headed. I just fucking broke down, started crying and shit. There was no end to this. When the fuck is help coming? Shit, how long are we going to do this?" Cross was ultimately evacuated to Camp Striker during this TCP rotation for a complete psychological evaluation and a stay at Freedom Rest.

With the TCP mission now indefinite, Fenlason instituted a complex system where nine out of the approximately thirty-five soldiers in 1st Platoon rotated back to the FOB every day for four or five hours to take a shower, grab a hot meal, make a phone call, use the Internet, pick up their laundry, or get supplies for the TCPs. That left, on any given day, two dozen or so soldiers spread across four battle positions, which resulted in some of the thinnest staffing scenarios the men had ever experienced. TCP2 and TCP6 were routinely left with three or four people to man each spot. Staffing became so strained that at least once a single U.S. soldier got stranded alone with four or five Iraqi soldiers at a checkpoint. Despite this regular, methodical rotation system, which required nine soldiers to travel back and forth to Yusufiyah every day, Fenlason not only never visited TCP2, he never arranged for the men to receive better defensive supplies or hot food because, he said, "You don't want to travel if you absolutely do not have to. You don't want to travel predictably. Those are two things that are going to get you blown up."

One major initiative Fenlason got under way was a local leaders' meeting. During the few times he went on patrols himself, he asked old men, anyone who looked as if they qualified as an elder, whether they would come to an informal meeting. Many men, including a veterinarian and the town's only doctor, said they would attend. The meeting took place late in the first week of March, with Fenlason and a translator alone in a large room at TCP1 with about a dozen Iraqi men who showed up. Fenlason asked them what they wanted. They responded, overwhelmingly, that they wanted security. They wanted the insurgents to go away. Fenlason tried to align America's interests with theirs, telling them that if they would just tell the Americans where the bad guys were, he and his men could go get them. "So we just kind of went around and around in circles for about two hours, just sort of saying the same things over and over again," he recalled. "They had some food that a friendly family next door had made, and the group ended with an agreement to meet again in a few weeks."

Goodwin was getting an uninterrupted stream of good news from Fenlason about how great everything was at the TCPs. "Fenlason was calling me," Goodwin recollected, "and he is saying, 'Hey, we're talking with so-and-so, we've got this, and we've got this.' It's like, holy crap. They're coming back with information that I just haven't seen in a while. I'm sitting there thinking, 'This platoon is doing great stuff.'"

Unfortunately, the men of 1st Platoon did not see it that way. "The chain of command cared more about what was happening in Rushdi Mullah than what was happening to us," said Cross. "The frustration got to the point where pretty much everybody at the TCP started taking it out on people coming through. It kind of became a competition, bragging who's fucking them up better."

Drinking and drug use were on the rise, frequently right under Fenlason's nose. "The vast majority of the Joes were drinking," Private First Class Steven Green acknowledged. "Most of the NCOs. Of course, the NCOs were all like twenty-two years old, though. Since I can chug a pint of whiskey, Sergeant Yribe would be like, 'Hey, chug that bottle.' By February or March, I was doing some type of intoxicant every day. A lot of Valiums, and a lot of these pink pills that were some kind of a hallucinogen. A lot of other guys were taking those too. Iraqi Army guys would sell them to us. TCP1 was where all of the drugs were coming from, because that's where the most IAs were, and then they were getting spread to the other TCPs."

Some soldiers had started getting drunk and going out looking for Iraqis to beat up. "Cortez, Barker, and them, they'd get on whiskey and shit," said Cross. "They'd get rowdy. Cortez and Barker at one point went on a two-man drunken patrol. They were like, 'Fuck this shit, let's go find some people and fuck them up.' They took off by themselves. We had to send another soldier, who was sober, over there to keep an eye on them so nothing happened." These rogue patrols were not uncommon. "They'd go out in Mullah Fayyad and beat up some people," recalled Collin Sharpness, the medic. "They'd tell me all about it when they got back. There was a lot of shit going on. You got a twenty-two-year-old, a twenty-three-year-old in charge of a bunch of nineteen-year-olds? Controlling a checkpoint? Who knows what they're doing?"

On March 9, with so many 3rd Squad soldiers on leave, Cortez needed two more soldiers from the other squads to fill his ranks. Private First Class Jesse Spielman begged Cortez to take him, just so he could get away from Fenlason. No matter how bad TCP2 was, it was better than being around him, Spielman said. Fenlason's approval was easy to secure. He simply didn't care what personnel, in what combination, went down to TCP2. "Turns out to be Spielman and Green," he said. "Which, sure, why not? As long as I've got nine, I don't really give a shit."

Around two or three in the morning of March 10, TCP1 got a call from TCP2 saying they had detainees they needed help bringing in. They had been on their way to the house of an informant known as Mr. B when someone fired a rocket at them. They followed the rocket back to the house they thought it came from and now they had some suspects. Sergeant Yribe got Babineau and a couple of guys in a truck to go help out the guys from 3rd Squad. They didn't really know where the house was, so Babineau and Yribe got out and started filing down some of the alleyways as Cortez guided them in over the radio using landmarks. Finally, they were within shouting range.

"Cortez, that you?"

"Yeah, over here!"

Yribe walked into the house. Cortez, Spielman, a couple of other soldiers, and an interpreter were all there. In the room there were some electrical works, fuse boxes, wiring. Definitely shady, Yribe thought, so, okay, good grab. But walking in, Yribe could smell alcohol. And looking around, he could see that the soldiers had been drinking. The guys down at TCP2 were drinking at least every other day these days. Tonight they were so drunk they were practically falling down. They were trying to stand the detainees up, so they could punch them again or kick them, but they were so wasted, sometimes they wouldn't even connect and fell to the floor themselves. Realizing just how serious the situation was in terms of their safety as well as their getting into trouble, Yribe tried to take control. He had no problem roughing up Iraqis. Catching a guy who shot at you, or tried to blow you up, and putting a lot of hurt back on him? Not a problem. But you have to do it in a controlled, even methodical way. This was way, way, insanely out of control and, maybe more important, they were in danger of getting caught.

"What the fuck are you doing?" Yribe asked. "Cortez, you need to get a grip."

"What?" said Cortez, slurring.

"You guys are way out of line. What if it was anybody but me and Babs who came after your call? You'd be fucked. Where is your brain? We need to get these guys back and you need to get your stupid asses back to TCP2."

"Fuck you, motherfucker." Cortez always was a belligerent drunk.

"Whoa, who are you talking to here, dude?" Yribe responded.

"You're a fucking dick," Cortez slurred. Every time Yribe turned around, one or the other of the soldiers would shout at the Iraqis.

"Fucking motherfucker! You probably helped kill Nelson and Casica!" Spielman yelled as he tried to stomp on one of them.

"Bro, you just need to stop, all right?" Yribe repeated to Cortez. "You're drunk. You don't know what the fuck's going on. I'm trying to make it to where you don't get busted here, okay?" There was a brand-new soldier there, Private Nicholas Lake, who, according to platoon rules, had not earned the right to beat suspects. He was guarding the women and the children.

"All these Hadjis are motherfuckers!" one of the other drunk soldiers yelled. "We ought to just kill them all now." Another soldier butt-stroked one of the guys across the jaw. Blood went flying across the room. The man was knocked out cold, his jaw hanging in an unnatural way.

"Dude," Yribe yelled, "did you just kill him?" He hadn't, but the man was knocked out. Babineau and Yribe managed to wrangle the detainees and herd the drunk soldiers back to the truck. The whole time, Cortez was indignant that Yribe was not being cooler about this, saying he would have expected him to have his back. Spielman was an emotional drunk, telling Babineau how much he loved him and how Babineau had always been there for him. Yribe and Babineau got the guys from 3rd Squad back to TCP2, and they passed the detainees over to the IAs. No beating was ever reported.

20

The Janabis

O N MARCH 12, Green was pulling predawn guard in the gun truck at TCP2. He'd been up for eighteen hours. "I've had it," he thought to himself. This was it. After the morning IED sweep down Sportster and back, he was hanging out with Barker and Cortez in the courtyard area of the TCP, where Barker would always hit golf balls with a club he had scrounged somewhere. Whenever soldiers found Barker's balls on patrols and IED sweeps, they'd bring them back to the TCP.

"When I'm on guard next time," Green told them, "I'm going to waste a bunch of dudes in a car. And we'll just say they were running the TCP."

"Don't do that!" Cortez exclaimed. "Don't do it while I'm here. I'm supposed to be running this shit. I don't want to get in trouble."

Barker agreed. "I've got a better idea," he said. "We've all killed Hadjis, but I've been here twice and I still never fucked one of these bitches." Cortez's interest was piqued. They talked about it, the three of them, semiseriously but somewhat distractedly as they did other things throughout the rest of the morning. Sometimes Barker and Cortez would confer privately, sometimes Green and Barker would, and sometimes all three of them would talk.

Barker had already picked the target. There was a house, not far from here, that would be perfect, he said. They had been on a patrol there just a little while ago. There was only one male and three females in the house during the daytime—a husband, a wife, and two daughters. One was young, but the other was a teenager or in her twenties, it was hard to tell with all the clothes the women wore, as they frequently lamented. But Barker thought she was pretty hot, at least for a Hadji chick. Barker told them that they should go over there right now.

Witnesses were a problem, however. They knew that they couldn't leave anyone alive. Barker asked Green if he was willing to take care of that, even if there were some women and kids involved. Barker knew Green was always begging to kill Iraqis, if only someone would say the word.

"You'll kill them, right?" Barker asked.

"Absolutely," Green replied. "It don't make any difference to me," Green said. "A Hadji is a Hadji."

They refined their plan. Barker and Cortez told Green where the father hid the family's AK-47. They described the layout of the house and instructed Green on how to kill the family: Lay everyone down on their faces, put pillows over their heads, and shoot them once right in the back of the head real close, they said.

Over several hours and several conferences, they went back and forth on whether to do it or not.

Invoking the privileges of rank, Cortez asserted, "If we are going to do this, I am going to go first." Barker was pushing hard, and Green was game, but Cortez was waffling. Finally Cortez said, "No, fuck it, this is crazy. Fuck this. There is no way we are doing this shit."

At around noon, with a new wave of boredom taking hold, the three of them, along with Private First Class Jesse Spielman, sat down outside with a cardboard box as a table to play Uno. They drank Iraqi whiskey. Barker had bought five or six 12-ounce cans of the stuff from an IA at the very reasonable price of $5 per can. There was some bottled whiskey on hand too. Most of them mixed the whiskey in an empty one-liter water bottle with some Rip It, a carbonated energy drink. Green liked his whiskey straight. Over several hands of cards, they got drunk as they talked about all the things they usually talked about. Girls, cars, music, sports, how much they hated this place, how much they hated Fenlason, how much they hated Hadj.

During most of the game, Private First Class Bryan Howard had been on his cot, listening to his CD player in another room. Howard was just eighteen, a brand-new private who had arrived in November. Though he had missed only a little more than a month of the deployment, he was still considered a new guy. He was hazed often and not included in a lot of things.

The men, as they played, got drunker and drunker. Cortez later rated their level of intoxication at a 6 or 7 on a scale of 10. Barker said he felt about the equivalent of having six to eight beers.

During one of the rounds, Cortez popped up and declared, "Fuck it, we are going to do this." He outlined the mission and he divvied up the duty assignments just like a legit patrol. He and Barker would take the girl, Green would kill the rest of the family, Spielman would pull guard, and Howard would stay back and man the radio. He told everyone to grab their rifles and get ready to head out.

Spielman, who had not heard of the plan until now, did not bat an eye. "I'd be down with that," he said. As he packed up the cards and put them away, Cortez went out to the truck to check on Private Seth Scheller, who was the only one on guard. Scheller was also a brand-new private and he had been in the truck all morning.

Cortez returned and said, "If we are going to do this, let's go before I change my mind." He and Barker started changing their clothes, putting on their black, silk-weight Polartec tops and bottoms and balaclavas to obscure their faces. They wanted to look like insurgents, they said, and ordered Spielman and Green to do the same. Green objected, saying he wasn't changing. At least take your patches off, Cortez said, which Green did. Spielman wore only his ACU bottoms and a T-shirt, while Green kept his whole uniform on. Cortez insisted they cover their faces, so Green tied a T-shirt around his head and Spielman put on a pair of sunglasses, remarking that that was good enough.

Green grabbed a shotgun, and Cortez and Barker snagged M4s.

Barker took Howard's because it had fewer accessories attached to it and was therefore lighter. Spielman picked up an M14, a larger, heavier rifle than the M4 frequently used as a longer-range weapon.

Cortez briefed Howard. Cortez told him they knew about an Iraqi girl who lived nearby and they were going to go out and fuck her. To Howard, it was the most insane thing he'd ever heard. He did not believe them, but he also could not believe that they were actually leaving for somewhere, leaving him and Scheller alone. Cortez gave him the radio and told him to call if there were any patrols or Humvees coming through.

The men, armed and disguised, headed out the back of the TCP.

Forty-five-year-old Qassim Hamzah Rashid al-Janabi was not originally from the Yusufiyah area. The ancestral seat of his branch of the Janabi tribe was Iskandariyah, fifteen miles to the southeast. Qassim grew up in a large, poor family comprised mostly of farmers. He was a gentle and thoughtful child according to his sister, and in his early adulthood, he was a guard at the Hateen Weapons facility near Iskandariyah. During Saddam's time, Iskandariyah was one of the capitals of the Iraqi military-industrial complex, and Hateen was one of the region's major employers. When he was in his late twenties, his parents matched him with a cousin eleven years his junior, Fakhriah Taha Mahsin Moussa al-Janabi. They had a large wedding in 1987, even though the Iran-Iraq War was still raging and times were tough.

Qassim and Fakhriah had dreams. They wanted to own a house, have a large family, and earn enough money to provide anything their children desired, including college educations. After the 1991 Gulf War, the UN sanctions made life even tougher. Qassim, like everyone, just struggled to make ends meet. In the mid-1990s, the couple moved to Yusufiyah, to be closer to Fakhriah's family and to look for different work. During this period, the couple lived in several different homes and he held a number of jobs, sometimes as a farmhand, sometimes as a construction laborer. If their financial life was difficult, one part of their dream was coming true: they were building a big and handsome family.

A daughter, Abeer, was born in August 1991. She was tall for her age, somewhat gangly, and plagued with asthma, but Abeer was nonetheless beautiful, with big doe eyes, a small mouth, and gentle features. She was a spirited child who was, in the words of her aunt, "proud of being young." Soon after Abeer came a son, Muhammad, another son, Ahmed, and another daughter, Hadeel.

In 2000, Qassim came into a job that provided a measure of stability. A landlord in Baghdad hired him to look after his five-acre plot of orchards and farmlands where he grew pomegranates, dates, and grapes, among other crops, in a hamlet near Yusufiyah called Al-Dhubat. The landlord paid Qassim about $50 a month to look after the grounds, but he also allowed the Janabis to live in the small, one-story, one-bedroom furnished farmhouse on the land for free. Qassim split the harvest with the landlord. Depending on the season, his half could yield Qassim an extra $30 a month.

Qassim's family stayed in touch with his relatives in Iskandariyah and Fakhriah's relatives in Yusufiyah, visiting on holidays and weekends. They were always poor—so poor that Qassim never paid off a motorcycle he had bought from a relative for $20. The relative was so fond of the couple that he simply forgave the debt. Despite their poverty, the family was happy, the sons said. Qassim would take the boys to the market, play soccer with them, and help them with their homework, while Fakhriah stayed at home, teaching her daughters to cook the big meals that were her specialty. The children loved the small orchards, where they would play hide-and-seek among the rows of scraggly trees.

When the Americans invaded, people in the neighborhood and throughout the region were optimistic. The U.S. bombing campaigns had ruined what little infrastructure there had been under Saddam, but the people were sure that the Americans would bring not just peace and democracy but all of the electricity and water they would ever need, as well as new roads and sewer pipes. But soon, as they waited and waited, they realized, in fact, that was not going to happen—and that's when the trouble started. The area began to fall apart from neglect and violence.

"When the Americans entered the country, they dissolved the military, the police, everything," said Abu Muhammad, Fakhriah's cousin who lived in Mullah Fayyad then. "The borders were open and chaotic. And terrorists and Al Qaeda were ready to enter the country." Strangers started coming to town, beating people up, killing them. "And the people accepted it, because there was no other option. Fanaticism and radicalism, things we never had before, started happening. Even the government was built on radicalism."

In the fall of 2005, the people of Yusufiyah started seeing a lot more Americans, but even this brought no relief. It was no exaggeration to say, in many locals' eyes, that the Americans were as bad as the insurgents. Not only did the locals not feel protected, they felt persecuted. The patrols the Americans ran were brutish. "When they came to search a house, they would come without warning," remarked Abu Muhammad. "They would throw a flash-bang grenade by the door, storm in, scare the whole family." The Americans would break things or even steal money and jewelry as they upended the house looking for evidence. They'd leer at the women, point guns at the men, shout at them in English. If the homeowners were lucky, after the soldiers had found nothing, they would get an insincere apology. Qassim's son Muhammad said whenever the soldiers came to the house, he was terrified. They would point guns straight at his father's chest and shout at him, even though his father had done nothing, yelling, "You are Ali Baba, you are Ali Baba," the pidgin Arabic-English phrase for "criminal."

Whenever the extended family got together, the relatives would talk about how bad things had gotten and what could be done. But what could be done? Nothing. Qassim's brother-in-law was gunned down in cold blood by the Americans in Iskandariyah in early 2005, said his sister. The U.S. Army, she continued, admitted it made a mistake but never did a thing to make restitution, never did anything to the soldiers involved. Other family members got hauled off to jail for no reason, with no indication when they would ever be coming home. One member of the extended family got picked up just because there was a dead body outside his house, as if murderers dump their victims right outside their own homes. It made no sense.

Fakhriah was particularly worried about Abeer. Now fourteen years old, she was on the verge of womanhood and had started looking beyond the boundaries of her family. She dreamed of getting an education, marrying a well-to-do man, and moving to the city, where she could escape the tedium of country life. But her fragile beauty was attracting a lot of unwanted attention. Soldiers, whenever they saw her, would give her the thumbs-up and say, "Very good, very nice." Muhammad and Ahmed once watched a soldier run a finger down the terrified Abeer's cheek.

By early March, the harassment of Abeer was getting so bad that Abu Muhammad told the family to leave Abeer with him. There were more people at his house and it was less secluded. Abeer stayed there only one night, on March 9 or 10. Qassim came the next day to pick her up. Abeer's parents had decided to bring her back home. It was no problem, Qassim said, Abeer would be fine. Since they had taken the girls out of school awhile ago, Qassim was able to watch them all day. With his protection, Qassim assured Abu Muhammad, they would be fine.

The house was only a few hundred yards to the northwest, across a couple of farm fields and dirt trails. Like the natural pathfinder he was, Barker knew the way over and under every ditch, ravine, and bridge. They hurried there, doing the half-walk, half-jog pace known as the Airborne Shuffle. Barker knew the route to that little cluster of houses so well that he had taken his Gerber hand tool. He knew they would encounter a chain-link fence en route. Halfway through cutting it, his hand got tired, so he passed the tool off to one of the others to finish the job. They passed another fence that had been cut on a previous patrol. They passed three houses, knowing from trips through the area before that one of those was abandoned and one was still being constructed.

Sneaking up on the dingy home, Cortez and Barker broke to the right around a small shack in the front. Spielman and Green broke left. Spielman and Green found the little Hadeel and father Qassim in the driveway. Green grabbed the man and Spielman grabbed the girl and they marched them inside. Barker and Cortez cleared the house, checking the foyer, the hallway, and moving past the kitchen, where Cortez stopped to grab the woman, Fakhriah, and Abeer. Green and Spielman entered the house while Barker continued with the sweep, checking the bathroom and the toilet room, the bedroom and the living room. Then he headed up the stairs to the roof, checked the roof, and went back down the stairs.

The others had corralled the whole family into the bedroom. After they had recovered the family's AK-47 and Green had confirmed that it was locked and loaded, Barker and Cortez left, yanking Abeer behind them. Spielman pulled the bedroom door shut and then set up guard in the doorway between the foyer and the living room while Cortez shoved Abeer into the living room. Cortez pushed Abeer down on the ground and Barker walked over to her and pinned her outstretched arms down with his knees.

In the bedroom, Green was trying to get the man, woman, and child to lie down on the floor. They were scared, screaming in Arabic. Green was shouting back, "Get down, get down now!"

Back at the TCP, Howard was trying to get Cortez on the radio, each time saying there was a convoy coming and they needed to come back. They never responded. No Humvees actually came during the ten to fifteen minutes that they were gone, but Howard was panicked. Scheller and he were out there all alone.

In the living room, Cortez pulled Abeer's tights off. She was crying, screaming in Arabic, trying to struggle free as Barker continued to hold her in place. Cortez was masturbating, trying to get an erection. He started to make thrusting motions. "What the fuck am I doing?" he later recalled thinking at the time. "At the same time, I didn't care, either. I wanted her to feel the pain of the dead soldiers."

In the bedroom, Green was losing control of his prisoners. They weren't getting down on the ground. Terrified, they were yelling, and they weren't responding to Green's orders. The woman made a run for the bedroom door. Green shot her once in the back and she fell to the floor. The man, agitated before, now became unhinged. Green turned the AK on him and pulled the trigger. It jammed. He tried to clear it several times, but it kept sticking. Panicking, as the man started advancing on him, Green switched to his shotgun.

Green couldn't remember if there was anything in the chamber, so he pumped once and a full shell ejected. Then, Green said, "I shot him the way I had been taught: one in the head and two in the chest." The first shot blasted the top of the man's head off. He dropped backward to the floor as buckshot from the following shots continued to riddle his body.

Then Green turned toward the little girl, who was spinning away from him, running for a corner. Green returned to the AK and tried to clear it again, and this time it worked. He raised the rifle and shot Hadeel in the back of the head. She fell to the ground.

"I was hyped up, the adrenaline was really high," Green remembered later. "But as far as the actions of doing it, it's something that I had been through a million times, in training for raiding houses. It was just eliminating targets, and those were the targets that they had told me to eliminate. It wasn't complicated."

Spielman ran over to the locked bedroom door and pounded on it. Green opened the door. Spielman asked if he was okay and Green said he was. Spielman looked at the carnage in the room and was furious. He spotted the unexpended shotgun round, picked it up, and said, "What the fuck is this?" Green explained that the AK had jammed. Spielman asked Green how many shotgun blasts he had fired and began searching the room for the casings.

As Green was executing the family, Cortez finished raping Abeer and switched positions with Barker. Barker's penis was only half hard. Despite all her squirming and kicking, Barker forced himself on Abeer and raped her.

Green came out of the bedroom and announced to Barker and Cortez, "They're all dead. I killed them all." Barker got up and headed toward the kitchen. He wanted to look outside the window, see if anything was happening outside. As he did that, Green propped the AK-47 he was carrying against the wall, got down between Abeer's legs, and, as Cortez held her down, Green raped her.

The men were starting to get antsy. Spielman returned from the bedroom with several shells. The group had been there several minutes now.

"Come on, come on, hurry up," Cortez said, "hurry up and finish." Green stood up and zipped his fly as Cortez pushed a pillow over her face, still pinning her arms with his knees. Green grabbed the AK, moved Cortez's knee out of the way, pointed the gun at the pillow, and fired one shot, killing Abeer.

The men were becoming extremely frenzied and agitated now. Spielman lifted Abeer's dress up around her neck and touched her exposed right breast. Barker brought a kerosene lamp he had found in the kitchen and dumped the contents on Abeer's splayed legs and torso. Spielman handed a lighter to either Barker or Cortez, who lit the flame. Spielman went into the bedroom and found some blankets to throw on the body to stoke the fire. As the flames engulfing Abeer's body grew, Green, hoping to blow up the house, opened the valve on the propane tank in the kitchen and told everybody to get out of there.

The four men ran back the way they had come. When they arrived at the TCP, they were winded, nervous, and scared. Howard was relieved to see them. They were out of breath, manic, animated. But as the elation accompanying their safety took hold, they started celebrating. They began talking rapid-fire about how great that was, how well done. Green was jumping up and down on a cot and they all agreed that that was awesome, that was cool.

Barker and Cortez took off their long-underwear outfits and scrubbed down their genitals and bodies with bottled water. They collected their clothes to burn in the pit behind the TCP. Cortez told Spielman and Green to burn their clothes, too, but Green resisted, saying what he was wearing was the only uniform he had. Cortez then handed the AK to Spielman and told him to get rid of it. Spielman walked over to the canal and heaved it in.

Once their adrenaline started to wear off and they began to calm down, as they were standing around the burn pit, Cortez told everyone that they could never speak about what had happened. They agreed that if it ever came up, they would say that they didn't know anything about it. Green said that if it ever went beyond that, just to blame everything on him. He would say he and he alone did it.

It was getting close to dinnertime. Barker started to grill some chicken wings. Spielman tried to go to sleep and Green relieved Scheller on guard. Green asked Scheller if he had heard any shots or anything suspicious. Scheller said he hadn't.

Several hours later, as Yribe was walking back to TCP2 after investigating the crime scene, he mulled over what he had seen. The house was ghastly for sure, but it wasn't the worst thing ever. And yet, there were a couple of things about it that were odd. You don't see a lot of girls that little murdered in Iraq, he thought to himself. It happens, but it's not common. Maybe the killers didn't expect the house to be filled with females? Maybe they were disturbed mid-crime and panicked? And the burning of the other girl's body, that was strange too. Burning was a huge desecration, so big, Yribe knew, that Hadjis usually saved that insult for the rare American corpse they could get their hands on. And then there was the shotgun shell. Shotguns are not common in Iraq. The shotgun is almost exclusively an American weapon, mostly to shoot open doors and gates. The shell was locally made, green with a brass tip, called a "Baghdad round" because it had "Baghdad" stamped on it. Soldiers sometimes traded them with contractors on the larger FOBs for their novelty value. God knows, contractors can get pretty lawless themselves, but there were no contractors in the area; they were too scared to go down here.

As Yribe approached TCP2 along the canal road to drop off Spielman and Cortez, Green was waiting in the street. He didn't have any armor on, and he was looking up and down the street expectantly, nervously. He pulled Yribe aside and asked him what was going on, what he saw. Yribe gave him a twenty-second rundown, saying it was pretty ugly, especially with kids and all getting whacked, but other than that, it was just another murder like all the other murders. They had a phrase for it: "Yusufiyah happens."

"I did that shit," Green said.

"What?" Yribe said.

"I killed them," Green repeated. Barker was standing next to Green, but didn't say a word.

"What?" Yribe asked again. "What are you talking about?"

"That was me. I did it," Green said. "I killed that family."

Caught off guard, Yribe dismissed the idea immediately as more of Green's crazy talk. This is exactly the kind of stupid shit Green would say. And it was insane. How could a scrawny guy just slip away from a TCP by himself in the middle of the day and rape and murder a family? It just didn't figure. But Green kept insisting, and he knew details. He knew there were two parents and two girls, he knew there was a burned body, and he knew where the bodies were located in the house. Yribe was taken aback, but then he figured it was possible to have listened over the radio net as he was relaying the scene back to company headquarters. Yribe told Green to shut the fuck up, he didn't have time for his bullshit right now.

The next day, Cortez found his way up to TCP1 on a resupply or some other mission. He went to Yribe. He was in tears. He said he was so shaken up by what he had seen in the house—the littlest girl reminded him of his niece, he said—he needed to go to Combat Stress, but Fenlason wouldn't let him. Gimme a second, Yribe said. Yribe went to Fenlason and pleaded Cortez's case. The dude is really messed up, Yribe said, I think he really needs it. Fenlason relented and he sent Yribe to cover TCP2 while Cortez went to Mahmudiyah to see the psychiatrist there.

Yribe was anxious to get to TCP2. He had been thinking all night about what Green had told him, and it was bothering him. Yribe did not share any of it with Captain Goodwin when he briefed him on the crime scene. What was there to tell? That Green was talking shit again?

He figured that Cortez must have gotten rid of the green shotgun shell, because it wasn't in the small packet of evidence they had turned in. Once Yribe got to TCP2, however, he yanked Green's elbow.

"Now," Yribe demanded, "tell me everything, every single detail."

"No," Green said, "never mind. Forget I said anything. I'm either leaving Iraq in a body bag or as a free man. Just forget it."

"You tell me what happened," Yribe insisted, "or I will put you in that body bag myself."

Green started to talk. Again, Barker was there for the whole conversation, and again, Barker did not say a word. Green started telling Yribe everything he had told him the previous night, about the house, the four victims, details about the arrangement of the bodies, and what they were wearing, but in far greater detail than had ever been passed over the radio, such detail that only someone who had been there could possibly know. As he talked and retraced his steps, Green adamantly insisted that he had slipped away unnoticed while the other men were sleeping and acted alone. Barker volunteered nothing, and Yribe asked him no questions. The thing that really convinced Yribe, though, was not just what Green was saying but how he was saying it. Ordinarily, Green was manic and boastful, either jokey or angry or hysterical. Right now, however, Green was just serious, sober, matter-of-fact.

When Green was finished, Yribe stood up and told him, "I am done with you. You are dead to me. You get yourself out of this Army, or I will get you out myself."

21

Twenty-one Days

GOODWIN HAD LOW expectations of Fenlason's meeting in Mullah Fayyad, but he was delighted to hear how well it had gone. "It was awesome," Goodwin said. "Grass-roots politics right there." When the group of Iraqi attendees made good on their promise to have a second meeting a few weeks later, Goodwin was there. Fenlason, working with the Civilian Affairs captain on FOB Mahmudiyah, secured $15,000 worth of medical supplies for the local doctor. When the men of 1st Platoon later found out about that, their rage was nearly uncontrollable. *They can get fifteen grand for a Hadji doctor,* they muttered to each other, *but they can't fill our fucking HESCO baskets?!*

The events of the second meeting roughly mirrored the first, but that was fine. Everybody understood that no breakthroughs were going to happen overnight. This was the beginning of a long process. The Americans discussed how they wanted help locating insurgents. The Iraqis wanted safety and basic utilities restored. There was a circularity to the proceedings, but in all, Goodwin was enthused. "They voiced their concerns, and we addressed them," he said. "I said I would try to fix what I could. And I made promises where I could. We were moving forward."

Before the meeting broke up, however, the group talked about a couple of remaining issues. The men asked Captain Goodwin if he could
get his soldiers to stop beating them up. He thought they were talking
about arrests, where things maybe got a little rough. But then they clarified. No, they said. Sometimes, American soldiers would hit them and
kick them with no provocation whatsoever at traffic checkpoints. Worse,
sometimes they would appear at their homes in the middle of the night
and pummel them for no reason at all, not even as part of an arrest.
Goodwin knew that insurgent groups frequently used Iraqi uniforms,
or were, in fact, actual Iraqi policemen whose true loyalties lay with the
Mahdi Army, the Badr Corps, or some other militia. But U.S. Army uniforms were harder to come by than Iraqi ones, and anyway, he would
have thought Iraqis could tell the difference. He chalked it up to the
out-of-control rumor mills and conspiracy theories rampant in Iraq.

"You can trust me when I say that they're not my guys," he told them.

"But they look like you," they said.

"Trust me," he said. "They are not my guys."

Finally, there was the matter of the murder of a family in the small
nearby town of Al-Dhubat a few days ago. Did anyone, the Americans
asked, know anything about that? Violence was rife, it was true, but this
crime seemed, well, odd, for several reasons. The Iraqi elders said they
had no leads, nothing to offer, except to say it was horrible, what inhuman things the insurgents could do. Is it any wonder no one feels safe?

Those opinions conformed to all the data that had been collected so
far. The Iraqi Army had begun interviewing neighbors and family members the morning after the murders. Theories about who committed
the crime were so conflicting as to be inconclusive. Some said the family was killed by the Iraqi Army. Others said it was the Americans. Some
said it was the Badr Corps or the Mahdi Army. Others said it was a tribal
feud or a family grudge gone bad. There were no eyewitnesses, or at
least none who could offer a consistent story about what they saw. Since
the bodies had been removed so quickly (the family was buried in a
nearby cemetery the day after, with only stones as grave markers), and
since so many soldiers had tramped through the house, there was liter-

ally no usable physical evidence beyond a few AK-47 shell casings. A U.S. intelligence officer in the area a few weeks later asked about the incident and got much the same answers from the locals. Although the investigator found the atmosphere tense and unnervingly anti-American, nobody claimed Americans were the perpetrators in any greater numbers than for any of the other theories. Without conclusive evidence, and with no one presenting a compelling rationale that would favor one hypothesis over another, it was instantly a cold case, like literally tens of thousands of murders in Iraq that year. The resources devoted to any further investigative work on the crime plummeted to zero.

Yribe, like most of 1st Platoon, never liked or respected Fenlason. He was a know-it-all with not nearly enough battlefield experience to be telling him or anyone else in the platoon what to do, Yribe felt. And Yribe thought Fenlason was way too soft on Hadj, preferring to make time with them to score points with the higher-ups than to do anything that might actually benefit his own men.

On March 19, 1st Squad was doing a cordon-and-knock mission in one of the small villages around Mullah Fayyad and Yribe was surprised to see Fenlason come along for this one. They had searched about fifteen or twenty houses when, at one home, no one was answering the door. After they pounded and pounded, finally someone opened up.

"The Americans want to search the house," said the interpreter. "Do not be afraid." As soldiers fanned out, Yribe walked down a hallway. He knocked on the last door. It was locked. While he was jiggling the handle and laying his shoulder into it, getting ready to knock it in, an old man behind the door holding a pistol pulled it open. As Yribe's momentum carried him, surprised and with his weapon down, into the room, the two men practically bumped into one another, and the old man fired.

Yribe's rifle was not pointed forward, it was across his chest, barrel down, so his reflexive motion was not to pull the trigger but to stroke the man across the face with the butt of his rifle, knocking him back hard and opening a gash above his eye. Yribe got on top of him and got ready to keep pounding him. Fenlason and 1st Squad leader Chaz Allen were there, though, and threw Yribe off the man, yelling, "Stop!"

Yribe patted himself down to see if he was shot. The old man had missed. Yribe looked down and saw Fenlason giving first aid to the man, helping him up, giving him water. Yribe was enraged.

"What the fuck are you doing?" Yribe asked. "We should kill him." He had to walk out of the room or he was going to go berserk on both of them. Fenlason called some other soldiers to take the man outside and have him patched up by Doc Sharpness until they decided what to do with him.

"Fuck this! Fuck this! Fuck this!" Yribe yelled.

"Hey, pal, slow down," said Fenlason. "You need to cool off. What is the problem?"

"The problem is we should kill that motherfucker, not take him in. He fucking tried to shoot me."

Allen pulled Yribe aside and said, "When you entered that room, where was your weapon? You had it slung down like Mr. Cool Guy. If your weapon had been up at eye level where it should have been, you could have shot him and it would have been a clean shot. But we all know you can't go back in there and kill him now." Some of the other guys started teasing Yribe about it.

"Dude, you had a chance," they said, "and didn't fucking kill a guy? A guy who actually had a gun! What a fucking loser."

"No," quipped Watt, "that's not his M.O. Yribe only shoots women and children."

"That's fucking cold, Watt," Yribe said.

At the end of the mission, Fenlason called Goodwin and asked him what he wanted to do with the old man. He was seventy-two, he was hard of hearing, and he was scared out of his mind. He shouldn't have had a pistol, granted, but Fenlason seriously doubted he was an insurgent. He suggested they confiscate his pistol and just let him go. Goodwin agreed.

Yribe did not like that one bit, and he stewed in the Humvee all the way back to TCP1. By the time they arrived, he was fuming. It was cut-and-dried in his mind: This dude tried to kill a U.S. soldier. He is an enemy and should be treated that way. In the central area of TCP1, he began spouting a nonstop tirade about how this whole mission was fucked if they just kept letting go people who tried to do U.S. soldiers harm. Fenlason was a pussy. The whole chain of command was filled with gutless wonders.

This was all well within Fenlason's earshot, so Fenlason came to the central area of the TCP and said, "You need to cool it, Tony." Yribe, however, would not let it rest, and since he commanded a lot of sway among the younger men, Fenlason noticed he had a lot of disgruntled soldiers on his hands.

"Shut the fuck up!" Yribe yelled. "Don't even talk to me!"

"Who do you think you're talking to here, pal?" Fenlason responded.

"Fuck you. You are a piece of shit. If you come one more inch closer, it's going to be the worst fucking day you've ever had. I want out of your platoon. There is no way I can work for a piece of shit like you." One of the other sergeants started pushing Yribe out the door, telling him to go get his head together somewhere else.

Their scuffle almost reignited several times, because every time Yribe started to leave, Fenlason would say something like, "You better walk away," which would only cause Yribe to come scrambling back with: "No. Now I am staying. You have to make me leave, but you're too much of a pussy." This went on for several rounds before some other sergeants finally dragged Yribe away for good.

"You are done, Tony," Fenlason said as they finally hauled him out of there. Staff Sergeant Allen tried to calm Yribe down.

"Hey man, you can't be blowing up like this," he cautioned.

"Sergeant Allen, I don't know you," Yribe answered. "I haven't worked with you very long. But I respect you right now. But I'm not going to respect this guy. This guy will get everyone killed."

"Well, that's not for you to decide, is it? You're an E-5, he's an E-7. We work for him."

"I'm not going to work for him. I can't work for you either. If you're going to work for him, I can't work for you."

"Roger that, then," Allen fired back. "Then I don't need you."

Fenlason was already moving against Yribe. He could not tolerate that kind of insubordination. He had Allen and Staff Sergeant Payne write up statements that night, and he forwarded them to Goodwin. He thought for certain Yribe would be in for some sort of disciplinary action, or even a psychological evaluation, but after a brief double check of what had happened, Goodwin decided not to take any punitive action against Yribe. Yet after a rupture like that, there was no way Goodwin could leave Yribe in 1st Platoon.

Third Platoon's Phil Blaisdell said that he'd be willing to take Yribe. He sat Yribe down and told him he had no idea what had just happened between Fenlason and him. Frankly, he didn't want to know and he didn't care. "With me," Blaisdell said, "you start with a fresh slate. Follow orders, do a good job, get along with the rest of the platoon, and I am sure everything will be fine."

Goodwin's decision not to punish Yribe rankled Fenlason, but he saw the overall outcome—Yribe left, Fenlason stayed—as a turning point in the dynamic of the platoon. Fenlason had proved that he was not going anywhere, and that his authority could survive a full-scale coup attempt by the most powerful representative of the old 1st Platoon mentality. "That was when people began to realize that the immovable object was in fact immovable," he said. "That was the day there was no doubt that it was my platoon. We were done negotiating."

Fenlason's platoon was still very much in trouble, however, and he remained willfully ignorant of the extent of its problems. In order to take Yribe, for example, Blaisdell had to give someone up: Sergeant Daniel Carrick, who was considered one of the best young NCOs in the company, if not the battalion. He was Ranger qualified and had been to all the right schools and had gotten all the right skill badges very quickly. His culture shock upon arriving at 1st Platoon was extreme. Showing up more than six months into their deployment, Carrick never had much chance of being taken seriously by his fire team. Dealing with the aura left by Yribe was his first big challenge. Again and again, he would hear, "Sergeant Yribe wouldn't do it that way," or "Sergeant Yribe didn't care about stuff like that." He had to tell them that he didn't give a fuck about how Sergeant Yribe would do it because he was not Yribe, Yribe was not here any longer, and this was how they were going to do it now. But more than that, he was alarmed at how angry they were—at Hadj, at the chain of command, at life. "There were a lot of guys at 1st Platoon who would love to go on patrol, but only because they wanted to fuck something up," he said. "They wanted to punch somebody in the head or they wanted to shoot up somebody's car." In his eyes, a lot of the lower-enlisted were clearly thugs and degenerates back home and they had never been properly instilled with Army discipline in the first place. Here, they were out of control. "After being with them for a month, I was just like, 'These guys are the biggest group of bitches and psychopaths that I ever could have fallen into,' " as he put it. "They would get booze, and how do you stop this when Joes just do whatever they want? As a leader, what do you do? I didn't know. I knew about it, and I would tell them to knock that shit off, but I could never find the stuff. So what am I going to do?"

Other team leaders likewise acknowledged that they knew drinking or drug use was going on but that it was difficult to prevent. During the three-week TCP rotation in March, Sergeant John Diem had two soldiers melt down on him on two consecutive days. One day, the first suddenly became uncontrollable and inconsolable. "It was like a hysteria, left and right emotions, for hours," Diem said. "I told him to lie on his bunk and we'd take care of guard. I didn't understand it. I had known him for six months, I'd always been able to depend on him. Then, one day, he just went off the bend. I thought it was an extreme combat stress injury. So we got him out of there, somewhere where he could be closely watched. The very next day, we were doing a route clearance, and somebody tells me that one of my guys is asleep in a Humvee. So I go down there, and I fucking get on top of the Humvee, and I'm yelling, 'Hey dickhead!' And I'm yelling at him and he's not moving. He's breathing, but that's it. He's not aware of what's going on at all. So I give him a couple shots upside the K-pot [helmet] to check for responsiveness. And he's like, 'Stop hitting me. Stop hitting me.' Like almost completely unresponsive, like a catatonia, like a . . . like a . . . drug overdose. So I put him to bed. I get another guy out there on guard. I toss these two guys' shit and we find pill packs of some shit that I've never seen before. And those two guys lived with me. I had thought they couldn't make a move without me knowing. But I came to learn that it was pretty free game. It was something that you could get if you even half-ass wanted it."

Many soldiers assert that substance abuse was pervasive. "It was fairly common," said one. "That's how they began to deal and cope with certain things: All the soldiers who had been killed, the long hours they were pulling. Some of the soldiers used painkillers or drank because it was their only escape. That is what they had to do in their own mind to keep themselves from freaking out. Still, I was extremely upset and mortified by the idea that people would do that—all the times you thought your life was safe while you slept and they were on guard, it wasn't."

In Iraq, stray dogs are rampant and a constant nuisance. Most are mangy, disease-ridden, and nasty, and they run in large, wild packs. But some, every once in a while, manage to have good looks, clean coats, and friendly natures. These strays were frequently snatched up by soldiers and turned into pets. Although keeping dogs was always against the rules, many of the on-the-ground commanders recognized the undeniable positive impact they had on morale—several platoon-level leaders had stories of stumbling upon a soldier who had just lost a comrade in battle tucked away in some lonely corner of a base, cradling a dog in his arms, just petting it and sobbing into its fur—so they frequently just looked the other way. There were two dogs that hung around TCP1—an adult and a puppy. But the puppy got sick and started to lose its fur. Fenlason sent the word out: The puppy needs to be put down, and the faster you put it out of its misery, the easier it will be on canine and human alike.

It was the third week of March, 1st Squad was still at TCP1, and Fenlason could hear some guys tromp up the stairs. A few minutes later they came back down. He could hear them talking in excited but hushed tones, catching snippets of some guys giggling and saying, "That was cool," and others saying, "That shit was fucked up." Fenlason recognized it as the murmur of soldiers who were up to no good. He came out of his office and demanded, "What the hell is going on here?"

"Nothing, Sergeant," somebody replied.

"Don't bullshit me," Fenlason pushed. "What the hell is going on?"

"Green threw the puppy off the roof," somebody answered.

"He did what?" Fenlason asked, incredulous, to a wide round of more murmurs and shuffling.

"C'mere, you jackass," he said to Green.

"What, Sergeant?" Green responded, giggling. "You said to get rid of it."

"And do you think seeing if it could fly is what I had in mind?" Green found this line funny, but Fenlason wasn't laughing. Fenlason was so dismayed by Green's cavalier attitude to his own cruelty, he told Combat Stress about the incident. Green, meanwhile, was trying to comply with Yribe's order to get out of the Army. Between the puppy incident and Sergeant Yribe pushing him to find a way to get discharged, Green headed back to the Combat Stress tent the next time he was at FOB Mahmudiyah. "I got my duffel bags, all my stuff, and took it with me to Mahmudiyah. I was telling everybody I'm not coming back," Green said. "And they were like, 'You'll be back.' And I was like, 'Just watch.'"

Green had not seen Combat Stress since December 21, and a new team had taken over in January, headed by Lieutenant Colonel Elizabeth Bowler, a forensic psychiatrist and reservist who ordinarily worked in the California prison system, and Staff Sergeant Bob Davis, also a reservist. On March 20, Green showed up at the Mahmudiyah Combat Stress office. In the block marked Reason for Visit on his intake form, he wrote: "Anger, dreams, emotions over dead friends." And in the block marked Who Referred You and Why, he wrote: "Both team leaders Sgt. Diaz and Sgt. Yribe. Don't know exactly but they just said I needed to go."

In his initial interview, however, he told Davis, "I was told to see you because I killed a puppy." Through the course of the session, Green said he didn't understand what the big deal was. Everybody was killing dogs down there, he just happened to kill his in ten minutes rather than a couple of seconds. It all ends the same way, so what difference did it make? Seeing a red flag, Davis tried to explain why it made a world of difference. In his intake questionnaire, Green described his mood as "good a lot and then it flips to where I don't care and I want to kill all the Hadj." Bowler gave Green some Ambien to help him sleep and a course of antidepressant medication—Lexapro—and she kept him on the FOB for more evaluation.

Over the next few days, the Combat Stress team met with Green several more times and concluded that he wasn't registering the moral implications of the incident. "If he had ever said, 'Look, I was just trying to impress my buddies by showing my capacity for cruelty,' we would have let him go back to work," recounted Davis, "because it would have shown understanding of what the fuss was about." But the conversations progressed into more-troubling territory. Green said that the puppy could have just as easily been an Iraqi and it still wouldn't have made a bit of difference.

Bowler told Kunk of her diagnosis of Green: a preexisting antisocial personality disorder, a condition marked by indifference to the suffering of others, habitual lying, and disregard for the safety of self or others. People with this diagnosis are colloquially referred to as sociopaths or psychopaths. The diagnosis of personality disorder carries an immediate expulsion from the Army, and they began the process of removing Green from the service. In fiscal 2005, 1,038 soldiers—or 0.21 percent of those on active duty—were discharged with this classification. Even though Green had committed rape and quadruple homicide just eleven days earlier, Bowler's mental-health-status evaluation sheet that initiated the personality disorder discharge stated that his current potential for harm to others was "low." Green's separation from the Army had begun. He would never return to Bravo Company.

Green disputed the diagnosis. "I don't have antisocial personality disorder," he said. "That's like a sociopath. In regular day-to-day life, I'm not remotely like that. I don't even want to hurt people's feelings. If I say my opinion and someone gets offended, that's one thing, but intentionally to hurt someone? No, that's ridiculous. I didn't agree with the diagnosis, but I didn't care. It was getting me out of the Army."

He remained at Mahmudiyah for a few more weeks for observation and processing. By April 14, he was headed out of Iraq and back to the States, and at Fort Campbell on May 16 he was honorably discharged from the Army and sent back into society.

As Green was undergoing his psychological evaluations at Mahmudiyah, the rest of 1st Platoon had rotated back from the TCPs to Yusufiyah on March 21. Goodwin couldn't have been more pleased, but he thought three weeks was the maximum that men could stay out there without a break.

"I thought it was a great success," Goodwin said. "After they came back, I talked to the platoon that evening and told them that they did an outstanding job." Justin Cross had just returned from a week of Freedom Rest and psychological evaluation in Baghdad, but he was there for the pep talk, which he said was the first time most of the platoon had heard why they had all been out there so long. "Finally, after it was over, we finally found out what Sergeant Fen's master plan was out there. It just pissed everybody off that he didn't tell us when we were out there what we were doing."

Fenlason was pissed too. He wanted 1st Platoon to stay out at the TCPs longer. He was, he felt, just weeks away from making a real breakthrough in Mullah Fayyad. "A third meeting and we could have damn near formed a city government," he believed.

When Goodwin told him to move off of the TCPs, his response was "That's bullshit, we're close." When Goodwin said his mind was made up, Fenlason replied, "Well, then, you'll give back Mullah Fayyad."

For the remaining five months of the deployment, TCP rotations never lasted longer than a week, and Bravo Company never organized another community leaders' meeting in Mullah Fayyad.

APRIL–JUNE 2006

22

"We Had Turned a Corner"

THE HUNT FOR Zarqawi had begun shortly after the invasion of Iraq, in the summer of 2003, when the U.S. military joined two special operations forces units into what was then called Task Force 6-26. Over the years, the Task Force had gone through several name changes, becoming Task Force 145, then Task Force 121, and then Task Force 77. As the war ground on, and with Zarqawi still on the loose, the unit grew in size and mandate. By early 2006, Task Force 77 had expanded into four subordinate groups with rough geographic areas of responsibility. The Task Force's members, known as "operators," averaged at least a mission a day, usually conducted in the small hours of the morning. Task Force Central, which covered the Triangle of Death, was organized around a Delta Force squadron with Army Rangers in support.

Because of Zarqawi's feuds with the Anbar sheikhs and other Sunnis revolted by his hyperviolence, his areas of safe operation were narrowing, and the Triangle of Death was one of the last locales where he could find refuge. With information that he was spending more time there, the Task Force picked up its rate of operations in the area accordingly. The Task Force's methodology of pursuit was simple yet relentless: capture an enemy safe house, detain suspects, and exploit the resulting intelligence to set up a new hit as soon as possible, preferably in just a few hours. The Task Force described this combination of intelligence and action as "the unblinking eye."

Task Force 77's cooperation with the regular Army units holding a particular area was cordial but fairly one-way. The operators did not ask the local commanders' permission to come in; they usually just notified them that they were doing so. If a mission went poorly and men or machines were damaged, the local commander would be expected to have a QRF on standby, but beyond that, the commanders were expected to stay out of the way.

For the men of Bravo, "the cool guys," as they called the operators, were an ever-present but mysterious backdrop to their war. In the spring of 2006, the cool guys started zipping in and out of 1st Battalion's AO with increasing regularity. Unless they were assigned to a rescue mission, most of the men had only a dim awareness of when or even if TF-77 was in the area, but the operators always seemed to be popping up.

Zarqawi, Al Qaeda, and other terrorist organizations did not go dormant in the face of increased pursuit, however. In fact, they stepped up their activities in the Yusufiyah area and started taking out some very big American targets. Just before 5:00 p.m. on April 1, a rocket or RPG fired from a white Bongo truck shot down an Apache attack helicopter about one mile northwest of Rushdi Mullah. A video posted on Al Qaeda–related Web sites on April 5, complete with jihadi music and the Mujahideen Shura Council logo, depicted a gruesome scene. The helicopter was a mound of twisted rubble, flaming like a lava flow. Several black-clad fighters, with bandoliers, AKs, and covered faces, swarmed upon the wreckage. Some yelled "Allahu Akbar!" as they pulled out the body of one of the pilots and dragged him across the ground. It was the first time a U.S. helicopter had been shot down since January, but for the next few months, Al Qaeda's Aeisha Brigade, which was headquartered in the Yusufiyah area and specialized in antiaircraft operations, would become particularly successful at bringing down helicopters in the area.

"There were helicopters falling out of the sky a lot, which isn't supposed to happen," said Goodwin. The Aeisha Brigade was well organized, had outstanding concealment tactics, and possessed more sophisticated weaponry than average for an insurgent cell. Their presence was an indication of just how badly Al Qaeda wanted to hold this piece of land. "They started putting antiaircraft guns out there," remarked First Strike's intelligence officer, Leo Barron. "Rarely did you see many aircraft getting shot down anywhere else. This was pivotal terrain, and they were willing to expend those kinds of assets."

Numerous units from across the division were dispatched to the Apache crash scene, including Bravo Company's 2nd Platoon. The recovery effort would stretch for two days, hampered by muddy conditions, numerous IEDs, and frequent fire from insurgents. Both pilots would be pronounced dead, the body of one recovered on the scene and the other never found. With roads impassable, and helicopter delays interminable, the salvage effort had all but ground to a halt until 2nd Platoon, desperate not to spend a second night in the bush, carried helicopter wreckage on stretchers across muddy fields to the removal trucks for four hours.

On April 13, against great odds, contrary to the advice of many doctors, and despite all the unit commanders' assurances that no one expected him to return or would think less of him if he didn't, Rick Skidis returned to Iraq and resumed his role as Bravo's first sergeant. After getting blown up in November, he had battled through numerous surgeries to his leg and went through months of therapy to get back and finish the deployment with his beloved Bravo. Upon returning, Skidis noticed a definite change in his men. They were battle hardened and battle weary. "I saw a lot of stress," he recalled. "I saw a lot of tired guys, a lot of guys that had done a lot of fighting. They had been honed, they had matured, they had been working their asses off." And, he noticed, their work had made noticeable gains. "You could drive down Fat Boy. It was okay. You could drive down Sportster and it was pretty much okay."

As one first sergeant was returning, however, another was departing. Throughout the winter and into the spring, Kunk's battles with Charlie Company commander Captain Bill Dougherty and First Sergeant Dennis Largent were frequent and heated. They argued about tactics, priorities, IED sweeps, manning rosters, anything. While both men refused to be intimidated by the Kunk Gun, Largent was particularly emphatic about going back on the attack against Kunk, accusing him of a bullheadedness that was tantamount to incompetence because he insisted on policies that Charlie's leaders believed were misguided, if not needlessly dangerous. Through it all, however, Dougherty and Largent were concerned that their conflicts with the boss were having an adverse effect on the company, bringing more scrutiny and ultimately more pain down on their guys.

Others saw this happening as well. "Kunk was starting to have an impact on that company's performance and morale, because of the way he would treat the CO and the first sergeant," commented HHC commander Shawn Umbrell. Word had gotten out among Charlie that Kunk had it in for them, that he thought they were jacked up. Like Bravo, they were detaching themselves from the battalion, but unlike Bravo, they had more esprit de corps to carry them through, even if it was borderline mutiny sometimes. Occasionally Charlie soldiers flew a Cobra flag from their crow's nests and guard towers instead of the American flag. "He just hates us because we're the People's Army" became a battle cry among the Cobras. Those gestures of defiance drove a further wedge between the company and the battalion. Both Edwards and Kunk could frequently be heard screaming, "I am sick of this People's Army bullshit!"

Largent was in a dilemma. He believed that Kunk was a bad commander and a danger to the soldiers. He had tried reasoning with him, he had tried arguing with him, he had tried ignoring him, and he had tried defying him. As his disillusionment grew, so did his bitterness and hatred of Kunk. And that, he realized, was clouding his judgment and his ability to work in Charlie's best interests.

By spring, Charlie's relationship with the battalion had crumbled to the point that issues such as Internet access, which on the modern battlefield has real morale implications for soldiers, still got blown out of all proportion. Earlier in the year, during a visit from some general down in Lutufiyah, Largent mentioned that FOB Lutufiyah did not have good communications connections. And, as generals do, the general said to his aide, get this unit's info and get them one of those Internet trailers down here as soon as possible. E-mail addresses were exchanged, promises were made. Largent and the men of Charlie were pumped. Largent, dying to bring anything the men could be excited about into their lives, followed up with the general's aide like a demon. He inquired frequently: When's it coming? When's it coming? During this period of intense anticipation, a Charlie convoy that had been up to Mahmudiyah came back to report: Hey, the battalion has a shiny new Internet trailer that they are using up at their FOB. The outpouring of negative emotions from Charlie was intense, and the backlash back from the battalion was worse.

"Now, is that my Internet?" said Dougherty. "I don't know. There are theories that say it was ours because we were tracking the shipment of it, with air bill numbers or whatever. And guys got pissed. There was a tidal wave of 'They've got our Internet.' Maybe. Maybe not. I don't know. But I had a hard time convincing them of that, and I can't legislate how my men think. So they got it in their heads that Battalion stole their Internet. Then Colonel Kunk picked up on it and he got mad at me because he thought I was spouting all these terrible, terrible things about Battalion because of it. It just spun out of control."

Kunk vehemently denied the accusation that Battalion took first pick of anything. "We always pushed all resources down to Bravo Company or Charlie Company first—be it Internet, big-screen TVs, no matter what it was," Kunk said. "The Internet and all that had been provided down there and they were not taking advantage of it, and still saying that they didn't have what everyone had at Mahmudiyah." HHC commander Umbrell watched the fiasco escalate, powerless to stop it because the relationship between Kunk and Edwards and Dougherty and Largent had degraded so badly. "The relationship had deteriorated to the point where it wouldn't be improved unless both parties agreed it was going to be improved," he noted. "And neither one of them was backing down."

Largent was desperate for ideas to remedy the situation. He appealed, he thought in confidence, to an officer from the brigade whom he had always trusted. He approached him and asked, "Sir, we've got these problems. What can I do about it? Can you give me some insight here?" Largent believed he was betrayed: not long after, Kunk confronted him about going behind his back. They had a relationship-ending argument, during which Largent told Kunk he couldn't work for him anymore. He contacted Brigade Sergeant Major Brian Stall, who came down to see Largent in Lutufiyah the next day.

"I can't work for this fucking guy anymore," Largent told Stall. "We are headed down a road to where something bad is going to happen, because he is not listening to anybody. He's not understanding the tactical situation out here. I've done everything I can. This is going to end badly, and there's nothing more I can do to fix it." Largent was gone from Lutufiyah and moved to new duties within a week. About Largent's departure, Kunk said, "He wasn't getting the job done. The environment was tough. And there's a thing about enforcing standards and discipline and doing the right things. And it wasn't getting done. It was time for a change."

The Rushdi Mullah missions had become so frequent that First Strike decided in mid-April to seize a house permanently and make it a patrol base. Instead of having different units running through there at irregular intervals, they now had a fixed location that Alpha, Bravo, and Charlie would occupy on an alternating basis. The battalion never really had enough men to hold on to that patrol base and control of the town completely, but almost everybody viewed the initiative favorably because the battalion's activities were obviously disruptive to a very large insurgent population. Soldiers even liked the Rushdi Mullah missions. They were dangerous and scary, but they were more like the kind of war they had trained for. It was real enemy territory where soldiers could maneuver and fight against enemies who were recognizable yet defeatable. Give me a gun battle over an IED any day, was every soldier's preference.

First Platoon became a regular and reliable part of those rotations. For Goodwin, April seemed to be a crucial turning point. He felt that 1st Platoon was, after much pain and resistance, adapting to Fenlason's way of doing business and coming back on line as a well-performing unit. "We had three platoons at that point," he said. "It felt good. We were not just sitting there getting punched in the face. We're actually going out, looking for him, punching him back."

Around the same time, Task Force 77 was making more dramatic strikes into the area looking for Zarqawi. In February, they had identified certain houses in the Yusufiyah area that insurgent leaders were using. At 2:15 a.m. on April 16, TF-77 operators raided one such safe house. They got into a firefight, during which several suspected insurgents were killed and several more were taken into custody, though Zarqawi was not among them. He was, the Americans later learned, less than half a mile away at the time. Nine days after that, TF-77 mounted another raid on a house several miles from where the Apache had crashed on April 1. They were fired upon as they arrived and killed five men outside the house. With persistent fire coming from within the house, they called in an air strike, which reduced the house to rubble and killed seven more men and one woman. A press release issued by the military said every male found in the rubble was carrying an AK-47 and wearing a weapons vest.

With uncanny timing, a video starring Zarqawi appeared on Islamist Web sites the same day. It was his most public communiqué ever and the first to show his uncovered face. During the thirty-four-minute video, Zarqawi speaks directly into the camera for long stretches, meets with some masked lieutenants, pores over maps, and squeezes off machine gun bursts in the empty desert. He has a mustache and a beard and wears black fatigues, an ammunition harness, and a black skullcap. He is serious but robust looking. Healthy, even plump. The message is a condemnation of the United States and George W. Bush and an exhortation to the Iraqi insurgency. There are elements of bitterness—he is very harsh with Sunnis who have begun participating in the political process. They have, he says, "put a rope around the necks of the Sunnis," and he vows to target anyone who cooperates with the Shi'ite-dominated, U.S.-backed government. A debate raged within military and intelligence circles about whether Zarqawi's dramatic step into the spotlight connoted desperation or bravado.

In mid-April, some Charlie Company soldiers were busted for possession of Valium. The AR 15-6 investigation revealed that they had gotten it when they spent a short time at the TCPs filling in for Bravo. According to the soldiers' statements, the IAs offered them drugs within their first few hours of arrival. HHC commander Shawn Umbrell, who conducted the investigation, said he mentioned to Goodwin that if it happened to Charlie Company so quickly out there, then it was likely that Bravo's guys were being exposed to that temptation on a regular basis. Many IAs were known users and abusers of both drugs and alcohol. Fenlason, for his part, said he never entertained the notion that 1st Platoon might be abusing substances at the TCPs. "Do I know I have an alcohol problem or a drug problem?" he asked. "No, I don't. Did I conceive of it? No, I didn't. Did the IA have drugs? Yeah. They had all kinds of stupid shit down there. But, no, it never occurred to me."

That changed in mid-May when a 1st Platoon Bravo soldier, high on Valium, left his guard station at TCP3 in the middle of the night without his weapon and wandered two hundred yards down the road until he got caught in a strand of concertina wire. Sergeant Carrick found him snared out in the street, babbling gibberish, thinking he was still on a patrol that had happened days ago. Carrick sent him up to the medic at TCP1 because he thought he had had a mental breakdown. Doc Sharpness checked him out and concluded, no, he was not having a breakdown. He was high. Fenlason and Goodwin ordered urinalysis tests for the whole platoon and three soldiers failed.

In mid-May, Task Force 77 initiated another round of offensives against Al Qaeda throughout First Strike's AO. Beginning on the evening of the 13th, the United States claimed it killed a high-value target known as Abu Mustafa (who it believed was involved in the April Apache crash) and fifteen other insurgents in four coordinated raids in Lutufiyah. In keeping with TF-77's "unblinking eye" approach, the operators used information gleaned in those raids to immediately mount another raid beginning the afternoon of the 14th, this time on a safe house not far from the power plant.

As coalition forces approached, they started taking fire. Al Qaeda's Aeisha Brigade had commandeered several rooftops and from there shot at the helicopters with missiles and machine guns. At 5:30 p.m., they hit one of TF-77's Little Bird helicopters just east of the power plant. That copter was able to self-recover and take off again. At 5:40 p.m., however, the insurgents hit another Little Bird. This one crashed badly only a few hundred yards northwest of Rushdi Mullah. TF-77 called in a fighter-bomber air strike, which included at least one 500-pound bomb that ripped apart several homes and resulted in dozens of dead and wounded. An MNF-I (Multi-National Force–Iraq) press release said that "approximately 20 terrorists" were killed, but locals insisted that the dead were mostly noncombatants.

Several units from throughout the division were dispatched to assist in the recovery of the Little Bird and its two dead pilots, including, once again, Bravo's 2nd Platoon. In a repeat of the recovery mission in April, the salvage crews took far longer to get to the site than expected due to the dozens of IEDs and numerous firefights they met along the way. At about 3:00 p.m. on the second day, 2nd Platoon got word that the trucks were only an hour or two away. But by 7:00 p.m., after hitting two more IEDs, they still had not arrived and were not likely to make it there until morning. At that point, 2nd Platoon told the convoy to stay there, they would bring the helicopter to them. They found the house of a farmer with whom they had developed a good relationship. "We told him we'd pay him if he would let us borrow his tractor and trailer," said 2nd Platoon's Sergeant Jeremy Gebhardt. "And he said, 'No, no, I'll drive. Let's go.' So he drove out there and we loaded up his tractor with helicopter parts." They finished the job of getting the debris to the wrecker just before 11:00 p.m.

A military spokesperson reiterated to the *Washington Post* what
MNF-I's press release had said, that there were no civilian casualties related to this battle. This is not true according to 3rd Platoon soldiers
who were down at the JS Bridge during this time. Platoon Sergeant
Phil Blaisdell recalled, "The fucking bomb hit this one family's house,
killed like five kids. The wife survived, but her arm was broken. They
brought all those kids down to the JSB in the back of a Bongo truck,
just all fucked up. How do you face a guy that just lost his entire family except one son and his wife?" The man asked Blaisdell if they could
cross the bridge, which was ordinarily closed, to bury their children in
a cemetery that was on the other side. Blaisdell let them pass.

Fenlason and Norton were happy that 1st Platoon was participating more
fully in the company's battle rhythms, including the multiday rotations
out to Rushdi Mullah. To them, it was a sign that they were rehabilitating
the platoon. They had a couple of very successful runs up there, doing patrols, gathering intelligence, rolling up bad guys. "It was important, proving that we're not a jacked-up unit," said Norton, "proving we could
accomplish multiple-day operations miles away from any sort of higher
leadership."

Virtually every aspect of the platoon was on the upswing. Two months
after he kicked Yribe out, Fenlason felt like the men were finally getting
on board. Soldiers were shaving, wearing their uniforms correctly, cutting their hair. Their attitude was improving, they were letting go of
some of their anger and bitterness. "We still couldn't take much of a set-
back, but we had turned a corner," he said. "We were well on the road
to recovery." Others noticed it too. Sergeant Major Edwards told Fenlason several times that he was now running one of the top five platoons
in the whole battalion. Even some of the men say that May did seem like
the beginning of a new chapter. They had been in country seven
months, they were on the back end now, and things were looking up.

In mid-May, 1st Platoon returned to Rushdi Mullah. During what
would turn out to be their last trip up there, several elements of 1st Platoon got into a serious firefight. On May 22, most of the platoon was

back at the patrol base after a round of morning patrolling. They were relaxing, trying to cool off. They had been taking some sporadic fire coming from behind the house for some time, but it was steadily getting more persistent, moving from harassment probes to more directed fire.

After checking with Norton and Fenlason, Lauzier grabbed Specialist Barker, Sergeant Diaz, and another soldier and they headed out to maneuver on the gunmen. Norton began prepping another fire team to flank from the other direction. Barker was in the lead, with Lauzier behind and Diaz and the other soldier making up a machine gun team in the back. They flanked out right from the house and into a farm field. To their surprise, this field was much lower than the surrounding ones, and their sight was further impaired by stands of elephant grass. But they spotted six or seven insurgents on a berm about 130 yards to the northeast. Diaz and the other soldier had started firing the machine gun and lobbing rifle-fired grenades when another group of insurgents began firing from a field only 50 yards to the west. They were caught in a brutal crossfire. They hit the ground. Pinned down, they were trying to return fire but their weapons started to jam. Both Lauzier's and Barker's M4s locked up. Diaz, meanwhile, realized that they hadn't brought a full load of machine gun ammo. At the same time, the insurgents were refining their fire, walking it closer to them. "The rounds were just cracking all over us," Lauzier said.

"Hey, I need fucking mortars now!" Lauzier yelled into the radio. The platoon's radioman requested mortars up to battalion headquarters.

"Denied. We have fast movers in the air," meaning there were jets in the vicinity, which is a collision risk with large caliber, high-flying mortars. But the mortars that travel with each company are small enough that they fly below jets' minimum altitude. Norton's fire team had the mortar team, led by Staff Sergeant Matthew Walter, with them.

Mortarmen are frequently maligned for being lazy. They have heavy equipment, and it is standard practice to spread the mortar-round loads out to all the men of the platoon, which they complain about. But Walters humped all, or almost all, of his own gear. He would frequently carry the mortar tube and a dozen rounds at a time, which is about 100 pounds. So the guys esteemed him greatly. As Norton was talking to Fenlason about what sort of help they could get Lauzier, Walter asked Norton if he could borrow three men. Walter grabbed the men and ran across the road. Since he could see the enemy's tracer rounds, and generally the source of fire, he set up his 60mm mortar tube. Norton followed about two minutes later.

"How far do you think that is? Four hundred meters?" Walter asked.

"Six hundred?" Norton said. They decided to average it. The big problem, however, was figuring out where Lauzier's team was. Since their weapons were jamming, and they were conserving the machine gun ammo, Norton and Walter couldn't tell, exactly, where their friendlies were. They tried to determine their location over the radio, but descriptions like "in a canal" or "to the right of the enemy fire" were not hugely helpful. At Norton's command, Lauzier ordered Diaz to fire one rifle-launched grenade at the insurgents, and Norton eyeballed their probable location back from that explosion. With all of those variables, Norton and Walter were fairly confident, but still, this was some risky business and Norton was uneasy. Lauzier, however, was insistent.

"We are getting cut up," he yelled into the radio. "Our weapons are jammed. We need support now. Repeat, now."

"All right, we are working on it," Norton responded. "I want you to lay everything you have on the exact spot where the insurgents are. And then we're going to drop mortars off of that. As soon as the mortars drop, I want you to break contact and clear the area, because we're going to sweep left to right toward the direction we think you are. Got me?"

"Roger," Lauzier responded. A few seconds later, Diaz's machine gun ripped toward the berm, and Norton and Walter finalized their adjustments. Walter dropped his first round. Away it flew and detonated on impact.

"Aaaaaaaaaaarrrrrhhhhh!" Lauzier screamed through the mic. It was a loud and ear-splitting wail. Through the crackle of the radio, it sounded like the scream of a man badly injured. Walter and Norton looked at each other. "Oh my God," Norton thought. He felt like he was going to puke. "We hit them. I just killed my own men."

"Lauzier! Lauzier! Are you there? Are you there?" Norton yelled into the mic.

"Aaaaaaaaaarrrrrhhhhh, yyyeeeaaahhh! Fucking bull's-eye, dude!" Lauzier yelled. "You hit him dead on! Fucking bull's-eye! Fire for effect!" Norton had never been more relieved in his life. Walter lobbed about four or five shells on and around the spot. Lauzier wanted to follow and make sure the insurgents were dead, but he didn't have any more working weapons. He told his men to break contact, and they headed back to the house. It is something he regretted years later, that he was not able to personally finish the insurgents off.

After three years of hunting, the U.S. military finally found and killed Zarqawi on June 7, in a farmhouse in a village thirty-five miles north of Baghdad. U.S. and Jordanian intelligence had gotten a number of key breaks in the weeks before. One source helped focus the Zarqawi-hunters on Sheikh Abdul-Rahman, often described as Zarqawi's spiritual adviser. A small Task Force 77 team had followed Abdul-Rahman to a farmhouse where they were certain he was meeting with Zarqawi. Worried that their prey might get away if they waited to muster enough troops to attempt an assault, they requested air support. Two Air Force F-16s were diverted from another mission, and at 6:21 p.m., one dropped first one, then another 500-pound bomb on the house. Amazingly, Zarqawi survived the initial blasts as Iraqi police and U.S. soldiers swarmed the scene, but he died from injuries within the hour. Everyone else in the house, including Abdul-Rahman and a small but never conclusively specified number of women, children, and other men, died in the blast as well.

Hopes that this alone would deal a decisive blow to the insurgency, or even AQI's activities, were fleeting. On June 12, the Mujahideen Shura Council released a statement on behalf of Al Qaeda in Iraq saying that a new emir of Al Qaeda in Iraq had been appointed. Attacks resumed unabated, and a month later U.S. Ambassador Zalmay

Khalilzad would tell the BBC that Zarqawi's death, "in terms of the level of violence . . . has not had any impact."

By June, First Strike had decided to shut down the Rushdi Mullah patrol base. It simply did not have enough men to hold the position and turn it into a fully functioning outpost. Constant operations here were sapping combat strength for missions elsewhere, so on June 11, Bravo Company's 2nd Platoon was in the process of tearing it down. They were breaking down some of the defensive positions, dismantling the concertina wire serpentines in the front, and preparing for a night mission later on. They would depart the next day.

At 3:00 p.m. on what had been an unusually quiet day until then, the house started taking fire from both the front and the rear. As the IAs on guard started returning fire, the only American on guard, Private First Class Tim Hanley, who was manning a bunker on the front gate, saw an orange thirty-ton dump truck approach from the northeast. When it got to the front drive, it turned right and began barreling toward the gate, plowing through what few strands of concertina wire were left. Hanley started banging away at the truck with his M240B machine gun. He damaged it and may have thrown it off course, but he could not stop it from slamming into the courtyard wall and exploding into a massive fireball. Platoon Sergeant Jeremy Gebhardt, who had walked to the front door to investigate the gunfire, was thrown across the room. Several other soldiers were picked up off of their feet, hurled against walls, and showered with debris, shrapnel, and glass. The blast shook the FOB at Yusufiyah five miles away. Amazingly, although fifteen U.S. soldiers, eight Iraqi soldiers, and one interpreter were injured, no coalition forces were critically hurt. The driver's body was ripped to pieces.

A medic ran to the front of the building, where Hanley had crawled out of the rubble of his bunker, with a ruptured eardrum and shrapnel in his neck. The truck's front axle and engine had landed directly on top of his post, which was fortified only with sandbags and plywood overhead covering. Looking at the crushed bunker, it was impossible to figure out how Hanley had survived. Hanley lost most of his hearing, however, and could have returned home, but he elected to stay with the men and finish the deployment.*

Iraqi prime minister Nouri al-Maliki was inaugurated on May 28, 2006, and the Shi'ite militias' carte blanche increased substantially. Sectarian killings continued to escalate throughout the country, with more than a hundred civilians dying every day in June. By early August, the U.S. military would acknowledge that more people in Baghdad were being killed by Shi'ite death squads than by Al Qaeda and Sunni insurgents. Yet throughout the summer, the Iraqi government and top U.S. commanders thwarted attempts by lower-level units attempting to rein in the Shi'ite paramilitaries: American forces were not allowed to target the Mahdi Army without direct approval from either Maliki or General George Casey.

On June 14, 2006, nearly 50,000 Iraqi and American troops launched Operation Forward Together, an initiative designed to bolster security in the capital by increasing street patrols, beefing up checkpoints, and enforcing curfews. It was a failure. Two of the promised Iraqi brigades never showed up. After a day or two of calm, violence erupted in the capital again on June 17, when seven separate attacks—a suicide bombing, a mortar attack, three car bombings, a bus bombing, and a pushcart bombing—occurred in Baghdad, resulting in at least 36 dead and 75 wounded. And the attacks kept coming. Fifty gunmen wearing police uniforms kidnapped scores of factory workers on June 21. By July, Baghdad was averaging 34 attacks a day, compared with 24 a day in June. Despite the spike in violence, the war's planners insisted that the answer was fewer rather than more troops. On June 21, General George Casey briefed the Joint Chiefs of Staff and recommended reducing the 15 combat brigades currently stationed in Iraq to 10 brigades within six

---

*On September 25, 2007, Tim Hanley shot himself to death one year after returning from deployment. His was one of an epidemic of suicides to plague the Army and the 101st Airborne—including eighteen suicides at Fort Campbell through the middle of November 2009. One of those was Juan Hernandez, the soldier who had performed so valorously during Charlie Company's friendly fire incident on November 4, 2005. He shot himself to death in Coffee County, Tennessee, on October 5, 2009.

months. Six months after that, he proposed whittling that number down to 7 or 8. By December 2007, according to his timeline, only 5 or 6 brigades would remain. He similarly proposed cutting the number of bases from 69 to 11. With the violence still escalating, U.S. and Iraqi forces initiated Operation Forward Together II in August, using more troops shipped in from Anbar. One government report described this as "giving up ground to one enemy to fight another." That operation also failed.

23

The Alamo

On June 16, Bravo's 1st Platoon was back at the JSB, 2nd Platoon was manning the TCPs, and 3rd Platoon was patrolling Yusufiyah. Rick Skidis was on emergency family leave, so Fenlason was Bravo Company's acting first sergeant. A bunch of Freedom Rest passes had been approved simultaneously, so several more soldiers than anybody had anticipated were going to be gone from duty.

Fenlason was concerned about how shorthanded the company was, and he told Major Salome about it. "When you took out the people that were on leave, the people that were going on leave, and then you factored the passes into it, the company was going to be short the equivalent of a platoon for three weeks," Fenlason said. With attrition, scheduled leaves, and soldiers up at Striker for medical or other reasons, 1st Platoon had twenty-two of its assigned thirty-four men on the ground. In addition to security at the base itself, the AVLB, and TCP4, their missions included morning IED sweeps, at least two patrols a day to sensitive nearby facilities, resupply runs back to Yusufiyah, daytime neighborhood patrols in Quarguli Village, nighttime overwatches in that same village, and cordon and knock searches for bad guys as the case came up.

Heading into the evening of the 16th, Private First Class Thomas Tucker, Specialist David Babineau, and Private First Class Kristian Menchaca were guarding the AVLB. Menchaca hadn't even been on the regular duty roster for that shift, but he had volunteered so another soldier who was celebrating his birthday could enjoy it in the relative comfort of the JSB. The threesome had been on duty, in a single Humvee, for almost twenty-four hours. Their team leader, Sergeant Daniel Carrick, was on one of those four-day Freedom Rest passes and Staff Sergeant Chaz Allen, their squad leader, had told them to be extra alert, because when Cortez and two others were out there the night before, they had taken some small-arms fire and RPG fire.

Allen had nine men to cover the two positions and they had been doing it for days. It was a ridiculous staffing situation, but it was standard practice for this deployment. So at any given time, Allen had three men on the AVLB, three men on TCP4, and three in reserve.

Just before 8:00 p.m., he and two soldiers at TCP4 were about to relieve the soldiers on guard at TCP4. He asked somebody to do a radio check with the Alamo. A minute or so went by.

"Any luck?" he inquired. Negative, the soldier said. "Gimme the mic," he said. Just then, a torrent of gunfire opened up. Allen tried to raise them on the radio. Cortez climbed on the roof of the TCP with an M14. With that gun's scope, it was possible to see the position. He yelled down that he didn't see anyone.

Soldiers stationed at the JSB heard the barrage too. Lauzier figured it must be the IAs shooting at something from their location on the JSB itself. The birthday soldier had been planning on bringing steaks to the men at the AVLB for dinner as a thank-you, and he had taken their order over the radio a couple of minutes ago. He tried hailing them now, but there was no response. Norton ordered Lauzier, Barker, Hernandez, Sharpness, and couple of others to rush a convoy out there.

At TCP4, the same thing was happening. Cortez and a couple others jumped into a Humvee. It wouldn't start. The battery was dead. They piled back out and into the M113 armored personnel carrier and took off.

Just over halfway through the three-quarter-mile journey to the AVLB, the QRF from the JSB patrol base hit the brakes. There were two objects—they sort of looked like oil drums, which could be IEDs—blocking their path. Some of the men got out to investigate them. Though the drums turned out to be decoys, they would hold up the vehicles for an hour and a half. Lauzier, Barker, Hernandez, and Sharpness got out right away and decided to make it there on foot. They started out walking, but, increasingly worried, they began to run and finally sprinted the rest of the way.

Cortez and his men arrived first, around 8:15 p.m. There was no one there. Hundreds of brass shell casings were strewn about the ground. There were several large pools of blood. The men cordoned off the area and searched the vicinity. Cortez found Babineau about thirty yards away, facedown in the weeds and water on the banks of the canal. He had been shot multiple times up and down his back. Bullets had split his head open. There were two M4s on top of the hood and both right-hand Humvee doors were open. All three of the men's helmets were inside the Humvee. One had a packet of Skittles inside it. The soldiers had not been able to get a Mayday signal off over the radio, nor did they fire a shot. The Humvee's turret was locked and its M240B machine gun was on safe.

"They had their Kevlars off and no weapons," said Allen. "So nobody had situational awareness. Nobody was pulling guard. Sometimes people will say to me, 'It's a direct reflection of your leadership.' The first time somebody told me that, I almost fucking killed somebody. I wanted to just slit the motherfucker's throat. Mainly because you're basically stating that I allow things of this nature to take place, that I don't care."

The insurgents on the scene apparently had had enough time to sift through the truck and the men's personal effects looking for valuables, taking what they wanted. In addition to everything on the ground, and the guns on the hood, there was a PlayStation Portable on the floor of the Humvee, but two pairs of night-vision goggles and a bulletproof vest were gone.

Lauzier's fire team arrived a few minutes after Cortez's. They could hear yelling. "Menchaca! Menchaca! Tucker! Tucker!" Cortez was at the banks of the canal. He was trying to pull Babineau out of the water.

"Where are Tucker and Chaca?" Lauzier asked.

"I don't know," Cortez said, crying. "They're not here. They are not here."

Lauzier's team began to search the area. They headed out to the nearest houses to question, and kick the shit out of, anyone they saw. The Iraqi soldiers stationed on the JS Bridge itself said that they hadn't heard or seen anything, which, to the Americans, was a stone-cold lie. Either they were in on it, or they had decided to stay out of it, but there is no way they could have failed to hear the bullets. Sharpness put Babineau in a body bag, and the rage he felt was nearly uncontrollable.

"I pulled my fucking weapon up, I put it on fucking semi, and I was ready to just start spraying," he said. Much of 1st Platoon wound up staying out all night looking for their comrades. "We spent the whole night questioning people," recalled one soldier. "You're not supposed to tactically question people in combat unless you're an interrogator. We were straight-up interrogating people. Beating people's asses with weapons, threatening to kill them if they didn't talk. It was thug style, like a gang war, because we wanted our guys back alive and the chances of that were dwindling every second that went by."

While the rest of 1st Platoon was responding to the crisis, Private First Class Justin Watt and Sergeant Tony Yribe were up at FOB Mahmudiyah at the same time. Both were heading up to Striker: Watt, to get some dental work done, while Yribe was having his back looked at; the blast that had killed Britt and Lopez had caused a nagging injury. They had scored a semiprivate hooch in a tent occupied by some Psychological Operations soldiers they had befriended. It was early evening and Yribe was talking to some friends out in front of the tent when a bunch of Alpha guys started running past, heading for the helicopter landing zones and motor-pool staging areas, strapping on helmets and Velcroing vests as they went.

"What the hell is going on?" Yribe called out after some of them.

"Dead and wounded down by the JSB," they yelled as they ran past. The JSB? That's 1st Platoon, Yribe realized. He ran to the TOC to get the fuller story. Watt was sleeping when Yribe came back to wake him up.

"Watt, Watt! Hey, Watt!" he said. "Hadj just attacked Tucker, Babs, and Chaca down at the Alamo and they don't know where Tucker and Chaca are. Babineau's dead." Getting captured was every soldier's worst fear, worse than dying in a firefight or even getting blown to pieces by an IED. Insurgents were known to be lusty, committed torturers without mercy. Soldiers frequently commented that they would kill themselves before they'd allow themselves to be captured. So the news that Tucker and Menchaca were missing was, perversely, worse than hearing that they were already dead.

The two whipped outside and tried to find a ride or a flight down to the JSB to help with the search. Alpha was spinning up a massive Quick Reaction Force. Yribe and Watt asked everybody they saw if they could get a ride. No one had any seats. Finally, an officer told them that they weren't going anywhere anyway. Hundreds of soldiers were already flooding the area and no one thought bringing two more who were close friends with the kidnapped was going to help anything. So throughout that night, they had little to do but scrounge for updates and talk in their bunks.

"It just drives me crazy that all the good men die and the shitbag murderers like Green are home eating hamburgers," said Yribe.

"Murderers?" Watt asked.

Yribe told Watt about the day at the checkpoint, how he had found the shotgun shell, how Green had confessed to him, how Yribe had followed up the next day, and how, once he was convinced that Green really did it, he told Green that he needed to get out of the Army or he would get him out himself.

Watt couldn't believe what he was hearing. On the one hand, it sounded like something Green was capable of. On the other hand, it was unbelievable because it didn't add up.

"How in the fuck is Green going to single-handedly escape the wire without an NCO knowing, murder four fucking people by himself, without other people knowing, and then infiltrate that same wire?" he asked.

Green swore that he acted alone, Yribe said, and that Cortez and Barker had nothing to do with it. But they must have, Watt asserted—it doesn't make any sense otherwise. No, Yribe insisted, they wouldn't do that. And anyway, Yribe said, the less I know about it—and the less you know about it—the better. Just forget I said anything.

But Watt couldn't forget it. That night, he lay on his cot thinking about Tucker and Menchaca, who he, and everybody else, suspected were being tortured at that moment. And he thought about Green doing much the same thing to a whole family of Iraqis. Tucker and Menchaca were some of the best guys Watt had ever known. Tucker always talked about fishing and the pickup trucks he liked to work on. And Menchaca was quiet but respected, a friend to everyone. He was from Texas, but he still had a heavy Mexican accent that he turned up even heavier when he was goofing around. He had gotten married just a month before deployment. Babineau, though, had been married for years and was a father of three and shouldn't have even been there. He had been "stop-lossed," the policy that allowed the Army to forcibly retain soldiers scheduled to be discharged if their unit was deploying within a certain window of time. Watt couldn't stop thinking about that: Babineau was here on stolen time. Babs had done his eight years already, and now he was dead.

Goodwin showed up at the JSB with 3rd Platoon around 9:00 p.m. He had been in constant radio contact since the first call, but almost immediately, commanders several levels above him had taken control. When a "MisCap-DuStWUn" ("Missing, Captured–Duty Status, Whereabouts Unknown") happens, the Army moves fast. An Apache Longbow arrived within minutes. A Predator unmanned drone started hovering overhead within half an hour, tracking any suspicious activities. Relief units from the 2-502nd started arriving at each TCP location and halted all motor traffic throughout the area. An Iron Claw team and other, larger relief units were heading to Yusufiyah as their staging base. An Iraqi special operations forces unit went into action, and dive teams and division-level QRFs at Striker began gearing up.

"At that point," Goodwin said. "I didn't know what to do. Honest. I was talking to so many people on the radio, I was having a hard time keeping straight who I was talking to. It was insane." Within another hour, Colonel Kunk and Sergeant Major Edwards showed up too. "They took over the show and began to abuse 1st Platoon," Goodwin recalled. "Anytime they had a free moment, they were yelling at Norton, about how much 1st Platoon sucked and how worthless they all were. Anything that they were told by 1st Platoon, they considered lies or they just chose not to listen to them."

In less than five hours, approximately 400 soldiers had searched three objective areas in the vicinity of the attack site. Throughout the night, elements of the 101st Airborne and the 4th Infantry conducted searches, set up blocking positions, or prepared for mobilization at dawn.

As had become the norm during critical times for the 1-502nd, Alpha Company got the call to take the lead. They moved up fast as part of a multiunit clearing effort of Malibu. Bravo's 3rd Platoon walked up Malibu as well, following the guidance of helicopters and drones. Blaisdell remembered searching the house of a Quarguli sheikh on Malibu with whom they were on relatively friendly terms. Because he forgot to strap up his helmet, it popped off just as he was flinging himself over the courtyard wall. He and his helmet landed at the feet of the sheikh, who was waiting for them. Blaisdell had never seen a sheikh in his underwear before. "I knew he knew a lot of what was going on, but he wasn't going to tell us anything," he said. "That would have been a death sentence for him and his family."

After a brief operational pause in the earliest hours of the morning, Alpha and several other units moved northwest (more than 8,000 coalition troops would ultimately aid in the search), discovering bloody drag marks on the road leading to the power plant. As they searched throughout the morning, they found pieces of a U.S. body armor vest, a white Bongo truck with a thick pool of blood in the flatbed near an office building on the plant's grounds, and blood on the handrail of a bridge over a canal at the plant's front entrance.

With temperatures soaring past 110 degrees, Alpha took small-arms fire and mortar fire throughout the day. While Alpha inspected a village on the north side of the power plant and other nearby environs, massive air assaults cleared wide swaths of countryside almost continuously.

Colonel Ebel, Lieutenant Colonel Kunk, and Major General James Thurman, commander of the 4th Infantry Division, flew up to the Russian power plant looking for a status update from Alpha commander Jared Bordwell. "I had an Army Dive Team and a PJ [Air Force Para Jumper] Dive Team with me, diving in that canal up by Caveman," said Bordwell. "And we had just been in a firefight with some guys earlier in that morning. And they wanted to know what was going on and what we thought. And I started to brief General Thurman, and he just cut me off and started briefing me. He started briefing me on what had been reported—from me, up to him—and based on what had gotten changed along the way, he was telling me that I was wrong. And Colonel Kunk and Colonel Ebel just sat there. It was frustrating to see my two senior leaders not say anything. They just let the general tell me what I thought, which wasn't accurate by any means."

After searching well into the next day, most of the men of 1st Platoon returned to the JSB to try to get some food and rest for an hour or two before heading back out. But Kunk and Edwards were unhappy with the state of the base. "The first thing that sergeant major does is yell at us about the JSB being dirty. The very first thing," said 2nd Squad's Chris Payne. "He doesn't pull the guys together and say, 'Hold your heads up, we'll do what we can do to find these guys.' Neither did the battalion commander. Something to unify the platoon. It didn't happen. All that happened was that the men got yelled at." Under orders from Sergeant Major Edwards, Payne went down to the Bat Cave and hauled all the rest of the men out of their racks and they started picking up cigarette butts.

Since he was acting first sergeant, Fenlason did not get out to the JSB until the next day. "Kunk had moved his TOC down there," he said. "So now you got Edwards, Kunk, Salome, and all their little wizards down there. All I did was go in and take my ass beatings. They didn't want us around them. All they wanted us to do was cook their fucking food. I remember Kunk screaming at me one night because we didn't make enough food for his people, giving me the 'Here we are looking for your goddamn soldiers' routine while I am trying to explain that he's never told me how many people he's actually got down here. And Edwards is screaming at me every which way."

"That was it for me," said one 1st Platoon Bravo soldier. "I was done after that. I didn't give a fuck about anybody but my platoon. Other platoons, I didn't give a fuck. I didn't talk to anybody else after that. Other platoons were looking at us: no sympathy. They were looking at us like it was all our fault, giving us the 'Do you know how much pain you caused?' routine. It was just bad."

24

Dilemma and Discovery

MULTIPLE SWEEP AND search operations were conducted simultaneously throughout the next forty-eight hours on both sides of the Euphrates, but physical clues and human intelligence kept leading back to the vicinity of the power plant. As that was happening, Watt was obsessively mulling over everything Yribe had told him, even after they made it up to Striker the next day. It continued to nag at him. He weighed all the scenarios, he tried to evaluate all possibilities, and it just didn't compute, that one guy could get into a house and control an entire family in that situation. There was no way Green could have done it alone. No way. There just had to have been more people. He brought it up with Yribe several times, and each time Yribe refused to entertain the notion. Yes, Yribe said, he took Green's word on how it went down. No, he never asked Barker and Cortez about it. Why not? Tons of reasons, Yribe said: Because he didn't really want to know, because God would sort it out in the end, because the last thing 1st Platoon needed was more trouble, because it was already ancient history. And because it was none of his business—and it was none of Watt's business either.

The search for Tucker and Menchaca was continuing. There were

TVs in the Striker chow hall tuned to Fox News or CNN and people would just keep on feeding their faces. Watt couldn't believe it. He was so angry at these soft, smug rear-echelon motherfuckers. Look at them, he thought. Two missing soldiers were not going to get in the way of their sundae with sprinkles. He wanted to get up on a table and scream at them about how this entire room of fat, pasty fuckfaces was not worth a single one of those guys.

Going to Striker was like going to a different planet, he thought. Anytime any soldiers from 1st Platoon were up there, some NCO from the finance corps or quartermaster corps could be virtually guaranteed to stop them in the chow hall and get on their case for wearing the old green patches on their uniforms rather than the ones designed for new ACU digital pattern uniforms. First Platoon's fury would be hard to contain. "Eat my balls, dude," they would say. "You're lucky I even have a fucking patch. This is the one patch that got handed down to me through twelve people so you could check what division I am from before deciding it was cool to be a cocksucker. I don't have any other fucking patches because all of my other fucking uniforms got toasted when our fucking FOB burned down."

Even worse was when the "Fobbits" from Striker, as they were called, would be forced to come to Yusufiyah. They would arrive in their crisp uniforms and their shiny Humvees and bust out their cameras taking pictures of all the combat squalor. The piles of wreckage, the mangled Humvees, the scruffy soldiers. Watt couldn't stand it. It was like it was all a show for them, all a story they could tell their friends back home about how they had really seen some shit back in Iraq, man. And Watt knew these rear-echelon retards' friends would then all buy them rounds of drinks and toast their buddies, the war heroes. It made him seethe.

Just yesterday he nearly murdered someone. A female NCO in line at the Green Beans coffee shop was complaining about the communications blackout in effect because the names of the missing soldiers had not yet been released. She was irritated that she couldn't turn in a paper for an online correspondence course she was taking. Watt exploded.

"Are you fucking serious, you fucking bitch?" he yelled. "I'll tell my friends to die at a more convenient time for you, you fucking piece of shit." He physically went for her, intending to do her some sort of harm he wasn't even in control of, and he had to be dragged out of the place. Luckily, there were a bunch of infantry NCOs there, so they let Watt's outburst slide as long as he just got out of there. As he reluctantly slinked off, he was glad to hear them tell her, in a much more polite manner, that she really should shut the hell up.

Around lunchtime on June 19, Watt ran into Bryan Howard and Justin Cross. They were returning from leave and appreciated the chance to commiserate with a guy going through the same thing they were. Tucker and Menchaca had still not been found, but all around Striker, it seemed like just another day to everyone else. Since Watt spent much of the deployment as the platoon's radioman, he had a better memory for where people were located on particular days than the average soldier. As they were talking, Watt remembered that while both guys were members of 3rd Squad at the time, Howard had been a part of the group at TCP2 that day back in March.

Cross wandered off at one point, and Watt tried to get Howard to talk about that day. But he decided he had to do it craftily, as if he knew more than he actually did. They discussed all of the messed-up stuff they had seen, and Watt insinuated something about, well, the really messed-up stuff that had happened in March. What are you talking about? Howard asked. You know, Watt said, behind TCP2, with the family, the ones that got waxed that day. And the girl, the girl that got burned? Convinced that Watt did indeed know the whole story, Howard talked about it all, at length. He filled in many of the missing pieces about Cortez and Barker and even the extent of Howard's own involvement. He had had to hold down the TCP with just Scheller—and the radio that the others down at the girl's house weren't responding to anyway. He told Watt about how he still didn't really believe them until they returned, with the blood-stained clothes.

That night, Watt recounted to Yribe what Howard had relayed to him. Yribe said he couldn't really believe it, but he didn't see what good was going to come from digging it up. While it was bothering

Watt to the point of obsession, Yribe's philosophy was it had nothing to do with him.

"Watt, dude, were you there?" Yribe asked.

"No."

"Have you talked to anybody who was personally there, at the house, when it happened?"

"No."

"What you know is what somebody heard from somebody else. That's what you know, right?"

"Yeah."

"So you don't really know a lot, do you?"

"I guess not."

Watt didn't know much, but he just *knew* it was true. For a while, he did try to forget about it. But he kept coming back to the father, that was the thing that kept him up at night. He couldn't sleep at all anymore, and that was the image that haunted him. It was horrible, what happened to them all, especially the girl, but Watt kept focusing on the father. Watt wasn't a parent, he wasn't even married, but he supposed it was simply because he was a man that the father was the one he identified with the most. He imagined the powerlessness, the literal impotence, of having armed men break into your house and there being nothing you could do to protect your family. Watt ran it over in his mind again and again. What would that feel like, to realize that you and the people you love were about to be blown away? When did all hope vanish? When did the Iraqi man realize that he, and his whole family, were going to die? When the gun started going off, or before? When the bullet slammed into his skull, or before? "I'd just imagine what it would be like to spend my last moments on Earth like that," he said. "And I couldn't think of a worse way to go."

Watt called his father, who had been an airborne combat engineer in the late 1970s. He asked his dad what he would do if his brothers in arms had done something really bad.

"What is it?" his father asked.

"I really shouldn't say," Watt told him, "but it is bad beyond anything you could imagine. What would you do?" Watt asked.

"You should let your conscience be your guide," his father said. "If it is as heinous as you say, you can't let your loyalty to your men get in the way of doing what is right."

Watt resolved that he couldn't just let this pass. "If I kill someone in combat," he reasoned, "that's the risk that the other guy involved has agreed to take. And I stand just as much of a chance of getting my ticket punched as the guy I am trying to kill. But civilians are different. The guys who did this had to pay. Not to say that if I never turned them in, they wouldn't be paying for it, in their own heads. Your own conscience is worse than any punishment that anyone else can lay on you. I think that's part of why Yribe was saying he wouldn't turn them in. But that's not good enough. Not for that shit. Not after I and all the rest of us busted our balls the entire time. I didn't get to go out on a kill spree because I was hurting. We all sucked up the same bullshit and we didn't get to wig out."

Finally, after a midafternoon sweep through Rushdi Mullah on Sunday the 18th, two detainees helped pinpoint the location of Tucker's and Menchaca's bodies, which were located on Monday, June 19, just before 8:00 p.m., about two miles northeast of the power plant. Because it was possible they had been booby-trapped with IEDs, they had to be examined by an Iron Claw team and it took another several hours before their remains could be recovered.

Judging from a video shot by the insurgents, this seems to be the vicinity where the bodies were mutilated. There were about a dozen men milling around the already dead and desecrated bodies. Both soldiers appeared eviscerated and half-naked, dirty with caked blood and mud, just as one would appear after being dragged behind a truck. Tucker was decapitated, and a man, after holding his severed head aloft like a trophy, placed it on Tucker's own body. Another set of hands attempted to light both soldiers' ACUs on fire. The tape is particularly revolting because the men are so nonchalant. They are slightly agitated but don't seem worried, hurried, or anxious. As dusk appears to be falling in the background, they are in a subdued yet celebratory mood, half-singing, half-shouting "Allahu Akbar! Allahu Akbar!"

According to a briefing by Major General William Caldwell and an appearance on *Larry King Live,* coalition forces conducted over twenty-five combat operations, cleared twelve villages, and conducted eleven air assaults over seventy-two hours. The Air Force logged about four hundred flight hours of fixed-wing and about two hundred hours of unmanned drone flight time. One coalition force member died and twelve were wounded. One armored vehicle was destroyed and another seven were damaged. They encountered a total of twenty-nine IEDs, of which they discovered seventeen, and twelve detonated. They killed two Al Qaeda operatives, questioned dozens of people, and detained thirty-six.

Before the bodies were found, the Mujahideen Shura Council (MSC) had issued a statement saying the men had been captured and more information would be forthcoming in a few days. The day after, another statement appeared, also purportedly from the MSC, stating that the new leader of Al Qaeda in Iraq had slaughtered the two himself. Significantly, considering insurgents would later claim they mounted this attack as revenge for the rape of Abeer and the murder of her and her family, neither communiqué made any mention of the March atrocity.

In keeping with the pattern of making changes only after a tragedy had occurred, or, as 1st Squad leader Sergeant Chaz Allen put it, "Nothing is taken seriously until something serious happens," tons of defensive equipment flooded down to the JSB and the TCPs, and a new staffing directive was issued: Every TCP needed to have at least eight men and two trucks at all times, no exceptions. Rather than this being welcome news, virtually everyone in Bravo despised the new manning constraints because, without more troops, too, just conforming to the regulation was nearly impossible. "It was killing people on sleep. It was exhausting them even more," said one platoon leader.

25

"Remember That Murder

of That Iraqi Family?"

A COUPLE OF days after Tucker and Menchaca had been found, Fenlason and Norton were still decompressing. They had just lived through the most intense emotional and professional experiences of their lives. Simply dealing with the loss of three guys was enough, but to be the constant focus of, and focus of abuse from, Kunk and Edwards and Ebel and who knows who else all the way up to Division had been hard to take. No doubt, there would be investigations. The knives were going to come out, that was certain. They welcomed it in some regards. At one point, Fenlason was so fed up with Edwards's riding him that he told him that he just wasn't going to talk to him until the investigating officer showed up. When Edwards and Kunk had finally moved their TOC back to Mahmudiyah, Fenlason and Norton could try to focus—again—on getting the platoon back on its feet. They honestly didn't know if it could be done this time.

Watt had looked at it from every angle. He had searched for all the ways to avoid it, but he knew he had to tell. Why did he track down Howard, trick him into revealing everything? He wished he hadn't. He wished he could un-know what he knew. But now that he was convinced that Barker, Cortez, and Green had raped that girl and killed her and her family, there was no way he couldn't tell. He was worried. Paranoid is not too strong a word. This was serious stuff and he was choosing to put himself in the middle of it. He was accusing his own brothers in arms of murder. The way everyone was tweaked—everybody had become borderline insane to begin with over the course of the last eight months, and now they were all grieving over Tucker, Menchaca, and Babineau—he truly could not predict how anyone was going to react to what he had to say. He wanted to keep it out of his immediate chain of command. He was worried that the reflexive impulse among junior leaders would be to protect the unit, either to dismiss what Watt was saying without investigating it or to cover it up. But he was also worried that those he was accusing might try to hurt or even kill him. He wanted to get the information in the hands of someone with the authority to actually do something about it, yet outside the regular battalion structure.

On June 23, as Watt was finally heading back from Striker to the JSB, the convoy stopped at FOB Yusufiyah to pick up Staff Sergeant Bob Davis from the Combat Stress team. After the catastrophic loss to the platoon, he was heading down to the JSB too, to visit the men.

Watt made a beeline for Davis, pulled him aside, and said, "Hey, I need to talk to you." Once Davis had gotten the broadest outline—that Watt was not involved and had no evidence, but that he had heard a plausible story that some 1st Platoon members had committed a very serious crime and that he wanted Davis's help in reporting it—he told Watt to stop right there. This was neither a confession nor a counseling session. He was required to report any crime a soldier told him he had committed or had firsthand knowledge of. But all Watt was telling him was hearsay, so Davis wasn't sure how to handle the matter.

"I need to check with my own XO [executive officer] on how to proceed, and I don't have a way to contact my own chain of command right now," he told Watt. "I am not blowing this off, but I am gonna have to get back to you."

This was not the response Watt was looking for. Now that he had committed to telling, he was bursting the whole ride down to the JSB. His mind was racing. He needed to talk to someone he could trust. Upon his arrival at the JSB, he got sent to TCP4 as part of an element to relieve a team headed by Sergeant John Diem. Watt was so happy to see Diem. There was literally no one in the world Watt trusted more than Diem. No one had their head screwed on straighter than Diem. No one's moral compass was truer.

As they were doing the handoff, Watt said to Diem, "Things might get hairy in the next couple of days, so I want you to have my back. I need you to promise me that you'll protect me."

"What the hell are you talking about?" Diem asked.

"I have some information about some fucked-up stuff that guys in this unit did, I can't tell you about it now, but in a couple of days, some people might have it in for me, so you need to protect me."

"Bullshit. You are going to tell me—now—what in the fuck you are talking about."

And Watt did.

Diem went back to the JSB and immediately went on four hours of guard. While on guard, Diem decided he could not honor the promise Watt had extracted from him not to tell anyone. This was too serious. Watt's head was not in the game, for starters, and distracted soldiers make mistakes. Plus, if Watt was in danger from some of the men, he would be more so if rumors started leaking. The only option was to get the whole mess right in front of the chain of command's nose as soon as possible. Four hours later, as soon as he came off guard, he went straight to Fenlason's office. Norton was there, and the two were talking.

"What's up, Diem?" one of them asked. He said he needed to talk to them. Sure, they said.

"You remember that murder of that Iraqi family? Back behind TCP2 that happened several months ago?" Diem asked.

Vaguely, they said. Rings a bell. What about it?

Well, Diem continued, it had just come to his attention, but he had good reason to believe that the perpetrators might not have been Iraqis.

"What?" they said. "What exactly are you saying here?"

Diem said that Watt had just come to him. Watt was not involved, but he had spoken to two soldiers with firsthand knowledge of that day who said that Green, Cortez, and Barker killed that family. He didn't have any evidence and this was all thirdhand, Diem said, but he thought Fenlason and Norton should take it seriously. They said they would, but Diem had to tell them everything he knew. And he did, describing everything Watt had told him. He acknowledged his info was sketchy, and he wasn't even sure exactly how many soldiers were involved. They talked for a while and tried to consider all angles, including what the best next step was.

"How about this?" Diem asked, thinking of Howard. "If you will give me twenty-four hours, I think I can get one of the soldiers Watt talked to to come and talk to you."

"Yes," Fenlason said, without hesitation. "Do it." The closer they could get to firsthand sources, he thought, the better off everybody would be. The rest of the afternoon, Fenlason and Norton worked quietly, trying to make sense of what they had just heard. At dinner that night, they separated themselves from the rest of the platoon as they ate, and Fenlason broke the silence. He had been thinking about it, and he wasn't sure they should be doing any waiting, firsthand source or not. He looked at Norton and said, "Hey, boss, we can't do this. We gotta get this booger off of our plate. We need to make this motherfucker someone else's problem and quick."

"I was just thinking the same thing," Norton replied. Fenlason called Goodwin over the radio.

"Sir, I think you need to put together a patrol and get back down here as soon as possible."

"Why?"

"Sir, I'd rather not say over the open radio network," Fenlason responded, "but trust me, you need to get down here."

"You're going to have to give me something a bit better than that, Sergeant," an annoyed Goodwin replied.

"Sir, let's just say that it is worse than what just happened down here this week."

"There are soldiers missing?" Goodwin asked, alarmed.

"No! Negative! N. O. No. No, sir. It is different entirely, but it is serious."

"I am not going to play Twenty Questions with you, Sergeant."

"Let me just say one word, sir," Fenlason said. "Haditha." Haditha is a town in western Iraq, but the name had become shorthand for an international media scandal involving a group of Marines who had killed twenty-four men, women, and children there in November 2005. A *Time* magazine article in March 2006 cast doubt on the military's version of events, which initially claimed no one but insurgents had been killed, and an investigation of that incident had been ongoing ever since.

"Haditha?"

"Haditha, sir. It makes Haditha look like child's play." This was driving Fenlason crazy. Anyone who was listening would know something serious was going down.

"Haditha?"

"Sir, I'd rather not go into this over the radio. Just, really, sir, you need to get down here."

"All right," Goodwin responded, still baffled, "I'm on my way."

Several soldiers, of various levels, who heard the exchange asked each other, "What the fuck was that all about?"

Goodwin arrived a few hours later with 3rd Platoon, and Blaisdell was pissed. It sounded a lot like more of Fenlason's me-first dramatics, as if 3rd Platoon had nothing better to do than cater to Fenlason's histrionics. As soon as they pulled in, Blaisdell whipped out of the truck.

"Dude, who in the fuck do you think you are?" Blaisdell yelled. "This had better be fucking good, 'cause you got a lot of balls."

"You need to calm down and back down," Fenlason said. "Sit down and shut up. This is bigger than anything you can fucking possibly fathom. So you don't say a goddamn thing right now. Just sit down and be quiet and listen."

And Blaisdell did, because he could see in Fenlason's eyes that this was as serious as he said. Fenlason and Norton briefed Goodwin and Blaisdell. They actually went through it two or three times. The first time, Goodwin just listened, eyes wide and mouth open. After that, he was taking notes and asking questions.

Just after midnight on the 24th, Goodwin called Kunk and told him what he thought had happened. The connection was bad and Goodwin was emotional, but Kunk got the gist, that some of the soldiers may have committed a very serious crime. He said he would be down there in the morning. After briefing Majors Wintrich and Salome and calling the deputy brigade commander up at Camp Striker, he departed Mahmudiyah with Edwards just before 9:30 a.m. They hit an IED near TCP3, which delayed their arrival until after 11:00. After meeting with Norton, Fenlason, Goodwin, Blaisdell, Davis, and Edwards, to get as full a story as anyone had at the time, Kunk decided to question each of the soldiers whose names had come out so far individually.

Yribe was at TCP4, helping with the now drastically understaffed 1st Platoon, so Blaisdell went to fetch him. Kunk told Yribe, as he did each soldier he spoke to that day, that he was there conducting a Commander's Inquiry to investigate a rape and murder that may have been committed by U.S. soldiers. The purpose of the Commander's Inquiry was to see if he thought that there was any basis for further investigation by the Army's law enforcement officers. He read them their rights, and all agreed to talk to him freely and none asked for a lawyer. Before questioning each of them, he also gave them a little speech. In a statement he later filed, Kunk wrote, "I explained to them that the most important thing a man can go to his grave with is his own honor and integrity. How serious and the possible effects of these alleged allegations could have on the mission in Iraq and our own soldiers in First Strike. That bad news does not get better with time and that being honest and going the harder right were the most important things now."

With varying degrees of vehemence and evasiveness, each soldier whom Watt implicated claimed to have no knowledge of what Kunk was talking about. Yribe said he had heard some rumors about Green being

involved, but he didn't have any knowledge of that, and he denied finding a shotgun shell at the crime scene.

When Yribe returned to TCP4 after being questioned, as he got out
of the Humvee he gave Watt a look like "What the fuck?"

"What?" Watt said.

"What the fuck did you say?" Yribe asked.

"Nothing. What are you talking about?"

"Kunk is asking about that night, that family. Did you fucking tell
them?"

"No!"

"Then who did?"

"I don't know," said Watt, scrambling to push the heat off of him.
"Maybe Howard?"

"Well, I think I am okay. I was able to catch Barker and talk to him,
to make sure of what we were saying. I hope Cortez doesn't talk."

Watt was terrified for his safety. This had all gotten rolling very
quickly. Were they going to leave him out here? he wondered. If these
dudes would kill a kid, he thought, why wouldn't they kill the soldier
who snitched? Everyone had grenades. It would be the simplest thing to
just pull the pin on his vest as he was sleeping, and then say, stupid private doesn't even know how to keep his frags taped.

Howard was the second person to be questioned, and he told Kunk
that Green laughingly said he had done it. But Howard didn't believe
him and dismissed it. Howard did, however, admit to drinking alcohol down at the TCPs, along with Barker, Cortez, and Green. Barker,
when questioned, was insolent and uncooperative to the point of
being insubordinate. He denied any involvement, although, he repeatedly said, he had heard some "names" of people who were involved. Whenever he was asked "What names?" he just replied, "You
know, guys talk, just names." Kunk and Edwards traveled to the AVLB,
where Cortez was stationed. Cortez told Kunk that the crime scene
was gruesome, but he didn't know anything about Americans having
a hand in it.

Kunk and Edwards then went to TCP4 to talk to Watt. At that mo-

ment, Kunk didn't think there was anything to the allegations. It bog-
gled the imagination, what Watt was alleging. As he spoke to Watt, Kunk
was increasingly frustrated because Watt didn't have command of even
the most basic facts. "His story made no sense," Kunk said. "None whatsoever. There was no logic, any rhyme or reason to it."

Watt was flustered and scared. He wanted to know if Kunk was going
to keep the soldiers segregated, because he was concerned they would
talk and get their stories straight. Kunk thought Watt was getting way
ahead of himself. He was making some serious allegations and Watt
didn't even have his own story straight.

"Do you understand what you are doing here?" Kunk thundered.

Kunk was far from convinced that there was anything to Watt's tale,
but there was enough doubt and confusion that he decided to recommend a fuller investigation. He would take Watt with him to Mahmudiyah for the time being. Kunk was close to doing nothing at all
about the allegations, but, he said, "I either had to prove that this happened, or prove that it didn't happen. Because I could not allow there
to be a lingering rumor that something like that happened."

Kunk notified the brigade, and the brigade notified the division. At
4:20 p.m. on June 24, General Thurman informed the Army's Criminal
Investigation Division (CID), and at 7:40 p.m. they got their first briefing
from Kunk about the rape and quadruple murders that American soldiers may have committed.

On June 25, 1st Platoon rotated from the JSB to Yusufiyah and then
went to Mahmudiyah the next day for the memorial for Tucker, Menchaca, and Babineau. Second Platoon took over at the JSB. A lieutenant
colonel down there from brigade headquarters asked the platoon
leader, Lieutenant Paul Fisher, why none of his men had shaved. Fisher,
after the Alamo bridge incident, after all of the work and all of the loss,
couldn't hide his exasperation.

"We drink all the water we have, sir, so that we don't dehydrate," he
said. "We have been running nonstop since our guys got abducted. We
are not really concerned about our looks right now."

"I am just trying to keep the heat off of you, Lieutenant," the lieutenant colonel said. "You guys are not looked upon too favorably these days."

By June 26, all of 1st Platoon had moved to Mahmudiyah, ostensibly for the Tucker, Menchaca, and Babineau memorial. But the commanders were also taking a wait-and-see approach on whether any of the investigations led to something concrete. During this time, the rumor mill among the men of 1st Platoon was working overtime, and many had pieced together the broad outlines. Watt had pretty much disappeared, and one by one Cortez, Barker, Yribe, and Howard were all being yanked from their duties. Agents from CID interviewed Watt twice on the morning of the 25th. At 5:30 p.m., separate agents began interrogating Yribe and Howard simultaneously. After nearly five hours, Howard had confessed the major elements of what happened on March 12, implicating all of the other parties, including, for the first time, Spielman. He too was yanked from duties. Over the next five days, and over multiple interrogation sessions (none of which were filmed or recorded by CID agents, despite the agency's manual urging them to "strongly consider" doing so in cases of violent crime), Barker, Cortez, and Spielman all corroborated Howard's overall narrative, but each, in various ways, resisted fully implicating himself.* They would disagree, and lawyers would argue, about some of those details at their trials, and after, for years to come.

Simultaneously, CID and battalion staff were working to find family members related to the murdered family, to inquire about exhuming the bodies to retrieve evidence and to make financial reparations and offer condolences for the crime. The Janabi family was only mildly cooperative. On the advice of their imam, they forbade digging up the corpses, and only a few family members (including Abu Muhammad) could be convinced to testify in various court proceedings. The U.S.

---

*Private Seth Scheller, the other soldier abandoned at TCP2 with Howard on March 12 (but stationed away from him in the Humvee), told investigators he knew nothing about the crimes, either on the day they happened or any time after. The co-accused all corroborated this, and he was excluded from all further inquiries.

Army paid the Janabi family $30,000 for the murders of Qassim, Fakhriah, Abeer, and Hadeel.

The memorial service for Tucker, Menchaca, and Babineau was held on June 26. It is standard for one soldier, usually a close friend, to eulogize each of the deceased. The men came to Fenlason to say they wanted Yribe to speak for Babineau. Fenlason hesitated. Yribe, after all, was under investigation for some sort of role in the crimes that wasn't yet clear. Fenlason ultimately decided not to make an issue of it. "I remember thinking, Tony being Tony, and the personality and the reverence that some of the soldiers still look at Tony with, that it might actually be helpful," he recalled. "If Tony can bring it closure, then we're going to do it that way. I didn't like it, but I believe it was the right decision for the soldiers."

In his remarks, Tony said, "We have endured much pain and many losses throughout this deployment. Babs and I talked several times while we were on guard about what we would like to have said if something were to happen to one of us. He told me that he would want 1st Platoon to know, and I quote, 'If I were to go, it would be on my own terms. They will never take me alive.' " Many men said it was one of the most wrenching memorials they had ever experienced.

Fenlason had gotten word earlier in the day that 1st Platoon was not going to go back to Yusufiyah. They were staying in Mahmudiyah. Almost exactly nine months into year-long deployment, 1st Platoon's war was effectively over.

Captain Goodwin and First Sergeant Skidis were discussing how and when to tell the platoon about their fate when Fenlason lost it.

"Fuck you," he told Skidis. "Nobody is telling anybody about what's going to happen with my platoon except me." After the memorial, Fenlason gathered all of his men in a tent and delivered the news. "We are not going back home to Yusufiyah," he told them. "I don't know why. My guess is, with all the people being investigated, and all the interviews that are going to have to be done, it has been deemed impractical. I don't know what we are going to do here. That is all I know at the moment." He left on his midtour leave the next morning.

The men were bewildered. Some of them were upset that they were not able to go back and "finish the job," as Army vernacular puts it, but most were so emotionally and physically exhausted that they had ceased to care what happened to them. But a few realized right away: They were almost certainly going home alive.

A few days after the memorial, the men of 1st Platoon were summoned to the chapel tent for a meeting with Lieutenant Colonel Kunk and some other senior leaders. It was apparently designed as a kind of town hall meeting, to bring everybody up to speed on what was happening to the platoon and why.

He began by telling them, with complete unconcern for the men who spoke up, "You are right to think that there is a lot of suspicion and finger-pointing going on, because Diem and Watt came forward to tell the chain of command that five of your shitbag friends probably raped a girl and killed her whole family. And these guys are cracking, it looks like they are guilty." But the meeting quickly degenerated into the Kunk Gun unloading on the whole platoon.

"We thought we were going to get the 'Keep your heads up' speech," said one soldier. "We thought we were going to be told, 'We're going to keep you here in Mahmudiyah now because we don't want anything else to happen to you,' or something like that. Well, it wasn't that at all. It was an ass chewing. He just crushed us." It was, said the men of 1st Platoon, the culmination of all of the vilifications and disparagements they had ever received from Kunk. It was a tirade of abuse, scorn, and personal attack. And the message was clear: 1st Platoon was to blame for 1st Platoon's problems.

"You, 1st Platoon, are fucked up! Fucked up! Every single one of you!" he yelled as he scowled across the room. "When did I say it was okay to have one vehicle at the Alamo?" he demanded to know. When someone pointed out the number of times he had driven past when there was only one truck there, he exploded. In a torrent of profanities and at top decibel, Kunk told them that their friends were dead because of their failings; he told them they were quitters, crybabies, and complainers; and he told them they were a disgrace and were being kept at Mahmudiyah because they could not be trusted outside the wire.

Some men tried to protest how little support and how few men they had, others asked not to be judged by a criminal few in their midst. But the session soon devolved completely into a cacophony of shouts and accusations. Several men broke down in tears.

Kunk later maintained that he did not remember specifics of what was said that day, but he agreed that it was contentious. "Being honest and being forthright, it's tough sometimes but that's what we have to do in this business."

After it was all over and Kunk and the senior leaders left, the chaplain came in and said, "I don't agree with what just happened in here, but if you guys need any help, you can come and see me."

"That was one of the defining emotional moments of the tour for me," observed Sergeant John Diem. "If you talk to others about it, they will most likely say, 'We just got done with the memorial, and they were telling us how fucked up we were,' and they will leave it at that. But nobody will step back and look at it like, 'Wait a second. Did they maybe have a point? Were they trying to say something that was important? That maybe we had become something monstrous?' Now, the one thing that was absent was if Colonel Kunk had gotten up there and said, 'I fucked up too. I have allowed you guys to turn into monsters. And I had completely forsaken you when you needed the support that only I had the power to provide. But I lacked the character to do it. All of you have failed. Me, and we, as a family, as 1st Battalion, Bravo Company, 1st Platoon, all the way down the line, have failed. At some point we failed to have the character to make the right decisions to make it so that this never happened. Mine was the crowning failure, but not the only one.' If, at any point, that had come out of his mouth, a lot of people would have snapped out of it, like that. But nobody's got the grit to say that. Everybody wants to say, 'But it wasn't my fault.' Including him."

In the aftermath of 1st Platoon's back-to-back debacles, in addition to the criminal investigations against Cortez, Barker, Spielman, Yribe, and Howard, there were two AR 15-6 investigations conducted. The first, begun on June 18, centered on "the decisions made and guidance given" about staffing at the AVLB. That investigation was finished in eleven days.

During his interview with the investigating officer, Lieutenant Colonel Timothy Daugherty, First Lieutenant Norton explained his predicament: "I had twenty-three individuals at the JSB, including the medic. With all the IEDs going off on Sportster, I am not sending less than three vehicles back to the FOB. That takes nine guys out of the fight. That leaves guards on guard for six to eight hours. As much as I push up requests, the response is, 'Just go out and get after it.' In order to do all those missions, still make trips to the FOB, and switch out the guards, it wasn't enough bodies. It was pushed up and they acknowledged it, but it was just one of those things you had to do. I am 100 percent sure that I would have done nothing different that day. As a leader, you've got to look at what you've got and where you can put it. That was the best I could do at the time, sir. I have no regrets of my decisions or anything I did that day."

Daugherty's report put the blame squarely on the platoon's and the company's shoulders, declaring, "This was an event caused by numerous acts of complacency and a lack of standards at the platoon level." It recommended that Kunk receive a letter of concern, the lowest and least serious form of admonishment, one that carries no real punitive weight or long-term negative implication for an officer's career (Kunk said he never received such a letter). It recommended that Goodwin and Norton receive letters of reprimand (although it specifically recommended that Norton not be relieved from his position).

For many, this smacked of another instance of pushing the blame for bad news as far down the chain of command as possible. "Everybody from the battalion commander on down had been past that OP [observation post] and knew that it was bad, knew that it was a target of opportunity to get plucked," said Alpha Company's Jared Bordwell. "But during that whole investigation process, it was all focused on how messed up Bravo Company was. And there was some fault on their end, but there was some fault on the upper end too that I don't think was ever acknowledged."

Years later, Colonel Ebel remained irritated about this investigation. He was not interviewed, and he considered the attack at the Alamo not a lapse of discipline but a well-selected target of opportunity by a savvy enemy. "It was a very hasty investigation," he said. "And it was aimed at holding someone accountable for what essentially I determined was tactical risk. The enemy voted in what was a very volatile and dynamic battlefield."

The second investigation, begun in early July, focused on the rape-murders, specifically looking into "how four soldiers abandoned their post at TCP2 . . . without being detected" and "the frequency and measures that the chain of command (officers and non-commissioned officers) actually checked on and supervised B/1-502 IN's tactical sites." This report was completed by investigating officer Lieutenant Colonel John McCarthy in just five days. Because Sergeant First Class Fenlason was on leave at the time of the investigation, McCarthy never interviewed him and he interviewed only eight members of 1st Platoon total. The report makes no mention of how long the duty rotation at the TCPs actually was in March, never mentions that Lieutenant Norton was on leave at the time of the crime, never mentions that Norton had no part in lengthening the TCP rotation beyond a week, and claims that "Fenlason was generally commented by soldiers in the platoon as coming by the TCPs one to two times a week." The soldiers' sworn statements do not support this assertion, it is implausible that they would say such a thing about Fenlason considering he was widely ridiculed for never leaving TCP1, and he himself later admitted that he never visited either TCP2 or TCP6 during that entire March rotation.

The second AR 15-6 also put the blame on the company-level leaders and below. Of the numerous procedural failures, it said, most notable "was the failure to supervise the operations and enforce standards at the TCPs by the company commander and platoon leader and platoon sergeant." This investigation recommended that Goodwin be removed from command and that the platoon be busted up. "1LT Norton and SFC Fenlason should be moved to other duties," it said. "SSG Allen and SSG Payne should be moved to a new unit. 1SG Skidis believes SSG Lauzier has performed well and considers him the strongest squad leader in the platoon."

Norton and Goodwin knew they were marked men. "Shit rolls downward" is an old Army phrase. They were certain they were going to get hit, they just didn't know how badly. When Norton sat down with one of the investigators, he said that he knew he was a walking bull's-eye. He said he knew that the investigator was there to build a case against him. The investigating officer adopted a tone of bonhomie and straightforwardness with Norton, assuring him, no, no, no, almost conspiratorially, that that was not so.

"I can throw rocks at some of you or pebbles at all of you," he said, and he told Norton that he intended to throw pebbles. The results of the investigation confirmed Norton's suspicions. This was going to be a stoning all along. There was nothing Goodwin and Norton could do but wait until the brigade and the division decided on how to respond to the recommendations of the investigators. "I knew I was going to get fired," said Goodwin. "It was just a matter of when."

JULY–SEPTEMBER 2006

26

The Fight Goes On

FIRST PLATOON REMAINED at Mahmudiyah, where they would stay for the remaining two and a half months of the tour, doing not much more than pulling guard on the FOB. Charlie Company, who had handed over significant portions of their territory to the Iraqi Army, picked up the JSB from Bravo Company so that Bravo's 2nd and 3rd Platoons could focus on the traffic control points and Yusufiyah.

Sequestered from the rest of 1st Platoon, Watt spoke frequently with Lieutenant Colonel Elizabeth Bowler, the psychiatrist who headed up the battalion's Combat Stress team. After starting strongly, Bowler's relationship with Kunk had deteriorated drastically over the past few months. They clashed often. Kunk was frequently abusive, disparaging, and disrespectful of her. She was, through one of the oddities of the Army Reserve world, and by virtue of her education, the same rank as Kunk, and she frequently acted like it. Others on the FOB found this grating, notwithstanding any issues she may have had with Kunk. She had a brusque and superior manner with some of the company commanders, whom she technically outranked, and they found that ridiculous.

Upon Bowler's first meeting with Watt, she became concerned about his mental health, and his safety. The stress of turning in his friends was weighing heavily on him. She thought that the risks he faced from soldiers seeking revenge were real enough, and debilitating enough to his psyche, that he should be moved to Baghdad, if not evacuated from the theater entirely.

Kunk, however, called her a drama queen and told her that she was going far beyond her authority to be suggesting something like that.

"He's lucky I don't take him up on charges for making false official statements!" Kunk bellowed, a comment that Bowler did not understand but that disquieted her very much. In the civilian world, as a prison psychiatrist, she worked with skillful liars every day, and she was quite sure Watt was not lying about anything. Kunk later denied that he threatened such a thing. "That's ludicrous," he said.

On June 30, Associated Press reporter Ryan Lenz, who was embedded with a different unit north of Baghdad, wrote a brief story about the investigation now unfolding on Mahmudiyah, relying on anonymous sources who had intimate knowledge of the details of the case. He wrote a much fuller account the next day. What would come to be known as (oddly, for its geographic inaccuracy) the Mahmudiyah Massacre, ballooned into an international scandal in a matter of days. Lenz's stories included accurate, minute details about the crime: one of the bodies being burned by a flammable liquid, one of the victims being a young child, and one of the accused having already been discharged from the Army. The story infuriated Kunk, who thought the investigation was too premature to appear in the news. Since Lenz had recently been embedded with the 1-502nd, there was rampant speculation that his source was someone on FOB Mahmudiyah. Kunk became convinced that Bowler was the source, something that both she and Lenz have denied.

Back in the States, Green saw the news stories streaming out of Iraq on all the cable news channels about the investigation. While he suspected it was just a matter of time before he was arrested, a part of him actually thought no one would bother with him. "My mind was so fucked up about Iraqis, I wasn't even really sure I was going to get in trouble. To my mind, it was like, 'No one's going to be mad about Iraqis. They're Iraqis.' " In fact, the Army's Criminal Investigation Division had notified the FBI about Green on June 27, and they had been working on an affidavit and arrest warrant ever since.

Since his discharge on May 16, Green had wandered around aimlessly. "I was still kind of tripping from the war. All I was doing was drinking and smoking weed and driving around with a pistol and an AK in my car. That was it, all day long." He visited a cousin, who was appalled that he didn't have any change of clothes, so she took him shopping and bought him several outfits. He met up with old friends, who thought he looked haggard and unwell. Occasionally, when he was drinking, he would tell one or the other of them that he had seen horrific things, including a rape by American soldiers. In the morning, he would tell them to forget he had said anything.

In early July, Green flew to Washington, D.C., to attend David Babineau's funeral at Arlington National Cemetery. While in the area, he stayed with Noah Galloway, the 2nd Platoon soldier who had lost an arm and a leg during the December 19, 2005, IED explosion. After the funeral, Green drove to Nebo, North Carolina, to visit his maternal grandmother. That's where FBI agents stormed the property and arrested him. "I wish you had called," he told the agents. "I would have turned myself in."

In the first few days of July, Cortez, Spielman, and Barker were all moved to Camp Striker, where they would spend the rest of their deployment. They'd had their weapons confiscated and been placed under arrest since they first started confessing, but since their chances of fleeing from Camp Victory were deemed to be infinitesimal, they were not placed in pretrial confinement. Although they had to have an armed escort with them at all times, they were allowed, more or less, to go wherever they wanted on the base, and since they had no real duties except to meet with the Army defense lawyers assigned to their case and continue to be questioned by CID, they could do pretty much as they pleased. They were simply agog at how comfortable life was up at Striker, where the chow halls had steak and lobster night every Friday, some of the soldiers were actually pretty girls whom they could at least look at if not talk to, and many of the palaces converted into barracks or offices still had functioning swimming pools. What would become of Howard and Yribe was still very much unclear, but Barker, Cortez, and Spielman knew, one way or another, that this was almost certainly their final few weeks of anything that resembled freedom.

First Platoon may have been relegated to pulling guard duty on FOB Mahmudiyah, but for the rest of Bravo and the rest of the battalion, the fight was as hard as ever. Bravo's 2nd and 3rd Platoons continued to engage and patrol around Yusufiyah, while Alpha, Charlie, and Delta also tried to keep their sectors running.

In fact, the battle was getting tougher. All throughout Iraq, sectarian violence was increasing. The summer of 2006 would usher in some of the fiercest and bloodiest partisan slaughters of the entire conflict. Baghdad became an open battlefield, with the Mahdi Army and Sunni groups engaging in gun battles and trading tit-for-tat car bombings that would kill dozens and wound scores more at a time. This kind of violence hit the Mahmudiyah area hard. On July 17, a large group of Sunni insurgents drove into the market in Mahmudiyah and killed over seventy people, mainly Shi'ites, with grenades and rifles.

And the headlines about the rape and murders committed by 101st Airborne soldiers in the Triangle of Death weren't making anyone's job any easier. The Iraqi government and the locals were outraged. Kunk claimed that the Mahmudiyah government and the Iraqi Army were understanding. They were upset, he said, but they understood that criminals exist and perpetrate crimes in every society and subculture, including armies, and they did not view the crime as representative of the unit as a whole.

The locals were harder to convince. Al Qaeda exploited the outrage for maximum propaganda value. On July 10, the Mujahideen Shura Council issued a five-minute video depicting the mutilated corpses of Tucker and Menchaca. The tape's audio includes clips of Osama bin Laden's and Zarqawi's speeches, as well as the message that the video was being presented as "revenge for our sister who was dishonored by a soldier of the same brigade." The narration stated that the MSC had known that Americans were behind the rape when it happened, but "they kept their anger to themselves and didn't spread the news, but were determined to avenge their sister's honor." This seems unlikely, however, considering that the first message claiming responsibility for the attack in June did not mention revenge or provide any other indication that insurgents were aware that Americans had perpetrated the March 12 massacre. On September 22, the MSC released a longer clip that included an animation of Green's mugshot (which was widely available on the Internet by this time) being engulfed in flames, footage of Tucker and Menchaca being dragged behind a truck, and a television interview by Al Jazeera with Muhammad Taha al-Janabi, one of the murdered family's relatives.

The crime had a palpable negative effect on the men on the ground in the Yusufiyah area. "We were having some form of violence pretty much every day of the week during the month of August," said one platoon leader in the area. "Before that, it wasn't great, but it hadn't been that bad. Until the horrible events of June, things were getting better." Charlie, which absorbed parts of Bravo's AO, felt renewed bitterness from the locals. "Let me tell you, those were some pissed-off folks," said Charlie's executive officer, First Lieutenant Matt Shoaf.

Violence targeted against coalition forces would continue to the very end. Alpha lost a soldier, Private First Class Brian Kubik, during another dramatic firefight in Rushdi Mullah. On August 30, Al Qaeda attacked fourteen Iraqi Army checkpoints simultaneously, though the attacks have to be considered a failure because Al Qaeda didn't manage to injure a single soldier.

Even though 1st Platoon was not engaged in direct combat operations anymore, they were living a new nightmare all their own. For months many people in the battalion and brigade had considered 1st Platoon to be First Strike's problem children. Now, however, the men of 1st Platoon were outright pariahs. "That was the worst part, being in Mahmudiyah getting treated like shit by guys that didn't see a quarter of the shit we saw," said one 1st Platoon soldier. "We were looked at as the enemy after that." Even 2nd and 3rd Platoons got caught in the perception that all of Bravo was a disgrace. "When the sector got divided up to other companies, we started hearing, 'Oh, we're down here to save Bravo Company's ass,' " remarked 2nd Platoon's leader Paul Fisher. "It was awful. It was an awful time."

Kunk moved Norton to a job running parts of FOB Mahmudiyah's headquarters over the night shift. Norton was stunned at how bad the perception was of the two forward-deployed companies. "I started working up in the TOC," recalled Norton. "And the perspective up there of Bravo and Charlie Company was so negative. I tried to tell people there, 'These are companies in your battalion, this is your unit, they are not the devil, you know?' "

Norton's move to the TOC left Fenlason, upon his return from leave, to run the platoon pretty much alone. "We were just existing at that point," he said. "I talked to the squad leaders every night about the stuff we needed to get done. We had some equipment issues. We didn't have all of our stuff. I didn't know at that time that the reason we couldn't go back to Yusufiyah was CID was going through everybody's stuff. It had basically been locked down as a crime scene. I didn't know that there was an FBI team that was going to come in. I didn't know any of that stuff. We didn't have a lot of allies. I just didn't have a lot of friends at that point. Nobody wanted to be me, that's for goddamn sure," added Fenlason. "I wasn't getting a whole bunch of people coming up telling me, 'It's going to be all right, brother.' The only person that did that when we were in country was Phil Blaisdell. Blaisdell never, ever left FOB Mahmudiyah if he was up there without stopping in and visiting us. Rick Skidis can't say that. John Goodwin can't say that. And I'm grateful for that. The fact that he didn't abandon us says a lot about Phil Blaisdell."

Sergeant Major Edwards hatched a plan to break up the platoon. He was going to send the squad leaders throughout the brigade, and the soldiers would be divided up among the battalion. But the plan floundered because the other first sergeants from the battalion vociferously resisted. They didn't see the point, this late in the deployment. Plus, nobody wanted to take in any 1st Platoon soldiers. Just leave them where they are, the first sergeants argued to Edwards. It is too complicated to try to integrate new blood, especially given the circumstances and especially this late. Just leave them alone. Ultimately, Edwards relented.

On FOB Mahmudiyah, HHC commander Shawn Umbrell was in charge of overseeing the wayward 1st Platoon. His priority, he explained, was to treat them as normally as possible. "We got some pretty weird guidance from Battalion. We were told to come up with a training plan, indicating how we were going to reinstill discipline," he said. "And my first sergeant told them, 'The soldiers don't need a training program. What the soldiers need are leaders who can show them what right looks like. Until now, they haven't had that.' "

That is something Umbrell thought about ever since. "Clearly a lot of what happened can be attributed to a leadership failure," he remarked. "And I'm not talking about just at the platoon level. I'm talking about platoon, company, battalion. Even I feel in some way indirectly responsible for what happened out there. I mean, we were all part of the team. We just let it go. And we let it go, and go, and go. And these things happened. And you can say, 'It was Green's fault. He was a criminal.' But it goes beyond that. We failed those guys by letting them be out there like that without a plan."

27

"This Was Life and Death Stuff"

FRUSTRATED, BORED, ANGRY, and demonized, much of 1st Platoon were at each other's throats during this period. While most of the soldiers agreed that Watt did the right thing, there was talk that a few were plotting to take violent revenge on him. Watt had been moved to a different area of the FOB, but anybody who wanted to find him on Mahmudiyah could. Private First Class Shane Hoeck, one of Watt's best friends, tipped him off, telling him to watch his back; some soldiers were saying some stuff about making him pay.

But that wasn't the only way platoon unity was fracturing. A rumor got around that CID thought 1st Platoon was a kind of Murder, Inc., kill squad, complete with blood rituals and civilian-murder initiation requirements for new soldiers. Word was, CID was trolling now for any suspicious killings that they could turn into murder probes. Early on, investigators had heard rumors that there was more to the story about the woman Sergeant Tony Yribe had shot and killed at TCP3 on November 18, 2005. Some soldiers alleged that the account of the vehicle refusing to stop that day was not merely a lie to make an accident sound more plausible, but a cover for a cold-blooded murder. By July 17, CID had begun investigating the incident as a potential murder, questioning everyone who was there multiple times during an inquiry that would drag on for more than two years before being dropped for lack of evidence.

Paranoia skyrocketed. Lauzier, for one, was not coping well. He felt a blinding anger and crushing disappointment at what Cortez and Barker were accused of. TCP2 was 3rd Squad's mission that March day; Cortez was his designated proxy while he was on leave. It was a personal betrayal. But he also felt tremendous guilt. If one of the truest tests of leadership is how your people perform when you are not around, how could his example be considered anything other than a failure? It was debilitating, disorienting, dispiriting. How could they do this? he wondered. How could they think they would get away with it? How could they not consider how it would impact the rest of the unit? Was this what he led them for? Is this what he taught them? And, as he ground himself up inside, no one was putting his arm around Lauzier's shoulder, telling him not to take it so hard. In fact, he was treated like an outcast and encouraged to think of himself that way by this chain of command and the ironclad Army traditions that hold that you are directly responsible for everything your immediate subordinates do or fail to do. "In a way, the individual soldier is a perfect being," remarked Justin Watt. "The soldier is never late, the soldier never makes a mistake—any failure on the soldier's part is a failure of his direct supervisor. That's what Lauzier was dealing with."

A few weeks earlier, Lauzier had been one of the best-regarded squad leaders in the company. On June 13, for example, Kunk approved a recommendation from Bravo's leadership that Lauzier receive a Bronze Star for meritorious service throughout the deployment, and he passed that recommendation up to brigade headquarters. On the routing sheet, Kunk wrote, "SSG Lauzier led from the front in the most lethal area of AO Strike. He is a warrior. Outstanding duty performance under the most dangerous environments." Now he was being treated like a cancer, under suspicion for being the ringleader of some kind of death squad. His interviews with CID were more like interrogations, as if they were trying to pin something major on him too. "This isn't over, you know," investigators would say to him at the end of every session. That phrase alone almost gave him a nervous breakdown. He couldn't bear to hear it.

His men found his obsessive tendencies steering into borderline psychosis. If any of his possessions looked different from the way he had left them, he would freak out, yelling, "Who is the mole, who is working for CID!?" Once, he left a piece of official paperwork with his home address and his parents' address on his cot for a few minutes. When he returned and the paper was gone, he pulled his 9mm pistol on the handful of 1st Squad and 3rd Squad men standing there.

"I don't know who is fucking with me," he said, "but if anything happens to my wife or my family, I will waste everything the motherfucker who did it holds dear and kill him last." Stunned, the men put their hands up and sputtered that they did not know what he was talking about. Cross approached, trying to calm Lauzier down, but Lauzier cocked his pistol. "Take one more fucking step, Cross, and I will shoot you right here. I've got nothing to lose." Cross backed off and Lauzier lowered his gun. Shortly after that episode, Lauzier decided he was probably long overdue for his first visit to Combat Stress.

Watt was having trouble coping with the strain of being a whistleblower as well. Despite his ultimate conviction that he had done the right thing, the feeling that he had been a rat was inescapable. And the thought that some of his former friends wanted to kill him was utterly terrifying. Over several consultations with him, Lieutenant Colonel Bowler became worried about Watt's mental state. She felt Kunk was not taking the psychological burden of what he'd done seriously enough. She likewise thought the whole battalion was taking the threat that Watt felt far too cavalierly. She increasingly implored Watt to protect himself legally. Demand a lawyer, she told him. They are not going to protect you, they may even come after you. Do not talk to Kunk or CID again without a lawyer, she advised.

When Kunk got wind that Watt was acting on that advice, demanding a lawyer before he said another word, he became unhinged.

"Hey, Sergeant Davis," Kunk asked Bowler's deputy, "is your doctor a lawyer?"

"No, sir," Davis responded.

"Well then, what the fuck is she doing handing out legal advice?"

"I don't know, sir."

"Get your commander down here as soon as possible." When Davis did so, Kunk told the mental health commander, "If you don't get her off my FOB in the next forty-eight hours, I will have her up on charges like that." The commander went back to the Combat Stress tent and told Bowler to pack her stuff, she was going back to Baghdad.

Though banished, Bowler over the next several weeks kept in touch with Watt via e-mail, in which she continued to beseech him to get legal help. She also tried to arrange for him to get sent out of theater, something she said should have happened as a matter of course. On Camp Victory, she spoke to another Combat Stress psychiatrist about Watt's case, who spoke to an attorney, and, again via e-mail, she relayed the attorney's advice to Watt. She told him to write a sworn statement about the threats he was receiving, and then the battalion would be forced to take action.

On July 25, Watt did just that, writing a sworn statement about a specific incident that had happened the night before. At about 8:00 p.m. the previous evening, Hoeck approached him in the chow hall to say that while several 1st Platoon soldiers were grumbling about Watt's being a snitch, Private First Class Chris Barnes in particular was talking about making him sorry, whether here in Iraq or once they returned home. Another soldier told Watt that Barnes had been trying to find Watt's new tent.

When Watt told Sergeant Major Edwards later that night what he'd heard, Edwards replied, "That should be the least of your worries. It's the people who talk that you don't need to worry about." Edwards told Watt, "I'll take care of it," but offered no specifics.

Barnes later acknowledged, "I might have said something to someone else. Supposedly I said 'I'm going to cut his fucking throat.' I might have said it, being pissed off. But I never actually threatened Watt." Barnes said he never intended to do Watt any harm, but to this day he doesn't support Watt's decision to come forward. "What they did was wrong," he explained. "But war is fucking hell, and the shit they went through, if they went crazy, whether it's three minutes or three fucking hours, I can see how it happened to them. I would never have turned them in. They're your brothers, you know? There has to be some kind of loyalty there that you don't break no matter what. Let God judge them. If they're not sorry, they'll go to hell. And if they are, if they really are, they're going to have to live with that for the rest of their life."

Bowler had arranged for two members of a Combat Stress team who were heading down to Mahmudiyah on other business to meet with Watt. After speaking with them about Watt, she was confident they would recommend he be moved up to the Victory Base Complex, away from the battalion. To Watt, it looked like a done deal.

But it was far from a done deal. When the two mental health specialists returned to Camp Victory, Bowler was expecting to see Watt in tow. He was not there. When she asked about him, one of them, a psychiatrist, replied, "He's doing great, he's doing fantastic. He is a strong young man with a lot of inner strength."

Bowler was floored. Whatever may have happened, she was certain that Watt could not have given the impression that he was doing fine. "I was stunned," she said. "What kind of mental gymnastics did they have to go through as clinicians to come back and tell me that he was doing great, fine, fantastic?" When she started to protest that that was impossible, she was, she said, told to back off; she was overly involved in this matter. Shortly thereafter, she was ordered to have no further communication with Watt. "It was crazy," she felt. "A whistle-blower in a case like this should have been moved out of theater immediately. All of these friends of these people who are now arrested and charged with rape and murder are running around with guns and he's the whistle-blower? The way Watt was treated was just unthinkable."

The same day that Watt met with the psychiatrist, Sergeant Major Edwards informed him that he was being sent down to Lutufiyah, where he would complete his tour as a member of Charlie Company.

After expecting to get the ax immediately, Goodwin was at first confused and then hopeful as July turned into August and no moves were made against him. The end of the deployment in September was looming ever

closer. The advance parties of the 10th Mountain Division, which was relieving First Strike, would be showing up in their AO soon for their right-
seat, left-seat rides. After expecting every day to be his last, Goodwin had
begun to allow himself the fantasy that he might be allowed to finish the
deployment in command of Bravo Company. "I was like, wow, maybe I'm
going to make it through this," he said.

That was not to be. On August 15, Kunk came to Yusufiyah for a routine circulation through the AO. But the next day, he came back for an
unscheduled visit. The soldiers working the radios at Bravo's TOC let
Goodwin know that Kunk was en route.

"He is coming down to Yusufiyah?" Goodwin asked.

"Roger that, sir."

"What for?"

"We don't know, sir. They didn't say." Goodwin knew that was it. He
walked back to his hooch and started packing up his stuff. When Kunk
arrived, they talked privately for half an hour, during which the battalion commander told Goodwin that he was out of a job. "Kunk was probably the most cordial he has ever been to me in his life that day,"
Goodwin remembered. "We had a very decent conversation. Almost person to person."

Sent back up to Striker, Goodwin had time to draft rebuttals to the
AR 15-6s and the letter of reprimand he had received. His rebuttals
were, Goodwin said, filled with emotion, finding errors and bad leadership at every level in the chain of command.

Ebel called Goodwin into his office. "So this is how you feel?"
Ebel asked.

"Sir, that's exactly how I feel," Goodwin responded.

"To include Battalion, Brigade, and Division?"

"Sir, I'm not backing down," Goodwin replied. "I fucked up. Tim
fucked up. Squad fucked up. Battalion fucked up. You fucked up. Division fucked up. There were mistakes at every level."

"It didn't really help my cause," Goodwin mused later. Perhaps not,
but it probably didn't hurt, either, since Ebel never thought Goodwin's
conduct warranted harsh judgment. Colonel Ebel, who had always

resisted removing Goodwin from command, clarified that even now Goodwin "was not relieved in its purest sense. He had just met his time-line" for one year in charge of a company and was simply being reas-signed. "I told him I won't relieve him because the fact is this guy's a hero too," he said. "He had incidents of breaches of discipline I had wit-nessed in other commands. His just happened to all fall at the wrong time and the wrong place." Bravo Company's executive officer, Justin Habash, who had been promoted to captain in July, was given command of the company.

On August 14, First Lieutenant Tim Norton had received a letter of reprimand from General Thurman citing both the AVLB attack and the rape-murders. On August 16, he got a letter from Ebel suspending him from his position. Like Goodwin, he also was never technically "re-lieved for cause" from his position. He was simply suspended and never reinstated. No punitive or disciplinary action was ever taken against Ser-geant First Class Jeff Fenlason. He finished the deployment as 1st Pla-toon's platoon sergeant, and he continued in that role after the unit's return to the States.

On August 21, Captain Bill Dougherty, the commander of Charlie Com-pany, took it upon himself to write a personal e-mail to Rick Watt, Justin Watt's father. The ongoing rape-murder investigation was making inter-national headlines and Justin's name had surfaced in the press as the whistle-blower. Dougherty wanted to assure the elder Watt that his son had found a supportive home.

"I have told your son that I am proud of him for coming forward," Dougherty wrote. "It took moral courage. I am sure that you are proud of him and I am glad to have him in my company. I know that he has been through a lot and I am looking out for him to make sure he is ok. . . . I can assure you that the Soldiers in Charlie Company all agree that he did the right thing and support him fully."

Dougherty encouraged Rick Watt to stay in touch regarding his son, and he passed along word that Goodwin and Norton had been relieved of their positions (he did this, he later said, in case Rick Watt was won-dering why he had not heard from either man himself). Dougherty assured him that Justin "is not wrapped up in anything concerning them being fired. Right now he is driving on with normal activities of an Infantryman serving in South Baghdad."

It was the only direct communication that Rick Watt had received (and would ever receive) from anyone in a leadership position in 1st Battalion. Rick Watt was desperately worried about his son's well-being and had been writing e-mails to commanders and senators, trying to get his son removed from Iraq entirely. Delighted finally to have any validation or expression of support for his son's actions from someone in a position of authority, Rick Watt passed the letter on to Gregg Zoroya, a reporter from *USA Today*.

When *USA Today* ran a story about Justin Watt's anguish, the paper included a short snippet of Dougherty's e-mail. Kunk and Ebel were furious. Rather than commend Dougherty for thinking of Watt's and his family's well-being (though perhaps recommending he do a better job of ensuring that his correspondents kept his e-mails confidential), Ebel issued Dougherty a letter of reprimand for "the gross error in judgment you displayed recently by sending an e-mail communication to PFC Justin Watt's father." Even though Rick Watt prevailed upon Zoroya not to mention anything in print about Goodwin's situation, Ebel accused Dougherty of betraying his peer, writing, "You acted recklessly and worst of all you did so without any consideration for the professional courtesy and loyalty due your fellow commander and this brigade. . . . The most profound impact of your poor choice is the attention that your negative comments will draw away from the hard-won accomplishments of the Soldiers of Strike Brigade: secure streets, open shops, flourishing businesses, and hopeful people." The reprimand was, to Dougherty, as demoralizing as it was nonsensical: There was nothing attributed to Dougherty in the article that could be even remotely construed as negative. It was baffling.

As the deployment wound down, men from all of the FOBs began handing over responsibility to the 10th Mountain Division throughout early September, packing up and preparing for the trip home.

After two weeks of transition, the last remnants of First Strike left

Mahmudiyah in mid-September and arrived at Fort Campbell shortly after. For a frontline deployment such as this one, it was common for NCOs or officers in positions of squad leader or above to receive a Bronze Star. First Platoon's squad leaders—Chaz Allen, Eric Lauzier, and Chris Payne—were not awarded Bronze Stars. First Lieutenant Tim Norton also did not receive a Bronze Star for his 2005–2006 tour of duty, but Sergeant First Class Fenlason did.

Following several weeks of battalion-wide leave, the usual changes in leadership and the routine discharges and transfers of men into and out of the unit commenced, but with this added difference: Bravo Company's 1st Platoon was being disbanded and would be reconstituted with almost entirely new personnel. Despite all they had been through, it was, for many of the men, one of the saddest, toughest days of the entire experience. Bravo's new company commander, Justin Habash, choked up as he delivered the news. "Nothing I could say to them would erase their feelings of betrayal or feeling like the black sheep for all that they had been through," Habash said, "but they were not to blame for the murder or other things that they felt they were carrying black marks for." He declared the breakup an unnecessary step, opining that 1st Platoon could and should be allowed to continue the rebuilding it had already begun.

That would not come to pass. Most of the men of 1st Platoon soon got scattered throughout Fort Campbell and across the rest of the Army, and the 1-502nd Infantry Regiment began the business of training up for their inevitable return to Iraq. First Strike would deploy again, this time to Baghdad, in the fall of 2007.

"This was life and death stuff," concluded Sergeant John Diem with respect to the 2005–2006 deployment, of which he and all the men of Bravo are still trying to make sense. "You line up three people in a row, and one of them dies. That's the kinds of numbers we are talking about. In ways that are important to young men, like what you do, what you stand for, and what you are willing to put on the line, this was the defining moment in a lot of people's lives. And I don't think their actions will withstand their own scrutiny. I know mine don't. But I know what kills soldiers now. I know what kills them. Not in the physical sense, but in the psychological sense; what causes soldiers to fail themselves, and what command can do to set them up for failure or not. It was the feeling of isolation at all levels of command that caused what happened. There's only one reality. There's only one thing that is happening, and there's only so many variables that surround it. It can be figured out and responsibility can be meted out and then problems can be fixed. If people continue to treat this like a mysterious event that came out of nowhere, and we don't change how we lead soldiers, and we don't honestly look at what caused this to happen, it's going to happen again. I mean, this isn't the only time. It's just the most notorious time."

The Triangle of Death Today

and Trials at Home

EVEN BEFORE THE broad-scale troop increases in early 2007 known as the surge, there was an awareness among military planners that one U.S. battalion in the Triangle of Death was not enough. Although the 1-502nd had trained two Iraqi battalions (one in Lutufiyah and one in Mahmudiyah) to the point that they could operate with substantial autonomy, when the 2nd Brigade of the 10th Mountain Division (the 2-10th) arrived in the area in August and September of 2006 to relieve the 101st Airborne's Second Brigade, they dispatched two battalions to occupy the same space that First Strike had held down on its own.

The 10th Mountain Division arrived, as units usually do, with a certain arrogance. In an October 2006 interview with *Stars and Stripes*, brigade commander Colonel Mike Kershaw downplayed the mythic stature that the Triangle had taken on, saying it was "not the worst place I've ever been in the war on terror." He likewise claimed that the rape-murders of March 12, 2006, hardly came up in his discussions with the locals. One of his officers affirmed, "I ask, but they don't want to talk about it. They're just not dwelling on that." Perhaps no one wanted to discuss the crime with the U.S. Army. But locals were, in fact, dwelling on the desecration and humiliation, and insurgent groups continued to extract as much propaganda value from the atrocity as possible. In November 2006, for example, the Islamic Army in Iraq (IAI) broadcast a video unveiling a homemade rocket it named "The Abeer," which it said had a range of 12.4 miles and carried 44 pounds of explosives.

With an extra battalion in the Triangle, the 2-10th could do things First Strike had only dreamt of. In late October, for example, the 10th Mountain took over the Yusufiyah Power Plant in a massive (though largely unopposed) attack and turned it into a large American base. Likewise, the unit started building permanent patrol bases in Rushdi Mullah, along Route Malibu, and at other locations that the 1-502nd, with 700 to 1,000 fewer men, had barely been able to patrol, let alone occupy for extended periods of time.

As the 2-10th was settling in during the fall of 2006, however, Washington was finally coming to terms with the fact that America was losing the war. During the winter of 2005–2006, for example, there had been about 500 attacks a week on U.S. and allied forces. By late summer 2006, there were almost 800 every week. Roadside bombs were at an all-time high, and 1,000 civilians were dying in Baghdad alone every month.

In late 2006, a small coterie of exasperated civilian and military planners had broken through to President George W. Bush with a new message: The current strategy was doomed. Drastic steps had to be taken. Too much emphasis, they said, had been placed on killing enemies and handing over power to Iraqi troops, most of whom were not prepared to operate independently. Right now, they asserted, Iraq needed more, not fewer, U.S. troops and the Americans needed to pay more attention to the paramount imperative of keeping the Iraqi population safe. An insurgency needs the people's support to thrive, and a secure, confident populace is more likely to quash an insurgency than nurture it.

In November 2006, Bush fired Secretary of Defense Donald Rumsfeld, and in January he replaced General George Casey, the top general in Iraq, with General David Petraeus. As part of the new strategy, Petraeus was authorized to deploy an additional 30,000 U.S. troops to augment the 130,000 already in the country, and he ordered strict adherence to the doctrines contained in *U.S. Army Field Manual 3-24: Counterinsurgency,* the new handbook he had just finished editing. The counterinsurgency dicta contained in the book, many of which are intentionally paradoxical, were communicated down to the lowest private: "Sometimes, the more you protect your force, the less secure you may be"; "Sometimes, the more force is used, the less effective it is"; and "Sometimes, doing nothing is the best reaction."

Despite the fresh approach, the situation on the ground got worse before it got better, and violence increased steadily through the first half of 2007. As Thomas E. Ricks chronicled in *The Gamble,* "The period from mid-2006 to mid-2007 would prove to be the bloodiest twelve months that Americans had seen thus far in the war, with 1,105 killed."

Despite the extra troops and the optimism with which the 2-10th Mountain arrived, they had their share of setbacks during this bloody year as well. Ultimately, the brigade lost sixty-nine men and suffered the most infamous soldier abduction since the Alamo incident. Before dawn on May 12, a group of up to twenty insurgents attacked a 10th Mountain convoy on Route Malibu—less than five miles from the Alamo ambush site. After at least one IED detonated and after a barrage of small-arms and grenade fire, four American soldiers and one Iraqi soldier were dead, and three Americans were missing.

As thousands of U.S. forces scoured the area, the Al Qaeda–affiliated Islamic State of Iraq released a communiqué over the Internet, taunting, "Searching for your soldiers will lead to nothing but exhaustion and headaches. You should remember what you have done to our sister Abeer in the same area." On May 23, Private First Class Joseph Anzack was found dead, floating in the Euphrates about a mile from the attack site, but the remains of the two others, Sergeant Alex Jimenez and Private First Class Byron Fouty, were not recovered for more than a year.

While a devastating and demoralizing event, this abduction proved to be a coda for one of the war's darkest periods, not a harbinger of more to come. Beginning in the summer of 2007, the weekly violence

tallies across much of the country started to drop. And they kept dropping. And dropping, and dropping. Within a few months, violence had
dipped to levels not seen since early 2006. No doubt the increased
American troop presence helped, but so dramatic and persistent a decline could not be attributed to 30,000 extra U.S. soldiers alone.

In fact, several other factors were at play. First was the grim reality
that after four years of constant sectarian conflict and low-grade civil
war, the country had, effectively, been ethnically cleansed. Entire towns
and regions had been re-sorted and segregated into religiously homo-
geneous enclaves. The demographics of Mahmudiyah, for example, had
been changing dramatically from a mixed city to a Shi'ite bastion even
while the 1-502nd was there, and although Sunnis managed to carve
out select strongholds for themselves, the years-long process of murder
and migration was finally hitting its stasis.

Second, what would become known as the "Sons of Iraq" programs
began taking hold nationwide. They started during the fall of 2006 in
Anbar, when, with the blessing and financial support of local U.S. commanders, a grouping of twenty-five tribes formed the Anbar Salvation
Council to fight off Al Qaeda. The success of that grassroots project inspired American senior commanders to nurture and promote similar
ones across the country. Seeing the Sunnis' increasing schism with Al
Qaeda as an opportunity to bring disaffected tribes back into the fold,
the United States began paying Sunni tribes (and some Shi'ite tribes)
$300 per man, per month, to run checkpoints, scout for IEDs, and oth-
erwise accept responsibility for the safety of their own neighborhoods.
Cynics said this amounted to little more than the Army paying its enemies not to fight. Most commanders needed little prodding to agree
that this was true, but they recited more counterinsurgency koans to assert that the payoffs were, if anything, long overdue rather than misguided. "The best weapons do not shoot," they would say, or, another
favorite: "Money is ammunition." At the program's peak, there were
more than 100,000 such Sons of Iraq on the American payroll, and they
had a profoundly positive impact on safety.

The third factor contributing to the dramatic drop in violence was

Muqtada al-Sadr's relative withdrawal from constant, violent confrontation. Ever since 2004, he had been an unpredictable irritant to the
United States. For years he declared unilateral cease-fires and then can-
celed them; he'd go quiet or even disappear for months, only to return
with more fiery speeches and rabble-rousing. He could never seem to
decide if he wanted to be a revolutionary or a part of the mainstream political process. With significant exceptions—such as the Shi'ite uprising
in March 2008 that came to be known among American soldiers as
"March Madness"—al-Sadr seemed to settle on a long-term policy of
avoiding rather than provoking violence. Some commentators insisted
that al-Sadr was merely biding his time until the United States withdrew
from Iraq entirely to make a full-scale violent bid. Others maintained
that al-Sadr had simply missed his window of opportunity and he and his
movement were suffering from a long, steady, and permanent erosion
of power and prestige. Either way, his relative dormancy has kept Iraqi
and American body counts far lower than they might have been.

The decreases in violence continued well into 2008. In November
2007, the 101st Airborne Division's 187th Infantry Regiment relieved
the 2-10th Mountain Division. Upon their arrival in South Baghdad, the
187th was astonished at how much safer the area was than what they
had expected. The operations officer from one 187th battalion told me,
that while planning for the deployment at Fort Campbell, he'd anticipated that his unit would live the entire year "off the hook," meaning
they would travel absolutely everywhere by helicopter. But, he said, the
187th soon discovered to their delight they could drive virtually everywhere they wanted with impunity.

When I arrived to embed with the 187th in May 2008, I, too, was bewildered by how non-deadly the "Triangle of Death" had become. Rides
down Sportster or Fat Boy were not terror-inducing tempts of fate. They
were routine, and routinely uneventful. The Sons of Iraq were in full
swing here, and there were tribal checkpoints on almost every piece of
road in the region. Some roads, such as Sportster, seemed to have a checkpoint every quarter mile or so. The AK-47-toting men manning the gates
and moving the pylons waved the Americans through with wide smiles.

There were dangers, of course, big ones, and nighttime raids on suspected insurgents were a frequent occurrence. But the soldiers of the 187th clearly did not fear that every day might be their last. They were in excellent spirits. Their biggest complaint was boredom. Commanders often told me that combating complacency was their primary soldier-management problem. Considering the alternatives, they added, it was a very good problem to have.

Daytime foot patrols were breezy, casual affairs. Entire squads or platoons would head out into Mahmudiyah or Yusufiyah amid streets filled with people and markets offering a hodgepodge of modest but colorful wares. Junior officers spent a lot of time meeting and negotiating with local sheikhs about what materials they needed to improve their own security.

"You need a tower?" one U.S. officer asked a Sons of Iraq leader. "HESCO baskets? Sandbags? If this lieutenant over here doesn't get you the sandbags you need within a week," the American said, pointing to one of his own men, "you can shoot him." Laughs all around.

The soldiers were fully aware that their new allies were former insurgents who had, until very recently, attempted to kill them or their predecessors, yet they remained surprisingly nonchalant and resigned, saying if that's what the mission now required, if that's what will get us home faster, then so be it.

The détente was working. The captain whose company occupied FOB Yusufiyah (and who was, in fact, a good friend of Captain John Goodwin) told me in June 2008 that his company had not suffered a serious IED in months and that no one in his company had fired a weapon, or been fired at, in more than six weeks.

When I asked the men about their staffing situation, they had few complaints. When I questioned a group of them if they ever went on three-, four-, or five-person patrols (as Bravo, 1-502nd, often had), they looked at me like I was insane and delivered a mini-lecture on the Army's philosophy of troop maneuver.

"We never go anywhere with less than a squad," one staff sergeant told me, as if I was the dumbest civilian on the planet.

"If you are running around with three or four people," chimed in a lieutenant, "then you got a leadership problem somewhere."

The men of the 187th were extremely respectful of the hardships that previous units had suffered. Once, I was standing atop several stories of scaffolding that still surrounds the five-story turbine hall of the Yusufiyah Power Plant, which was now called COP (Coalition Outpost) Dragon. The views of the Euphrates and the surrounding countryside were majestic. One of the battalion's senior officers used the opportunity to offer poetic praise about those who had come before.

"If peace is a structure," he said, "then maybe we topped it off, installed the roof, and here we are, enjoying the view. And the 10th Mountain put in the beams and built most of the floors. But don't let anyone tell you that the 502nd didn't clear the brush and lay the foundation. If it weren't for them, we wouldn't be here now."

As we were standing atop the power plant, the 502nd was actually less than twenty miles away. During the same deployment cycle in which the 187th was in South Baghdad, the Black Heart Brigade was in Baghdad proper, in a largely Shi'ite neighborhood of the city called Kadhimiyah. They had experienced a spike in violence during the March Madness uprising, but otherwise this tour had been far, far quieter than their previous rotation. "It took a while to adjust, to realize that your life isn't always in danger," one unidentified Bravo sergeant who had been on the 2005–2006 deployment told a reporter from the *Long War Journal*, a blog about terrorism and the wars in Iraq and Afghanistan, when speaking about the difference he saw in 2007–2008.

While the fast, drastic reduction in violence that occurred in Iraq in late 2007 was a tremendous milestone and achievement, there is a tendency among the military and American politicians to triumphantly overstate the gains. The mere absence of rampant murder does not produce a stable, healthy society on its own, and Iraq was and is a very long way from being a free, fair, prosperous, and democratic civil society.

During my visit to the area, sectarian resentments were festering and tribal harmony remained a long way off. Though slowly sputtering back to life, the economy was still barely functioning. Public services remained woefully inadequate or nonexistent. Sewage flowed into the street and the hum of generators to supplement the pitiful electric service was ever present. Courts, government offices, and schools were underfunded and understaffed, if they were open at all.

With the multipartite cease-fire hardening into the norm, however, and violence at four-year lows across the nation, the United States began in late 2008 dismantling much of the surge it had begun less than two years before. With attacks down over 80 percent in Babil province (where much of the Triangle of Death is located), U.S. forces handed full responsibility for the territory back to the Iraqis in October 2008. By January 2009, there were only one-third the U.S. troops in the Triangle than had been there a year before.

In June 2009, the United States further withdrew across Iraq, retrenching to large bases and largely staying out of day-to-day security operations except in a few restive areas. For some months before, the United States had likewise begun scaling back on the Sons of Iraq initiative, a move that has not, as many predicted, resulted in a wholesale return among former insurgents to their murderous ways. There are still bombings in Iraq, sometimes very lethal ones, but they remain, for now, fairly isolated incidents.

While Iraq may never become the model of Middle Eastern democracy and capitalism that the Bush administration envisioned, the current consensus among military chiefs as well as politicians and planners of every political affiliation is that the situation there is stable enough to allow the United States to withdraw completely without considering it a defeat. With the war in Afghanistan deteriorating rapidly and taking on a renewed urgency with the Obama administration, the United States remains on schedule to remove all American troops from Iraq by the end of 2011.

For some, however, the war will never be over.

Although there was virtually zero usable forensic evidence from the March 12, 2006, rape-murder crime scene (the AK-47 was never recovered, attempts to tie trace sample evidence from the scene to the DNA of the coconspirators were inconclusive, and the Janabi family forbade investigators from exhuming the victims to search for more clues), the Army's cases against James Barker and Paul Cortez were particularly strong. The two men's confessions and the confessions of others so thoroughly implicated them both that their defense teams concluded that saving them from execution was the overwhelming priority. Both soldiers offered to plead guilty to conspiracy to commit rape and murder and other charges, as well as to cooperate with all subsequent trials, in exchange for a term of years if the Army agreed not to pursue the death penalty. The Army accepted, and it sentenced Barker and Cortez to 90 years and 100 years, respectively, at Fort Leavenworth's Disciplinary Barracks, the military's only maximum-security prison.

During his one-day court-martial in November 2006, Barker told the court, "I have tried so many times to understand how I was able to do something so mean, so horrible. I simply have no answer when I think of why. When I think about my last deployment to Iraq, I see only darkness in my heart. Though I was never killed, I can see that part of me had died." Both Barker and Cortez will be eligible for parole after 10 years, and every year after that.

In March 2007, Bryan Howard pleaded guilty to conspiracy to obstruct justice and to being an accessory after the fact. He was sentenced to 27 months in prison at Fort Leavenworth. With time reduction for good behavior and time already served, he was discharged from the Army and released on parole after 17 months. Today, he is working for his father's heavy machinery rigging business in Huffman, Texas.

Because of gaps and inconsistencies in many of the soldiers' confessions and all the participants' ongoing revisions regarding the events of March 12, 2006, there remained some doubt about what, exactly, Jesse Spielman knew about what the others were planning that day and when he knew it. Contesting the bulk of the charges against him, including all felony charges, Spielman's lawyers claimed that he did not know where the rogue patrol was going on March 12 and that he did not know what was going to happen once it arrived at the Janabi residence. The attorneys contended that no one explained anything about the murderous mission to Spielman, and that once at the house, he was too surprised and scared to do anything about it. A military panel did not believe these claims of innocence, found him guilty of all charges, and sentenced him to life in prison (though his sentence was later reduced to 90 years). He too will be eligible for parole after 10 years, and every year after that.

Because Steven Green had been discharged from the Army in May 2006, his case proved to be a much more complicated undertaking that took nearly three years to bring to conclusion. As the Army began investigating Barker, Spielman, and Cortez, military prosecutors realized they had no jurisdiction over Green and notified the U.S. Attorneys' Office that a suspected rapist and murderer was at large in the United States. The FBI arrested Green in July 2006 as the Justice Department declared it planned to prosecute him under the Military Extraterritorial Jurisdiction Act (MEJA) of 2000 in the Federal District Court of Western Kentucky, the court district closest to Fort Campbell, Green's last permanent residence in the United States.

The Justice Department was operating in uncharted territory. There is surprisingly little precedent on how to handle charges against a soldier accused of committing a crime on active duty overseas but who had returned to the United States, been discharged, and was living as a civilian before the crime was discovered. In fact, only one other former service member, ex-Marine sergeant Jose Luis Nazario, had been tried under MEJA. Accused of killing unarmed detainees in Fallujah in 2004, he was acquitted for lack of evidence by a civilian jury in August 2008. Unlike with the Nazario case, however, the Justice Department announced it was pursuing the death penalty against Green, making him the first former service member ever to face the possibility of execution in a civilian court for his conduct during war.

Public defenders Scott Wendelsdorf and Pat Bouldin brought on Darren Wolff, a former Marine lawyer now in private practice. As had Cortez's and Barker's lawyers, Green's team concluded that the confession evidence was so strong that simply keeping their client alive would be a victory. In two motions to dismiss the case, they contested the constitutionality and jurisdiction of MEJA, arguing that the law was not designed for cases like Green's and should not be applied to him. Indeed,

MEJA was written to close a loophole that had enabled military contractors as well as spouses and dependents of service members to escape punishment for crimes committed abroad. Republican senator Jeff Sessions from Alabama, who introduced MEJA to Congress, confirmed the law was intended to have a somewhat narrow focus. Said Sessions, "I don't think any of us at the time the legislation passed were contemplating that a potential criminal act that occurred while a person was on active duty in combat would be tried in a civilian court." Regardless, Thomas Russell, chief judge of the Western Kentucky District Court, rejected Green's lawyers' challenges to MEJA, and the case proceeded.

Green's defense team twice offered to have Green plead guilty if the government would take the death penalty off the table, and twice the Justice Department declined. To this day, Wolff maintains that Justice's push for death was a politically motivated appeasement to the Iraqi government and Iraqi public opinion. Noting that the Iraqi minister of human rights attended the first day of Green's trial, and that Barker and Cortez never had to face the death penalty, Wolff said, "When it became obvious that this case was not about fairness or equity," Justice's rejection of Green's pleas was "about appeasing the overseas communities who have been calling for Mr. Green's execution."

The defense attorneys also tried several times to have Green reinducted into the Army and tried by court-martial. In letters to Fort Campbell's staff judge advocate, the secretary of the army, and the secretary of defense, they argued that a military court was the only appropriate venue for this case, but they also knew that the post–World War II Army was much less likely to execute a criminal than civilian courts were. (The last soldier put to death was Private John Bennett, for rape, in 1961.) The Army declined the offer to take Green back.

After ruling out an insanity defense, Wendelsdorf, Bouldin, and Wolff decided that their best hope before the jury was to emphasize what Bouldin called during the trial's April 2009 opening statements "the context of the crime": the horrible conditions that Bravo labored under, Green's abysmal upbringing, the leadership failures that plagued every level of the 1-502nd, and the clear, repeated warning signs of Green's murderous obsessions that his superiors routinely ignored.

During several dramatic and contentious weeks of testimony in a Paducah, Kentucky, courtroom, the defense ran, to the best of its ability, a trial within a trial against the Army's negligence in allowing the atrocity to happen, while prosecutors, countering repeatedly that there was only one man on trial, focused on the heinousness and inexcusability of Green's behavior.

Brought to Kentucky by the Justice Department, several members of the Janabi family, including Abu Muhammad, the children's paternal grandmother, and sons Ahmed and Muhammad, testified during the trial, movingly describing the innocence of their kin and the barbarity that had been visited upon them.

The jury of nine women and three men found Green guilty of all counts of conspiracy, rape, and murder, but they hung, six against six, on the issue of whether to sentence him to death. A jury unable to reach unanimity on the question of execution triggered an automatic sentence of life in prison without parole. In a comprehensive posttrial questionnaire, many of the jurors demonstrated sympathy for many of the mitigating factors the defense had introduced, and half of the twelve agreed with the statement "This case should have been tried in the military justice system."

One week after the trial, the Janabis were allowed to address the court and Green during a preliminary sentencing hearing in Louisville. Though the session lasted only a few hours, it was an electric, raucous, and dramatic event as they voiced their displeasure that Green would not be executed. When given the chance to address Green directly, one of the sons, Muhammad, glared menacingly at the man who had killed four of his family members but declined to say anything to him.

Hajia, the children's grandmother, wailed and shouted, as a court interpreter translated, "This man has no mercy in his heart, he does not have honor, and yet you let him breathe air until he dies naturally? He is a stigma on the United States. He is a stigma on the whole world. He is a bastard, and a criminal and a dog!"

Ululating and keening, she abruptly left the witness stand and attempted to approach Green at the defense table. "Show him to me!" she shouted. "Show him to me, I want to see him!" A couple of federal marshals attempted to block her path and grab her by the arms, but she would not be deterred. Ultimately, she had to be wrestled to the floor by nearly a dozen court officials, who then virtually carried her, still screaming, back to the gallery.

The mother's cousin, Abu Muhammad, spoke last, praising his slain family members and criticizing the jury's reluctance to execute Green. He concluded by turning to Green and saying, "Abeer will follow you and chase you in your nightmares. May God damn you."

Atrocities are committed in every war. They are a seemingly ineradicable by-product of the barbaric yet quintessentially human institution of organized, leader-mandated, group-on-group killing. But why do some fighting men give in to the final inhumanity of combat—raping and murdering the innocent—while others who experience the same loss, suffer the same hardship and feel the same hatred resist the temptation to defile the defenseless, abandon their honor, debase themselves, and shame their kin and country? Why did Achilles desecrate Hector's corpse when some other Greek and Trojan heroes maintained their dignity and their integrity in the waning days of the *Iliad*? Homer himself offers no satisfying answers. Since then, historians, psychologists, generals, and judges have investigated the causes of uncountable war crimes by fallen fighters far less august than Achilles with the same unsatisfying results. Why are some men mentally equipped to handle the harrowing rigors of war at its worst yet others are unable to endure? Why did James Barker, Paul Cortez, Steven Green, and Jesse Spielman do what they did on March 12, 2006? In their trials, neither Barker, Cortez, nor Spielman could articulate an answer to that seemingly simple, straightforward question.

"I have been in jail for five months, and I ask myself that every day," Cortez told the prosecutor when asked why he even went to the Janabi house. "I still don't have no answer."

And do such men feel any remorse? Barker, Cortez, and Spielman have all said that they do, apologizing in court to the Janabis and Iraq in general as well as to their own families, their comrades in arms, the Army, and America for both the wanton destruction they inflicted and the disgrace they brought on themselves and so many others. Of course, only they know how sincere their words of contrition really were.

At the end of his preliminary sentencing hearing, after the Janabis had spoken, Green was given the opportunity to make a statement himself. Since he had not taken the stand during his own trial or testified at any of the other coconspirators' courts-martial, this was the first public statement he had ever made.

Reading from a sheet of paper, Green emphasized, "What I am about to say is completely my own. No one told me what to say. No one wrote this for me. Not my lawyers, not the government, not anybody." He addressed the family, saying, "I am truly sorry for what I did in Iraq and I am sorry for the pain my actions, and the actions of my codefendants, have caused you and your family. I imagine it is a pain that I cannot fully comprehend or appreciate. I helped to destroy a family and end the lives of four fellow human beings, and I wish that I could take that back, but I cannot. As inadequate as this apology is, it is all I can give you. I know you wish I was dead, and I do not hold that against you. If I was in your place, I am convinced beyond any doubt that I would feel the same way. . . . I know that if I live one more year or fifty more years that they will be years that Fakhriah, Qassim, Abeer, and Hadeel won't have. And even though I did not learn their names until long after their deaths, they are never far from my mind. But in the end, whether in one year or fifty, I will die. And when I die I will be in God's hands, in the Kingdom of God, where there will be justice, and whatever I deserve, I will get. On the day of judgment, God will repay everyone according to his works, and affliction and distress will come upon every human being who does evil. I know that I have done evil, and I fear that the wrath of the Lord will come upon me on that day. But, I hope that you and your family at least can find some comfort in God's justice."

Steven Green is currently serving five consecutive life sentences with no possibility of parole.

POSTSCRIPT

Chaz Allen: Allen is a squad leader in the 75th Cavalry Regiment, 502nd Infantry Regiment, 101st Airborne Division at Fort Campbell, Kentucky.

James Barker: Barker is serving a 90-year prison sentence at the U.S. Disciplinary Barracks at Fort Leavenworth, Kansas. He will be eligible for parole in 2016.

Phil Blaisdell: Blaisdell deployed to Iraq as Platoon Sergeant of the 1-502nd's Scout Platoon in the fall of 2007. Promoted to First Sergeant in December 2007, he finished his tour as the First Sergeant of a 2-502nd company in Haswah, Iraq (just south of Lutufiyah). He is currently a company First Sergeant at the U.S. Army Airborne School at Fort Benning, Georgia.

Jared Bordwell: Promoted to Major in March 2008, Bordwell deployed to Iraq with a Ranger battalion from October 2008 to February 2009. He is currently attending the Command and General Staff College (CGSC) at Fort Leavenworth.

Paul Cortez: Cortez is serving a 100-year prison sentence at the U.S. Disciplinary Barracks at Fort Leavenworth. He will be eligible for parole in 2016.

John Diem: Diem worked on the 1-502nd's headquarters staff during the battalion's deployment to Baghdad in 2007–2008. Promoted to Staff Sergeant in December 2008, he is today a squad leader in the 1-502nd's Bravo Company at Fort Campbell.

Bill Dougherty: Promoted to Major in March 2008, Dougherty attended CGSC in 2009. He is currently working toward a master's degree in military studies at the School for Advanced Military Studies, also at Fort Leavenworth.

Todd Ebel: Ebel commanded Task Force Ramadi, a 140-member task force from all four branches of the military that provided a variety of support services to coalition forces in Anbar province in 2008. He is now director of the School for Command Preparation at CGSC.

Anthony Edwards: In 2008 and 2009, Edwards was Brigade Command Sergeant Major for the 205th Infantry Brigade at Camp Atterbury, Indiana, a National Guard and Army Reserve training center.

Jeff Fenlason: Fenlason is the 101st Airborne Division's Small Arms Master Gunner, a position he has held since January 2007, including a deployment to Afghanistan from March 2008 to January 2009. He was promoted to Master Sergeant in January 2009.

Rob Gallagher: Promoted to First Sergeant in June 2009, Gallagher is a company First Sergeant in the 101st Airborne Division's 506th Infantry Regiment at Fort Campbell.

Jeremy Gebhardt: Gebhardt has deployed to Iraq and Afghanistan on multiple occasions since 2007. Promoted to Master Sergeant in 2008, he is an operational specialist in the Asymmetric Warfare Group, a unit that identifies critical threats and enemy vulnerabilities through first-hand observation.

John Goodwin: Goodwin is currently a battalion operations officer at Fort Carson, Colorado.

Steven Green: Green is serving five consecutive life sentences without the possibility of parole at the United States Penitentiary in Terre Haute, Indiana.

Justin Habash: Honorably discharged from the Army as a Captain in June 2007, Habash is working toward a Ph.D. in philosophy at Duquesne University in Pittsburgh, Pennsylvania.

Bryan Howard: Sentenced to 27 months in prison in March 2007, Howard was released on parole after 17 months for good behavior and the time he had spent in pretrial confinement. Today he works as a heavy machinery rigger in Huffman, Texas.

Tom Kunk: Kunk served as Rear Detachment Commander for the 101st Airborne Division when most of the division rotated back to Iraq during 2007–2008. He was promoted to Colonel in July 2009 and is today the chief of current operations in the Army's Operations, Planning, and Training office at the Pentagon.

Dennis Largent: Largent was promoted to Sergeant Major in February 2007. He is currently deployed to northern Iraq as Operations Sergeant Major with a 1st Armor Division brigade out of Fort Bliss, Texas.

Eric Lauzier: Diagnosed with PTSD and suffering from a deployment-related back injury, Lauzier was medically retired from the Army in December 2008. Living in West Virginia, he is studying to become an MRI and radiology technician.

Phil Miller: Promoted to Sergeant First Class in October 2008, Miller is a Ranger instructor in Dahlonega, Georgia.

Tim Norton: Honorably discharged from the Army in June 2008 as a First Lieutenant, Norton is an insurance claims adjuster in the Boston area and an agricultural investor with Lonnie Hayes, his Charlie Company platoon sergeant, who retired from the Army and is a farmer in southern Illinois.

Chris Payne: Payne deployed to Iraq with the 3-187th Infantry Regiment, 101st Airborne Division in the fall of 2007. A member of a counter-IED advisory team, he was badly injured by an IED blast in November 2007 during a foot patrol just across the Euphrates from the Yusufiyah Thermal Power Plant. He lost his left leg above the knee, and several reconstructive surgeries were required to restore 50 percent use of his left arm. He was promoted to Sergeant First Class in September 2009 and was medically retired from the Army the same month. He is living in Tennessee and working toward his bachelor's degree with the intention of becoming a pharmacist.

Rob Salome: Promoted to Lieutenant Colonel in August 2009, Salome is the Army attaché to Vice President Joseph Biden.

Matt Shoaf: Promoted to Captain in July 2006, Shoaf served as Charlie Company commander from November 2006 to March 2007. Currently stationed at Fort Bragg, North Carolina, he has decided to leave the Army and will begin a master's degree in electrical engineering at Vanderbilt University in the fall of 2010.

Jesse Spielman: Spielman is serving a 90-year prison sentence at the U.S. Disciplinary Barracks at Fort Leavenworth. He will be eligible for parole in 2016.

Shawn Umbrell: Umbrell was promoted to Major in November 2007 and deployed to Iraq in early 2008 with a Ranger battalion. He attended CGSC in 2009 and is currently deployed in Afghanistan with the 5th Stryker Brigade, 2nd Infantry Division, out of Fort Lewis, Washington.

Justin Watt: Diagnosed with PTSD, traumatic brain injury, and an IED-related stomach injury, Watt was medically retired from the Army as a Specialist in December 2007. Today he is partner in a custom-built PC assembly and service business in Salt Lake City, Utah.

Fred Wintrich: Promoted to Lieutenant Colonel in October 2007, Wintrich served as 2nd Brigade's Executive Officer during its 2007–2008 deployment to Baghdad. He is currently Garrison Executive Officer at Fort Campbell.

Tony Yribe: Originally charged with dereliction of duty and making false official statements for his role in covering up the March 12, 2006, rape-murders, Yribe was granted immunity from prosecution and an other than honorable discharge from the Army for his testimony in the Barker, Cortez, Green, Howard, and Spielman trials. He remained under investigation for the November 2005 killing of a woman at TCP3 until August 2008, when all charges were dropped for insufficient evidence that the shot was anything other than an accident. Separated from the Army in September 2008, he is today living in Bellevue, Idaho, and is planning to return to school.

LIST OF CHARACTERS

**502nd Infantry Regiment/2nd Brigade Combat Team
("Strike Brigade," "Black Heart Brigade," "the Deuce"),
101st Airborne Division**
Colonel Todd Ebel, commander
Command Sergeant Major Brian Stall, brigade sergeant major

**1-502nd Infantry Regiment
("1st Battalion," "First Strike")**
Lieutenant Colonel Tom Kunk, commander
Command Sergeant Major Anthony Edwards, battalion sergeant
  major
Major Fred Wintrich, executive officer
Major James "Rob" Salome, operations officer
Captain Leo Barron, intelligence officer

Headquarters and Headquarters Company ("HHC")
Captain Shawn Umbrell, commander
First Lieutenant Brian Lohnes, scout platoon leader
Sergeant Cory Collins
Specialist Josh Munger
Specialist Benjamin Smith
Private First Class Tyler MacKenzie

Alpha Company
Captain Jared Bordwell, commander
Private First Class Brian Kubik

Bravo Company ("Bulldogs")

Captain John Goodwin, commander
First Sergeant Rick Skidis, first sergeant
Sergeant First Class Andrew Laskoski, first sergeant
First Lieutenant Justin Habash, executive officer
Specialist Ethan Biggers, radio transmission operator

1st Platoon

First Lieutenant Ben Britt, platoon leader
First Lieutenant Tim Norton, platoon leader
Staff Sergeant Phil Miller, platoon sergeant
Sergeant First Class Rob Gallagher, platoon sergeant
Sergeant First Class Jeff Fenlason, platoon sergeant
Specialist Collin Sharpness, medic
Staff Sergeant Travis Nelson, 1st Squad leader
Staff Sergeant Chaz Allen, 1st Squad leader
Staff Sergeant Chris Payne, 2nd Squad leader
Staff Sergeant Eric Lauzier, 3rd Squad leader
Staff Sergeant Matthew Walter
Sergeant Kenith Casica
Sergeant Roman Diaz
Sergeant John Diem
Sergeant Tony Yribe
Specialist David Babineau
Specialist James Barker
Specialist Paul Cortez
Specialist Thomas Doss
Specialist James Gregory
Specialist Anthony Hernandez
Specialist William Lopez-Feliciano
Private First Class Chris Barnes
Private First Class Justin Cross
Private First Class Steven Green
Private First Class Shane Hoeck
Private First Class Bryan Howard
Private First Class Kristian Menchaca

Private First Class Jesse Spielman
Private First Class Thomas Tucker
Private First Class Justin Watt
Private Nicholas Lake
Private Seth Scheller

2nd Platoon

First Lieutenant Jerry Eidson, platoon leader
First Lieutenant Paul Fisher, platoon leader
Sergeant First Class Jeremy Gebhardt, platoon sergeant
Staff Sergeant Les Fuller, squad leader
Specialist Noah Galloway
Private First Class Ryan Davis
Private First Class Tim Hanley

3rd Platoon

Second Lieutenant Mark Evans, platoon leader
Sergeant First Class Phil Blaisdell, platoon sergeant
Staff Sergeant Chris Arnold
Staff Sergeant Joe Whelchel
Sergeant Daniel Carrick
Specialist Anthony "Chad" Owens
Specialist Kirk Reilly
Specialist David Shockey
Specialist Jay Strobino

Charlie Company ("Cobras," "the People's Army")

Captain Bill Dougherty, commander
First Sergeant Dennis Largent, first sergeant
First Lieutenant Matt Shoaf, executive officer
Sergeant First Class Lonnie Hayes, platoon sergeant
Staff Sergeant Jason Fegler
Sergeant Juan Hernandez

Delta Company

Captain Lou Kangas, commander
First Lieutenant Garrison Avery

Specialist Marlon Bustamante
Private First Class Caesar Viglienzone

Combat Stress Practitioners
Lieutenant Colonel Elizabeth Bowler, forensic psychiatrist
Lieutenant Colonel Karen Marrs, psychiatric nurse practitioner
Staff Sergeant Bob Davis

2-502nd Infantry Regiment
("2nd Battalion," "Strike Force")
Lieutenant Colonel Rob Haycock, commander

MILITARY UNITS AND RANKS

Typical Light Infantry Unit Sizes and Leadership

Division

Size: 18,000–24,000 soldiers (4 brigades)

Led by: a Major General and a Command Sergeant Major

Brigade

Size: 3,000–6,000 soldiers (6 battalions)

Led by: a Colonel and a Command Sergeant Major

Battalion

Size: 700–1,000 soldiers (4 line companies, 1 headquarters company, and 1 logistics company)

Led by: a Lieutenant Colonel and a Command Sergeant Major

Company

Size: 125–140 soldiers (3–4 line platoons, plus headquarters)

Led by: a Captain and a First Sergeant

Platoon

Size: 25–40 soldiers (3–4 squads)

Led by: a First or Second Lieutenant and a Sergeant First Class or Staff Sergeant

Squad

Size: 7–11 soldiers (2 fire teams)

Led by: a Staff Sergeant or Sergeant

Fire Team

Size: 3–5 soldiers

Led by: a Sergeant or Specialist

Rank Structure
Officer Ranks

General (O-10)

Lieutenant General (O-9)

Major General (O-8)

Brigadier General (O-7)

Colonel (O-6)

Lieutenant Colonel (O-5)

Major (O-4)

Captain (O-3)

First Lieutenant (O-2)

Second Lieutenant (O-1)

Enlisted Ranks

Sergeant Major (E-9)

Master Sergeant or First Sergeant (E-8)

Sergeant First Class (E-7)

Staff Sergeant (E-6)

Sergeant (E-5)

Specialist or Corporal (E-4)

Private First Class (E-3)

Private (E-2)

Recruit (E-1)

ACRONYMS AND ABBREVIATIONS

ACU	Army combat uniform
AFP	Agence France-Presse
AIF	anti-Iraqi forces
AO	area of operation
AQI	Al Qaeda in Iraq
AVLB	armored vehicle–launched bridge
BCT	Brigade Combat Team
BDA	battle damage assessment
CIB	Combat Infantryman's Badge
CID	Criminal Investigation Division
CMO	civil-military operations
CO	commanding officer
COIN	counterinsurgency
COP	Coalition Outpost
COSR	Combat and Operational Stress Reaction
CPA	Coalition Provisional Authority
CUB	Commanders Update Briefing
EOD	Explosive Ordnance Disposal
FOB	forward operating base
HHC	Headquarters and Headquarters Company
IA	Iraqi Army
IAI	Islamic Army in Iraq
IED	improvised explosive device
IGC	Interim Governing Council
JAM	Jaish al-Mahdi (Mahdi Army)
JRTC	Joint Readiness Training Center
JSB	Jurf al-Sukr Bridge
LZ	landing zone

MisCap-DuStWUn	Missing, Captured–Duty Status, Whereabouts Unknown
MiTT	military transition team
MNF-I	Multi-National Force–Iraq
MRE	meal, ready to eat
MSC	Mujahideen Shura Council
NCO	noncommissioned officer
NTC	National Training Center
OIF	Operation Iraqi Freedom
ORHA	Office of Reconstruction and Humanitarian Assistance
PJ	[Air Force] Para Jumper
PLDC	Primary Leadership Development Course
POO	point of origin
PSD	Personal Security Detachment
QRF	Quick Reaction Force
RIP-TOA	Relief in Place, Transfer of Authority
ROE	rules of engagement
RPG	rocket-propelled grenade
SAW	squad automatic weapon
TCP	traffic control point
TOC	tactical operations center
VBIED	vehicle-borne improvised explosive device

ACKNOWLEDGMENTS

FIRST AND FOREMOST, I want to thank the men of the 1-502nd Infantry Regiment. When I began this project I did not know what to expect, but I did not think that very many men from the unit would want to speak to me. I was surprised, gratified, and ultimately humbled by just how many wound up responding affirmatively to my queries. They trusted me with their stories and they opened up about their experiences, knowing that much of their deployment was uncomfortable, controversial, and disquieting. They knew that this book would not necessarily present all their actions in a flattering light, and yet they talked to me anyway, at great length and in great detail.

Many men, especially those from other platoons or other companies than 1st Platoon of Bravo Company, wanted the world to know that there was more to their war than the rape-murders and the Alamo incident. And the men of 1st Platoon wanted what happened to be put in context. All any of them have ever asked of me is that I do my best to be accurate, that I neither prettify nor vilify their experiences, that I tell their story as truthfully as I could. I am deeply indebted to them, and I hope that I have succeeded.

Thanks go to all those who participated in or were affected by First Strike's deployment who graciously agreed to be interviewed: Abu Somer, Allen the Interpreter, Chaz Allen, Chris Arnold, Kayla Avery, James Barker, Chris Barnes, Leo Barron, Gary Bartlett, Richard Baxter, Mark Belda, Phil Blaisdell, Jared Bordwell, Elizabeth Bowler, Daniel Carrick, Renee Casica, Sean Cavenaugh, Steve Cisneros, Paul Cluverius, Dave Cochrane, Eric Conrad, Justin Cross, Anthony Davis, Bob Davis, Phil Deem, Roman Diaz, John Diem, Bill Dougherty, James Downs, Christopher DuBois, Todd Ebel, Jerry Eidson, Anthony Evans, Mark

Evans, Jeff Fenlason, Paul Fisher, Les Fuller, Noah Galloway, Jeremy Gebhardt, John Goodwin, Steven Green, John Greis, Justin Habash, Paul Haefele, Walled Mahmoud Hamza, Tyler Hanna, Lonnie Hayes, Nancy Hess, Shane Hoeck, Ryan Hoefer, Bryan Howard, Tim Iannacone, Mark Ivey, Lou Kangas, John King, Tom Kunk, Brian LaFond, Dennis Largent, Andrew Laskoski, Eric Lauzier, Brian Lohnes, Nathaniel Loper, Matt Marcelino, Phil Miller, Joe Mirkovich, Shelly Nelson, Tim Norton, James Page, Roselia Palma, Richard Patenia, Chris Payne, Leif Peterson, Jeff Preston, Rob Salome, Antonio Sandoval, Dennison Segui, Collin Sharpness, Matt Shoaf, Rick Skidis, Daniel Sparks, Jay Strobino, Mike Taylor, Christopher Thielenhaus, Chris Till, Shawn Umbrell, Paul Vermillion, Justin Watt, Rick Watt, Joe Whelchel, Mark Whiteman, William Wilder, Robert Williams, Fred Wintrich, and Tony Yribe.

This project would be nothing without John Glusman, a profoundly talented and enthusiastic editor, who seemed to understand this project at its very root the moment he read the proposal and we first spoke. Ever since then, I have thanked the heavens for his involvement. He believed in it, championed it, nurtured it every step of the way. He inspired me to work harder and dig deeper than I thought possible, and he always encouraged me to follow the story wherever it led, even after we had long departed the original parameters of the proposal. His team at Harmony Books, including Anne Berry, Domenica Alioto, David Tran, Mark McCauslin, and Campbell Wharton, have been more helpful than I could have possibly imagined.

I am similarly indebted to Elizabeth Sheinkman, an old friend and an extraordinary agent, who is a wise guide and a fierce advocate, and whose coworkers at the Curtis Brown Agency, especially Felicity Blunt, are similarly a pleasure to work with.

I am grateful to my editors and colleagues at *Time* magazine, particularly Michael Elliott, Bobby Ghosh, and Howard Chua-Eoan. They knew I was taking myself out of *Time*'s bullpen to work on this book, yet they extended to me all of the door-opening, safety-guaranteeing, wheelgreasing privileges that come with remaining a member of the Time organization for my two trips to Iraq. Without them, those reporting excursions would have been impossible, and their immediate and un-questioned extension of assistance to me was a demonstration of the fraternity of journalism at its best.

At *Time*'s Baghdad bureau, the reporting and logistical assistance, and the simple companionship provided by its foreign correspondents Mark Kukis, Abigail Hauslohner, and Yuri Kozyrev, were impressive and inspiring, proving that grace under pressure defines not just courage but class. Speaking of courage, however, there are few people on the planet braver than innocent Iraqis, especially those who work for West-ern news organizations. I cannot fathom how *Time*'s Baghdad staff—Ali, Sami, Mazen, Omar, and Rahd—managed to stay loyal, motivated, sane, and, I dare say, upbeat given the constant threats that have borne down on them—and killed several of their colleagues—but I did and would forever trust them all with my life. They are personal heroes of mine. *Time*'s South Baghdad stringer Ahmed also assisted with finding inter-view subjects from the Yusufiyah area.

I am grateful to Lieutenant Colonels Andrew Rohling, William Zemp, and Michael Getchell, commanders of the 3-187th Infantry Reg-iment, the 3-320th Field Artillery Regiment, and the 2-502nd Infantry Regiment, respectively, and all of their men for being supremely hos-pitable embed hosts as I familiarized myself with the Triangle of Death.

Tara Sad, Bethany Hebert, Ben and Jackson Daviss, and Galen Butcher unflaggingly, relentlessly, doggedly turned several hundred hours of interviews into 4,000 pages of transcripts quickly, cleanly, and often on a rush basis. Tara, in particular, was a confidante and adviser, someone I could always bounce ideas off of or seek an opinion from; she was one of the few people from outside the 1-502nd who, in a way, knew all of the soldiers by listening to their interviews. She took a keen in-terest in the soldiers and their lives.

I am grateful to Andrew Tilghman of *Stars and Stripes* and Ryan Lenz of the Associated Press, who were embedded with the 1-502nd at dif-ferent times during the battalion's deployment in 2005 and 2006, for both the stories they wrote and the personal insights they have shared with me since then. Likewise, Sean Naylor of *Army Times* provided good advice about how best to journalistically navigate the thickets of Freedom of Information Act requests, Army Public Affairs Offices, and other oddities of journalism about the military. Also extending help were Ned Parker of the *Los Angeles Times* and Michael Ware of CNN. Thanks go as well to Dave Alsup of CNN, Brett Barrouquere of AP, and Evan Bright, boy wonder high-school blogger who documented the Steven Green trial with impressive thoroughness and zeal.

My old friend Mike Bergner opened his home to be my base for three months when I was literally homeless and flying around the country interviewing soldiers—I could not be more grateful for his hospitality. While on the road, I benefited from the kindness of many friends, especially Paul and Erin Scott in Berkeley and Zack Meisel and Cori Schreiber in Philadelphia. John and Elaine Watson rented an apartment in their fourteenth-century farmhouse in North Stainley, Yorkshire, England, to me during the winter of 2008 and 2009 as I wrote the first draft of the manuscript. It is the most perfect writer's retreat there has ever been. Hugh, Pat, and the entire Greensit family in nearby Masham were and are the best second family in the world and I am blessed to have been so welcomed by them.

The lawyers associated with all of the cases surrounding the rape-murders of the Janabis have been extremely helpful with background insights and advice, including Bill Casara, William Fischbach, Marisa Ford, Steve McGaha, Juan Roman, Megan Shaw, Brian Skaret, and Elizabeth Walker. Lawyers Patrick Bouldin, David Sheldon, and Darren Wolff deserve special mention for being remarkably generous with their time, trust, and expertise.

To Jim Culp I am singularly and forever indebted, as he prodded me to investigate this story in the first place and suggested—nay, insisted—that there was far more to the tale than could be contained by a magazine article. He was right.

I would also like to thank terrorism expert Evan Kohlmann for his assistance in trying to make sense of the Iraqi insurgency, and terrorism blogger Bill Roggio for his views on the complexities of "The Long War." I am grateful to forensic expert Dr. Michael Baden for his analysis of the March 12 crime scene photos and to Mike Bealing and Julius Domoney for their photo research assistance.

Cathy Gramling at the 101st Airborne Public Affairs Office and Val Florez of the 101st Airborne's Freedom of Information Act Office were extremely helpful running down obscure facts and documents.

I would like to thank my parents and sisters Laura and Sharon for the unflagging support and encouragement they have provided me my entire life. In particular, however, I want to thank my brother Ted, a retired armor Army lieutenant colonel, who was frequently my first stop to ask about the mysteries of the military, and an early reader of the manuscript.

And nearly last, but in almost every regard first, I want to thank Charlotte Greensit for her truly bottomless love, patience, support, counsel, and cheer. This book could not have been possible without her. She is, in every way, a partner and a soul mate.

Finally, I would like to thank the Janabi family: cousin Abu Muhammad (who asked that I use a pseudonym for even his nickname), aunt Ameer, grandmother Hajia, and sons Ahmed and Muhammad. I am glad that they chose to speak to me when they have spoken to so few journalists. Their grief continues. I have a particular hope that Ahmed and Muhammad may find peace in their hearts and a future free from hatred.

NOTES ·

A Note on Sources

THE MATERIAL ABOUT the 2005–2006 deployment of the 1-502nd Infantry Regiment is primarily the product of my own reporting in both the United States and Iraq from mid-2006 to late 2009, including two reporting trips to Iraq, one of which involved a three-week stay with 101st Airborne Division units in Mahmudiyah, Yusufiyah, Lutufiyah, the Russian power plant, and other Triangle of Death environs in May and June of 2008.

The sources for most of the information contained in this book are overwhelmingly the soldiers and officers of the 1-502nd themselves. I met scores of men from this unit for in-person interviews. Dozens more who could not connect with me in person agreed to interviews over the phone.

Many of them shared with me their letters, journals, and photos. Some passed along still-classified documents, including the battalion's major events database known as its "Sig Acts" (significant actions) file, debriefing PowerPoint slides (known as "storyboards"), detailed maps, work e-mail exchanges, and internal reports—all at great professional risk. These documents, which contained invaluable details such as specific times and pinpoint locations of a wide variety of events, informed virtually every scene of the book, but because of their sensitivity I have chosen not to include them in the notes.

Formal and informal interviews with the relatives and friends of many of the soldiers helped round out their portraits as well. A few sources have asked not to be identified by name, but they were a tiny minority. The overwhelming majority of interview subjects readily agreed to be identified, and most interviews were conducted entirely on the record. Unless otherwise stated, I conducted all the interviews referenced in the notes that follow. I have not detailed the interview dates because doing so would be unwieldy and impractical: many interview subjects sat for several days of interviews, often several months apart, and answered follow-up questions via e-mail and telephone.

Supplementing my own interviews and firsthand reporting, I relied heavily on the voluminous transcripts of the many court proceedings that resulted from the March 12, 2006, rape-murders as well as the recordings of fact-finding interviews conducted in July and August 2006 by then-Captain James Culp and David Sheldon, who served as James Barker's defense lawyers. Likewise, I frequently relied upon the signed sworn statements soldiers routinely submitted in relation to AR 15-6 investigations or criminal investigations, as well as the summaries and findings from the AR 15-6s themselves. These interviews, court transcripts, and sworn statements were particularly helpful for providing the viewpoints of the few soldiers who elected not to speak with me.

To round out these sources and for historical context, I have also made frequent use of the research generated by many government agencies, think tanks, and mainstream news outlets as well as a number of the many excellent general histories of the war that have already been published. These sources are presented more fully in the bibliography.

Foreword

xiii *In late September 2008:* Lesley Stahl and Richard Bonin, "General O," *60 Minutes,* September 28, 2008.

xvi *During their year-long:* Leo Barron, interview.

xvi *Twenty-one men:* 101st Airborne Public Affairs Office.

xvii *Including Iraqi locals:* Richard Patenia, interview.

xvii *More than 40 percent:* Ryan Lenz, "Army Works to Offset Combat Stress in Iraq," Associated Press, June 4, 2006.

xvii *For 1st Battalion:* Fred Wintrich, interview.

xvii *By the end: Presentation of the AR 15-6 Investigation Results to the Family of Specialist David Babineau,* PowerPoint slides, undated.

xx *(One expert estimates:* J. Robert Lilly, "Rape and Murder in the European Theater of Operations, WWII," January 31, 2007.

xxi *Bravo Company commander:* John M. McCarthy, "AR 15-6 Investigation Concerning Leadership Actions in Effect of B/1-502 IN on or about 12 MAR 2006," July 10, 2006.

xxi *Perhaps so:* Joseph Giordono, "8,000 Troops Widen Search for Missing GIs," *Stars and Stripes,* June 20, 2006.

Prelude

1 *About an hour later:* Abu Muhammad [pseud.], interview.

2 *There was another knock:* Ibid.; testimony during Article 32 Hearing and at *U.S. v. Green.*

2 *Socked by dust storms:* Crime scene photos.

3 *Abu Muhammad had seen:* Abu Muhammad [pseud.], interview.

3 *Each body was:* Crime scene photos.

3 *In her right hand:* Abu Muhammad [pseud.], interview; testimony during Article 32 Hearing and at *U.S. v. Green;* crime scene photos.

4 *"Yribe! Hey, Yribe!:* Tony Yribe, interview and testimony at *U.S. v. Spielman.*

1: "We've Got to Get South Baghdad Under Control"

11 *When Colonel Todd Ebel:* Todd Ebel, interview.

11 *The deterioration of Iraq:* Tommy Franks and Malcolm McConnell, *American Soldier* (New York: HarperCollins, 2005), pp. 147, 474; Thomas E. Ricks, *Fiasco* (New York: Penguin Press, 2006), p. 395; BBC.com, "UK Fatalities in Afghanistan and Iraq."

11 *After the initial euphoria:* Charles H. Ferguson, *No End in Sight: Iraq's Descent into Chaos* (New York: PublicAffairs, 2008), pp. 33–34.

11 *The first American:* Bob Woodward, *State of Denial: Bush at War, Part III* (New York: Simon & Schuster, 2006), pp. 117, 170, 180.

12 *The White House:* Rajiv Chandrasekaran, *Imperial Life in the Emerald City* (London: Bloomsbury, 2007), pp. 52, 76–84; Ferguson, *No End in Sight,* pp. 156, 164, 190–224.

12 *The people who worked:* Chandrasekaran, *Imperial Life,* pp. 1–20, 153–63.

12 *Due to the CPA's:* Ferguson, *No End in Sight,* pp. 296–97.

13 *The CPA failed:* Stewart W. Bowen, Jr., *Hard Lessons: The Iraq Reconstruction Experience.* U.S. Special Inspector General for Iraq Reconstruction (Washington, D.C.: U.S. Government Printing Office, February 9, 2009). Electricity was an obsession for Bremer, but only to the extent

that his staff could best prewar generation levels of approximately 4,000 MW (one megawatt equals roughly the power needed by about 1,500 homes). "The CPA effort to get electricity production up to 4,400 MW was fleetingly successful in October 2003," says *Hard Lessons,* "but the short-term actions taken to meet that goal proved counterproductive to long-term progress." To date, electrical generation in the country has never topped 5,000 megawatts.

13 *Bremer and the CPA:* Chandrasekaran, *Imperial Life,* pp. 208–9.

13 *He created an Interim:* L. Paul Bremer and Malcolm McConnell, *My Year in Iraq: The Struggle to Build a Future of Hope* (New York: Threshold Editions, 2006), p. 93.

13 *While the Bush:* Evan Kohlmann, interview.

14 *The insurgency was not limited:* Patrick Cockburn, *Muqtada al-Sadr and the Fall of Iraq* (London: Faber & Faber, 2008); Bremer, *My Year in Iraq.*

15 *The first response:* James Fallows, "Why Iraq Has No Army," *Atlantic Monthly,* December 2005.

15 *Well into 2007:* Thomas E. Ricks, *The Gamble* (New York: Penguin Press, 2009), p. 156.

15 *In August 2003:* U.S. State Department Office of the Historian, "Significant Terrorist Incidents, 1961–2003: A Brief Chronology," March 2004, http://www.state.gov/r/pa/ho/pubs/fs/5902.htm.

16 *When CENTCOM commander:* Michael Gordon and Bernard Trainor, *Cobra II: The Inside Story of the Invasion and Occupation of Iraq* (New York: Pantheon, 2006), p. 487.

16 *In his memoir:* Ricardo S. Sanchez and Donald T. Phillips, *Wiser in Battle: A Soldier's Story* (New York: HarperCollins, 2008), pp. 261–63, 276.

16 *One Human Rights Watch:* Human Rights Watch, *Leadership Failure: Firsthand Accounts of Torture of Iraqi Detainees by the U.S. Army's 82nd Airborne Division,* September 22, 2005.

17 *Many in the government:* Human Rights Watch, *"No Blood, No Foul": Soldiers' Accounts of Detainee Abuse in Iraq,* July 2006.

17 *President Bush ordered:* Sanchez, *Wiser in Battle,* p. 356; Ricks, *Fiasco,* pp. 330–43.

17 *In October 2003:* Chandrasekaran, *Imperial Life,* pp. 214–15.

17 *Ultimately, Bremer handed:* Ricks, *Fiasco,* pp. 390–93.

17 *Casey arrived with:* Ibid., p. 413.

18 *A counterinsurgency rule:* James T. Quinlivan, "Burden of Victory: The Painful Arithmetic of Stability Operations," *Rand Review,* Summer 2003.

18 *During the planning:* Ferguson, *No End in Sight,* pp. 25–32.

18 *The subject was:* Bremer, *My Year in Iraq,* p. 357.

18 *In late 2005:* Bob Woodward, *The War Within: A Secret White House History 2006–2008* (New York: Simon & Schuster, 2008), p. 33.

19 *In 2005, the number:* Ricks, *Fiasco,* p. 414.

19 *His plans to reduce:* Woodward, *The War Within,* p. 59.

19 *The 101st Airborne's:* James Page, interview; 101st Airborne Public Affairs Office.

20 *Petraeus would become:* Ricks, *Fiasco,* p. 228.

20 *Books such as:* Stephen E. Ambrose, *Band of Brothers* (New York: Simon & Schuster Paperbacks, 2004).

20 *But that strength:* Page, interview.

21 *During the invasion:* Thomas L. Day, *Along the Tigris* (Atglen, Pa.: Schiffer Publishing, 2007), p. 127.

21 *The son of a lieutenant colonel:* Ebel, interview.

21 *Along his rise:* Ibid.

22 *The Black Hearts name:* Page, interview.

23 *Knowing that the 101st:* Ebel, interview.

2: The Kunk Gun

24 *As part of General Casey's:* Todd Ebel, interview.

25 *When Tom Kunk:* Tom Kunk, interview.

27 *Kunk served in:* Ibid.

28 *As the battalion:* Fred Wintrich, interview.

28 *First Strike's operations officer:* Rob Salome, interview.

29 *Commanding HHC:* Shawn Umbrell, interview.

29 *Captain Bill Dougherty:* Umbrell and Bill Dougherty, interviews.

30 *"There was still:* Dougherty, interview.

30 *Years before:* Dennis Largent and Tim Norton, interviews.

32 *Immediately, 1st Battalion's:* Umbrell and Jared Bordwell, interviews.

33 *Bordwell went afoul:* Bordwell, interview.

33 *That approach:* Bordwell, Dougherty, Umbrell, Largent, John Goodwin, Mark Belda, and others, interviews.

34 *By Army culture:* Belda, interview.

34 *He routinely ridiculed:* Norton, written sworn statement in McCarthy, "AR
      15-6 Investigation"; Matt Shoaf and Eric Lauzier, interviews.

34 *If anyone disagreed:* Dougherty, interview.

34 *If, initially:* Belda, interview.

34 *The relationship continued:* Bordwell, interview.

34 *The captains became:* Umbrell, interview.

34 *Several first sergeants:* Belda, interview.

35 *First Sergeant Largent:* Largent, interview.

35 *As the senior company:* Umbrell, interview.

36 *Kunk never had:* Salome and Wintrich, interviews.

36 *Other subordinates not:* Leo Barron and Dennison Segui, interviews.

36 *This is a discrepancy:* Brian Lohnes, interview.

37 *HHC commander Shawn:* Umbrell, diary entry.

37 *"Ebel said it was:* Kunk, interview.

37 *"We started having:* Steve Cisneros, interview.

37 *"Open-source information:* Shoaf, interview.

38 *"I lost my first sergeant:* Bordwell, interview.

38 *As the wheels-up date:* Umbrell, diary entry.

3: "This Is Now the Most Dangerous Place in Iraq"

41 *In one sense:* Charles Tripp, *A History of Iraq* (Cambridge: Cambridge
      University Press, 2007); William R. Polk, *Understanding Iraq* (New York:
      Harper Perennial, 2006).

43 *You cannot easily get:* Tom Kunk, testimony at *U.S* v. *Green;* Kunk, Jared
      Bordwell, Bill Dougherty, and Leo Barron, interviews.

43 *Some families from:* Ali A. Allawi, *The Occupation of Iraq* (New Haven,
      Conn.: Yale University Press, 2007), p. 244.

44 *Eight miles west:* Lauren Frayer, "Derelict Power Plant Symbol of Iraq
      Woes," Associated Press, February 11, 2007; Sergei L. Loiko and John
      Daniszewski, "Russia Launches 'a Planned Withdrawal' of Its Citizens
      from Iraq," *Los Angeles Times,* March 7, 2003.

45 *Two of the most powerful:* Evan Kohlmann, "State of the Sunni Insurgency
      in Iraq, 2006," December 29, 2006; Dr. Ali Al-Naimi (spokesman of IAI),
      interview with Kohlmann, July 2008.

45 *After the American invasion:* Mary Anne Weaver, "The Short, Violent Life
      of Abu Musab al-Zarqawi," *Atlantic Monthly,* July–August 2006.

46 *Near Yusufiyah:* Mike Starz, interview and diary entry.

47 *One suicide bomber:* Ireland Online, "Suicide Bomber Attacks Iraqi Wedding Party," January 21, 2005.

47 *The Sunni groups:* Associated Press, "Iraq's 'Triangle of Death' Includes Bounties," November 19, 2004; Alissa J. Rubin, "Religious Hostility Surfacing," *Los Angeles Times,* December 20, 2004.

47 *Roads were littered:* Rubin, "Religious Hostility Surfacing," *Los Angeles Times,* December 20, 2004.

48 *The area was just as dangerous:* Associated Press, "Iraq's 'Triangle of Death' Includes Bounties," November 19, 2004; Anthony Shadid, "Iraq's Forbidding 'Triangle of Death': South of Baghdad, a Brutal Sunni Insurgency Holds Sway," *Washington Post,* November 23, 2004; Ahmed Mukhtar, "Deadly Triangle," *Al-Ahram Weekly,* November 4–10, 2004.

48 *On October 3, 2004:* Agence France-Presse, "Two Bodies, Including Beheaded Man, Found South of Baghdad," October 3, 2004.

48 *As the United States:* Thanassis Cambanis, "2 Pictures Emerge of Militants' Power," *Boston Globe,* October 18, 2004.

49 *In the fall:* Kim Sengupta, " 'This is now the most dangerous place in Iraq. We are coming up against Zarqawi's people,' " *The Independent,* November 22, 2004; Military Channel, *Combat Zone* (season 1, episode 7), "Triangle of Death," 2007; John F. Burns, "With 25 Citizen Warriors in an Improvised War," *New York Times,* December 12, 2004; Anthony Shadid and Bradley Graham, "Troops Hit Sites South of Baghdad: Raids Involve U.S., British, Iraqi Forces," *Washington Post,* November 24, 2004; CNN.com, "Iraq: New Push Against Insurgents," October 5, 2004.

49 *The Marines decamped:* John King, interview.

49 *Throughout 2005:* Charles H. Ferguson, *No End in Sight,* pp. 362–63.

4: Relief in Place, Transfer of Authority

51 *On September 29:* Shawn Umbrell and Les Fuller, diary entries.

52 *Lieutenant Colonel Kunk decided to:* Tom Kunk and Umbrell, interviews.

53 *Kunk gave Charlie:* Kunk, interview.

53 *This was Bravo Company:* John Goodwin, interview.

55 *The 48th lost four:* Moni Basu and Anna Varela, "Four More from 48th Killed in Iraq," The 48th Goes to War blog, *Atlanta Journal-Constitution Online,* July 31, 2005; Jeremy Redmon, "New Buddy Sorely Missed," The 48th Goes to War blog, *Atlanta Journal-Constitution Online,* October 27, 2005; Jeremy Redmon, "48th Will Redeploy in Iraq by Thanksgiving,"

The 48th Goes to War blog, *Atlanta Journal-Constitution Online,* October 4, 2005, http://www.ajc.com/news/content/news/index/iraq.html.

56 *One 101st soldier:* Daniel Carrick, interview.

56 *Another said some:* Justin Cross, interview.

56 *The 48th men:* Umbrell, interview.

56 *The living conditions:* Chris Payne, Carrick, Eric Lauzier, Rick Skidis, Justin Habash, and others, interviews.

56 *First Strike's intelligence:* Leo Barron, interview.

57 *The 48th intelligence:* Todd Ebel, interview.

57 *First Battalion's eight-man:* Barron, interview.

57 *As the battalion:* Kunk, interview.

57 *And what little:* Kunk and John King, interviews.

57 *There was no:* Ebel, interview.

57 *Many, the Americans':* King, interview.

57 *Kunk suspected:* Ebel, interview.

57 *Two of the battalion:* Kunk and Ebel, interviews.

58 *Delta's company commander:* Lou Kangas, interview.

58 *Within a few days:* Jared Bordwell, interview.

58 *Down in Lutufiyah:* Bill Dougherty, interview.

58 *On the battalion level:* Rob Salome, interview.

58 *As Goodwin and:* Goodwin, interview.

58 *The magnitude of Goodwin's:* Ibid.

59 *Twenty-four-year-old:* Jon Mark Beilue, "Ben Britt: Never a Taker, Always a Giver," *Amarillo Globe News,* January 1, 2006.

60 *"He wanted a piece:* Tony Yribe, interview.

60 *Despite Miller's considerable:* Kunk, interview.

60 *Miller jumped at:* Phil Miller, interview.

60 *When Second Lieutenant Mark:* Mark Evans, interview.

61 *If First Strike's:* Ebel, Kunk, and Goodwin, interviews.

63 *"We couldn't get:* Ebel, interview.

64 *On his early:* Kunk, interview.

64 *Upon Bravo's arrival:* Goodwin, interview.

5: 1st Platoon at the JS Bridge

65 *Goodwin decided to send:* John Goodwin, interview.

65 *Living conditions were:* Chris Payne, James Downs, Eric Lauzier, and others, interviews.

66 *"From the moment:* Justin Habash, interview.

67 *First Platoon filled:* Lauzier and Phil Miller, interviews.

67 *Forty-one years old:* Shelly Nelson, Collin Sharpness, Miller, and Phil Deem, interviews.

68 *Nelson's Alpha Team:* Miller, eulogy of Casica, *Remembering Our Fallen Heroes: Staff Sergeant Travis L. Nelson and Sergeant Kenith Casica,* DVD, December 16, 2005; Renee Casica, Lauzier, and Payne, interviews.

69 *Spielman's grandmother was:* Nancy Hess, interview.

69 *He married just:* Sarah Bowles and Hadley Robinson, "Trying to Understand the Mahmudiyah Massacre," *Gelf Magazine,* May 6, 2009.

69 *His superiors found:* Tony Yribe and Lauzier, interviews.

69 *Private Steven Green:* U.S. v. *Green.*

70 *Along the way:* Green, interview.

71 *With the Army strapped:* Andrew Tilghman, "The Army's Other Crisis," *Washington Monthly,* December 2007.

71 *One lieutenant was surprised:* Mark Evans, interview.

71 *Second Squad was:* Payne, interview.

72 *He was Sergeant:* Miller, interview.

72 *Captain Goodwin came:* Goodwin, interview.

72 *This was his second:* Lauzier, interview.

73 *Woe to the smart:* Shane Hoeck, interview.

73 *He had several:* Lauzier, interview.

74 *Lauzier called Yribe:* Ibid.

74 *"I would joke:* Goodwin, testimony at Article 32 Hearing.

74 *Yribe saw no need:* Yribe, interview.

74 *Living in motel:* U.S. v. *Cortez;* Payne, interview.

75 *"You take him:* Payne and Lauzier, interviews.

75 *Childhood friends:* Roselia Palma, interview; Doug Hoagland, "Soldier's Story Is Written in Contrasts," *Fresno Bee,* July 30, 2006.

75 *But as he grew:* David Walker, testimony at U.S. v. *Barker.*

75 *He married and joined:* Barker, interview.

75 *Private Justin Watt:* Justin Watt and Lauzier, interviews.

6: Contact

77 *Only two or three:* Eric Lauzier, Tony Yribe, and Justin Watt, interviews.

78 *Miller took Lauzier:* Phil Miller, interview.

78 *Between those duties:* Watt, testimony at Article 32 Hearing.

78 *Miller was appalled:* Miller, interview.

78 *They were dependent:* John Goodwin, interview.

78 *Miller didn't find:* Miller, interview.

79 *"Supposedly they weren't:* Justin Habash, interview.

79 *But Kunk wasn't:* Tom Kunk, interview.

79 *Miller and the squad:* Miller, interview.

79 *That's precisely the way:* Kunk, interview with defense lawyers.

79 *But to Miller:* Miller, interview.

80 *A few days after:* Phil Deem, Lauzier, and Watt, interviews.

81 *From the start:* Habash, interview.

81 *It wasn't more:* Mark Evans, interview.

82 *"Take whoever was:* Goodwin, interview.

82 *Men up and down:* Yribe, interview.

83 *The Iraqi Army:* Les Fuller, diary entry.

84 *"It's like someone:* Ryan Hoefer, interview.

85 *On October 25:* Evans, interview.

88 *While Kunk and the rest:* Yribe and Lauzier, interviews.

89 *Once Ebel learned:* Todd Ebel, interview.

89 *Miller was not:* Miller, interview.

7: Route Sportster and Bradley Bridge

93 *On October 29:* Matt Marcelino, interview.

93 *After toying with:* John Goodwin, interview.

94 *But the ideal:* Tom Kunk, interview.

94 *"We thought it was:* Phil Blaisdell, interview.

94 *TCP1 and TCP4 had:* Goodwin, interview.

95 *Goodwin worried:* Goodwin, interview.

95 *"Before," said 2nd Platoon's:* Jeremy Gebhardt, interview.

96 *Second Platoon's platoon leader:* Jerry Eidson, interview.

96 *Kunk maintained that:* Kunk, testimony at Article 32 Hearing.

96 *In that regard:* Todd Ebel, interview.

96 *"It was obvious:* Jared Bordwell, interview.

96 *Charlie Company First Sergeant:* Dennis Largent, interview.

97 *A major component:* Kunk, interview.

97 *"Colonel Kunk put his:* Bordwell, interview.

97 *One of Edwards's:* Ebel, interview.

97 *MacKenzie was Justin Watt's:* Justin Watt, interview.

98 *Heading back to Mahmudiyah:* John C. Stroh, "AR 15-6 Investigation: PSD IED Strike 02NOV05," November 4, 2005; Tim Norton and Largent, interviews.

101 *It was Ebel:* Ebel, interview.

101 *With many relief units:* Norton, interview.

101 *After the cleanup:* Largent and Bill Dougherty, interviews.

102 *"It affected everybody:* Chris Barnes, testimony at *U.S.* v. *Green.*

102 *Two days later:* "AR 15-6 Investigation (A/2-101 and C/1-502 Friendly Fire Incident, 04 November 2005)," November 19, 2005; Matt Shoaf and Dougherty, interviews.

106 *As the Bravo Company:* Justin Habash, Rick Skidis, Dennison Segui, and Blaisdell, interviews.

8: Communication Breakdowns

108 *"His reaction:* Dennis Largent, interview.

108 *The company commanders:* Jared Bordwell, interview.

109 *"We would sit down:* Ibid.

109 *"Both assumed the negative:* Ibid.

109 *"The battalion sergeant major:* Chris Payne, interview.

109 *Kunk threatened:* John Goodwin, Bill Dougherty, Tom Kunk, and Todd Ebel, interviews.

109 *When Kunk made his:* Goodwin, interview.

110 *Many company-level leaders:* Shawn Umbrell, interview.

110 *But Kunk did not:* Kunk and Lou Kangas, interviews.

110 *Umbrell tried to:* Umbrell, interview.

110 *As the battalion's:* Rob Salome, interview.

111 *According to Salome:* Ibid.

112 *As Squad Leader Eric:* Eric Lauzier, interview.

112 *Before late June:* McCarthy, "AR 15-6 Investigation Concerning Leadership Actions in Effect of B/1-502 IN on or about 12 MAR 2006," July 10, 2006.

112 *Squad leaders routinely:* Lauzier, testimony at *U.S.* v. *Barker* and interview.

112 *The TCPs were also:* Phil Miller, interview.

113 *The overwhelming majority:* Lauzier and Justin Watt, interviews.

114 *"Every morning before:* Lauzier, letter, Army Medical Evaluation Board on behalf of Justin Watt.

114 *"Let me put it:* Watt, interview.

115   *"How many times:* Justin Cross, interview.

115   *Lauzier, as one of:* Lauzier, interview; letter, Army Medical Evaluation Board on behalf of Justin Watt.

115   *Ebel understood that:* Ebel, interview.

116   *Lauzier would study:* Lauzier, interview.

116   *"My vehicle got hit:* Bordwell, interview.

116   *"Bullshit!" he would shout:* Largent and Mark Belda, interviews.

116   *When presented with:* Largent, Dougherty, and Tim Norton, interviews.

117   *Operations Officer Salome:* Salome, interview.

117   *Executive Officer Fred:* Fred Wintrich, interview.

117   *Salome conceded:* Salome, interview.

118   *"Several times, Kunk:* Belda, interview.

118   *Charlie's First Sergeant:* Largent, interview.

118   *Charlie's Executive Officer:* Matt Shoaf, interview.

9: The Mean Squad

119   *In the early days:* Eric Lauzier, interview.

119   *The Arabic interpreters:* James Barker, interview.

120   *"They'll push your buttons:* Justin Watt, interview.

120   *"You didn't come:* Lauzier, interview.

120   *"I would drink:* Watt, interview.

120   *Occasionally, one or:* Lauzier, interview.

121   *"It is well:* Ibid.

121   *On November 11:* Watt, interview.

122   *Six days later:* Tony Yribe, Lauzier, and Watt, interviews; Yribe, testimony at *U.S.* v. *Spielman.*

123   *Within an hour:* Barton Tate, "AR 15-6 Investigation #06-25: Escalation of Force Resulting in the Death of a LN," November 23, 2005.

10: "Soldiers Are Not Stupid"

125   *Often, the Bravo:* Eric Lauzier, interview.

126   *"Colonel Kunk wanted:* Jerry Eidson, interview.

126   *"Area Denial" was:* Jared Bordwell, interview.

127   *"Soldiers are not stupid:* Lauzier, interview.

127   *But 2nd Platoon's:* Eidson, interview.

128   *"If I were up:* Dennis Largent, interview.

128 *But unlike Goodwin:* Largent, Bill Dougherty, and John Goodwin, interviews.

128 *Early on, for example:* Bordwell, interview.

129 *Increasingly frustrated:* Largent and Dougherty, interviews.

130 *"If I gave Dougherty:* Rob Salome, interview.

130 *Largent had little patience:* Largent, interview.

130 *"I'm going to be honest:* Matt Shoaf, interview.

131 *"We were real:* Tony Yribe, interview.

131 *Earlier that day:* Shawn Umbrell, interview.

131 *And, after weeks:* Goodwin, Umbrell, and Bordwell, interviews.

11: Nelson and Casica

135 *After First Strike:* Leo Barron and Tom Kunk, interviews.

135 *Within Bravo's area:* Kunk, interview.

136 *It was from these:* Ibid.

136 *Throughout November:* John Goodwin, interview.

137 *"Battalion's idea was:* Chris Payne, interview.

137 *December 10 started:* Justin Watt, interview.

137 *Platoon Sergeant Phil:* Phil Miller, interview.

138 *Every company has:* Tim Norton, interview.

138 *Pulling up to TCP2:* Miller, interview with defense lawyers; Richard Casper, "AR 15-6 Investigation #06-043, Deaths of SSG Nelson, Travis and SGT Casica, Kenith, B/1-502d Infantry Regiment," February 2, 2006.

138 *Not long after:* Casper, "AR 15-6 Investigation."

140 *Most of the:* Tony Yribe, interview.

140 *Up at Yusufiyah:* Eric Lauzier, interview.

140 *Yribe, driving down:* Yribe, interview.

140 *Watt got out:* Watt, interview.

141 *Britt was still:* Watt and Yribe, interviews.

141 *Yribe's and Miller's:* Miller, Yribe, Collin Sharpness, and Watt, interviews; Andrew Tilghman, " 'I Came Over Here Because I Wanted to Kill People,' " *Washington Post,* July 30, 2006.

141 *In the back:* Yribe, interview.

142 *The Humvee pulled:* Dennison Segui, interview.

142 *Miller had to be:* Miller, interview.

142   *"The focus of the:* Marc Cooper, "AR 15-6 Investigation: Quality of Mental
      Health Care Provided in the Iraq Theater of Operations," July 26, 2006.

142   *Lauzier likened them:* Lauzier, interview.

142   *"All they would do:* Ryan Hoefer, interview.

142   *"They wanted to go:* Miller, interview with defense lawyers.

142   *Upon the squad's:* Steven Green, interview.

143   *"That was the point:* Chris Till, interview.

143   *"That's when things:* Payne, interview.

143   *Just a few:* Green, interview.

144   *"Goddamn it, that's not true:* Kunk, testimony at Article 32 Hearing and
      interview with defense lawyers.

144   *"Fuck the Hadjis:* Green, interview.

144   *The officer who:* Casper, "AR 15-6 Investigation."

145   *"The real fault:* Watt, interview.

145   *Any argument that:* Kunk, interview with defense lawyers.

145   *"If you are the:* Yribe, interview.

145   *"Staff Sergeant Nelson:* Steven Green, eulogy, *Staff Sergeant Travis Nelson
      and Sergeant Kenith Casica Memorial,* DVD, FOB Mahmudiyah, December
      16, 2005.

146   *A lieutenant from:* Michael Taylor, diary entry.

146   *Already displeased with:* Kunk, "Performance Counseling Memorandum
      for Captain John Goodwin," included in McCarthy, "15-6 Investigation."

146   *Miller heard about:* Miller, interview.

147   *Britt spoke with:* Kunk and Miller, interviews.

147   *Britt returned to tell:* Miller, interview with defense lawyers.

12: "It Is Fucking Pointless"

149   *Shortly after coming:* Eric Lauzier, Justin Watt, and Shane Hoeck,
      interviews.

152   *On that election day:* Nimrod Raphaeli, "The Elections in Iraq—The
      Roots of Democracy," Inquiry and Analysis Series No. 258. Middle East
      Media Research Institute, December 21, 2005.

152   *To Abu Musab al-Zarqawi:* D. Hazen, "Al-Zarqawi: A Post Mortem,"
      Inquiry and Analysis Series No. 284. Middle East Media Research
      Institute, June 30, 2006.

152 *Al Qaeda's senior:* Combating Terrorism Center at West Point, "Letter Exposes New Leader in Al-Qa'ida High Command," September 25, 2006; DeYoung, Karen, "Letter Gives Glimpse of Al-Qaeda's Leadership," *Washington Post,* October 2, 2006; Bassem Mroue, "Letter Criticized al-Qaida Head in Iraq," Associated Press, October 3, 2006.

152 *A month after:* Jonathan Finer, "How U.S. Forces Found Iraq's Most-Wanted Man," *Washington Post,* June 9, 2006; Evan Kohlmann, Global Terror Alert, April 7, 2006.

153 *On December 19:* Jerry Eidson, interview.

154 *Fuller, a devout Christian:* Les Fuller, diary entry.

154 *Eidson was now:* Eidson, interview.

155 *Lieutenant Ben Britt:* Tony Yribe, Watt, and Lauzier, interviews.

156 *He was fond:* Roman Diaz, interview.

157 *But only Green:* Paul Vermillion, interview.

157 *Everybody was frustrated:* Diaz, interview.

157 *At the prodding:* Steven Green's medical papers; Karen Marrs, testimony at *U.S.* v. *Green.*

158 *"I told her:* Green, interview.

158 *According to Goodwin:* John Goodwin, testimony at *U.S.* v. *Barker.*

158 *Goodwin, like most:* Goodwin, interview with defense attorneys.

158 *When Staff Sergeant:* Bob Davis, interview.

158 *While Sergeant First Class:* Phil Blaisdell, interview.

160 *Second Platoon's Sergeant:* Paul Fisher, interview.

13: Britt and Lopez

161 *"I just have a feeling:* Tony Yribe, interview.

161 *In the medic area:* Collin Sharpness, interview.

161 *They started:* Paul F. Schmidt, "AR 15-6 Investigation of the 22 December IED Attack on 1/B/1-502 Infantry Resulting in the Deaths of 1LT Benjamin Britt and SPC William Lopez-Feliciano," January 2, 2006.

162 *Everybody started turning:* Yribe, interview.

162 *They had already:* John Goodwin, interview.

162 *"I don't care:* Chris Till, interview.

163 *Laskoski said:* Yribe, interview.

163 *Britt was thrown:* Chris Barnes, testimony at *U.S.* v. *Green.*

164 *Within a second:* Yribe, interview.

164 *Goodwin had hoped:* Goodwin, interview.

165 *Private First Class Chris Barnes:* Barnes, testimony at *U.S.* v. *Green.*

165 *Yribe turned and said:* Yribe, interview.

165 *After a minute:* Goodwin, interview.

166 *Phil Miller also sought:* Phil Miller, interview.

166 *Goodwin went down:* Goodwin, interview.

166 *The carnage in front:* Yribe, interview.

167 *Captain Jared Bordwell:* Jared Bordwell, interview.

167 *That night:* Yribe, interview.

167 *Colonel Marrs agreed:* Karen Marrs, testimony at *U.S.* v. *Green.*

167 *Kunk and Edwards approached:* Goodwin, interview.

168 *When asked about:* Tom Kunk, interview.

168 *Other times:* McCarthy, "AR 15-6 Investigation," July 10, 2006.

168 *Goodwin insisted:* Goodwin, interview.

168 *Around-the-clock:* Shawn Umbrell, interview.

169 *First Strike units:* Kunk, interview.

169 *Others disagreed:* Goodwin, interview.

14: Leadership Shake-up

170 *When the platoon:* Todd Ebel, testimony at *U.S.* v. *Green.*

170 *During the meeting:* Ebel, testimony at *U.S.* v. *Howard.*

171 *Ebel was reassured:* Ebel, testimony at *U.S.* v. *Green.*

171 *Green said Ebel's:* Steven Green, interview.

171 *But scientists have been:* John Keegan, *The Face of Battle* (New York: Penguin Books, 1976), pp. 335–36.

172 *During World War II:* Dave Grossman, *On Killing: The Psychological Cost of Learning to Kill in War and Society* (New York: Back Bay Books, 1996), p. 44.

172 *Deployments where every day:* Ibid.

172 *Foremost among their:* John Diem, interview.

173 *This "shrinkage of the:* Jonathan Shay, *Achilles in Vietnam: Combat Trauma and the Undoing of Character* (New York: Scribner, 2003), p. 23.

173 *Paul Cortez rated:* Paul Cortez, testimony at *U.S.* v. *Spielman.*

173 *Suspects were routinely beaten:* Tony Yribe and Nicholas Lake, testimony at *U.S.* v. *Spielman.*

173 *"If you weren't there:* James Downs, interview.

173 *A common attitude was:* Yribe, testimony at *U.S.* v. *Spielman.*

173 *"The platoon rejected:* Diem, interview.

174 *"Having to reseed:* Fred Wintrich, interview.

174 *"Maybe we should:* Ebel, interview.

174 *"The exact words:* Rob Gallagher, interview with defense attorneys.

175 *Both Blaisdell and Gebhardt:* Jeremy Gebhardt and Phil Blaisdell, interviews.

175 *"The company commander:* Gallagher, interview with defense attorneys.

176 *"I don't think:* Chris Till, interview.

176 *"I have been in:* Gallagher, testimony at *U.S.* v. *Spielman.*

176 *After losing four men:* Phil Miller, interview with defense attorneys.

176 *He undermined Gallagher's authority:* Wintrich, interview.

176 *Gallagher spent:* Gallagher, interview with defense attorneys.

176 *According to Lauzier:* Eric Lauzier, interview.

177 *Kunk called Norton:* Tim Norton, interview.

178 *He didn't demand:* Phil Deem, interview.

178 *"He merged with the:* Till, interview.

178 *That's not exactly true:* Miller, interview.

179 *After the Britt and Lopez:* Wintrich, interview.

179 *Actually, there was one:* Paul Fisher, interview.

15: Gallagher

185 *Within a couple of days:* Rob Gallagher, testimony at *U.S.* v. *Barker.*

185 *He considered FOB:* Gallagher, testimony at *U.S.* v. *Spielman.*

186 *"I addressed that:* Gallagher, interview with defense lawyers.

186 *When he voiced:* Gallagher, testimony at *U.S.* v. *Barker.*

186 *Laskoski, for his part:* Andrew Laskoski, interview with defense lawyers.

186 *Looking more closely:* Gallagher, testimony at *U.S.* v. *Barker.*

187 *Gallagher would clear:* Laskoski, interview with defense lawyers.

187 *He began butting heads:* Gallagher, interview with defense lawyers.

187 *"He was the only:* Paul Vermillion, interview.

187 *And despite how foolhardy:* Gallagher, testimony at *U.S.* v. *Barker* and *U.S.* v. *Spielman.*

187 *Gallagher had little:* Tom Kunk, interview with defense lawyers.

188 *Many members of 1st:* Tim Norton, Chris Payne, and Eric Lauzier, interviews.

188 *"Everything that ever:* Payne, interview.

188 *Gallagher thought Norton:* Gallagher, interview with defense lawyers.

188 *Norton didn't have:* Norton, interview.

189 *Around this time:* Phil Miller, interview with defense lawyers.

189 *Allen was all:* Chaz Allen, interview.

190 *Second Brigade's Command:* Kunk, interview with defense lawyers.

190 *Miller didn't see:* Miller, interview.

190 *After rotating down:* Gallagher, testimony at *U.S.* v. *Spielman.*

190 *How to properly treat:* U.S. Army Field Manual 3-90: Tactics (Washington, D.C.: Department of the Army Headquarters), July 2001.

190 *Obviously, there are:* Rob Salome, interview.

191 *Kunk asserted that:* Kunk, interview; John M. McCarthy, "AR 15-6 Investigation Concerning Leadership Actions in Effect of B/1-502 IN on or about 12 MAR 2006," FOB Kalsu, Iraq, July 10, 2006, p. 5.

191 *Goodwin, for his part:* John Goodwin, interview.

191 *So it is unclear:* Gallagher, testimony at *U.S.* v. *Spielman.*

191 *Second and 3rd Platoons:* Jeremy Gebhardt, interview.

191 *Blaisdell would employ:* Phil Blaisdell, interview.

191 *Regardless of how:* Paul Fisher, Gebhardt, Norton, and Lauzier, interviews.

191 *Captain Shawn Umbrell:* Shawn Umbrell, interview.

192 *Their relationship:* Gallagher, testimony at *U.S.* v. *Barker.*

193 *Lieutenant Norton remembered:* Norton, interview.

193 *Gallagher could not figure:* Gallagher and Lauzier, testimony at Article 32 Hearing.

195 *Gallagher had tried:* Gallagher, interview with defense attorneys.

195 *After hearing about:* Laskoski, interview with defense attorneys.

195 *Reviewing the map:* Goodwin, interview.

196 *A soldier in Gallagher's:* Ryan Hoefer, interview.

196 *"Rob," Goodwin called:* Norton and Goodwin, interviews; Laskoski, interview with defense attorneys.

196 *Even before Goodwin:* Kunk, Jeff Fenlason, and Eric Conrad, interviews; Kunk, testimony at *U.S.* v. *Green.*

197 *Blaisdell and Gebhardt:* Blaisdell, interview.

197 *Several times throughout:* Laskoski, interview with defense attorneys.

197 *Second Squad leader:* Payne, interview.

198 *Fenlason's briefing from Stall:* Fenlason, testimony at Article 32 Hearing.

198 *"I knew what I needed:* Fenlason, interview.

199 *"He helped stand up:* Umbrell, interview.

199 *Charlie First Sergeant:* Dennis Largent, interview.

199 *"I'm just a sergeant:* John Diem, interview.

200 *Gallagher knew that:* Gallagher, testimony at *U.S.* v. *Spielman.*

16: February 1

203 *When one of the:* Shawn Umbrell, interview.

203 *Kunk saw that:* Tom Kunk, testimony at Article 32 Hearing; Timothy J. Daugherty, "AR 15-6 Investigation: 16 June AIF Attack on Jerf Al Sakr Bridge."

203 *Keep working with him:* Todd Ebel, interview.

203 *"I think you:* John Goodwin, interview.

203 *During Vietnam:* 4th Infantry Division Public Affairs Department, *Ivy Update,* online video about Freedom Rest. Undated.

204 *"Thanks very much:* Goodwin and Kunk, interviews.

204 *On the evening:* Goodwin, interview.

205 *At 8:45 a.m:* Daniel Carrick, Tony Yribe, and Eric Lauzier, interviews.

206 *Sergeant First Class Blaisdell:* Tim Norton and Phil Blaisdell, interviews.

207 *In a decision:* Dennison Segui, interview.

207 *Norton arrived:* Norton and Roman Diaz, interviews.

208 *"Jesus Christ:* Norton, interview.

208 *As Babineau was:* Chris Arnold, interview.

208 *The rest of Blaisdell's men:* Blaisdell, interview.

209 *Whelchel, Specialist Kirk:* Jay Strobino, Joe Whelchel, and Arnold, interviews.

210 *Outside the farmhouse:* Norton, interview.

210 *The two insurgents outside:* Strobino and Whelchel, interviews.

213 *Blaisdell responded:* Norton, interview.

213 *This was far:* "AR 15-6 Investigation #06-091: Death of a SM (KIA)," February 15, 2006.

214 *The 1st Platoon:* Strobino and Norton, interviews.

214 *Back at Freedom Rest:* Goodwin, interview.

215 *There was a lull:* Norton, Blaisdell, Arnold, Whelchel, and Diaz,

interviews; Wes Moerbe, "AR 15-6 Investigation #06-92: Death of SM (DOW) Findings and Recommendations," February 14, 2006.

219 *Goodwin was still:* Goodwin, interview.

219 *Owens was dead:* Norton and Blaisdell, interviews; Wes Moerbe, "AR 15-6 Investigation," February 14, 2006.

220 *Back at LZ:* Goodwin, interview.

220 *Third Platoon left:* Norton and Umbrell, interviews.

17: Fenlason Arrives

223 *On February 4:* John Goodwin, interview.

224 *First Platoon's 3rd Squad:* James Barker, interview.

225 *Everybody had known:* Jason Abbott, "AR 15-6 Investigation #06-097: Loss of Sensitive Items (FOB Yusufiyah Fire)," February 18, 2006.

225 *The loss was devastating:* Tim Norton and Goodwin, interviews.

226 *Most of 2nd Platoon:* Goodwin, interview.

226 *Battalion Operations Officer:* Rob Salome, interview.

226 *A box of socks:* Phil Blaisdell, interview.

226 *One soldier says:* Chris Barnes, testimony at *U.S.* v. *Green.*

226 *Until housing tents:* Salome, interview.

227 *After the immediate:* Jeff Fenlason, interview with defense attorneys.

227 *Fenlason told Blaisdell:* Blaisdell, interview.

228 *"So, who the fuck:* Collin Sharpness, interview.

228 *Fenlason knew:* Fenlason, interview.

228 *Payne tried:* Chris Payne, interview.

228 *"I heard you like:* Eric Lauzier, interview.

228 *Fenlason came to see:* Fenlason, interview.

228 *Lauzier thought Fenlason:* Lauzier, interview.

229 *"I would say:* Lauzier, testimony at Article 32 Hearing.

229 *Lauzier was not:* Fenlason, interview with defense attorneys.

229 *Throughout the rest:* Payne, interview.

229 *Staff Sergeant Chaz Allen:* Chaz Allen, interview.

230 *During one of:* Fenlason, interview with defense lawyers; Barnes and Paul Vermillion, interviews.

231 *Norton and Fenlason had:* Norton, testimony at Article 32 Hearing; interview.

232 *"Sergeant Fenlason didn't:* Daniel Carrick, interview.

232 *Fenlason conceded:* Fenlason, interview.

232 *In the early morning:* Evan Kohlmann, Global Terror Alert, April 7, 2006; Andrew Tilghman, "The Myth of AQI," *Washington Monthly,* October 2007.

233 *More Iraqi civilians:* Louise Roug, "Targeted Killings Surge in Baghdad," *Los Angeles Times,* May 7, 2006.

233 *According to Captain Leo:* Leo Barron, interview; *Stars and Stripes,* February 27, 2006.

233 *On February 7:* Eric Conrad and Tom Kunk, interviews; Andrew Tilghman, *Stars and Stripes,* February 25, 2006.

233 *That first mayor:* Kunk, interview.

233 *Prior to the Samarra:* Barron, interview.

234 *On February 28:* Lauzier and Barker, interviews.

234 *But Lauzier couldn't bear:* Lauzier, interview.

235 *"Lauzier was very:* Roman Diaz, interview.

235 *Halfway into his:* Lauzier, testimony at Article 32 Hearing.

235 *Increasingly alienated:* Lauzier, interview.

236 *"He would have done:* Barker, interview.

236 *When asked what:* Cortez, testimony at *U.S. v. Cortez.*

236 *"They were a bunch:* Carrick, interview.

236 *"Yes, he had control:* John Diem, interview.

236 *Cortez was particularly:* Lauzier, interview.

18: Back to the TCPs

241 *"About thirty days into it:* John Goodwin, interview.

241 *"First Platoon had become:* John Diem, interview.

242 *Private First Class Justin Cross:* Justin Cross, interview.

242 *"You can't think:* Tony Yribe, interview.

242 *"I don't know:* Justin Watt, interview.

242 *Cross described:* Cross, interview.

242 *Charlie Company's First:* Dennis Largent, interview.

243 *Specialist James Barker:* James Barker, interview.

243 *"You can see:* Fred Wintrich, interview.

243 *"A lot of people:* Diem, interview.

244 *Sergeants would egg:* Steven Green, interview.

244 *Brigade commander Colonel:* Todd Ebel, interview.

244 *"We would turn:* James Downs, interview.

245 *"I probably didn't help:* Jared Bordwell, interview.

245 *At the beginning:* Jeff Fenlason, interview with defense attorneys.

245 *Fenlason would not have:* Fenlason, interview; interview with defense attorneys.

246 *To mitigate this danger:* Eric Lauzier, Yribe, Watt, and Cross, interviews.

246 *With Lauzier on leave:* Fenlason interview, and interview with defense attorneys; Phil Blaisdell, interview.

246 *Said one squad leader:* Matt Marcelino, interview.

246 *Indeed, Cortez was not:* Paul Cortez, testimony at *U.S.* v. *Spielman.*

246 *Fenlason maintained that:* Fenlason, interview with defense lawyers.

247 *"I kept asking:* Cortez, testimony at *U.S.* v. *Cortez.*

247 *In* Achilles in Vietnam*:* Jonathan Shay, *Achilles in Vietnam,* pp. 5, 19.

247 *Even though TCP2:* Fenlason, testimony at Article 32 Hearing; interview; interview with defense lawyers.

247 *"Fenlason was reliable:* Barker, interview.

248 *"This could be:* Andrew Tilghman, "Air Assault Spearheads Push to Hurt Insurgency South of Baghdad," *Stars and Stripes,* March 4, 2006.

248 *Parts of Bravo's:* Goodwin, Jeremy Gebhardt, and Les Fuller, interviews.

248 *Just after 4:00 p.m.:* "AR 15-6 Investigation #06-124: Serious Injury to U.S. Service Member," December 22, 2006.

249 *He needed to stretch:* Goodwin, Gebhardt, and Fuller, interviews; "AR 15-6 Investigation #06-124."

250 *"That shooting became:* Bordwell, interview.

250 *The first lieutenant:* "AR 15-6 Investigation #06-124."

250 *"If you were there:* Fuller, interview.

250 *On the morning:* Timothy J. Daugherty, "AR 15-6 Investigation," June 29, 2006.

19: The Mayor of Mullah Fayyad

251 *During this TCP rotation:* Jeff Fenlason, interview with defense lawyers; interview.

252 *Goodwin was encouraged:* John Goodwin, interview.

252 *Fenlason got this:* Phil Blaisdell and Jeremy Gebhardt, interviews.

253 *Charlie Company's First Sergeant:* Dennis Largent, interview.

253 *Those not stationed:* Paul Cortez, testimony at *U.S.* v. *Cortez.*

253 *Fenlason said he couldn't:* Fenlason, interview with defense attorneys.

253 *Private First Class Justin Cross:* Justin Cross, interview.

253 *With the TCP mission:* Cortez, testimony at *U.S.* v. *Spielman;* Eric Lauzier, Tony Yribe, and Fenlason, interviews.

254 *Despite this regular:* Fenlason, interview with defense lawyers.

254 *One major initiative:* Fenlason, interview.

254 *Goodwin was getting:* Goodwin, interview.

255 *Unfortunately, the men:* Cross, interview.

255 *Drinking and drug use:* Steven Green, interview.

255 *Some soldiers had:* Cross, interview.

255 *These rogue patrols:* Sharpness, interview.

255 *On March 9:* Cortez, testimony at *U.S.* v. *Spielman.*

256 *Fenlason's approval:* Fenlason, interview.

256 *Around two or three:* Yribe, interview; testimony at *U.S.* v. *Spielman.*

256 *The guys down at:* James Barker, testimony at *U.S.* v. *Spielman.*

256 *Tonight they were:* Yribe and Nicholas Lake, testimony at *U.S.* v. *Spielman;* Yribe, interview.

20: The Janabis

The subject of one Article 32 Hearing and five trials (*U.S.* v. *Barker, U.S.* v. *Cortez, U.S.* v. *Spielman, U.S.* v. *Howard,* and *U.S.* v. *Green*), March 12 is more thoroughly documented than any other event of the deployment. All of those court transcripts have contributed to my attempt to present that day as a seamless whole, but there are numerous discrepancies. James Barker, Paul Cortez, and Jesse Spielman have all, at several junctures, contradicted each other, their own previous court testimony, and the multiple sworn statements they filled out when they confessed. And, over the course of the trials, some differences about what happened that day hardened into irreconcilable alternate versions. More notable, however, are the recollections of Steven Green (who has never testified, even in his own trial, but whom I have interviewed for about six hours), which diverge substantially at several key junctures from the prevailing narrative that emerged over the other trials. I have selected and presented the chain of events that I find most credible, but I have flagged the most prominent alternate versions in the notes below.

258 *On March 12:* Green, interview.

259 *Barker had already:* Barker, testimony at *U.S.* v. *Green.*

259 *Witnesses were a problem:* Green, interview.

259 *Invoking the privileges:* Barker, testimony at *U.S.* v. *Cortez.*

259 *Barker was pushing:* Green, interview.

259 *At around noon: U.S.* v. *Barker; U.S.* v. *Cortez; U.S.* v. *Spielman;* Green, interview. Barker's trial, which came first, introduced the card game as the time and place where the plan was initially hatched, and Barker fingered Green as both the plot's mastermind and the group's motivator. Cortez, at his trial, followed suit. Spielman, both at his trial and after, contended that nothing about the crime was discussed over cards and that he knew nothing of the plan even after it had already begun. Over the course of the trials, which were spread out over eighteen months, Barker took increasing responsibility for being one of the attacks' principal architects.

260 *During most of the game:* Bryan Howard, testimony at *U.S.* v. *Green.*

260 *Cortez later rated:* Cortez, testimony at *U.S.* v. *Spielman.*

260 *Barker said he:* Barker, testimony at *U.S.* v. *Barker.*

260 *During one of:* Green, interview.

260 *Spielman, who had not:* Green, interview; Cortez, testimony at *U.S.* v. *Spielman.*

260 *Cortez returned and:* Barker, testimony at *U.S.* v. *Cortez.*

260 *He and Barker:* Green, interview. Cortez has never spoken about any discussions before the card game, and he has claimed that he was merely a follower throughout the entire event. He has also testified that he knew a rape was going to happen but not murder, and he has denied declaring that he intended to rape the girl first.

261 *Cortez briefed Howard:* Howard, testimony at *U.S.* v. *Spielman.*

261 *Forty-five-year-old:* Abu Muhammad, Ameer al-Janabi, Muhammad al-Janabi, and Ahmed Al-Janabi, interview; testimony at *U.S.* v. *Green.*

264 *The house was only:* Green, interview; *U.S.* v. *Barker; U.S.* v. *Cortez; U.S.* v. *Spielman.*

265 *"What the fuck:* Cortez, interview with doctor, quoted during testimony at *U.S.* v. *Cortez.*

265 *In the bedroom:* Green, interview. During *U.S.* v. *Green,* Spielman testified that he only knocked on the door to check if Green was okay and then went back into the living room.

266 *As Green was:* Green, interview; *U.S.* v. *Barker; U.S.* v. *Cortez; U.S.* v. *Spielman.*

267 *The four men:* Green, interview; Howard, testimony at *U.S.* v. *Spielman* and *U.S.* v. *Green.*

268 *Once their adrenaline:* Green, interview; Howard, testimony at *U.S.* v. *Spielman.*

268 *Green asked Scheller:* Green, interview.

268 *Several hours later:* Tony Yribe, testimony at *U.S.* v. *Spielman* and *U.S.* v. *Green,* interview; Green, interview.

21: Twenty-one Days

271 *Goodwin had low:* John Goodwin and Jeff Fenlason, interviews.

271 *The events of the:* Ibid.

273 *Yribe, like most:* Tony Yribe, Fenlason, and Chaz Allen, interviews.

274 *"Dude, you had:* Justin Watt, interview.

274 *At the end:* Fenlason, Yribe, and Allen, interviews.

276 *Goodwin's decision:* Fenlason, interview.

276 *His culture shock:* Daniel Carrick, interview.

277 *During the three-week:* John Diem, interview.

278 *"It was fairly:* James Downs, interview.

278 *There were two dogs:* Fenlason, interview.

279 *Green, meanwhile:* Steven Green, interview.

279 *On March 20:* Green medical papers.

279 *In his initial interview:* Bob Davis, interview; Green medical papers.

280 *Over the next few:* Davis, interview.

280 *Bowler told Kunk:* Green medical papers.

280 *In fiscal 2005:* Julie Rawe and Aparisim Ghosh, "A Soldier's Shame," *Time,* July 17, 2006.

280 *Even though Green:* Green medical papers.

280 *Green disputed:* Green, interview.

281 *"I thought it was:* Goodwin, testimony at Article 32 Hearing.

281 *Justin Cross had just:* Justin Cross, interview.

281 *Fenlason was pissed:* Fenlason, interview.

22: "We Had Turned a Corner"

285 *The hunt for Zarqawi:* Mark Bowden, "The Ploy," *Atlantic Monthly,* May 2007.

285 *As the war ground on:* Sean Naylor, "Closing In on Zarqawi," *Air Force Times,* May 8, 2006.

286 *Zarqawi, Al Qaeda:* Jim Miklaszewski, "Video Posted of Downed
     Helicopter," *NBC Nightly News.* Undated, accessed online,
     http://www.msnbc.msn.com/id/21134540/vp/12172474#12172474.

286 *It was the first:* Stars and Stripes, Mideast edition, "Apache May Have Been
     Shot Down in Iraq," April 3, 2006; Evan Kohlmann, "Biography of an Al-
     Qaida Operative 'Martyred' in Iraq: Abu Rabieh al-Ghamdi (Saudi
     Arabia)," Global Terror Alert Web site; John Goodwin, interview.

287 *"They started putting:* Leo Barron, interview.

287 *Numerous units from:* Goodwin, Rob Salome, Jeremy Gebhardt, and Les
     Fuller, interviews.

287 *On April 13:* Rick Skidis, interview.

288 *As one first sergeant:* Dennis Largent, interview.

288 *"Kunk was starting:* Shawn Umbrell, Largent, and Bill Dougherty,
     interviews.

288 *Largent was in:* Largent, interview.

289 *"Now, is that:* Dougherty, interview.

289 *Kunk vehemently denied:* Tom Kunk, interview.

289 *HHC commander:* Umbrell, interview.

290 *Largent was desperate:* Largent, interview.

290 *About Largent's departure:* Kunk, interview.

291 *For Goodwin:* Goodwin, interview.

291 *Around the same time:* MNF-I press release, April 16, 2006; Naylor,
     "Closing In on Zarqawi."

291 *Nine days after that:* MNF-I press release, April 25, 2006.

291 *With uncanny timing:* Dexter Filkins, "Qaeda Video Vows Iraq Defeat for
     'Crusader' U.S.," *New York Times,* April 26, 2006; Karen DeYoung,
     "Zarqawi Taunts U.S. in Video: Leader of al-Qaeda in Iraq Vows to
     Thwart New Baghdad Government," *Washington Post,* April 26, 2006.

292 *In mid-April:* Umbrell, interview.

292 *Fenlason, for his part:* Jeff Fenlason, interview.

292 *That changed:* Daniel Carrick, Fenlason, and Collin Sharpness,
     interviews.

292 *In mid-May:* MNF-I press release, May 15, 2006; Dexter Filkins, "25
     Insurgents Killed in Battle South of Baghdad, U.S. Says," *New York Times,*
     May 16, 2006.

293 *Several units from:* Gebhardt, interview.

294 *A military spokesperson:* Nelson Hernandez and Hassan Shammari, "Scores Are Killed in Heavy Fighting South of Baghdad," *Washington Post,* May 16, 2006; MNF-I press release, May 15, 2006.

294 *This is not:* Phil Blaisdell and Christopher Thielenhaus, interviews.

294 *Fenlason and Norton:* Fenlason and Tim Norton, interviews.

294 *In mid-May:* Eric Lauzier and Norton, interviews.

297 *After three years:* Bill Powell and Scott MacLeod, "Zarqawi's Last Dinner Party," *Time,* June 11, 2006; Ellen Knickmeyer, "Zarqawi's Hideout Was Secret Till Last Minute," *Washington Post,* June 11, 2006.

297 *U.S. Ambassador Zalmay:* BBC.co.uk, "Zarqawi Death Has 'Little Impact,'" July 4, 2006.

298 *By June:* Gebhardt, Paul Fisher, and Fuller, interviews.

299 *Iraqi prime minister:* Anthony Cordesman, "CSIS Iraqi Force Development: Summer 2006 Update," August 23, 2006.

299 *Yet throughout the summer:* Linda Robinson, *Tell Me How This Ends* (New York: PublicAffairs, 2008), p. 22.

299 *On June 14, 2006:* Thomas E. Ricks, *The Gamble* (New York: Penguin Press, 2006), p. 50.

299 *After a day or two:* Cordesman, "Summer 2006 Update."

299 *Despite the spike:* Bob Woodward, *The War Within* (New York: Simon & Schuster, 2008), p. 59.

300 *With the violence still:* Stewart W. Bowen, Jr., *Hard Lessons* (Washington, D.C.: U.S. Government Printing Office, February 9, 2009), p. 278.

23: The Alamo

301 *On June 16:* Jeff Fenlason, interview.

301 *With attrition:* Tim Norton, interview.

302 *Menchaca hadn't even:* Phil Deem, interview.

302 *The threesome had been:* Chaz Allen, interview.

302 *Soldiers stationed:* Eric Lauzier and Deem, interviews.

302 *At TCP4:* Allen and Lauzier, interviews; Timothy J. Daugherty, "AR 15-6 Investigation: 16 June AIF Attack," June 29, 2006.

302 *Just over halfway:* Daugherty, "AR 15-6 Investigation"; Norton, Lauzier, Collin Sharpness, and Allen, interviews.

303 *Cortez and his men:* Daugherty, "AR 15-6 Investigation"; Allen, interview.

303 *"They had their:* Allen, interview.

303 *The insurgents on:* Daugherty, "AR 15-6 Investigation."

303 *Lauzier's fire team:* Lauzier, interview.

304 *Sharpness put Babineau:* Sharpness, interview.

304 *"We spent the whole:* James Downs, interview.

304 *While the rest:* Tony Yribe and Justin Watt, interviews.

306 *"At that point:* John Goodwin, interview.

307 *Bravo's 3rd Platoon:* Phil Blaisdell, interview.

307 *After a brief:* Daugherty, "AR 15-6 Investigation."

308 *With temperatures soaring:* Jared Bordwell, interview.

308 *After searching well:* Chris Payne, interview.

308 *"Kunk had moved:* Fenlason, interview.

309 *"That was it for me:* Deem, interview.

24: Dilemma and Discovery

310 *As that was happening:* Justin Watt, interview.

312 *That night, Watt:* Watt and Tony Yribe, interviews.

314 *Judging from a video:* Michael Ware, videotape CNN acquired from insurgents.

315 *According to a briefing:* William Caldwell, *Larry King Live*, CNN, June 20, 2006.

315 *the Mujahideen Shura:* Dexter Filkins, "U.S. Says 2 Bodies Retrieved in Iraq Were Brutalized," *New York Times,* June 21, 2006.

315 *In keeping with the pattern:* Timothy J. Daugherty, "AR 15-6 Investigation: 16 June AIF Attack," June 29, 2006; Chaz Allen, interview.

315 *Rather than this:* Christopher Thielenhaus, interview.

25: "Remember That Murder of That Iraqi Family?"

316 *A couple of days after:* Jeff Fenlason, interview.

316 *Watt had looked:* Justin Watt, interview.

317 *On June 23:* Bob Davis, interview.

317 *This was not:* Watt, interview.

318 *As they were:* John Diem, interview.

318 *"You remember that:* Fenlason, Diem, and Tim Norton, interviews.

319 *The rest of:* Fenlason, interview.

319 *Fenlason called Goodwin:* Fenlason and John Goodwin, interviews.

320 *Several soldiers:* Eric Lauzier, interview.

320 *Goodwin arrived:* Phil Blaisdell, Fenlason, and Goodwin, interviews.

321 *Just after midnight:* Tom Kunk, sworn statement, July 5, 2006, and interview.

322 *When Yribe returned:* Watt, testimony at *U.S.* v. *Barker* and interview.

322 *Howard was the second:* Kunk, sworn statement, July 5, 2006.

322 *Barker, when questioned:* Fenlason, interview with defense lawyers.

322 *Kunk and Edwards:* Kunk, testimony at *U.S.* v. *Green.*

323 *Watt was flustered:* Watt, interview.

323 *Kunk was far:* Kunk, interview and testimony at *U.S.* v. *Green.*

323 *On June 25:* Paul Fisher, interview.

324 *The U.S. Army paid:* Abu Muhammad [pseud.], interview.

325 *The men came:* Fenlason, interview.

325 *In his remarks:* Yribe, eulogy, *Memorial for SPC Babineau, PFC Menchaca, and PFC Tucker.* DVD. FOB Mahmudiyah, Iraq, June 26, 2006.

325 *Fenlason had gotten:* Fenlason, interview.

326 *A few days after:* Daniel Sparks, Daniel Carrick, Chris Payne, Diem, Lauzier, and others, interviews.

327 *Kunk later maintained:* Kunk, interview.

327 *After it was:* Diem, interview.

327 *In the aftermath:* Timothy J. Daugherty, "AR 15-6 Investigation: 16 June AIF Attack," June 29, 2006.

327 *During his interview:* Norton, sworn statement in Daugherty, "AR 15-6 Investigation."

328 *Daugherty's report:* Daugherty, "AR 15-6 Investigation."

328 *"Everybody from the battalion:* Jared Bordwell, interview.

328 *Years later:* Todd Ebel, interview.

329 *The second investigation:* John M. McCarthy, "AR 15-6 Investigation Concerning Leadership Actions," July 10, 2006; Fenlason, interview with defense lawyers.

329 *Norton and Goodwin knew:* Norton and Goodwin, interviews.

26: The Fight Goes On

333 *After starting strongly:* Elizabeth Bowler, interview.

333 *Upon Bowler's first:* Ibid.

334 *Kunk later denied that:* Tom Kunk, interview.

334 *On June 30:* Ryan Lenz, "Soldiers Investigated for Alleged Rape, Killing

Family in Iraq," Associated Press, June 30, 2006; "GIs May Have Planned Iraq Rape, Slayings," Associated Press, July 1, 2006.

334 *The story infuriated:* Bowler and Lenz, interviews.

334 *Back in the States:* Steven Green, interview.

335 *He visited a cousin:* U.S. v. *Green.*

335 *Cortez, Spielman, and Barker:* James Culp and James Barker, interviews.

336 *In fact, the battle:* Thomas E. Ricks, *The Gamble* (New York: Penguin Press, 2009), p. 47.

336 *On July 17:* Larry Kaplow, "The Last Day of the Iraq War," *Newsweek,* January 12, 2009.

336 *Kunk claimed that:* Kunk, interview.

336 *Al Qaeda exploited:* Agence France-Presse, "Al-Qaeda Posts Rape Revenge Video," July 11, 2006; Robert Reid, "Tape Claims 3 GIs Killed over Rape-Murders," Associated Press, July 11, 2006; SITE Intelligence Group, "The Mujahideen Shura Council in Iraq Issues a Video of the Mutilated Corpses of the Captured American Soldiers in Al-Yusufiyah," translation and description of jihadi video, July 10, 2006.

337 *On September 22:* SITE Intelligence Group, "In Memory of the Sunnah of Our Ancestors in Mutilation Video from the Mujahideen Shura Council in Iraq Featuring Attack upon Two Captured American Soldiers in Yusufiyah," translation and description of jihadi video, September 22, 2009.

337 *"We were having some:* Christopher Thielenhaus, interview.

337 *"Let me tell you:* Matt Shoaf, interview.

337 *On August 30:* Justin Habash, interview.

337 *"That was the worst:* Phil Deem, interview.

338 *"When the sector:* Paul Fisher, interview.

338 *Kunk moved Norton:* Tim Norton, interview.

338 *"We were just existing:* Jeff Fenlason, interview.

339 *On FOB Mahmudiyah:* Shawn Umbrell, interview.

27: "This Was Life and Death Stuff"

340 *Word was, CID:* Justin Watt and Eric Lauzier, interviews.

341 *Lauzier, for one:* Lauzier, interview.

341 *In fact:* Watt, interview.

341 *A few weeks earlier:* "The Bronze Star Medal to SSG Eric R. Lauzier, U.S. Army: Recommendation for Award," June 10, 2006.

341 *Now he was being:* Lauzier, interview.

342 *His men found his:* Justin Cross and Lauzier, interviews.

342 *Watt was having:* Watt, interview.

342 *When Kunk got wind:* Bob Davis, interview.

343 *On July 25:* Watt, sworn statement, July 25, 2006.

343 *Barnes later acknowledged:* Chris Barnes, interview.

344 *Bowler had arranged:* Watt, interview.

344 *When the two:* Elizabeth Bowler, interview.

344 *The same day:* Watt, interview.

344 *After expecting:* John Goodwin, interview.

345 *Colonel Ebel:* Todd Ebel, interview.

346 *On August 14:* Tim Norton, interview.

346 *On August 21:* Bill Dougherty, Rick Watt, and Justin Watt, interviews.

348 *Following several weeks:* Jeff Fenlason and Justin Habash, interviews.

348 *"This was life and death:* John Diem, interview.

Epilogue

350 *Even before:* Anita Powell, "Tall Task for 10th Mountain in Mahmudiyah," *Stars and Stripes,* Mideast edition, October 8, 2006.

351 *In November 2006:* Associated Press, "Iraqi Insurgent Group Unveils Rocket," November 4, 2006.

351 *With an extra battalion:* Josh White, "Troops Take On Insurgent Haven," *Washington Post,* October 24, 2006; Lauren Frayer, "Derelict Power Plant Symbol of Iraq Woes," Associated Press, February 11, 2007.

351 *As the 2-10th:* Thomas E. Ricks, *The Gamble* (New York: Penguin Press, 2009), p. 56.

351 *As part of:* Associated Press, "A Timeline of Iraq War, Troop Levels," April 08, 2008; *U.S. Army Field Manual 3-24: Counterinsurgency* (Washington, D.C.: Department of the Army Headquarters, December 2006).

352 *Despite the fresh approach:* Ricks, *The Gamble,* p. 33.

352 *Ultimately, the brigade lost:* Bing West, foreword to Dominic J. Caraccilo and Andrea L. Thompson, *Achieving Victory in Iraq: Countering an Insurgency* (Mechanicsburg, Pa.: Stackpole Books, 2008).

352 *Before dawn on:* Joel Roberts, "Terror Group Warns U.S. over Missing
     GIs," CBS.com, May 14, 2007; Thomas Frank, "The Trail Is Cold, but a
     Platoon Searches On for Two U.S. Soldiers Captured in a May Attack
     Tied to Al-Qaeda," *USA Today,* August 8, 2007; Damien Cave, "5 Killed
     and 3 Missing in Attack on American Patrol South of Baghdad," *New
     York Times,* May 13, 2007.

352 *On May 23:* Associated Press, "Bodies of Two Missing Soldiers Found in
     Iraq," July 11, 2008.

353 *Within a few:* Ray Odierno, Department of Defense news briefing,
     November 1, 2007. .

353 *They started during:* Mark Perry, "U.S. Military Breaks Ranks," *Asia Times
     Online,* January 23, 2008.

353 *At the program's peak:* Ricks, *The Gamble.*

356 *"It took a while:* Wesley Morgan, "Leaving Baghdad, Battalion Recalls a
     Long Deployment," *Long War Journal,* November 17, 2008.

357 *With attacks down:* Peter Graff, "U.S. Hands 'Triangle of Death' to Iraqi
     Troops," Reuters, October 23, 2008.

357 *By January 2009:* Larry Kaplow, "The Last Day of the Iraq War," *Newsweek,*
     January 12, 2009.

358 *In March 2007:* Reuters, "Soldier Gets 27 Months in Iraq Gang-Rape
     Case," March 21, 2007.

359 *In fact, only one:* Associated Press, "Federal Jury Acquits Ex-Marine in
     Iraqis' Deaths: Verdict Is the First Time a Civilian Jury Has Weighed In
     on the Law of War," August 28, 2008.

359 *Indeed, MEJA was:* Nicholas Casey, "Civilian Court Tries Case from the
     Fog of War: Ex-Marine Is Accused Under Law Aimed at Contractors,"
     Wall Street Journal, August 19, 2008.

360 *Green's defense team:* Darren Wolff, interview.

360 *After ruling out: U.S. v. Green.*

362 *"I have been:* Cortez, testimony at *U.S. v. Cortez.*

SELECTED BIBLIOGRAPHY

Books

Allawi, Ali A. *The Occupation of Iraq: Winning the War, Losing the Peace.* New Haven, Conn.: Yale University Press, 2007.

Ambrose, Stephen E. *Band of Brothers: E Company, 506th Regiment, 101st Airborne from Normandy to Hitler's Eagle's Nest.* New York: Simon & Schuster Paperbacks, 2004.

Atkinson, Rick. *In the Company of Soldiers: A Chronicle of Combat in Iraq.* London: Little, Brown, 2004.

Baker, James A., III, Lee H. Hamilton, et al. *The Iraq Study Group Report: The Way Forward—A New Approach.* New York: Vintage Books, 2006.

Bando, Mark. *101st Airborne: The Screaming Eagles in World War II.* St. Paul, Minn.: Zenith Press, 2007.

Bremer, L. Paul, and Malcolm McConnell. *My Year in Iraq: The Struggle to Build a Future of Hope.* New York: Threshold Editions, 2006.

Bryant, Russ, and Susan Bryant. *Screaming Eagles: 101st Airborne Division.* St. Paul, Minn.: Zenith Press, 2007.

Burke, Jason. *Al-Qaeda.* London: Penguin Books, 2007.

Caraccilo, Dominic J., and Andrea L. Thompson. *Achieving Victory in Iraq: Countering an Insurgency.* Mechanicsburg, Pa.: Stackpole Books, 2008.

Chandrasekaran, Rajiv. *Imperial Life in the Emerald City: Inside Iraq's Green Zone.* London: Bloomsbury, 2007.

Cockburn, Patrick. *Muqtada al-Sadr and the Fall of Iraq.* London: Faber & Faber, 2008.

Day, Thomas L. *Along the Tigris: The 101st Airborne Division in Operation Iraqi Freedom, February 2003 to March 2004.* Atglen, Pa.: Schiffer Publishing, 2007.

Diamond, Larry. *Squandered Victory: The American Occupation and the Bungled Effort to Bring Democracy to Iraq.* New York: Henry Holt, 2006.

Draper, Robert. *Dead Certain: The Presidency of George W. Bush.* New York: Free Press, 2007.

Fallows, James. *Blind into Baghdad: America's War in Iraq.* New York: Vintage, 2006.

Ferguson, Charles H. *No End in Sight: Iraq's Descent into Chaos.* New York: PublicAffairs, 2008.

Franks, Tommy, with Malcolm McConnell. *American Soldier.* New York: HarperCollins, 2005.

Galbraith, Peter W. *The End of Iraq: How American Incompetence Created a War Without End.* London: Pocket Books, 2007.

Gordon, Michael, and Bernard Trainor. *Cobra II: The Inside Story of the Invasion and Occupation of Iraq.* New York: Pantheon, 2006.

Grossman, Dave. *On Killing: The Psychological Cost of Learning to Kill in War and Society.* New York: Back Bay Books, 1996.

Grossman, Dave, and Loren Christensen. *On Combat: The Psychology and Physiology of Deadly Conflict in War and Peace.* 2nd ed. Warrior Science Publications, 2004.

Hedges, Chris. *What Every Person Should Know About War.* New York: Free Press, 2003.

Hersh, Seymour M. *Chain of Command: The Road from 9/11 to Abu Ghraib.* New York: Harper Perennial, 2005.

Hiro, Dilip. *Secrets and Lies: The True Story of the Iraq War.* London: Methuen/ Politico's, 2005.

Holmes, Richard. *Acts of War: The Behaviour of Men in Battle.* London: Cassell, 2004.

Horrie, Chris, and Peter Chippindale. *What Is Islam: A Comprehensive Introduction.* Revised and updated ed. London: Virgin Books, 2007.

Hunter, James. *The Servant: A Simple Story About the True Essence of Leadership.* Roseville, Calif.: Prima Publishing, 1998.

Keegan, John. *The Face of Battle.* New York: Penguin Books, 1976.

Packer, George. *Assassins' Gate: America in Iraq.* New York: Farrar, Straus and Giroux, 2005.

Pax, Salam. *The Clandestine Diary of an Ordinary Iraqi.* New York: Grove Press, 2003.

Polk, William R. *Understanding Iraq.* New York: Harper Perennial, 2006.

Ricks, Thomas E. *Fiasco: The American Military Adventure in Iraq.* New York: Penguin Press, 2006.

———. *The Gamble: General David Petraeus and the American Military Adventure in Iraq, 2006–2008.* New York: Penguin Press, 2009.

Riverbend. *Baghdad Burning: Girl Blog from Baghdad.* New York: The Feminist Press at the City University of New York, 2005.

———. *Baghdad Burning II: More Girl Blog from Baghdad.* New York: The Feminist Press at the City University of New York, 2006.

Robinson, Linda. *Tell Me How This Ends: General David Petraeus and the Search for a Way out of Iraq.* New York: PublicAffairs, 2008.

Sanchez, Ricardo S., and Donald T. Phillips. *Wiser in Battle: A Soldier's Story.* New York: HarperCollins, 2008.

Shadid, Anthony. *Night Draws Near: Iraq's People in the Shadow of America's War.* New York: Henry Holt, Picador, 2006.

Shay, Jonathan. *Achilles in Vietnam: Combat Trauma and the Undoing of Character.* New York: Scribner, 2003.

Steele, Jonathan. *Defeat: Why America and Britain Lost Iraq.* Berkeley, Calif.: Counterpoint, 2008.

Stiglitz, Joseph E., and Linda J. Bilmes. *The Three Trillion Dollar War: The True Cost of the Iraq Conflict.* New York: W. W. Norton & Company, 2008.

Tripp, Charles. *A History of Iraq.* 3rd ed. Cambridge: Cambridge University Press, 2007.

West, Bing. *No True Glory: A Frontline Account of the Battle of Fallujah.* New York: Bantam Dell, 2006.

Woodward, Bob. *Bush at War.* New York: Simon & Schuster Paperbacks, 2005.

———. *Plan of Attack: The Definitive Account of the Decision to Invade Iraq.* New York: Simon & Schuster Paperbacks, 2004.

———. *State of Denial: Bush at War, Part III.* New York: Simon & Schuster, 2006.

———. *The War Within: A Secret White House History 2006–2008.* New York: Simon & Schuster, 2008.

Government Publications, Reports, and Court Proceedings

Abbott, Jason. "AR 15-6 Investigation #06-097, Loss of Sensitive Items (FOB Yusufiyah Fire)." February 18, 2006.

"AR 15-6 Investigation (A/2-101 and C/1-502 Friendly Fire Incident, 04 November 2005)." November 19, 2005.

"AR 15-6 Investigation #06-091: Death of SM (KIA)." February 15, 2006.

"AR 15-6 Investigation #06-124: Serious Injury to U.S. Service Member." FOB Mahmudiyah, Iraq. December 22, 2006.

Article 32(b) Session Proceedings. Camp Liberty, Iraq. August 6–9, 2006.

Bowen, Stewart W., Jr. *Hard Lessons: The Iraq Reconstruction Experience.* Washington, D.C.: U.S. Government Printing Office, February 9, 2009.

Casper, Richard. "AR 15-6 Investigation #06-043: Deaths of SSG Nelson, Travis and SGT Casica, Kenith, B/1-502d Infantry Regiment." Camp Striker, Iraq. February 2, 2006.

Cooper, Marc. "AR 15-6 Investigation: Quality of Mental Health Care Provided in the Iraq Theater of Operations." July 26, 2006.

Crane, Conrad C., and W. Andrew Terrill. *Reconstructing Iraq: Insights, Challenges, and Missions for Military Forces in a Post-Conflict Situation.* February 2003.

Daugherty, Timothy J. "AR 15-6 Investigation: 16 June AIF Attack on Jerf Al Sakr Bridge." June 29, 2006.

Marrs, Karen L. "Remind: Addressing the Risk of Illegal Violence in Military Operations." *The United States Army Medical Department Journal,* July–Dec 2008, 43–49.

McCarthy, John M. "AR 15-6 Investigation Concerning Leadership Actions in Effect of B/1-502 IN on or about 12 MAR 2006." FOB Kalsu, Iraq. July 10, 2006.

Memorial for SPC Babineau, PFC Menchaca, and PFC Tucker. DVD. FOB Mahmudiyah, Iraq. June 26, 2006.

Moerbe, Wes. "AR 15-6 Investigation #06-092: Death of a SM (DOW) Findings and Recommendations." February 14, 2006.

Multi-National Force–Iraq Combined Press Information Center. "Coalition Forces Raid Insurgent Safe Haven." Press release. May 14, 2006.

———. "Iraqi Army Soldiers Secure Sadr-Yusufiyah." Press release. March 9, 2006.

———. "Update: AH-64 Crash, Two Pilots Killed." Press release. April 4, 2006.

National Strategy for Victory in Iraq. National Security Council. November 2005.

Presentation of the AR 15-6 Investigation Results to the Family of Specialist David Babineau. PowerPoint slides. Undated.

Schmidt, Paul F. "AR 15-6 Investigation of the 22 December IED Attack on 1/B/1-502 Infantry Resulting in the Deaths of 1LT Benjamin Britt and SPC William Lopez-Feliciano." Camp Striker, Iraq. January 2, 2006.

Small-Unit Leader's Guide to Counterinsurgency. United States Marine Corps. June 2006.

Small-Unit Leader's Guide to Urban Operations: Tactics, Techniques and Procedures. Newsletter No. 03-4. Center for Army Lessons Learned, Fort Leavenworth, Kans. May 2003.

Staff Sergeant Travis Nelson and Sergeant Kenith Casica Memorial. DVD. FOB Mahmudiyah, Iraq. December 16, 2005.

Stroh, John C. "AR 15-6 Investigation: PSD IED Strike 02NOV05." FOB Mahmudiyah North, Iraq. November 4, 2005.

Tate, Barton. "AR 15-6 Investigation #06-25: Escalation of Force Resulting in the Death of a LN." November 23, 2005.

Traffic Control Point Operations: Tactics, Techniques and Procedures. Handbook No. 06-15. Center for Army Lessons Learned, Fort Leavenworth, Kans. April 2006.

U.S. Army Field Manual 3-21.8: The Infantry Rifle Platoon and Squad. Washington, D.C.: Department of the Army Headquarters, March 2007.

U.S. Army Field Manual 3-21.10: The Infantry Rifle Company. Washington, D.C.: Department of the Army Headquarters, July 2006.

U.S. Army Field Manual 3-21.20: The Infantry Battalion. Washington, D.C.: Department of the Army Headquarters, December 2006.

U.S. Army Field Manual 3-24: Counterinsurgency. Washington, D.C.: Department of the Army Headquarters, December 2006.

U.S. Army Field Manual 3-90: Tactics. Washington, D.C.: Department of the Army Headquarters, July 2001.

United States v. *James P. Barker: Proceedings of a General Court-Martial.* Fort Campbell, Ky. November 15, 2006.

United States v. *Private First Class Bryan L. Howard: Proceedings of a General Court-Martial.* Fort Campbell, Ky. March 2007.

United States v. *Private First Class Jesse V. Spielman: Proceedings of a General Court-Martial.* Fort Campbell, Ky. July 13, 2001.

United States v. *Sergeant Paul E. Cortez: Proceedings of a General Court-Martial.* Fort Campbell, Ky. February 15, 2007.

United States v. *Steven Dale Green.* United States District Court, Western Division of Kentucky. Paducah, Ky. April–May 2009.

U.S. State Department Office of the Historian. "Significant Terrorist Incidents, 1961–2003: A Brief Chronology." March 2004. www.state.gov/r/pa/ho/pubs/fs/5902.htm.

Wright, Donald P., and Timothy R. Reese. *On Point II: Transition to the New*

Campaign—The United States Army in Operation Iraqi Freedom, May 2003– January 2005. Fort Leavenworth, Kans.: Combat Studies Institute Press, June 2008.

Newspaper, Magazine, Internet Articles, TV Segments, and Nongovernmental Reports

Agence France-Presse. "Al-Qaeda Posts Rape Revenge Video." July 11, 2006.

———. "Two Bodies, Including Beheaded Man, Found South of Baghdad." October 3, 2004.

APS Review Downstream Trends. "Iraq—Contractors from Friendly States." April 23, 2001.

Arraf, Jane, et al. "Iraq: New Push Against Insurgents." CNN.com, October 5, 2004.

Associated Press. "Al-Qaida Claims Killing of Two GIs: Military Awaits DNA Tests After Finding Mutilated, Booby-trapped Bodies." June 21, 2006.

———. "Bodies of Two Missing Soldiers Found in Iraq." July 11, 2008.

———. "Federal Jury Acquits Ex-Marine in Iraqis' Deaths: Verdict Is the First Time a Civilian Jury Has Weighed In on the Law of War." August 28, 2008.

———. "Iraqi Insurgent Group Unveils Rocket." November 4, 2006.

———. "Iraq's 'Triangle of Death' Includes Bounties." November 19, 2004.

———. "Rumsfeld Blames Iraq Problems on 'Pockets of Dead-enders.' " June 18, 2003.

———. "A Timeline of Iraq War, Troop Levels." April 8, 2008.

Atlanta Journal-Constitution Online. "AJC 48th Brigade Blog." http://www .ajc.com/news/content/news/index/iraq.html.

Barnes, Julian E. "20% of Iraq, Afghanistan Veterans Have Depression or PTSD, Study Finds." *Los Angeles Times,* April 18, 2008.

Barrouquere, Brett. "Killings Shattered Dreams of Rural Iraqi Family." Associated Press, May 23, 2009.

———. "Relatives of Slain Iraqis Confront Killer in Court." Associated Press, May 28, 2009.

Basu, Moni, and Ron Martz. "Building Iraqis' Trust a Difficult Mission: Progress in Iraqi Town Fades Since Georgia Guard Unit Headed Home." *Atlanta Journal-Constitution,* July 30, 2006.

Basu, Moni, and Anna Varela. "Four More from 48th Killed in Iraq." The 48th Goes to War blog, *Atlanta Journal-Constitution Online,* July 31, 2005.

BBC.co.uk. "Zarqawi Death Has 'Little Impact,' " July 4, 2006.

Beilue, Jon Mark. "Ben Britt: Never a Taker, Always a Giver." *Amarillo Globe News,* January 1, 2006.

Bowden, Mark. "The Ploy." *Atlantic Monthly,* May 2007.

Bowles, Sarah, and Hadley Robinson. "Trying to Understand the Mahmudiyah Massacre." *Gelf Magazine,* May 6, 2009.

Brown, Drew. "A Long Day on Patrol in Mahmudiyah." *Stars and Stripes,* Mideast Edition, July 15, 2007.

Burns, John F. "Iraq's Ho Chi Minh Trail." *New York Times,* June 5, 2005.

———. "With 25 Citizen Warriors in an Improvised War." *New York Times,* December 12, 2004.

Cambanis, Thanassis. "2 Pictures Emerge of Militants' Power." *Boston Globe,* October 18, 2004.

Carey, Benedict. "When the Personality Disorder Wears Camouflage." *New York Times,* July 9, 2006.

Casey, Nicholas. "Civilian Court Tries Case from the Fog of War: Ex-Marine Is Accused Under Law Aimed at Contractors." *Wall Street Journal,* August 19, 2008.

Cave, Damien. "5 Killed and 3 Missing in Attack on American Patrol South of Baghdad." *New York Times,* May 13, 2007.

CNN.com. "Iraq: New Push Against Insurgents." October 5, 2004.

Coll, Steve. "The General's Dilemma: David Petraeus, the Pressures of Politics, and the Road out of Iraq." *New Yorker,* September 8, 2008.

Cooper, Anderson, and Pierre Bairin. "Former Enemies Kiss in 'Triangle of Death.' " CNN.com, September 11, 2007.

Cordesman, Anthony H. "Iraqi Force Development: Summer 2006 Update." Center for Strategic and International Studies. Revised August 23, 2006.

———. "Iraq's Evolving Insurgency and the Risk of Civil War." Center for Strategic and International Studies. Working draft for outside comment. Revised January 26, 2007.

DeYoung, Karen. "Letter Gives Glimpse of al-Qaeda's Leadership: Letter Shows Worry over Iraq Infighting." *Washington Post,* October 2, 2006.

———. "Zarqawi Taunts U.S. in Video: Leader of al-Qaeda in Iraq Vows to Thwart New Baghdad Government." *Washington Post,* April 26, 2006.

DeYoung, Karen, and Walter Pincus. "Zarqawi Helped U.S. Argument That Al-Qaeda Network Was in Iraq." *Washington Post,* June 10, 2006.

Diamond, Larry. "What Went Wrong in Iraq." *Foreign Affairs,* September/ October 2004.

"Ethan Biggers Death Notice." *Dayton Daily News,* March 2, 2007.

Fallows, James. "Why Iraq Has No Army." *Atlantic Monthly,* December 2005.

Farmer, Blake. "Fort Campbell Faces Wave of Suicides." WPLN Radio news feature, April 16, 2009.

Filkins, Dexter. "Qaeda Video Vows Iraq Defeat for 'Crusader' U.S." *New York Times,* April 26, 2006.

———. "U.S. Says 2 Bodies Retrieved in Iraq Were Brutalized." *New York Times,* June 21, 2006.

———. "25 Insurgents Killed in Battle South of Baghdad, U.S. Says." *New York Times,* May 16, 2006.

Finer, Jonathan. "How U.S. Forces Found Iraq's Most-Wanted Man." *Washington Post,* June 9, 2006.

Frank, Thomas. "The Trail Is Cold, but a Platoon Searches On for Two U.S. Soldiers Captured in a May Attack Tied to Al-Qaeda." *USA Today,* August 8, 2007.

Frayer, Lauren. "Derelict Power Plant Symbol of Iraq Woes." Associated Press, February 11, 2007.

Gaughen, Patrick. "Backgrounder #8: 4th Brigade, 6th Iraqi Army Division." Institute for the Study of War. Undated.

Ghosh, Bobby. "Behind the Sunni-Shi'ite Divide." *Time,* February 22, 2007.

Giordono, Joseph. "Pentagon Identifies Two Pilots Killed When Copter Was Shot Down in Iraq." *Stars and Stripes,* Mideast edition, May 19, 2006.

———. "U.S. Troops Kill 12 Suspected Insurgents in Raid on 'Safe House.' " *Stars and Stripes,* Mideast edition, April 27, 2006.

———. "8,000 Troops Widen Search for Missing GIs: Militant Web Site Claims Soldiers Were Kidnapped." *Stars and Stripes,* Mideast edition, June 20, 2006.

Graff, Peter. "U.S. Hands 'Triangle of Death' to Iraqi Troops." Reuters, October 23, 2008.

Hazen, D. "Al-Zarqawi: A Post Mortem." Inquiry and Analysis Series No. 284. Middle East Media Research Institute, June 30, 2006.

———. "Sunni Jihad Groups Rise Up Against Al-Qaeda in Iraq." Inquiry and Analysis Series No. 336. Middle East Media Research Institute, March 22, 2007.

Hernandez, Nelson, and Hassan Shammari. "Scores Are Killed in Heavy Fighting South of Baghdad." *Washington Post,* May 16, 2006.

Hoagland, Doug. "Soldier's Story Is Written in Contrasts." *Fresno Bee,* July 30, 2006.

Human Rights Watch. *Leadership Failure: Firsthand Accounts of Torture of Iraqi Detainees by the U.S. Army's 82nd Airborne Division.* September 22, 2005.

———. *"No Blood, No Foul": Soldiers' Accounts of Detainee Abuse in Iraq.* July 2006.

International Crisis Group. *In Their Own Words: Reading the Iraqi Insurgency.* Middle East Report No. 50, February 15, 2006.

Ireland Online. "Suicide Bomber Attacks Iraqi Wedding Party." January 21, 2005.

Kagen, Kimberly, et al. "Iraq Situation Report." Institute for the Study of War, February 7, 2008.

Kaplow, Larry. "The Last Day of the Iraq War." *Newsweek,* January 12, 2009.

Kershaw, Michael. Department of Defense news briefing, October 4, 2007.

Knickmeyer, Ellen. "Details Emerge in Alleged Army Rape, Killings." *Washington Post,* July 3, 2006.

———. "Military-Style Assault Kills Dozens in Iraqi Marketplace." *Washington Post,* July 18, 2006.

———. "Zarqawi's Hideout Was Secret Till Last Minute." *Washington Post,* June 11, 2006.

Kors, Joshua. "How Specialist Towns Lost His Benefits." *The Nation,* April 9, 2007.

Krepinevich, Andrew F., Jr. "How to Win in Iraq." *Foreign Affairs,* September/October 2005.

Lenz, Ryan. "Army Works to Offset Combat Stress in Iraq." Associated Press, June 4, 2006.

———. "GIs May Have Planned Iraq Rape, Slayings." Associated Press, July 1, 2006.

———. "Soldier Accused of Murdering Iraqi Family Was Diagnosed as Homicidal Threat 3 Months Before." Associated Press, January 9, 2007.

———. "Soldiers Investigated for Alleged Rape, Killing Family in Iraq." Associated Press, June 30, 2006.

Lilly, J. Robert. "Rape and Murder in the European Theater of Operations, WWII." Unpublished paper prepared at the request of the Steven Green legal defense team, January 31, 2007.

Loiko, Sergei L., and John Daniszewski. "Russia Launches 'a Planned With-drawal' of Its Citizens from Iraq." *Los Angeles Times,* March 7, 2003.

Miklaszewski, Jim. "Video Posted of Downed Helicopter." *NBC Nightly News,* undated, accessed online. http://www.msnbc.msn.com/id/21134540/vp/12172474#12172474.

Military Channel. "Triangle of Death." *Combat Zone* (season 1, episode 7), 2007.

Morgan, David. "Study Says 300,000 U.S. Troops Suffer Mental Problems." Reuters, April 17, 2008.

Morgan, Wesley. "Leaving Baghdad, Battalion Recalls a Long Deployment." *Long War Journal,* November 17, 2008.

Morin, Monte. "48th BCT Nears End of Tough Tour in Iraq: Guard Unit Suf-fered Heavy Losses in Early Fighting." *Stars and Stripes,* Mideast edition, March 26, 2006.

———. "Medics Recall Their Own Close Brushes with Death in Iraq." *Stars and Stripes,* Mideast edition, March 21, 2006.

———. "Triangle of Death Now a Safe Passage for Pilgrims." *Stars and Stripes,* Mideast edition, March 11, 2007.

Mroue, Bassem. "Letter Criticized al-Qaida Head in Iraq." Associated Press, October 3, 2006.

Mukhtar, Ahmed. "Deadly Triangle." *Al-Ahram Weekly,* November 4–10, 2004.

Naylor, Sean. "Closing In on Zarqawi." *Air Force Times,* May 8, 2006.

Odierno, Ray. Department of Defense news briefing, November 1, 2007. *Iraq Situation Report.* Institute for the Study of War, February 7, 2008.

Perry, Mark. "U.S. Military Breaks Ranks." *Asia Times Online,* January 23, 2008.

Powell, Anita. "Sectarian Militias Seen Gaining Strength in Mahmudiyah." *Stars and Stripes,* Mideast edition, October 21, 2006.

———. "Tall Task for 10th Mountain in Mahmudiyah." *Stars and Stripes,* Mideast edition, October 8, 2006.

Powell, Bill, and Scott MacLeod. "Zarqawi's Last Dinner Party." *Time,* June 11, 2006.

Quinlivan, James T. "Burden of Victory: The Painful Arithmetic of Stability Operations." *Rand Review,* Summer 2003.

Raphaeli, Nimrod. "The Elections in Iraq—The Roots of Democracy." In-quiry and Analysis Series No. 258. Middle East Media Research Institute, December 21, 2005.

Rawe, Julie, and Aparisim Ghosh. "A Soldier's Shame." *Time,* July 17, 2006.

Redmon, Jeremy. "48th Will Redeploy in Iraq by Thanksgiving." The 48th Goes to War blog, *Atlanta Journal-Constitution Online,* October 4, 2005.

———. "New Buddy Sorely Missed." The 48th Goes to War blog, *Atlanta Journal-Constitution Online,* October 27, 2005.

Reid, Robert. "Tape Claims 3 GIs Killed over Rape-Murders." Associated Press, July 11, 2006.

Reuters. "Soldier Gets 27 Months in Iraq Gang-Rape Case." March 21, 2007.

Roberts, Joel. "Terror Group Warns U.S. over Missing GIs." CBS.com, May 14, 2007.

Roug, Louise. "Targeted Killings Surge in Baghdad." *Los Angeles Times,* May 7, 2006.

Rubin, Alissa J. "Iraqi Court Sentences Man to Die for Killing 3 G.I.'s." *New York Times,* October 29, 2008.

———. "Religious Hostility Surfacing." *Los Angeles Times,* December 20, 2004.

Russian News and Information Service. "Iraq in Talks with Russia on Completing Power Plant." March 12, 2008.

Schmitt, Eric, and Carolyn Marshall. "In Secret Unit's 'Black Room,' a Grim Portrait of U.S. Abuse." *New York Times,* March 19, 2006.

Sengupta, Kim. " 'This is now the most dangerous place in Iraq. We are coming up against Zarqawi's people.' " *The Independent,* November 22, 2004.

Shadid, Anthony. "Iraq's Forbidding 'Triangle of Death': South of Baghdad, a Brutal Sunni Insurgency Holds Sway." *Washington Post,* November 23, 2004.

Shadid, Anthony, and Bradley Graham. "Troops Hit Sites South of Baghdad: Raids Involve U.S., British, Iraqi Forces." *Washington Post,* November 24, 2004.

SITE Intelligence Group. "In Memory of the Sunnah of Our Ancestors in Mutilation Video from the Mujahideen Shura Council in Iraq Featuring Attack upon Two Captured American Soldiers in Yusufiyah." Translation and description of jihadi video, September 22, 2009.

———. "The Mujahideen Shura Council in Iraq Issues a Video of the Mutilated Corpses of the Captured American Soldiers in Al-Yusufiyah." Translation and description of jihadi video, July 10, 2006.

Spinner, Jackie. "Marines Widen Their Net South of Baghdad: Troops Say Offensive Is Vastly Different from Urban Warfare in Fallujah." *Washington Post,* November 28, 2004.

Stahl, Lesley, and Richard Bonin. "General O." CBS, *60 Minutes,* September 28, 2008.

Stars and Stripes, Mideast edition. "Apache May Have Been Shot Down in Iraq: Pilots Are Presumed Dead; Recovery Efforts Continue." April 3, 2006.

———. "Iraqi Unit Takes Over Another U.S. Base." June 20, 2006.

———. "U.S. Military Focuses on Missing Soldiers." May 17, 2007.

———. "U.S. Military Transfers Security Responsibility for Mahmudiyah Area." August 15, 2006.

Tilghman, Andrew. "Air Assault Spearheads Push to Hurt Insurgency in Area South of Baghdad." *Stars and Stripes,* Mideast edition, March 4, 2006.

———. "The Army's Other Crisis: Why the Best and Brightest Young Officers Are Leaving." *Washington Monthly,* December 2007.

———. " 'I Came Over Here Because I Wanted to Kill People.' " *Washington Post,* July 30, 2006.

———. "In Mahmudiyah, Tensions Were at a Boiling Point Before Samarra Mosque Attack." *Stars and Stripes,* Mideast edition, February 25, 2006.

———. "Insurgents Control Many Perilous Rural Roads in Iraq." *Stars and Stripes,* Mideast edition, February 24, 2006.

———. "The Myth of AQI." *Washington Monthly,* October 2007.

———. "Soldiers at Yusufiyah See It All Go Up in Smoke: Faulty Wiring Suspected in Fire at FOB Near Baghdad." *Stars and Stripes,* Mideast edition, February 20, 2006.

———. "Soldier's Death Leaves Others Thinking 'What If': Routine Search of Iraqi House Turned into a Fatal Firefight." *Stars and Stripes,* Mideast edition, March 15, 2006.

———. "U.S. Troops Avoid Both Sides of Sectarian Fight South of Baghdad: Tension Between Sunnis, Shias Rises in Mahmudiyah." *Stars and Stripes,* Mideast edition, February 27, 2006.

———. "U.S. Troops Helping Keep the Peace Inside Iraqi City: U.S. Troops Help Iraqi Forces Curb Sectarian Violence in Urban Areas." *Stars and Stripes,* Mideast edition, February 26, 2006.

———. "U.S. Troops in 'Triangle of Death' See Independent Iraqi Army as Distant Goal: Progress Noted, but Force's Equipment, Competence Level, Trustworthiness Debated." *Stars and Stripes,* Mideast edition, March 3, 2006.

Van Natta, Don, Jr. "Who Is Abu Musab al-Zarqawi?" *New York Times,* October 10, 2004.

Weaver, Mary Anne. "The Short, Violent Life of Abu Musab al-Zarqawi."
   Atlantic Monthly, July–August 2006.

White, Josh. "Ex-Soldier Charged in Killing of Iraqi Family." *Washington Post,*
   July 4, 2006.

———. "Troops Take On Insurgent Haven." *Washington Post,* October 24,
   2006.

Worth, Robert F., and Carolyn Marshall. "G.I. Crime Photos May Be Evidence." *New York Times,* August 5, 2006.

Yehoshua, Y. "Dispute in Islamist Circles over the Legitimacy of Attacking
   Muslims, Shiites, and Non-combatant Non-Muslims in Jihad Operations in
   Iraq: Al-Maqdisi vs. His Disciple Al-Zarqawi." Inquiry and Analysis Series
   No. 239. Middle East Media Research Institute, September 11, 2005.

Zoroya, Gregg. "Soldier Describes Anguish in Revealing Murder Allegations."
   USA Today, September 13, 2006.

INDEX